States and Their Nationals Abroad

In a novel contribution to the field of comparative foreign policy analysis, this book carefully delineates how states, regardless of regime, have formulated policies to deal with their national communities aboard. Some states, depending on their domestic political ideologies, cultures, and capabilities, have extensive institutional mechanisms in place for coming to the aid of their nationals abroad. Others, however, have also used these capabilities in adverse ways. Chapters focusing on individual countries explore the rationale behind state policies that differentiate treatment for distinct groups, such as tourists, migrants, and diasporas.

Amongst the intriguing findings is the fact that state capacity alone does not explain the ability or willingness of states to assist their nationals abroad in times of need. Furthermore, in some cases, communities abroad can also actively mobilize against their home state and thus play key roles in conflict and even regime change.

Klaus Brummer holds the Chair of International Relations at the Catholic University of Eichstätt-Ingolstadt. He served as coeditor-in-chief of *Foreign Policy Analysis* and was the 2021/22 German Academic Exchange Service Hannah Arendt Visiting Chair for German and European Studies at the Munk School of Global Affairs and Public Policy, University of Toronto.

Šumit Ganguly is Distinguished Research Fellow and the Director of the Strengthening the US–India Relationship Program at the Hoover Institution at Stanford University. He was an Alexander von Humboldt fellow at the University of Heidelberg in 2018–2019.

States and Their Nationals Abroad

Support, Co-Opt, Repress

Edited by

Klaus Brummer

Catholic University of Eichstätt-Ingolstadt

Šumit Ganguly

The Hoover Institution, Stanford University

CAMBRIDGE
UNIVERSITY PRESS

CAMBRIDGE
UNIVERSITY PRESS

Shaftesbury Road, Cambridge CB2 8EA, United Kingdom

One Liberty Plaza, 20th Floor, New York, NY 10006, USA

477 Williamstown Road, Port Melbourne, VIC 3207, Australia

314–321, 3rd Floor, Plot 3, Splendor Forum, Jasola District Centre, New Delhi – 110025, India

103 Penang Road, #05–06/07, Visioncrest Commercial, Singapore 238467

Cambridge University Press is part of Cambridge University Press & Assessment, a department of the University of Cambridge.

We share the University's mission to contribute to society through the pursuit of education, learning and research at the highest international levels of excellence.

www.cambridge.org
Information on this title: www.cambridge.org/9781009531979

DOI: 10.1017/9781009531986

When citing this work, please include a reference to the DOI 10.1017/9781009531986

First published 2025

A catalogue record for this publication is available from the British Library

A Cataloging-in-Publication data record for this book is available from the Library of Congress

ISBN 978-1-009-53197-9 Hardback
ISBN 978-1-009-53201-3 Paperback

Klaus Brummer dedicates this book to Sybilla, Cedric, Justin, and Jeremy.

Šumit Ganguly dedicates this book to his wife, Traci Nagle.

Contents

Figures

Tables

Contributors

YASEMIN AKBABA is Professor of Political Science in the Political Science Department at Gettysburg College, USA and coeditor of the journal *International Studies Perspectives*. Yasemin's research is at the nexus between international security and religion. She specifically studies the impact of religion on various political outcomes connected to ethnic and religious minorities, foreign policy analysis, and political mobilization. Yasemin has published several journal articles that have appeared in *Political Studies*, *Journal of Peace Research*, *Comparative European Politics*, *Foreign Policy Analysis*, *Politics and Religion*, *Nationalism and Ethnic Politics*, *Ethnopolitics*, *Civil Wars*, *International Interactions*, *Interdisciplinary Journal of Research on Religion*, *Politics, Religion & Ideology*, and others. She is coauthor, with Özgür Özdamar, of *Role Theory in the Middle East and North Africa* (2019). Yasemin is interested in research on teaching. She received Gettysburg College's Thompson Award for distinguished teaching and University of Missouri–Columbia's Excellence in Teaching Award.

NICOLAS BLAREL is Associate Professor of International Relations at the Institute of Political Science, Leiden University, the Netherlands. He studies foreign and security policy-making, the politics of migration governance, and the international politics of South Asia. He is currently working on mapping and theorizing Indian migration governance. Nicolas has published *The Evolution of India's Israel Policy: Continuity, Change, and Compromise since 1922* (2015); and coedited, with Šumit Ganguly and Manjeet Pardesi, the *Oxford Handbook of India's National Security* (2018) and, with Crystal A. Enis, *The South Asia to Gulf Migration Governance Complex* (2022). In addition, Nicolas has authored articles in the *European Journal of International Relations*, *Political Studies*, *Foreign Policy Analysis*, *International Studies Perspectives*, *International Politics*, *European Political Science*, *Rising Power Quarterly*, *Strategic Analysis*, *Politique Etrangère*, and *Hérodote*.

KLAUS BRUMMER holds the Chair of International Relations at the Catholic University of Eichstätt-Ingolstadt, Germany. He served as coeditor-in-chief of the journal *Foreign Policy Analysis* (2018–2020) and was President of the Foreign Policy Analysis section of the International Studies Association (2015–2016). As professor and guest lecturer, he has taught as the German Academic Exchange Service Hannah Arendt Visiting Chair for German and European Studies at the University of Toronto, Canada, and at Duke University, USA, among others. He has published in peer-reviewed journals such as the *British Journal of Politics and International Relations*, *Foreign Policy Analysis*, *Government and Opposition*, *International Affairs*, *International Studies Review*, *Journal of European Public Policy*, and *Journal of International Relations and Development*. Klaus is the author of *A Leader-Centered Theory of Foreign Policy Change* (2024); coauthor of *Foreign Policy Analysis* (2024); and coeditor, with Valerie M. Hudson, of *Foreign Policy Analysis beyond North America* (2015) and, with Sebastian Harnisch, Kai Oppermann, and Diana Panke, of *Foreign Policy as Public Policy?* (2019).

AMY FREEDMAN is Professor and Department Chair of the Political Science Department at Pace University, USA, and Research Fellow at the Weatherhead East Asian Institute, Columbia University, USA. She earned her MA and PhD at New York University, USA, and is the author of numerous books and articles on democracy and ethnic and religious politics in Southeast Asia, and on international relations in Asia. Selected publications include: *Political Participation and Ethnic Minorities: Chinese Overseas in Malaysia, Indonesia, and the United States* (2000). She coauthored, with Ann Marie Murphy, *Nontraditional Security Threats in Southeast Asia* (2017); and coedited, with Joseph Lee, *Empire Competition: Southeast Asia as Site of Imperial Contestation* (2022). Amy is also coeditor of the journal *Asian Security*.

ŠUMIT GANGULY is the Director of the Strengthening the US–India Relationship Program at the Hoover Institution at Stanford University. He previously taught at Indiana University Bloomington, USA, where he was the holder of the Tagore Chair in Indian Cultures and Civilizations and Distinguished Professor of Political Science. Šumit's most recent book, coauthored with Manjeet S. Pardesi and William R. Thompson, is *The Sino-Indian Rivalry: Implications for Global Order* (2023).

ANDREA GHISELLI is Assistant Professor at the School of International Relations and Public Affairs of Fudan University, China. He is also the Head of Research of the TOChina Hub's ChinaMed Project. Andrea's research interests include Chinese foreign policy, China's relations with the Middle East, and foreign policy analysis. Besides his monograph *Protecting China's Interests Overseas* (2021), his research has appeared in a number of political science, international relations, and China studies peer-reviewed journals.

DANIEL HERNÁNDEZ JOSEPH is a Mexican diplomat currently serving as Ambassador to the Philippines. Most of his career has been dedicated to consular protection and consular services. Daniel was Director General for Consular Protection at Mexico's Secretariat of Foreign Affairs (2007–2011), Deputy Chief of Mission at Embassy of Mexico in the USA (2016), Consul General in Boston (2011–2016), Head of Post in the Consulate in Laredo, Texas (1999–2006), Director for Consular Protection Policy (1995–1999), and Consular Protection Officer in the Consulates of Mexico in Houston (1982–1988) and Austin (1988–1994). He has participated in numerous bilateral negotiations on migration and consular protection with the US, Canada, Cuba, and several Central American nations. As Diplomat in Residence at American University in Washington, DC, USA (2006–2007), Daniel lectured on migration policies in North America and researched international land-border administration policies. In 2015, he published the book *Protección Consular Mexicana* (Mexican Consular Protection). He has published several articles on cultural affairs, media and communications, science diplomacy, migration, consular protection, and border issues and border security in Chile, the Netherlands, United States, and Mexico.

DREW A. HOGAN is a PhD student in political science at the University of Minnesota, USA. His research interests include US foreign policy, grand strategy, and rhetoric in foreign policy. Drew holds a BA in political science from Kenyon College and a MALD from the Fletcher School of Law and Diplomacy, USA. In the 2022–2023 academic year he was a Hans J. Morgenthau fellow at the Notre Dame International Security Center.

SAHAR KHAN is Senior Fellow and Deputy Director of South Asia at the Stimson Center, USA. Her research interests include state-sponsored militancy, anti-terrorism laws and legal regimes, and private military and security contractors in South Asia and Africa. Sahar's policy work is focused on US foreign policy in South Asia, Pakistan–US relations, and Pakistan's foreign policy. She holds a BA in economics, international studies, and politics and government from Ohio Wesleyan University; an MPP from the Harris School of Public Policy, University of

Chicago; and a PhD in political science from the University of California, Irvine, USA. She is also the Section Co-chair of the International Studies Association's South Asia in World Politics section and a Leadership Council member of the American Pakistan Foundation.

RONALD R. KREBS is Distinguished McKnight University Professor and Professor of Political Science at the University of Minnesota, USA. He is the author of *Fighting for Rights: Military Service and the Politics of Citizenship* (2006) and the award-winning Narrative and the Making of US National Security (2015); and is the coeditor, with Elizabeth Kier, of *In War's Wake: International Conflict and the Fate of Liberal Democracy* (2010) and, with Thierry Balzacq, of the *Oxford Handbook of Grand Strategy* (2021). Ron's articles on a wide range of subjects in global affairs and international security have appeared in leading scholarly journals, including *International Organization*, *International Security*, *European Journal of International Relations*, *International Studies Quarterly*, and *Security Studies*, as well as in leading general interest outlets such as *Foreign Affairs*, *Foreign Policy*, *Lawfare*, *The National Interest*, the *Washington Post*, and *Slate*. He is immediate past editor-in-chief of the leading scholarly journal *Security Studies*.

ETHAN LARSON is Case Writer at the Tobin Project in Cambridge, USA, a non-profit organization dedicated to education and research. Working with academic experts, he develops historical case studies for high school classrooms, focusing on the theme of democracy in a wide range of countries and contexts. His PhD dissertation, which he defended in 2020, is a history of the Yugoslav diaspora in the interwar period. He has published in *Nations and Nationalism*, *National Identities*, and *Dve Domovine* on topics ranging from international exhibitions to the image of Nikola Tesla in the United States and Yugoslavia. His research interests include migration, nationalism, and transnationalism in twentieth-century Eastern Europe and Russia.

ANN MARIE MURPHY is Professor at the School of Diplomacy and International Relations, Seton Hall University, USA, where she directs the Center for Foreign Policy Studies. She is also adjunct Senior Research Scholar at the Weatherhead East Asian Institute, Columbia University, Fellow of the Mansfield-Luce Asia Scholars Network, and was a 2019–2020 ASEAN Research Program Fulbright Scholar. Ann Marie earned her PhD in political science from Columbia University, USA. Her research interests include international relations and comparative politics in Southeast Asia, US foreign policy toward Asia, and governance of nontraditional security issues. Ann Marie is the coauthor, with Amy Freedman, of *Non-traditional Security Issues in Southeast Asia: The Transnational Dimension*,(2018); and the coeditor, with Bridget Welsh, of *Legacies of Engagement in Southeast Asia* (2008). Her articles have appeared in journals such as *Asian Security*, *Contemporary Southeast Asia*, *Orbis*, *Asia Policy*, *World Politics Review*, and *PS: Political Science & Politics*. Ann Marie is a founding partner of the New York Southeast Asia Network and is currently completing a book on the impact of democratic change on Indonesian foreign policy with the generous support of the Smith Richardson Foundation.

KELSEY P. NORMAN is Fellow for the Middle East at the Baker Institute for Public Policy, Rice University, USA and Director of the Women's Rights, Human Rights and Refugees Program. She holds a PhD in Political Science from the University of California, Irvine, USA. Kelsey has conducted extensive, empirically grounded research on refugees, migration, and state policy, reflected most recently in her book, *Reluctant Reception: Refugees, Migration and Governance in the Middle East and North Africa* (2021). Her research has also been published in academic journals, including the *European Journal of International Relations*, *International Studies Review*, *Journal of North African Studies*, *International Migration Review*, *International Journal of Migration and Border Studies*, and *Journal of Ethnic and Migration Studies*, among others. Kelsey has also published numerous policy-oriented articles in outlets including the *Washington Post*, *The Atlantic*, *Foreign Policy*, and *Foreign Affairs*.

KAI OPPERMANN is Professor of International Politics at the Chemnitz University of Technology, Germany. He has previously held positions at the University of Sussex and King's College London, UK, and the University of Cologne, Germany. Kai's research centers on the domestic sources of foreign policy and European integration, with a focus on British and German European and foreign policy. He won a Marie Curie Fellowship for a research project on EU referendums and worked as a specialist advisor to the House of Lords External Affairs Sub-committee in the UK. Kai's work has been published in international journals such as *European Journal of International Relations*, *West European Politics*, *Foreign Policy Analysis*, *Journal of European Public Policy*, and *British Journal of Politics and International Relations*. He is coauthor of *Foreign Policy Analysis* (2024), a coeditor of *German Politics*, and an associate editor of the *Oxford Encyclopedia of Foreign Policy Analysis* (2018).

MA. DIVINA GRACIA Z. ROLDAN is Full Professor at the Department of Political and Development Studies, College of Liberal Arts, De La

Salle University, Philippines, where she teaches graduate and undergraduate courses in the political science and development studies programs. She gained her PhD in Philippine studies, specializing in bureaucracy and external relations, at the University of the Philippines Asian Center. She is the book review editor of the *Philippine Political Science Journal* and has published in the *European Journal of Sustainable Development*, *Asia–Pacific Social Science Review*, *Philippine Political Science Journal*, *Asian and Pacific Migration Journal*, and *International Journal of Interdisciplinary Social and Community Studies*. Her research interests include governance and development, migrants, and information and communications technology for social inclusion.

JORGE A. SCHIAVON is Professor of International Relations at the International Studies Department, Universidad Iberoamericana, Ciudad de México (2023–). He was Professor of International Relations at the International Studies Division, Center for Research and Teaching in Economics (CIDE) (1999–2023), Coordinator (2013–2022) of the Interdisciplinary Program on Migration at CIDE (CIDE-MIG), Non-resident Fellow (2021–2023) at the Migration Policy Institute, and Executive Director of Mexico, the Americas and the World project (2010–), Mexico. At CIDE, he was President of the CIDE Foundation (2017–2019), Chair of the International Studies Department (2007–2010), Secretary General (Vice-Rector) (2004–2007), Director of Development and External Affairs (2002–2004), and Director of the BA Program in Political Science and International Relations (2000–2001). Jorge holds a Diploma in Public International Law from The Hague Academy of International Law, International Court of Justice, the Netherlands; a BA in International Relations from El Colegio de México, Mexico; an MA in political science from UCSD; and a PhD in political science and international affairs from UCSD. He is a member of the National Researchers System (SNI) in Mexico, Level III. Jorge was President of the Mexican International Studies Association (2011–2013), Founding President of the Latin American Federation of International Studies Associations (2012–2013), and Fulbright's Mexico Studies Chair (2019–2020) at the Center for U.S.–Mexican Studies at UCSD. He is author or editor of thirty-two academic books and over 150 articles and chapters on Mexican foreign policy, the history of Mexican international relations, migration, substate diplomacy (paradiplomacy); public opinion and foreign policy; regional integration in Latin America and North America; institutions, decentralization, and federalism in Latin America and North America; US–Mexico–Canada relations and Hemispheric

Latin American relations; and Mexican, North American, and Latin American political systems and foreign policies. Jorge has taught over 120 undergraduate and graduate courses, and participated in more than 500 conferences and lectures in over fifty countries.

JAMES STRONG is Senior Lecturer in British Politics and Foreign Policy at Queen Mary University of London. He holds a PhD in International Relations from the London School of Economics. His research looks at the relationship between domestic politics and foreign policy, with a specific focus on the foreign policy of the United Kingdom. James is the author of *Public Opinion, Legitimacy and Tony Blair's War in Iraq* (2017) and numerous articles on parliamentary and press contestation around UK military deployments. James is currently working on a second monograph studying the role played by the UK House of Commons in times of war from 1782 to 2018. He was Convenor of the Foreign Policy Working Group of the British International Studies Association from 2019 to 2021 and coeditor-in-chief of *Politics*, a journal of the Political Studies Association, from 2018 to 2021.

1 States' Interactions with Their National Communities Abroad

Klaus Brummer and Šumit Ganguly

Introduction

In April and May 2023, India rescued some 3,800 of its nationals from the escalating military conflict in Sudan. "Operation Kaveri" showcased the Indian government's "commitment to ensuring the safety and security of all Indians abroad" (*Times of India* 2023), as the country's foreign minister, Subrahmanyam Jaishankar, put it. About the same time, record numbers of Turks living in Germany participated in the two rounds of presidential elections in their country of origin. Being home to "nearly 1.5 million eligible voters, Germany was a major focal point for campaigning" (Politico 2023) for the ruling Justice and Development Party (AKP) under the leadership of Prime Minister Erdoğan, which has traditionally fared well in overseas voting in Germany and did so again this time around.[1] A few weeks earlier, two people were arrested in New York City based on the allegation of "operating an illegal overseas police station ... for a provincial branch of the Ministry of Public Security (MPS) of the People's Republic of China (PRC)." According to the US Department of Justice (2023), the office's purpose was to "monitor and intimidate dissidents and those critical of its [the PRC's] government."

Those examples illustrate that the interaction of states with their national communities abroad can manifest in very different ways. In some cases, states actively support and protect their communities abroad. In other cases, states co-opt and exploit their communities abroad in that they reach out to them in order to tap into, and thus benefit domestically, from their economic and financial potentials or, as in the previous case, to garner political support. In yet other cases, states repress or coerce communities abroad, thus conceiving the latter not as an asset but as a possible challenge or threat that needs to be controlled.

[1] In the run-off elections for the presidency, Erdoğan got 67.2 percent of the votes in Germany, compared to 19.6 percent in the United Kingdom and 17.3 percent in the United States (Schwanitz 2023).

The goal of this volume is to explore the drivers for such activities by states toward a diverse set of their nationals abroad, including tourists, migrants, and diaspora groups. Following the International Organization for Migration (IOM 2019: 49, 132, 216), those groups can be conceived as follows. A *tourist* is:

> A person who does not reside in the country of arrival and is admitted to that country temporarily (under tourist visas if required) for purposes of leisure, recreation, holiday, visits to friends or relatives, health or medical treatment, or religious pilgrimage. A tourist must spend at least a night in a collective or private accommodation in the receiving country and the duration of his or her stay must not surpass 12 months.

In turn, *migrant* is "an umbrella term, not defined under international law, reflecting the common lay understanding of a person who moves away from his or her place of usual residence, whether within a country or across an international border, temporarily or permanently, and for a variety of reasons." Lastly, *diaspora* is defined by the IOM as "migrants or descendants of migrants whose identity and sense of belonging, either real or symbolic, have been shaped by their migration experience and background. They maintain links with their homelands, and to each other, based on a shared sense of history, identity, or mutual experiences in the destination country."[2]

In this volume, we use the term "national communities abroad" to refer to those aforementioned groups collectively. The term is deliberately broad in scope, in both temporal and legal terms. In temporal terms, the addresses of states' actions could reside permanently in other countries, or they could be there temporarily for reasons of work or tourist travel. In legal terms, states' actions could aim at their citizens holding national passports (e.g., tourists or first-generation migrants), at people with dual or multiple citizenship, or at diasporas more broadly including second- and third-generation migrants who no longer hold citizenship of their parents' or grandparents' home state. Hence, the group under examination in this volume is broader than what Latha Varadarajan (2010: 6) calls the "domestic abroad," which is "produced through state policies and initiatives aimed at institutionalizing the relationship between nation-states and their diasporas," since it also includes members of a national community who stay abroad only temporarily, most notably for tourist travel. Having thus cast the net deliberately wide, it is for the individual country chapters to ascertain whether, and for what reason, states

[2] On the constructed nature of terms like "migrant" and "diaspora" and resulting identities among those groups, see, for example, Brubaker (2005).

develop "multi-tier policies" (Tsourapas 2015) through which they treat specific groups among their national communities abroad differently or whether they engage with diverse groups simultaneously and more or less equally in terms of instruments and intensity as well as over time or across space (i.e., states or regions).

While states interactions with their communities abroad is by no means a new phenomenon (e.g., Leira 2018: 150–153), we suggest that this activity is a highly relevant question today and, if anything, is likely to gain in relevance in the future even further. For starters, the number of international tourists has increased significantly over the last three decades. While there were 436 million tourists in 1990, the number had risen to 1.5 billion in 2019 (UNWTO 2008, 2020).[3] The number of international migrants has also risen sharply during the same time period. In 1990, the "international migrant stock" comprised of some 153 million people. In 2020, this number had increased to 281 million (UN 2020), which in turn has led "migrants' states of origin … taking an increasingly strong and proactive interest in these transnational connections" (Gamlen 2019: 3).

In addition to those quantitative increases, several political developments point to the current and future relevance of the topic under examination. Indeed, there has been a change in the perception of communities abroad on the part of states "from at best ignoring and at worst vilifying their expatriates, to a world where expatriate populations have the potential to be a vital resource for homeland populations and politicians" (Leblang and Glazier 2022: 36) – a perspective which aligns with a "neoliberal art of government [where] the population is perceived as a resource of productive forces to be mobilised for governmental purposes" (Tsinovoi and Adler-Nissen 2018: 213) and also connects to "fundamental shifts in the way in which nations are configured" (Varadarajan 2010: 6). At the same time, states do not always perceive communities abroad as assets but at times also as challenges or outright threats that need to be countered, with ensuing "extra-state practices [being] bound to increase in intensity, fostered by technological change, rising global levels of cross-border mobility, as well as a growing climate of illiberalism" (Tsourapas 2022: 315). Either way, states are and will be required to engage with their communities abroad. The evolution of a global migration regime centering around organizations such as the IOM and the World Bank has lent additional impetus for the creation of "diaspora institutions" through which states interact with their national

[3] Tourist travel has been projected to almost return to pre-pandemic levels in 2024 (UNWTO 2024).

communities abroad (Gamlen 2019: 38),[4] as has the increasing global acceptance of dual citizenship which, in addition to social and emotional attachments, also extends the legal links of communities abroad to their country of origin (Vink et al. 2019). Against those backgrounds, it seems highly pertinent to explore why and through which practices states engage with their national communities abroad.

At this point, two caveats are in order. First, while this volume emphasizes the activities of home states towards their national communities abroad, this is by no means to suggest that the latter are nothing but passive recipients of the home states' actions. To the contrary, communities abroad can exercise agency towards their countries of origin on a range of issues. The latter include providing information on their locations in governmental data bases in order to enable states to come to their support (Melissen and Caesar-Gordon 2016), influencing home states politics for example through extra-territorial voting (e.g., Brand 2010), and contributing to the home state's economic development through remittances, trade, and investments (Fernandes 2022). Communities abroad can also actively mobilize against their home state and thus play key roles concerning the initiation, perpetuation, or termination of political and at times also military conflict in their home state, thereby ultimately posing a challenge to regime survival (e.g., Shain 2007: ch. 4; Koinova 2013; Betts and Jones 2016; Kopchik et al. 2022; Bird 2023).

Second, while this volume emphasizes host states' interactions with their national communities abroad, there are a number of additional actors out there who enable or interfere in such interactions. They include: the host states of communities abroad whose sovereignty is infringed by home states' outreach to its communities (Tindall 2012: 106); third states with whom the home state might join forces, for example in crisis situations (Melissen and Okano-Heijmans 2018: 143); international governmental organizations such as the European Union (Bicchi and Schade 2022) or institutions that belong to the "global migration regime" (Gamlen 2019); and an array of non-state actors, including both national and international nongovernmental organizations (NGOs and INGOs) and private security contractors (e.g., Tsinovoi and Adler-Nissen 2018). The country chapters contained in this volume will highlight the agency of national communities vis-à-vis their home states as well as the influence of other actors on home states' interactions with their communities abroad whenever appropriate.

[4] According to Gamlen (2019: 30), 118 states had set up "diaspora institutions" in 2015, compared to just 15 in 1980. On the reasons why states set up such "expatriate-related institutions," see Brand (2006).

This volume connects to and expands on different strands of literatures that have explored states' engagement with their national communities abroad. For starters, there are conceptual works on the general motivations as well as on the specific factors that condition whether and how states reach out to their communities abroad (e.g., Délano and Gamlen 2014; Ragazzi 2014; Koinova and Tsourapas 2018). In turn, aspects specifically related to "support" have been discussed, for example under the heading of states' general "duty of care" (e.g., Melissen and Okano-Heijmans 2018; Græger and Leira 2020) or, more specifically, with respect to granting access to social protection to their citizens abroad (Vintila and Lafleur 2020; Lafleur and Vintila 2020a). Conversely, concerns of "co-optation" and even more so "repression" have been explored prominently in the literature on "transnational authoritarianism" (e.g., Glasius 2018; Tsourapas 2021a, 2022). The aforementioned discussions on the general motives on the part of states to engage with their communities are complemented by Gamlen's (2019) "new institutional explanation" for why states set up "diaspora institutions" to engage with their national communities abroad in the first place, which he suggests has happened in response to the rise of a global migration regime.

Empirically, scholarship has analyzed the activities of a range of individual countries towards its communities abroad (e.g., Brand 2006; Allison 2009; Délano 2011; Hernández Joseph 2012; Rifawan et al. 2017; Græger and Lindgren 2018; Gaur 2019; Asis 2020; Hameed 2021; Katigbak and Roldan 2021; Tsourapas 2021b; Arkilic 2022), with special emphasis being placed on China (e.g., Wang 2013; Zerba 2014; Boni 2019; Baum 2020; Ghiselli 2021). Other works examine the impact or the specific activities of international organizations (e.g., Geyer 2007; Ianniello Saliceti 2011; Mwagiru 2012; Moraru 2014; Gamlen 2019). Yet other publications focus on specific substantive themes, such as child abduction (Haugevik 2018), the protection of low-skilled workers (Okano-Heijmans and Price 2019), access to social protection (Lafleur and Vintila 2020b, c), or consular support in the aftermath of catastrophic events or emergencies (Tindall 2012).

What sets this volume apart from the aforementioned scholarship is its comparative approach across countries, covering both Western and non-Western states, combined with its multidimensional approach in terms of substantive areas of states' interactions with their national communities abroad comprising diplomatic and consular, economic and social, and security-related activities. In so doing, it heeds several interrelated calls in the literature. One is to engage in "comparative work" (Délano and Gamlen 2014: 47) when analyzing states' interactions with their citizens abroad. Another concerns the exploration of the reasons as to why some states do actively interact with communities abroad while others do not, thereby exploring the reasons for convergence or divergence in state behavior towards different groups of their communities abroad, in different substantive domains, and over time (Koinova and Tsourapas 2018: 312). A third one concerns the examination of "non-Western practices in the duty of care" (Melissen and Okano-Heijmans 2018: 141) as well as in other substantive areas in addition to "support" (Brand 2006: 1–2). A final one relates to focusing on the policies and politics of home or sending states as opposed to the immigration policies by host states (Brand 2006: 5). In so doing, the volume contributes to the aforementioned discussions on (sending and home) states' migration and diaspora policies and politics and on transnational authoritarianism. In addition, by examining a critical albeit understudied component of states' external affairs, the volume contributes from a comparative perspective (Brummer 2020) to our understanding of the drivers and outcomes of foreign policy, and to the field of Foreign Policy Analysis (FPA) more broadly (e.g., Alden and Aran 2017; Brummer and Oppermann 2024).

The remainder of this chapter proceeds as follows. The next section explores the general motivations and objectives as to why states interact with their national communities abroad ("support, co-opt, repress"). Then, the chapter discusses key practices and tactics that states can employ in this interaction along three substantive dimensions, namely: diplomacy and consular, economy and social, and security. Next, possible drivers that condition whether, how, and for what reason states interact with their communities abroad are presented. This is followed by a discussion on how the countries covered in this volume were selected. The concluding section presents the plan of the book and briefly summarizes the individual chapters.

States' Interaction with Their National Communities Abroad: Support, Co-optation, and Repression

As indicated by the examples presented at the outset of this chapter, states' activities towards communities manifest in very different ways. At times states do something *for* their communities abroad. At other times states want to *get something out of* their communities abroad. At still other times states deliberately *act against* their communities abroad. We refer to those different types of actions as "support" (do for), "co-optation" (get something out of), and "repress" (act against). The following paragraphs introduce those different general types of states' motivations in their interactions with their national communities abroad in greater detail. The next section then provides information on the specific practices and tactics that states employ in the pursuit of those objectives.

Support

States' actions towards their national communities abroad can be grounded in a genuine ambition to support, assist, and protect said group, or specific members thereof. Activities in this regard include consular measures such as replacing passports or efforts to augment rights and protections for workers. Occasionally, they also entail military measures, such as evacuation flights during times of political turmoil or in the aftermath of natural disasters.

By engaging in activities such as the aforementioned, states fulfil their "duty of care" (Melissen and Okano-Heijmans 2018; Græger and Leira 2020) towards their communities abroad, with special emphasis being placed on "citizens beyond the border" (Leira and Græger 2020: 2). In this sense, Kristin Haugevik (2018: 168) refers to a state's activities to assist and protect its citizens beyond its borders as "an extension of the social contract between state and subjects – a state's responsibility for its citizens' safety and well-being does not stop at the border."

From this grows an expectation on the part of citizens that their country will come to their assistance and support in cases of need, acting either as "caretakers" in routine, low-profile situations or as "rescuers" in extreme and high-profile contexts (Haugevik 2018: 168). By implication, if states refrain from coming to the support of their communities abroad, this could diminish their (domestic) legitimacy. At the same time, states might face a dilemma in this regard in that their activities might violate international norms pertaining to state sovereignty and nonintervention, which in turn might infringe on their own international status (Haugevik 2018: 169). Another dilemma might arise for states in that past efforts to support and protect their communities abroad lead to expectations of similar activities in the future, which might even be abused by third parties, for example with regards to "hostage diplomacy" (Hess 2022).[5] At any rate, the motivation of states to support should be particularly pronounced towards, albeit not categorically restricted to, those people among the national community abroad who hold formal citizenship, like tourists, expats, and first-generation migrants.

[5] With an eye on US measures to protect American-owned property overseas, Noel Maurer (2013) makes a similar argument grounded in path dependencies by suggesting that administrations were put under pressure to engage in such activities based on precedents set by their predecessors, a phenomenon that Maurer calls "empire trap."

Co-optation

States also engage their national communities abroad in more instrumental and transactional ways. Rather than doing something for them, as is the case for "support," states' primary concern is to get something out of their communities by means of co-optation and exploitation. From this vantage point, national communities abroad are perceived as an asset that the home state can tap into "in pursuit of power" (Gamlen 2019: 10). States are driven by economic, political, and social considerations, which in turn can have implications for the overall legitimacy of the state's political regime.

National communities abroad possibly hold huge economic and financial potential (e.g., Brand 2006: 17; de Haas 2010).[6] One dimension concerns remittances, which for some countries is a key component of their national budgets and which has also been shown to contribute to regime survival (Ahmed 2012).[7] Communities abroad could additionally serve as key sources for investments and donations in their country of origin. Further, states may seek to tap into the skills, knowledge, and expertise of their communities abroad, thereby reversing "brain drain" into "brain gain" (Kapur 2001).

In addition, states may seek to co-opt and exploit national communities abroad for political reasons, both foreign and domestic. States could mobilize their communities abroad, which are perceived as "a political leverage tool" (Arkilic 2022: 3), to advance their foreign policy interests by influencing policy-making in the host states, most notably towards itself (i.e., the home state) and possibly also towards relevant third parties (foes and friends of the home state alike) (e.g., Brand 2006: 16). This relates not only to members of national communities who reside permanently abroad but also to tourists who could, for example, be barred by their home state from entering certain countries, thereby "punish[ing] countries or territories whose actions or policies displease" the home state (Paradise 2022: 32). At the same time, states can seek to co-opt and instrumentalize communities abroad for domestic political reasons, including the retention of power, for example through overseas voting (e.g., Brand 2010).

The aforementioned economic and political considerations can be complemented by a social motive in that states might seek to tap into their

[6] On the broader questions of the effects of neoliberal restructuring of (the home) states and of capitalist social relations in the context of states' interactions with their communities abroad, see Varadarayan (2010).

[7] However, Escribà-Folch et al. (2018) have recently suggested that remittances could have the opposite effect as well, in the sense of increasing the likelihood of political protests in non-democratic regimes by increasing the resources available for such activities.

national communities abroad for reasons of national identity-building and national unity (Gamlen 2019: 11–12). Individually or jointly, home states' ability to co-opt the economic, political, and social potential of their national communities abroad can be a key factor for shoring up or even augmenting regime legitimacy and in the final analysis securing regime survival.

Repression

A third type of state interaction with their national communities abroad manifests in acts of repression, coercion, and control of said group, or specific groups or individuals within that group. The underlying rationale for such actions is that at least parts of the national community abroad are perceived by their home state as representing a challenge or outright threat, most notably a political or military one. This perception reinforces the previously mentioned conceptualization of communities abroad as being more than merely passive recipients of their home states' activities.

For example, communities abroad could stage protests against their home state in their host state, thereby threatening to undermine the former's legitimacy. They could also support or even organize military challenges (e.g., Betts and Jones 2016). Given the threats that emanate from such actions for regime legitimacy and ultimately regime survival, states perceive a need to counter those challenges.

The recent literature on "transnational authoritarianism" and ensuing "extraterritorial authoritarian practices" (e.g., Glasius 2018; Tsourapas 2021a; Wackenhut and Orjuela 2023) suggests that this need is particularly pronounced in non-democratic regimes. The latter do not ascribe certain (citizen) rights to their communities abroad but conceive of them, or rather certain parts, as "outlaws" or "traitors" (Glasius 2018: 186). The home state thus perceives a need to act against parts of their communities abroad in order to prevent political dissent or military challenges from arising. Overall, states, and authoritarian ones in particular, "seek to reap the material benefit of free movement while ensuring that migrant and diaspora groups pose little political or security threat to their survival" (Tsourapas 2021a: 621).

Specific State Practices towards Their National Communities Abroad

After having outlined the general types of states' interactions with their national communities abroad, the ensuing question concerns the specific activities that they may undertake. The following paragraphs introduce various practices and tactics that states employ to support, co-opt, and repress their national communities abroad.[8] The discussions are structured along three substantive dimensions that reflect core domains of statecraft (e.g., Goddard et al. 2019). Those dimensions are: diplomatic and consular; economic and social; and security. The discussions show that rather than being confined to a specific substantive dimension, the aforementioned motives of support, co-opt, and repress cut across them.

The Diplomatic and Consular Dimension

Diplomatic and consular measures are a key building block in states' interaction with their national communities abroad. Typically undertaken by "classical" diplomatic institutions of states (foreign ministries, embassies, consulates), they include a range of measures of support, such as replacing lost or stolen passports for tourists or offering assistance in legal matters, including instances of "hostage diplomacy." Diplomatic and consular practices can also be connected to the other two motivations in terms of co-optation and repression, for example by providing the infrastructure for overseas voting, by politicizing certain consular activities, or through the deliberate withholding and thus exclusion of certain parts of the national community abroad from certain services.

States can undertake various *diplomatic and consular activities* in support of their national communities abroad. Corresponding action is regulated by international conventions, most notably the Vienna Convention on Diplomatic Relations of 1961 and the Vienna Convention on Consular Relations of 1963. When enumerating the functions of diplomatic missions, the former convention states that: "Protecting in the receiving State the interests of the sending State and of its nationals, within the limits permitted by international law" (art. 3 para. 1b). In turn, the latter convention lists multiple "consular functions" (art. 5) that states may undertake to assist and support their citizens in the respective host states. Those include: the issuing of travel documents and visas; safeguarding the interests of minors; representing citizens before courts; as well as "helping and assisting" individual citizens in general. While not explicitly mentioned, diplomatic or consular support measures could also include supporting nationals in case of "hostage diplomacy" or the coordination and provision of emergency assistance after natural disasters or during times of violent conflict in the host country. Following Brand (2006: 7), "The extent and type of services offered by such government offices [like

[8] For an extensive list of possible "emigrant policies," see Pedroza and Palop-García (2017).

embassies and consulates] abroad are important indicators of a state's interest and involvement in its expatriate communities." Advances in communications technology have not only increased expectations by communities abroad towards their states for assistance (e.g., Melissen and Caesar-Gordon 2016: 322) but, while being demanding in terms of overcoming "communicative challenges" (Melissen 2020) and sometimes falling short (e.g., Katigbak and Roldan 2021: 364–365), have also generally enabled states to better live up those increased expectations (e.g., Bjola and Holmes 2015; Manor and Adiku 2021).

States exhibit considerable variation concerning the domestic legal foundations for conducting diplomatic and consular activities. While in some states such provisions are enshrined in foreign service laws (e.g., Germany) or even in constitutions (e.g., China), other states do not have such legal provisions (e.g., United Kingdom). In the latter cases, the provision of support to citizens abroad depends on voluntary efforts and essentially boils down to a policy decision (Geyer 2007: 2).

So far, the discussion has highlighted the supportive and essentially technical and by implication seemingly apolitical nature of diplomatic and consular activities. However, there is also an intrinsically political dimension to such activities (Melissen and Caesar-Gordon 2016: 322), which, in turn, opens up space for practices aimed at co-optation and repression.[9] An example of the politicization of seemingly innocuous technical undertakings comes in the form of "passportization." The latter refers to issuing and distributing passports to a certain group of people and illustrates a process of co-optation of communities abroad (and of the latter's political "creation" in the first place) for political ends. Such actions challenge the host states' sovereignty and can serve as a possible precursor for future broader political or military actions by "creating" citizens who subsequently can be referenced as being in need of protection, as has been the case for Russian activities towards Georgia and Ukraine (Allison 2009; Wrighton 2018).

Diplomatic and consular institutions and activities can also be employed to tap into the potential of, and thus co-opt, communities abroad particularly for political purposes. Key in this regard is the extension of voting rights to communities abroad and the provision of the necessary infrastructure to that end, which may include turning embassies and consulates into temporary voting stations. Communities abroad are

[9] Scholarship refers to "consular diplomacy" in order to highlight that, "Rather than discussing consular affairs and diplomacy in isolation, more evidence now articulates how transnational consular challenges may involve and at times complicate) inter-state collaboration" (Melissen and Okano-Heijmans 2018: 139).

particularly interesting for those in power in their home states if they are large in size and likely to support their home state's ruling government (Brand 2010: 84; Wellmann 2021). As Laurie Brand (2010: 86) argues, "domestic jockeying for electoral advantage" and the ensuing expectation "that those abroad would improve the electoral prospects of a particular party," thus consolidating or further strengthening the regime, is among the main reasons for the extension of voting rights to communities abroad, which has been done by democracies and non-democracies alike.

In addition, there are several practices in the diplomatic and consular dimension that states can employ to repress certain groups or individuals among their communities abroad. Those pertain not only to "discretionary consular services," by which Gamlen (2019: 248) refers to measures that "are not specifically condoned or prohibited by the Vienna Convention," such as data collection or the intensity of legal support. In addition, though, they can also concern "core" diplomatic and consular activities (e.g., Glasius 2018: 191; Wackenhut and Orjuela 2023: 153) and manifest, for example, in the deliberate withholding of diplomatic support in legal matters or the denial of consular services (e.g., non-renewal of passports). Another option is to exclude certain groups of people from overseas voting (e.g., based on profession or length of stay), which may be part of a larger drive of disenfranchising certain groups of communities both at home and abroad (Indian Express) and prevent "turning rights into ballots" (Finn and Besserer Rayas 2022).

The Economic and Social Dimension

States engage in a host of economic and social activities towards their national communities abroad, which in turn can be tied to different motivations of states. Supportive measures may include efforts to shore up the rights of national communities in host states through the signing of legal agreements. The line between doing something in support of communities abroad and getting something out of them is rather blurry, however, since efforts to shore up the rights and statuses of communities abroad concomitantly contain the promise for the host state of reaping bigger returns, for example through higher remittances. At the same time, states could repress parts of their communities abroad by deliberately excluding them from certain services or by barring certain activities on their part. While foreign ministries are key for diplomatic and consular activities, a broader array of "diaspora institutions" tends to be involved in economic and social affairs, comprising both dedicated diaspora ministries and additional "parent ministries" (next to the foreign ministry) “like health, welfare, labor, culture, and religion” (Ragazzi 2014: 75) that feature departments dealing with communities abroad (Gamlen 2019: 42–48; also Lafleur and Vintila 2020a: 27).

States can undertake a variety of activities to assist and support their national communities abroad in economic and social terms. They pertain, for example, to extending domestic benefits and services such as family or unemployment benefits, health care, social assistance, and pensions to their national communities abroad, thereby offering “deterritorialized social security as protection policy” (Lafleur and Vintila 2020a: 8). Importantly, though, the extent to which benefits and services are “portable” depends on whether a home state can enter agreements with host states where its communities reside.

Another key issue is the protection of the rights of “worker-citizens” (Okano-Heijmans and Caesar-Gordon 2016) abroad. This aspect is particularly salient for low-skilled workers who are not supported by their sending company (should there be one in the first place) and who also typically receive limited, if any support from their employers in the host state (Okano-Heijmans and Price 2019). A major instrument in this regard is the conclusion of labor agreements or of (nonbinding) memorandums of understanding between the home state and the host states of its national communities in which commitments and responsibilities concerning the protection of workers are established (e.g., Brand 2006: 6–7).

Agreements like those on social protection and workers’ rights are important not only for the individual members of the communities abroad in terms of support but also for the home state and its ability to co-opt and thereby materially benefit from its communities. Indeed, higher levels of protection of the rights of their communities abroad should increase the economic and financial benefit of the host state, for example through higher returns of remittances or investments by the communities abroad (e.g., de Haas 2010). Accordingly, states should focus their efforts of concluding such agreements with those states where large diaspora groups reside. However, the mere conclusion of agreements with host states is by no means a guarantee for the actual upholding of workers’ rights as problems of “non-payment of due wages, working hours longer than that specified in contracts, denial of weekly holidays, exit or re-entry visas, health and medical insurance as well as non-renewal of residence permits” (Hameed 2021: 447) can nonetheless persist.

In addition to benefiting economically and financially from them “from afar,” states can set up activities for their communities abroad that seek to incentivize the return especially of highly qualified individuals to their home state (Ragazzi 2014: 76). Measures which aim at the permanent return can be complemented by activities that seek to "engage [members of the diaspora] in temporary or virtual return programmes" (Koinova and Tsourapas 2018: 313).

Representing the flipside of the aforementioned activities to induce "brain gain" (Kapur 2001) by tapping into the potential of communities abroad, states could deliberately try to repress parts of their communities abroad by withholding or barring certain benefits and activities respectively. This could relate to actions both from and to the home state. The former entails the deliberate exclusion of certain groups of communities abroad from the provision of domestic benefits and services, thereby making the latter "non-portable" for political reasons. The latter includes, for example, the blocking of transfers of remittances to the country of origin.

The Security Dimension

Finally, states engage in various security-related measures towards their national communities abroad. As has been the case for the two preceding dimensions, states' actions can be tied to different motivations and objectives. While certain measures are aimed at protecting and at times literally saving members of their national community abroad from natural disasters or man-made threats, with the latter emanating from both other state actors and non-state actors (e.g., Leira 2018), others are driven by states' ambitions to either co-opt or repress members of their national community abroad, which in the most extreme cases mean the elimination of certain individuals. Whereas the supportive activities are typically situation-specific and limited in time, the other practices tend to be more systematic and long term. Importantly, while "diaspora institutions" are crucial for diplomatic and consular as well as economic and social measures, they are less relevant in the security realm where states' military or intelligence services play important roles.

Security-related measures of support[10] are often times necessitated by extreme circumstances, such as civil conflict or interstate war, natural disasters, or, as has been the case recently, a global pandemic. In such situations, states often times engage in interministerial efforts to coordinate their support for affected members of their communities abroad. Examples are evacuation flights which are organized by foreign ministries and conducted using either civilian aircraft or by drawing on the states' military. The latter is particularly relevant in situations of violent

10 Here we focus on threats to peoples' physical security, rather than following a broader, human-security oriented conceptualization of security.

conflict where the use of force may be required to take members of the national community out of harm's way.

In terms of travel and residency patterns, the geographical scope of security-related measures of support and protection is potentially global. Having said that, the ability of most states to project power across larger distances is rather limited or virtually nonexistent. By implication, inaction on the part of states may result not from a lack of will but a lack of capacity. At the same time, military activities sometimes become possible or are at least rendered easier by fortuitous circumstances, such as when military forces are already present in a country or region that succumbs to civil war or is affected by a natural disaster for other purposes which can then be used to extract nationals (e.g., Zerba 2014: 1107).

In addition to activities to support and occasionally outright save members of their communities abroad, states have developed an extensive arsenal of security-related instruments and practices which they can employ to co-opt and, more importantly still, repress groups or certain individuals among their communities abroad. In this sense, Wackenhut and Orjuela (2023: 147) refer to "a sizeable toolbox … to pursue their challengers and silence critique beyond their own borders, which includes assassinations, assaults, disappearances, renditions and unlawful deportations, abuse of Interpol's system of 'red notices', digital threats, spyware, passport and document control, and coercion by proxy." As indicated by the quote, recent technological advances have considerably expanded states' ability "to monitor, discipline, and punish dissenters abroad" (Tsourapas 2022: 308), hence their reach across borders. Communities residing in open societies, where they can mobilize and express their positions against their home state's regime freely, should be of particular interest to authoritarian states' security services in terms of monitoring and surveillance (Brand 2006: 218).[11]

Drivers of States' Interaction with Their National Communities Abroad

After having first outlined the general ways in which states might interact with their national communities abroad and the specific practices that states can employ in this regard, the ensuing question concerns the specific drivers which condition *whether, how, and for what purposes* states actually reach out to their national communities abroad. Possible

[11] However, a recent report by Freedom House suggests that the vast majority of acts of transnational repression (74 percent) has occurred in "non-free" countries (Gorokhovskaia and Linzer 2022: 4).

explanatory factors can be grouped into four categories. While the first points to characteristics of the national community abroad, the others address characteristics of home states themselves. Thus, we place emphasis on utilitarian explanations which focus on material factors and instrumental considerations on the one hand and on governance explanations of states' interactions with their national communities abroad which highlight multiple practices and channels of engagement on the other (Ragazzi 2014: 82; Koinova and Tsourapas 2018: 313–314).[12]

First, certain *characteristics of the national communities abroad* can render activities of states more or less likely. This includes geographic location. That is, where national communities reside or travel abroad influences the extent to which states may be required to come to their assistance. If citizens travel or reside primarily in developed countries, on the whole the host states themselves should be better equipped to provide protective measures and also be less prone to succumb to civil conflict or become the location of interstate war. Conversely, the less developed a state is, the less state capacity exists in the host state for providing support and protection to any kinds of people, especially foreigners, and the likelihood of violent conflict also often times increases. As a result, the necessity for home states to come to the support of their citizens should increase.

Another factor relates to the domestic relevance of communities groups in economic terms. Not least spurred by economic globalization, home states increasingly consider their communities abroad as valuable assets (e.g., Délano and Gamlen 2014: 44; Chaterjee and Das 2021: 579). Indeed, migrants and diaspora groups more broadly can be a major economic factor in the home state, as indicated, for example, by remittances and investments. Moreover, diaspora groups can prove helpful in opening up host-state markets or for transferring knowledge back to their country of origin. Such manifest or expected material benefits should incentivize states to engage with, and co-opt, their citizens abroad.

Second, certain *legal and institutional factors* could be key drivers for state action. Regarding the former, the key question is whether states are legally obliged to assist their citizens abroad. More specifically, are such provisions established in state's laws (e.g., the foreign service laws) or even national constitutions? The more formally binding the provisions are, the more likely states should become active. Conversely, if there are

[12] In terms of Brand's proposed explanations for state behavior towards its communities abroad, the volume connects the "international politics," "domestic political," and "security/stability" explanations (Brand 2006: 13–19).

no legal provisions, interacting with national communities abroad essentially boils down to a policy decision (Geyer 2007: 2), which could lead to lower levels of engagement.

A similar logic applies with respect to "diaspora institutions" (Gamlen 2019: ch. 2). Here, the key question is whether states have specific ministries dedicated to the interaction with their national communities abroad. By setting up such an institution, states signal how important the issue is for them, and should engage in substantial and sustained activities accordingly. Alternatively, the task could be handled "merely" by subunits (e.g., departments or desks) of ministries with more encompassing mandates such as the foreign ministry or ministries dealing with economic and social affairs, or they could be handled by "other diaspora institutions" (Gamlen 2019: 46) such as interdepartmental committees or advisory councils. The specific institutional set-up of diaspora institutions should be indicative of the political relevance and salience that states ascribe to their interactions with national communities abroad, which in turn should impact the intensity with which states engage in such actions, be it in terms of support, co-optation, or repression.

Third, states' ability to engage with their national communities abroad can be conceived as a function of *state capacity*. States with greater political functionality are more likely to feature stable and capable institutions, both domestically (ministries, etc.) and abroad (e.g., diplomatic and consular network), which in turn are required to provide sustained and high-quality engagement with communities abroad, be it for purposes of support, co-optation, or repression. Similarly, greater economic prowess puts states in a better position to engage in diverse and durable activities towards their communities abroad. The same should be true for states with greater capacity in the security realm (military, intelligence, police) and ensuing activities most notably in terms of repression.

Thus, generally speaking, states with greater state capacity should be better able to employ a broader array of instruments in that regard, and do so in a sustained fashion, than states with lower capacity. However, it might be the latter who are particularly interested in or even dependent on such outreach activities. Indeed, states' weakness at home might actually push them especially towards co-opting their national communities abroad to a much larger extent than is the case for states with high capacity. As Koinova and Tsourapas (2018: 315) put it, "To compensate for these limitations, they [weak states] engage diasporas abroad to fulfil missing functions and provide remittances to sustain livelihoods. Formal remittances and other capital contributions have been crucial to states' survival."

Finally, *regime type* can be another driver for states' interaction with its national communities abroad. As a baseline, all regimes strive for legitimacy. In turn, the provision of support to nationals abroad can be among the means to accomplish this goal. Indeed, citizens expect support from their governments: While "travelling or residing abroad [they] will in many cases have a legitimate expectation that their home state will provide them with assistance if needed" (Haugevik 2018: 171). If done successfully, the provision of support to communities abroad can consolidate or even augment a state's legitimacy. Having said that, a state's unwillingness or inability to come to the support of its citizens abroad could have the opposite effect by fostering the impression of "exploitative states that attempt to extract obligations without extending rights" (Gamlen 2006: 23).

Still, while all regimes should have at least some interest in the well-being of their communities abroad, the extent to which states are politically required to engage in measures of "support" for reasons of legitimacy may vary depending on regime type. Indeed, different requirements could follow from being a democracy or an autocracy. However, the direction in which those requirements point is not clear. For example, based on generally higher levels of responsiveness and accountability democratic states might feel more compelled to look after their communities abroad than non-democratic regimes. Having said that, in non-democratic states the lack of participatory rights might make it even more crucial for the regimes to provide "at least" physical protection to their communities abroad.

The expectations for the practices of co-optation and especially repression are more clear-cut. Indeed, the literature on transnational authoritarianism (e.g., Glasius 2018; Tsourapas 2021a) suggests that incentives to engage in such activities should be particularly pronounced in authoritarian regimes. Thus, practices to repress certain parts of their national communities abroad like "surveillance, threats, proxy punishment, enforced disappearances, coerced return, and lethal retribution" (Tsourapas 2022: 308) should be found primarily as part of non-democratic regimes.

Country Selection

This volume examines the interactions of a total of twelve countries located in four continents with their national communities abroad for purposes of support, co-optation, and repression. Five of the countries are members of the Organisation for Economic Co-operation and Development (OECD) and six belong to the G77 (plus Russia). Hence,

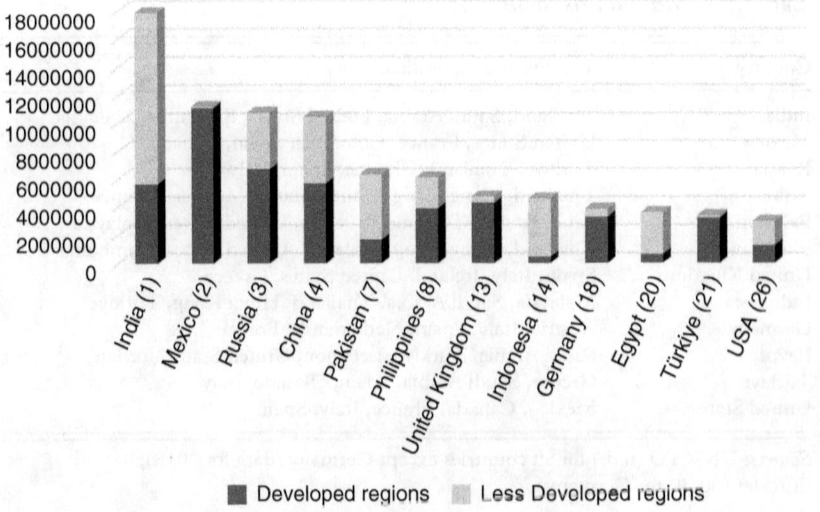

Figure 1.1 Nationals living abroad
Source: UN (2020). Numbers in parentheses after country name indicate the respective country's global ranking in terms of nationals living abroad measured in absolute numbers.

the volume heeds the calls found in the literature previously cited for both engaging in comparative work on states' relations with their national communities living abroad and for including non-Western cases when doing so (Délano and Gamlen 2014: 47; Melissen and Okano-Heijmans 2018: 141). All the states have in common large groups of their national communities living abroad. This can be illustrated by the number of citizens living abroad, which for the countries covered in this volume range from a minimum of some 3 million in the case of the United States to close to 18 million in the case of India (Figure 1.1). Measured in absolute numbers, the countries covered in this volume are all ranked among the top thirty worldwide. Incorporating tourists and members of the diaspora who do not hold formal citizenship of their country of origin increases the size of the respective groups still further.

Large groups of national communities abroad should, in principle, render the issue of interacting with those communities in other countries sufficiently salient for governments to engage in corresponding activities, thus rendering them most-likely cases. Of course, whether this is actually the case is a matter for empirical examination, hence this is one of the key analytical goals of this volume. The volume only considers countries which exhibit a minimum functionality in terms of state capacity since

Table 1.1 *Main tourist destinations*

Country	Top five tourist destinations
India	Thailand, Saudi Arabia, United States, Sri Lanka, Malaysia
Mexico	United States, France, Colombia, Spain, Canada
Russia	Türkiye, Thailand, Ukraine, Spain, Italy
China	Thailand, Hong Kong, United States, Malaysia, France
Pakistan	Saudi Arabia, Thailand, Türkiye, United States, Malaysia
Philippines	Thailand, Hong Kong, Malaysia, United States, Cambodia
United Kingdom	Spain, Italy, Ireland, United States, Greece
Indonesia	Malaysia, Saudi Arabia, Thailand, Hong Kong, Türkiye
Germany	Austria, Italy, Spain, Netherlands, France
Egypt	Saudi Arabia, Türkiye, Lebanon, United States, Jordan
Türkiye	Greece, Saudi Arabia, Spain, Ukraine, Italy
United States	Mexico, Canada, France, Italy, Spain

Sources: UNWTO (n.d.) for all countries except Germany (data for 2018); Eurostat (2019) for Germany.

this is deemed a prerequisite for any meaningful and sustained activities to interact with national communities abroad. Consequently, while also exhibiting large communities abroad, countries like South Sudan, Afghanistan, or Syria, which are barely functional as per, for example, the "Fragile State Index" (Fund for Peace 2022), are not considered.

In addition to those basic parameters, the countries covered in this volume exhibit a wide variation along the aforementioned drivers that possibly condition states' engagement with their communities abroad. Starting with the *characteristics of national communities abroad.* Here, the twelve countries exhibit significant differences, for example in terms of the geographic location of their communities residing permanently abroad (Figure 1.1). At one end of the spectrum, Mexicans reside almost exclusively in developed states and in the United States in particular. The United Kingdom, Germany, and Türkiye exhibit similar distributions. At the other end of the spectrum, the vast majority of Indonesians and Egyptians residing abroad are located in less developed states (UN 2020). A similar pattern emerges with respect to tourist travel (Table 1.1).

The national communities abroad of the twelve countries under examination also differ greatly in terms of their economic relevance for the home countries. Figure 1.2 illustrates this based on remittances, which display huge variation in terms of both absolute numbers and share of GDP. Regarding absolute numbers, India ranks top among the countries analyzed in this volume with remittances of more than $83 billion in 2020. In contrast, Türkiye received around $800 million. A different

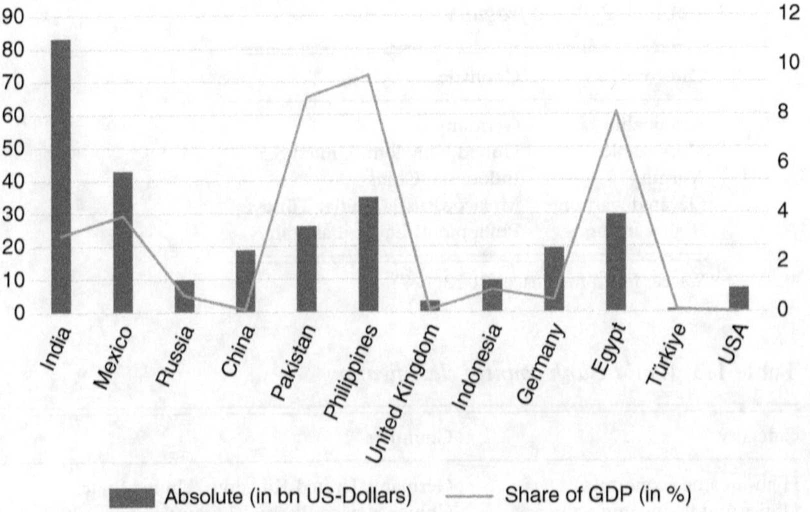

Figure 1.2 Remittances
Source: World Bank (2022a) (data for 2020).

pattern emerges, however, when the remittances are measures in terms of percent of GDP. Here, the Philippines, Pakistan, and Egypt top the list. In all three countries, remittances amounted to 8 percent or more of the respective GDP in 2020. Conversely, in countries like Türkiye but also China and the United States remittances made up 0.1 percent of GDP or less (World Bank 2022a).

The countries covered in this volume also show variation with respect to *the legal provisions* and *the institutional set-up* for interacting with their national communities abroad. Regarding legal provisions, the countries include those where corresponding obligations have been enshrined in constitutions (e.g., China, Türkiye) or in regular laws such as foreign service laws (e.g., Germany). At the same time, the volume includes cases where no legal provisions exist (United Kingdom) or where provisions are aimed at the protection of specific groups of the national community abroad, most notably migrant workers (e.g., Indonesia).

The countries covered in this volume show similar variation in terms of the "diaspora institutions" tasked with the interaction with the national communities abroad. On the one hand, there are countries where dedicated ministries have been set up to address the state's interactions with its communities abroad. Cases in point are: the Ministry of Overseas Pakistanis; the (albeit short-lived) Ministry of Overseas Indian Affairs; the Philippine's newly set up Department of Migrant Workers; or the Ministry

Table 1.2 *State fragility*

Category	Countries
Sustainable	Germany
More stable	United Kingdom, United States
Warning	Indonesia, China
Elevated warning	Mexico, Russia, India, Türkiye
High warning	Philippines, Egypt, Pakistan

Source: Fund for Peace (2022: 6–7).

Table 1.3 *World Bank country classification*

Category	Countries
High-income economies	Germany, United Kingdom, United States
Upper middle-income economies	China, Mexico, Russia, Türkiye
Lower middle-income economies	Egypt, India, Indonesia, Pakistan, the Philippines

Source: World Bank (2022b).

of State for Emigration and Egyptian Expatriate Affairs. In the other countries, the engagement with citizens residing abroad is handled by departmental units, with the foreign ministry being the key parent ministry.

The countries covered in this volume also vary significantly in terms of *state capacity*. This concerns both the overall functionality of the states and the specific indicators concerning the three substantive domains of actions covered in this volume (in short: diplomacy, economy, security). Differences in the overall functionality of the states can be illustrated by their ranking in the "Fragile State Index," as Table 1.2 illustrates.

In addition, the countries exhibit considerable differences in terms of the density and reach of their diplomatic and consular networks as indicated by the ranking in the "Global Diplomacy Index." China tops the list, followed by the United States (2nd), Türkiye (5th), Russia (6th), United Kingdom (7th), Germany (8th), India (12th), Mexico (14th), Indonesia (23rd), Pakistan (32nd), and the Philippines (41st) (Lowy Institute 2021).[13]

Moreover, the countries vary greatly in economic terms, as indicated, for example, by different classifications by the World Bank, including high, upper middle-, and lower middle-income countries (Table 1.3). They also differ markedly in their ranking on the "Human Development

[13] Egypt has not been included in the ranking.

Table 1.4 *Human development*

Category	Countries
Very high human development	Germany (9th), United Kingdom (18th), United States (21st), Türkiye (48th), Russia (52nd)
High human development	China (79th), Mexico (86th), Egypt (97th), Indonesia (114th)
Medium human development	Philippines (116th), India (132nd)
Low human development	Pakistan (161st)

Source: UNDP (2022). Specific country rank in parentheses.

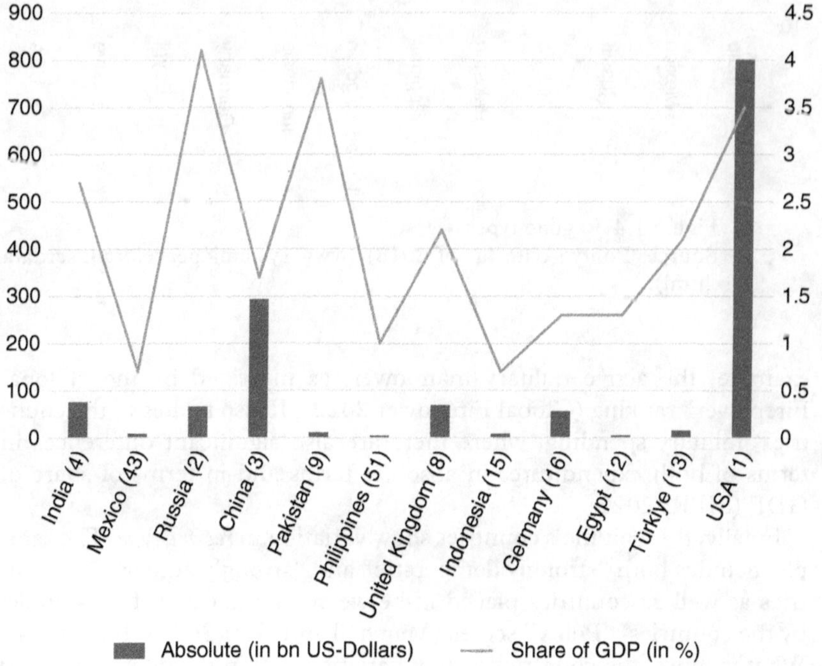

Figure 1.3 Military expenditures
Source: SIPRI (2022). Data for 2021. Absolute expenditures in current USD. Number in parentheses after country name denotes state's Global Firepower ranking (Global Firepower 2022).

Index." Here, countries range all the way from "very high human development" to "low human development (Table 1.4).

The countries covered in this volume also exhibit huge differences with respect to military capabilities (Figure 1.3). This concerns, for

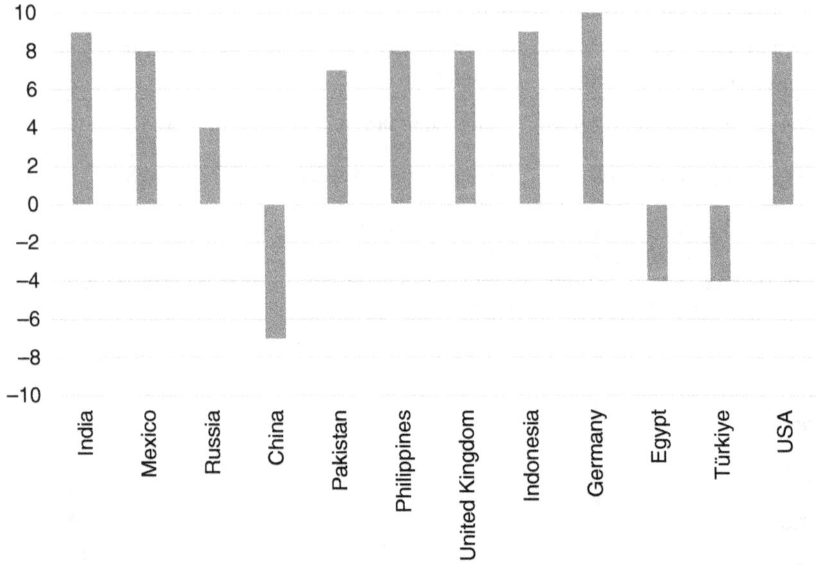

Figure 1.4 Regime types
Source: Polity5 data (as of 2018) (www.systemicpeace.org/inscrdata.html).

example, the active military manpower, as indicated by the "Global Firepower" ranking (Global Firepower 2022). It also relates to the countries' military spending, where there are also significant differences in terms of both expenditures in absolute terms and in terms of share of GDP (SIPRI 2022).

Finally, this volume's countries show variation in *regime type*. The sample includes both "strongly democratic" and "strongly autocratic" countries as well as countries placed in-between, as indicated, for example, by the countries' "Polity" scores (Marshall and Gurr 2020) (Figure 1.4). What is more, the countries exhibit variation within the democratic and autocratic groups. Regarding democracies, the volume entails both parliamentary (e.g., United Kingdom) and presidential (e.g., United States) systems. And in terms of variation among autocracies (e.g., Geddes 1999), it includes both party-based (China) and military (Egypt) types.

Plan of the Volume

To ensure comparability of findings across the chapters and coherence throughout the volume, each of the twelve country studies adheres to an identical structure consisting of six sections. Following brief introductions, the chapters present information on the respective countries' national communities abroad, for example with respect to overall numbers, main geographical locations, and possible waves in which outward migration has occurred. Next, the chapters provide detailed discussions on the activities of the countries along the three substantive dimensions previously introduced, thus diplomatic and consular, economic and social, and security activities. Discussions focus primarily but not exclusively on developments since the end of the Cold War. Each chapter ends with a conclusion that highlights the key motivations and practices of the respective countries towards their national communities abroad, together with a brief outlook on expected changes, or lack thereof, in the foreseeable future.

The line-up of the chapters is based on the absolute numbers of nationals living abroad (see Figure 1.1). Thus, Nicolas Blarel starts out with a discussion on India's activities towards its national communities abroad, for which he detects fundamental changes over time that more recently has led to a "re-engagement" by the Indian state (Chapter 2). Daniel Hernández Joseph and Jorge A. Schiavon follow with their discussion of Mexico, where the engagement of its nationals abroad – almost all of whom reside in a single country, namely the United States – not least through consular measures is a "foreign policy priority" (Chapter 3). In his chapter on Russia, Ethan Larson emphasizes the extent to which the country's past – referred to as "empire's echo" – informs its perception of, as well as drives its actions towards its national communities abroad, especially in the post-Soviet space (Chapter 4).

Examining China, Andrea Ghiselli characterizes the country's activities towards its national communities abroad as being "low cost and low key," which is striking given the prominence that the country ascribes to the protection of its nationals overseas and of its overseas interests more broadly (Chapter 5). Sahar Khan, in her exploration of Pakistan, emphasizes the crucial economic role that the country's national community abroad widely understood plays through remittances and investments, which makes efforts to "tap into the diaspora's economic potential" not only expedient but outright necessary (Chapter 6). In a similar vein, Ma. Divina Gracia Z. Roldan emphasizes in her discussion of the Philippines the crucial economic role of overseas Fillipino workers, which the country considers as "valued human assets" (Chapter 7).

In stark contrast, James Strong suggests for the United Kingdom that while the country provides "good information" to its nationals about the risks they may face abroad and how to mitigate them, it tries to avoid offering further support ("limited liability") unless it really cannot help it, in which case it does offer a "powerful safety net" (Chapter 8). Reversing emphasis yet again, Ann Marie Murphy and Amy Freedman emphasize in their chapter on Indonesia that the country is strongly engaged with its national communities abroad, particularly when it comes to "protecting migrant workers," which is expedient not only for economic but also for domestic political purposes (Chapter 9). Conversely, Klaus Brummer and Kai Oppermann argue that Germany, whilst having the material wherewithal to do much more towards its national communities abroad, is for the most part only "supportive in times of crisis" (Chapter 10).

In her chapter on Egypt, Kelsey P. Norman argues that the country has taken a bifurcated approach in its engagement with the national community abroad, which not only refers to categorizing the latter in temporary and permanent migrants but also in terms of actions in the form of "cultivating loyalty" on the one hand and "repressing when necessary" on the other (Chapter 11). In her discussion of Türkiye, Yasemin Akbaba argues that the roles, policies, and services of the country's institutions and what they do to protect Turkish citizens abroad have shifted in response to changes in the nature and volume of emigration, which has led to "reimagining the home state" (Chapter 12). For the United States, Drew A. Hogan and Ronald R. Krebs contend that despite its unmatched capabilities, the country has shown little inclination overall to engage its national communities abroad directly, thus making the country a "(mostly) hand-off superpower" (Chapter 13). The concluding chapter (Chapter 14), by Šumit Ganguly and Klaus Brummer, presents core findings in terms of the drivers of states' interactions with their national communities abroad and ends with suggestions for future research.

References

Alden, Chris, and Amnon Aran (2017) *Foreign Policy Analysis: New Approaches*, 2nd ed. London and New York: Routledge.

Ahmed, Faisal Z. (2012) The Perils of Unearned Foreign Income: Aid, Remittances, and Government Survival. *American Political Science Review* 106(1), 146–165.

Allison, Roy (2009) The Russian Case for Military Intervention in Georgia: International Law, Norms and Political Calculation. *European Security* 18(2), 173–200.

Arkilic, Ayca (2022) *Diaspora Diplomacy: The Politics of Turkish Emigration to Europe*. Manchester: Manchester University Press.

Asis, Maruja M. B. (2020) *Repatriating Filipino Migrant Workers in the Time of the Pandemic*. Migration Research Series No. 63. Geneva: International Organization for Migration.

Baum, Toshiro Jeffrey (2020) The Responsibility of Power: Shifts in Chinese Conceptualisation of the Legitimacy of Overseas Intervention to Protect Nationals Abroad. *Global Change, Peace & Security* 32(3), 259–273.

Betts, Alexander, and Will Jones (2016) *Mobilising the Diaspora: How Refugees Challenge Authoritarianism*. Cambridge: Cambridge University Press.

Bicchi, Federica, and Daniel Schade (2022) Whither European Diplomacy? Long-Term Trends and the Impact of the Lisbon Treaty. *Cooperation and Conflict* 57(1), 3–24.

Bjola, Corneliu, and Marcus Holmes (2015) *Digital Diplomacy: Theory and Practice*. Abingdon: Routledge.

Boni, Filippo (2019) Protecting the Belt and Road Initiative: China's Cooperation with Pakistan to Secure CPEC. *Asia Policy* 14(2), 5–12.

Brand, Laurie A. (2006) *Citizens Abroad: Emigration and the State in the Middle East and North Africa*. Cambridge and New York: Cambridge University Press.

Brand, Laurie A. (2010) Authoritarian States and Voting from Abroad. *Comparative Political Studies* 43(1), 81–99.

Brid, Lucia (2023) Motivations of Diaspora Support in Homeland Civil Conflict. *Journal of Peace Research* 60(2), 226–242.

Brubaker, Rogers (2005) The 'Diaspora' Diaspora. *Ethnic and Racial Studies* 28(1), 1–19.

Brummer, Klaus (2020) Comparative Analyses of Foreign Policy. In Luigi Curini and Robert Franzese (eds.), *The SAGE Handbook of Research Methods in Political Science and International Relations (Vol. 2)*. Los Angeles, CA: Sage, 1148–1166.

Brummer, Klaus, and Kai Oppermann (2024) *Foreign Policy Analysis*. Oxford: Oxford University Press.

Chaterjee, Shibashis, and Udayan Das (2021) Indian Foreign Policy as Public History: Globalist, Pragmatist and Hindutva Imaginations. *India Review* 20(5), 565–588.

Cusumano, Eugenio (2017) Diplomatic Security for Hire: The Causes and Implications of Outsourcing Embassy Protection. *The Hague Journal of Diplomacy* 12(1), 27–55.

de Haas, Hein (2010) Migration and Development: A Theoretical Perspective. *International Migration Review* 44(1), 227–264.

Délano, Alexandro (2011) *Mexico and Its Diaspora in the United States: Policies of Emigration since 1848*. New York: Cambridge University Press.

Délano, Alexandro, and Alan Gamlen (2014) Comparing and Theorizing State–Diaspora Relations. *Political Geography* 41, 43–53.

Escribà-Folch, Abel, Covadonga Meseguer, and Joseph Wright (2018) Remittances and Protest in Dictatorships. *American Journal of Political Science* 62(4), 889–904.

Eurostat (2019) *Trips of Residents of Western European Countries: Domestic, Outbound and Top 5 Outbound Destinations*. Available at: https://ec.europa.eu/eurostat/statistics-explained/index.php?title=Tourism_statistics_-_top_destinations#United_Kingdom.2C_Turkey_and_USA_-_top_3_destinations_outside_the_EU (last accessed January 24, 2023).

Fernandes, Deepali (2022) Diaspora and Transnational Communities' Economic Contributions. In Liam Kennedy (ed.), *Routledge International Handbook of Diaspora Diplomacy*. New York and London: Routledge, 123–141.

Finn, Victoria, and Andrés Besserer Rayas (2022): Turning Rights into Ballots: Mexican External Voting from the US. *Territory, Politics, Governance*, OnlineFirst, https://doi.org/10.1080/21622671.2022.2141849.

Fund for Peace (2022) *Fragile State Index Annual Report 2022*. Washington, DC: Fund for Peace.

Gamlen, Alan (2006) *Diaspora Engagement Policies: What Are They, and What Kinds of States Use Them?* Centre on Migration, Policy and Society. Working Paper No. 32. Oxford: University of Oxford.

Gamlen, Alan (2019) *Human Geopolitics: States, Emigrants, and the Rise of Diaspora Institutions*. Oxford: Oxford University Press.

Gaur, Seema (2019) Policies for Protecting Indian Migrant Workers in the Middle East. In S. Irudaya Rajan and Prem Saxena (eds.), *India's Low-Skilled Migration to the Middle East: Policies, Politics and Challenges*. Singapore: Palgrave Macmillan, 125–166.

Geddes, Barbara (1999) What Do We Know about Democratization after Twenty Years? *Annual Review of Political Science* 2: 115–144.

Geyer, Florian (2007) *The External Dimension of EU Citizenship: Arguing for Effective Protection of Citizens Abroad.* CEPS Policy Brief No. 136, July 2007. Brussels: Center for European Policy Studies.

Ghiselli, Andrea (2020) Market Opportunities and Political Responsibilities: The Difficult Development of Chinese Private Security Companies Abroad. *Armed Forces and Society* 46(1), 25–45.

Ghiselli, Andrea (2021) *Protecting China's Interests Overseas Securitization and Foreign Policy*. Oxford: Oxford University Press.

Glasius, Marlies (2018) Extraterritorial Authoritarian Practices: A Framework. *Globalizations* 15(2), 179–197.

Global Firepower (2022) *2022 Military Strength Ranking*. Available at: www.globalfirepower.com/countries-listing.php (last accessed December 16, 2022).

Goddard, Stacie E., Paul K. MacDonald, and Daniel H. Nexon (2019) Repertoires of Statecraft: Instruments and Logics of Power Politics. *International Relations* 33(2), 304–321.

Gorokhovskaia, Yana, and Isabel Linzer (2022) *Defending Democracy in Exile: Policy Responses to Transnational Repression*. Washington, DC: Freedom House.

Græger, Nina, and Halvard Leira (eds.) (2020) *The Duty of Care in International Relations: Protecting Citizens beyond the Border*. London and New York: Routledge.

Græger, Nina, and Wrenn Yennie Lindgren (2018) The Duty of Care for Citizens Abroad: Security and Responsibility in the In Amenas and Fukushima Crises. *The Hague Journal of Diplomacy* 13(2), 188–210.

Hameed, Sameena (2021) India's Labour Agreements with the Gulf Cooperation Council Countries: An Assessment. *International Studies* 58(4), 442–465.

Haugevik, Kristin (2018) Parental Child Abduction and the State: Identity, Diplomacy and the Duty of Care. *The Hague Journal of Diplomacy* 13(2), 167–187.

Hernández Joseph, Daniel (2012) Mexico's Concentration on Consular Services in the United States. *The Hague Journal of Diplomacy* 7(2), 227–236.

Hess, Maximilian (2022) Biden's Hostage Diplomacy Was a Historic Mistake. *Foreign Policy*, December 15. Available at: https://foreignpolicy.com/2022/12/15/biden-hostage-diplomacy-russia-griner-bout-putin/ (last accessed December 19, 2022).

Indian Express (2020) CAA+NRC Can Lead to 'Disenfranchisement' of Indian Muslims: US Body. Available at: https://indianexpress.com/article/india/caa-nrc-india-us-trump-6277969/ (last accessed December 21, 2022).

International Organization for Migration (IOM) (2019) *Glossary on Migration*. Geneva: IOM.

Jetly, Rajshree (2021) The Politics of Gwadar Port: Baluch Nationalism and Sino-Pak Relations. *The Round Table* 110(4), 432–447

Kapur, Devesh (2001) Diasporas and Technology Transfer. *Journal of Human Development* 2(2), 265–286.

Katigbak, Jovito Jose P., and Ma. Divina Gracia Z. Roldan (2021) Protecting Filipino Migrant Workers in Distress through Social Media Platforms. *Asian and Pacific Migration Journal* 30(3), 357–369.

Koinova, Maria (2013) Four Types of Diaspora Mobilization: Albanian Diaspora Activism for Kosovo Independence in the US and the UK. *Foreign Policy Analysis* 9(4), 433–453.

Koinova, Maria, and Gerasimos Tsourapas (2018) How Do Countries of Origin Engage Migrants and Diasporas? Multiple Actors and Comparative Perspectives. *International Political Science Review* 39(3), 311–321.

Kopchik, Connor, Erin K. Jenne, Kathleen Gallagher Cunningham, and Stephen Saideman (2022) Emerging Diasporas: Exploring Mobilization outside the Homeland. *Journal of Peace Research* 59(2), 107–121.

Lafleur, Jean-Michel, and Daniela Vintila (2020a) Do EU Member States Care about Their Diasporas' Access to Social Protection? A Comparison of Consular and Diaspora Policies across EU27. In Jean-Michael Lafleur and Daniele Vintila (eds.), *Migration and Social Protection in Europe and Beyond (Volume 2): Comparing Consular Services and Diaspora Policies*. Cham: Springer, 1–31.

Lafleur, Jean-Michel, and Daniela Vintila (eds.) (2020b) *Migration and Social Protection in Europe and beyond (Volume 2): Comparing Consular Services and Diaspora Policies*. Cham: Springer.

Lafleur, Jean-Michel, and Daniela Vintila (eds.) (2020c) *Migration and Social Protection in Europe and Beyond (Volume 3): A Focus on Non-EU Sending States*. Cham: Springer.

Leblang, David, and Jenny Glazier (2022) Diaspora Engagement Strategies: Theory and Case Study Evidence. In Liam Kennedy (ed.), *Routledge International Handbook of Diaspora Diplomacy*. New York and London: Routledge, 34–47.

Leira, Halvard (2018) Caring and Carers: Diplomatic Personnel and the Duty of Care. *The Hague Journal of Diplomacy* 13(2), 147–166.

Leira, Halvard and Nina Græger (2020) Introduction: The Duty of Care in International Relations. In Nina Græger and Halvard Leira (eds.), *The Duty of Care in International Relations: Protecting Citizens beyond the Border*. London and New York: Routledge, 1–17.

Lowy Institute (2021) *Global Diplomacy Index: 2021 Country Ranking*. Available at: https://globaldiplomacyindex.lowyinstitute.org/country_rank.html (last accessed December 16, 2022).

Manor, Ilan, and Geraldine Asiwome Adiku (2021) From 'Traitors' to 'Saviours': A Longitudinal Analysis of Ethiopian, Kenyan and Rwandan Embassies'

Practice of Digital Diaspora Diplomacy. *South African Journal of International Affairs* 28(3), 403–427.

Marshall, Monty G., and Tedd Robert Gurr (2020) POLITY5. Political Regime Characteristics and Transitions, 1800–2018. *Dataset Users' Manual.* Available at: www.systemicpeace.org/inscrdata.html (last accessed December 18, 2022).

Maurer, Noel (2013) *The Empire Trap: The Rise and Fall of U.S. Intervention to Protect American Property Overseas, 1893–2013.* Princeton, NJ and Oxford: Princeton University Press.

Melissen, Jan (2020) Consular Diplomacy's First Challenge: Communicating Assistance to Nationals Abroad. *Asia and the Pacific Policy Studies* 7(2), 217–228.

Melissen, Jan, and Matthew Caesar-Gordon (2016) "Digital Diplomacy" and the Securing of Nationals in a Citizen-Centric World. *Global Affairs* 2(3), 321–330.

Melissen, Jan, and Maaike Okano-Heijmans (2018) Introduction: Diplomacy and the Duty of Care. *The Hague Journal of Diplomacy* 13(2), 137–145.

Moraru, Madalina (2014) Securing Consular Protection of the EU Citizens Abroad: What Role for the EU? In Inge Govaere and Sara Poli (eds.), *EU Management of Global Emergencies: Legal Framework for Combating Threats and Crises.* Leiden: Brill Nijhoff, 147–193.

Mwagiru, Makumi (2012) The African Union's Diplomacy of the Diaspora: Context, Challenges and Prospects. *African Journal of Conflict Resolution* 12(2), 73–85.

Okano-Heijmans, Maaike, and Matthew Caesar-Gordon (2016) Protecting the Worker-Citizen Abroad: Duty of Care beyond the State? *Global Affairs* 2(4), 431–440.

Okano-Heijmans, Maaike, and Caspar Price (2019) Providing Consular Services to Low-Skilled Migrant Workers: Partnerships That Care. *Global Affairs* 5(4–5), 427–443.

Owolabi, Tife (2022) Gunmen Kidnap Three Chinese, Kill Two Locals at Nigerian Power Project. *Reuters*, January 6. Available at: www.reuters.com/markets/commodities/gunmen-kidnap-three-chinese-kill-two-locals-nigerian-power-project-2022-01-06/ (last accessed December 9, 2022).

Paradise, James F. (2022) China's 'Coercive Tourism': Motives, Methods and Consequences. *International Relations of the Asia-Pacific* 22(1), 31–68.

Pedroza, Luicy, and Pau Palop-García (2017) Diaspora Policies in Comparison: An Application of the Emigrant Policies Index (EMIX) for the Latin American and Caribbean Region. *Political Geography* 60, 165–178.

Politico (2023) *Record Number of Turks Vote in Germany in 'Fateful Election' for Erdoğan*, May 10. Available at: www.politico.eu/article/a-fateful-election-more-turks-than-ever-stream-to-the-polls-in-germany/ (last accessed May 26, 2023).

Ragazzi, Francesco (2014) A Comparative Analysis of Diaspora Policies. *Political Geography* 41, 74–89.

Rifawan, Affabile, Ivan Darmawan dan, and Riki Relaksana (2017) A Review on the Governance of Protection System for Indonesian Citizens Abroad. *Jurnal Asia Pacific Studies* 1(2), 155–168.

Saliceti, Alessandro Ianniello (2011) The Protection of EU Citizens Abroad: Accountability, Rule of Law, Role of Consular and Diplomatic Services. *European Public Law Review* 17(1), 91–109.

Schwanitz, Johanna (2023) Deutschland wählt Erdogan. *Frankfurter Allgemeine Zeitung*, May 31, p. 5.

Shain, Yossi (2007) *Kinship and Diasporas in International Affairs*. Ann Arbor, MI: University of Michigan Press.

SIPRI (2022) *SIRPI Military Expenditure Database*. Available at: https://milex.sipri.org/sipri (last accessed December 16, 2022).

Times of India (2023) India Closes Operation Kaveri, 3,862 Persons Rescued from Conflict-Torn Sudan, May 5. Available at: https://timesofindia.indiatimes.com/india/india-closes-operation-kaveri-3862-persons-rescued-from-conflict-torn-sudan/articleshow/100020413.cms?from=mdr (last accessed May 26, 2023).

Tindall, Karen (2012) Governments' Ability to Assist Nationals in Disasters Abroad: What Do We Know about Consular Emergency Management? *Journal of Contingencies and Crisis Management* 20(2), 102–114.

Tsinovoi, Alexei, and Rebecca Adler-Nissen (2018) Inversion of the 'Duty of Care': Diplomacy and the Protection of Citizens Abroad, from Pastoral Care to Neoliberal Governmentality. *The Hague Journal of Diplomacy* 13(2), 211–232.

Tsourapas, Gerasimos (2015) Why Do States Develop Multi-tier Emigrant Policies? Evidence from Egypt. *Journal of Ethnic and Migration Studies* 41(13), 2192–2214.

Tsourapas, Gerasimos (2021a) Global Autocracies: Strategies of Transnational Repression, Legitimation, and Co-optation in World Politics. *International Studies Review* 23(3), 616–644.

Tsourapas, Gerasimos (2021b) *Migration Diplomacy in the Middle East and North Africa: Power, Mobility, and the State*. Manchester University Press: Manchester.

Tsourapas, Gerasimos (2022) Diaspora Diplomacy under Authoritarianism. Practices of Transnational Repression in World Politics. In Liam Kennedy (ed.), *Routledge International Handbook of Diaspora Diplomacy*. New York and London: Routledge, 307–319.

United Nations Department of Economic and Social Affairs, Population Division (UN) (2020) *International Migrant Stock 2020: Destination and Origin*. Available at: www.un.org/development/desa/pd/content/international-migrant-stock (last accessed December 16, 2022).

United Nations Development Program (UNDP) (2022) Human Development Report 2021/22. New York: UNDP.

United Nations World Tourism Organization (UNWTO) (n.d.) Top 10 Destinations. Available at: www.unwto.org/tourism-data/global-and-regional-tourism-performance (last accessed January 24, 2023).

United Nations World Tourism Organization (UNWTO) (2008) *Tourism Highlights*. 2008 Edition. Available at: www.e-unwto.org/doi/epdf/10.18111/9789284413560 (last accessed May 30, 2023).

United Nations World Tourism Organization (UNWTO) (2020) World Tourism Barometer 18(7), December.

United Nations World Tourism Organization (UNWTO) (2024) *International Tourism to Reach Pre-pandemic Levels in 2024*, January 19. Available at: www.unwto.org/news/international-tourism-to-reach-pre-pandemic-levels-in-2024 (last accessed May 22, 2024).

US Department of Justice (2023) *Two Arrested for Operating Illegal Overseas Police Station of the Chinese Government*. Available at: www.justice.gov/opa/pr/two-arrested-operating-illegal-overseas-police-station-chinese-government (last accessed May 26, 2023).

Varadarajan, Latha (2010) *The Domestic Abroad: Diasporas in International Relations*. Oxford and New York: Oxford University Press.

Vink, Maarten, Arjan H. Schakel, David Reichel, Ngo Chun Luk, and Gerard-René de Groot (2019) The International Diffusion of Expateriate Dual Citizenship. *Migration Studies* 7(3), 362–383.

Vintila, Daniela, and Jean-Michel Lafleur (2020) The Immigration–Emigration Nexus in Non-EU Sending States: A Focus on Welfare Entitlements, Consular Services, and Diaspora Policies. In Jean-Michel Lafleur and Daniela Vintila (eds.), *Migration and Social Protection in Europe and Beyond (Volume 3): A Focus on Non-EU Sending States*. Cham: Springer, 1–39.

Wackenhut, Arne F., and Camilla Orjuela (2023) Engaging the Next Generation: Authoritarian Regimes and Their Young Diaspora. *European Political Science* 22(1), 143–158.

Wang, Duanyong (2013) The Safety of Chinese Citizens Abroad: A Quantitative Interpretation of the "Special Notices for Chinese Citizens Abroad" (2008–2010). *Journal of Current Chinese Affairs* 1, 167–198.

Wellmann, Elizabeth Iams (2021) Emigrant Inclusion in Home Country Elections: Theory and Evidence from Sub-Saharan Africa. *American Political Science Review* 115(1), 82–96.

World Bank (2022a) *Personal Remittances, Received (Current US$)*. Available at: https://data.worldbank.org/indicator/BX.TRF.PWKR.CD.DT (last accessed December 16, 2022).

World Bank (2022b) *World Bank Country and Lending Groups*. Available at: https://datahelpdesk.worldbank.org/knowledgebase/articles/906519-world-bank-country-and-lending-groups (last accessed December 16, 2022).

Wrighton, Sam (2018) Authoritarian Regime Stabilization through Legitimation, Popular Co-optation, and Exclusion: Russian *Pasportizatsiya* Strategies in Crimea. *Globalizations* 15(2), 283–300.

Zerba, Shaio H. (2014) China's Libya Evacuation Operation: A New Diplomatic Imperative – Overseas Citizen Protection. *Journal of Contemporary China* 23(90), 1093–1112.

2 India

Engaging and Re-engaging the Diaspora

Nicolas Blarel

Introduction

India has historically been the leading country of origin of international migrants with an estimated 32 million *overseas Indians* in 2018, including 18.6 million Persons of Indian Origin (PIO)[1] and 13.4 million Non-Resident Indians (NRI).[2] This significant Indian community abroad covers all continents and over 200 countries and contributes more to India financially every year than Foreign Direct Investment (FDI) and foreign aid combined, with an estimated $83 billion in remittances in 2021 (McAuliffe and Triandafyllidou 2021). The movement of Indians across the globe is an old phenomenon which can be traced back to the early nineteenth century and a series of policy decisions which forced or facilitated the migration of large numbers of Indian laborers who permanently settled across the different continents.

As Indian nationalists gained independence in 1947, they were concerned about governing Indian citizens in a newly defined territory but also abroad. However, due to finite material and institutional capacities, as well as a willingness not to interfere in the sovereign affairs of other states, engagement with nationals abroad remained limited. Since the early 1990s, in light of increasing remittances but also as a reaction to the emergence of a successful and influential Indian diaspora in the OECD countries, India has adapted its political, material, legal, institutional,

[1] A Person of Indian Origin is a citizen of any country (other than Bangladesh or Pakistan) who has (a) at any time held Indian passport or (b) the person or either of the person's parents or any of their grandparents were a citizen of India by virtue of the Constitution of India or the Citizenship Act, 1955 or (c) the person is a spouse of an Indian citizen or a person referred to in (a) or (b). See the definition offered by the Reserve Bank of India, available at: www.rbi.org.in/scripts/BS_ViewMasCirculardetails.aspx?id=8096#:~:text=Person%20of%20Indian%20Origin%20(PIO,c)%20the%20person%20is%20a.

[2] For the figures, see MEA 2019. These Ministry of External Affairs figures date back to 2018 and have not been officially updated, but are still cited by Indian authorities. A recent parliamentary panel has asked the MEA to prepare and update a database of Indians abroad (ANI 2022a).

and security apparatus to support and co-opt nationals abroad, notably in order to attract investments to India and to leverage the Indian communities' growing economic and political clout in their host countries.

Accordingly, India has established a multilayered framework and infrastructure to support its diverse overseas population. Since the 1980s, a variety of institutions have been created, modified, discontinued, or streamlined. As discussed in this chapter, some government initiatives were ad hoc and temporary in nature, and others were established in direct partnership with the private sector. The diverse needs of India's vast, heterogenous, and growing migrant, diaspora, and tourist populations have led to a wide set of policy initiatives. However, in spite of the various Indian governments' willingness to publicize India's proactive policies to engage its nationals abroad, limited material resources devoted to these initiatives has in turn limited their implementation.

This chapter aims to provide a broad overview of India's re-engagement of its community abroad. First, it offers an overview of Indian international migration. Second, it presents the set of diplomatic and consular initiatives gradually put in place to protect overseas Indians. This section looks at how India has moved from a policy of active disassociation with overseas Indians in the post-independence period to a growing recognition and support of its diaspora. Third, the chapter looks at initiatives since the early 2000s to (re-)engage India's global diaspora at the economic and social levels. This section will notably highlight the differences in consular services and diaspora policies tailored towards ethnic Indian populations whose forefathers migrated in the pre- or immediate post-independence period, Indian communities residing in OECD countries, and migrant workers temporarily located in countries in the Gulf States. Fourth, the chapter also outlines the ways the Indian government has used military force to assist Indians in distress abroad. A final section then discusses the main challenges and debates driving India's consular and diaspora policies.

Overview of the Indian Community Abroad

India has one of the densest and most complex migration histories. Indeed, there is a long history of Indian migration which predates the colonial period and the composition of flows has evolved over time (Tinker 1977; Narayan 2008, 1–6). However, it was only in the nineteenth century, during British colonial rule in India, that important changes in migration flow patterns led to the global dispersion of Indian communities that we know today. Three major periods of emigration can be identified, starting with the British colonial era.

The first was emigration as a result of direct colonial design in the nineteenth century, including coerced movement of indentured laborers to other parts of the British Empire. The main driver of this important wave of emigration from India was the abolition of slavery in 1833, but there were also self-sponsored migrants exploiting the limited "free" or passage migration within the British imperial system. Most were traders, entrepreneurs, and semi-skilled and skilled professionals (mainly goldsmiths, teachers, lawyers) "pulled" to migration due to the prospect of better living conditions in other colonies such as Canada, South Africa as well as the East African countries of Kenya, Tanzania, and Uganda (Pande 2013).

Second, the end of British colonialism and the creation of the modern Indian state led to a second wave of emigration. War-scarred Britain at the time was experiencing labor shortages, and as Commonwealth citizens, Indian nationals were able to move to the country with few restrictions. Migration to the United Kingdom became more difficult in subsequent years, as laws passed between 1962 and 1971 imposed new controls on movement from elsewhere in the Commonwealth, notably in response to the rise of the National Front and politicians like Enoch Powell who spoke of "rivers of blood" if immigration was not halted (Thandi 2015).[3]

A third wave rose in the post-1970s with the possibilities of employment in the OECD and Gulf countries. This third wave of emigration was mainly driven by new economic factors and opportunities. First, there were important migration flows to the Gulf countries in the 1970s responding to the labor needs in the growing oil-extraction business and related growth in the construction sector (Weiner 1978). Retail and construction trades such as carpentry, electrical wiring, and masonry were popular for many migrants lacking postsecondary education, while those with higher levels of training have gone to sectors such as health care. By 2018, an estimated 8.5 million Indians (30% of overseas Indians) resided in the Gulf region (MEA 2019). Similarly, along with migrants from Kerala, recent flows from Telangana, Andhra Pradesh, and Tamil Nadu have also accounted for an increase in semi-skilled workers being employed in the healthcare sectors (nurses) and retail in the Gulf States (Ennis and Blarel 2022).

This third wave of emigration has also included skilled workers (healthcare workers, engineers, finance professionals, service sector workers) and

[3] As of 2020, India remained the largest country of birth for immigrants in the UK. See the UK census data available at: www.ons.gov.uk/peoplepopulationandcommunity/populationandmigration/internationalmigration/bulletins/ukpopulationbycountryofbirthandnationality/2020.

international students who migrated to economically developed nations such as the United States, Canada, Australia and other OECD countries. Unlike previous migration waves and the emigration to the Gulf, these Indian nationals have built on new opportunities of the globalized workforce market, came from India's growing middle class (mainly from the states of Gujarat, Punjab, Maharashtra, and Karnataka), and shared strong educational and skills backgrounds (McCarthy 2020). As a result, India has the highest number of emigrants with a postsecondary degree, with more than 4 million residing in the OECD states as of 2018 (MEA 2019). In addition, India has been one of the fastest-growing outbound travel markets in the world since the 1990s. International tourism departures from India have grown from 3.7 million in 1997 to 26.7 million in 2019.[4]

According to UN data on international migrants, India has been the largest source country of emigrants, with close to 18 million persons born in India now living abroad, followed by 11 million Mexican (McAuliffe and Triandafyllidou 2021). This number includes both first generation NRIs and PIOs, but not overseas Indians who were born abroad. However, in contrast with other cases in this volume, the Indian government deliberately uses a broader definition of overseas Indians, and thereby of its "national community abroad" which includes all NRIs and PIOs. According to India's estimations, there were 32 million overseas Indians in 2018, of which 13.4 million were NRIs and 18.6 million were PIOs (Table 2.1). This chapter focuses on the Indian government's support of the population that it defines as overseas Indians and thus adopts the official terminology and figures (MEA 2019).

This overseas population is also diverse in terms of socioeconomic profiles. The professions that overseas Indians have taken have ranged from unskilled to highly skilled ones depending on their education and social background. On the one hand, unemployment in some Indian regions compelled laborers to move to the Middle East for work despite risks of oppressive working conditions; on the other hand, several high-skilled and highly educated Indians deliberately moved to take up some key executive and administrative positions in OECD countries.

With the largest number of international emigrants across the globe, India has also become the biggest recipient of international remittances since 2008 (McAuliffe and Triandafyllidou 2021). In 2021, the country recorded $83 billion in international remittances. This figure was only a small drop (0.2 %) from the previous year, despite the Covid-19

[4] Data retrieved from the UN Tourism (UNWTO) Dashboard. See: www.unwto.org/tourism-data/global-and-regional-tourism-performance.

Table 2.1 *Top 10 countries hosting overseas Indians*

Country	Non-Resident Indians (NRIs)	Persons of Indian Origin (PIOs)	Overseas Indian
United States	1,280,000	3,180, 000	4,460,000
United Arab Emirates	3,419,875	5,269	3,425,144
Malaysia	227,950	2,760,000	2,987,950
Saudi Arabia	2,592,166	2,781	2,594,947
Myanmar	9, 207	2,000,000	2,009,207
Canada	178,410	1,510,645	1,689,055
United Kingdom	351,000	1,413,000	1,764,000
Sri Lanka	14,000	1,600,000	1,614,000
South Africa	60,000	1,500,000	1,560,000
Kuwait	1,028,274	1,587	1,029,861

Source: Data compiled by the Ministry of External Affairs in 2018. The official Indian figures deliberately do not include Pakistan.

pandemic, and accounted for around 3% of India's GDP (World Bank 2021). Over the last decade, the sources of remittances have gradually shifted from largely low-skilled, informally employed workers in the Gulf Cooperation Council (GCC) countries to a dominant share of high-skilled jobs in high-income countries and regions such as the US, UK, Australia, New Zealand, and East Asia (Singapore, Japan). The overall share of remittances from Saudi Arabia, UAE, Kuwait, Oman, and Qatar, from where temporary laborers sent back money that was critical for their communities of origin, experienced a significant decline from 54 to 28 % between 2016 and 2021 (RBI 2021).

Due to these different historical waves of migration, the resulting heterogeneous composition of overseas Indians, and the growing economic significance of remittances coming from various destination countries over the last two decades, the scope and nature of India's consular policies and services have evolved over time.

Diplomatic and Consular Dimension

Before sketching out India's consular infrastructure, it is important to give details on the different legal and political terms that the Indian state had used to describe communities abroad which can trace their origins to modern-day India, as this has implications for knowing whom the Indian state aims to support, who can ask for Indian consular support, and for the nature of this consular assistance over time. As mentioned, India had an estimated 32 million "overseas Indians" in 2018, including 18.6 million

PIOs and 13.4 million NRIs. The Citizenship Act of 1955 originally recognized only one category of Indians, namely citizens. The term NRI itself is originally derived from a tax category, and refers to Indian citizens living in India for less than 182 days each year.[5] The term is therefore used to distinguish Indian citizens living abroad from those who have acquired a different citizenship, namely PIOs (Naujoks 2018: 92).

However, since 2006, the Indian government has deliberately promoted through official documents and policies a more expansive definition of "overseas Indians" (*Pravasi Bharatiya*) as being a larger community than just NRIs (Jayal 2016). The term "Overseas Citizen of India" (OCI) is misleading since India does not have and expressly prohibits a dual citizenship regime. Nevertheless, this inclusive definition of overseas Indians encompasses a larger diaspora spread across all continents: temporary NRI workers mainly based in the GCC countries, NRIs and PIOs in the US, Canada, Australia, and Europe, as well as PIOs in countries where large-scale emigration took place roughly during the British Indian system (Mauritius, South Africa, Fiji, Malaysia, Singapore). India's conceptualization of its diaspora has undergone a tremendous change over the last two decades, which has in turn led to the adoption of a host of new consular and diaspora policies, as discussed in the following sections.

India's consular and diplomatic services have therefore evolved to support these different categories of overseas Indians. Under the Citizenship Act of 1955, India initially recognized only one category of Indians, citizens (NRIs), and its consular services were therefore geared to assist this category of nationals abroad. This support via embassies and consulates in 160 countries, as well as honorary consuls in an additional 36 countries, has included traditional documentation services, such as the issuance of new passports, emergency travel documents, and financial and logistical support for sending mortal or cremated remains of the deceased to India for last rites. To increase efficiency, some consulates have outsourced these services to private companies. In some countries, consular assistance or diplomatic support has been available to help NRIs facing legal problems. Most legal assistance is however remedial and does not encompass intervention in the host state's internal affairs or judicial processes. For Indians in the GCCs, welfare and social protection schemes have also been offered (see the following section).

[5] The Section 115(C)(e) of the Indian Income Tax Act 1961 describes an NRI as "an individual, being a citizen of India or a person of Indian origin who is not a 'resident.'" See: https://incometaxindia.gov.in/pages/acts/income-tax-act.aspx.

However, due to limited material and institutional capacities, as well as political prudence when negotiating with international partners, these consular services have often been limited in nature. For instance, India did not directly intervene to support the interests of Indian-origin communities under threat in other states as in Uganda in 1972 or in Fiji in the 1980s (Lall 2003). Over time, India's Ministry of External Affairs (MEA) was also quite explicit in stipulating that while consular assistance could be claimed, diplomatic protection was a state prerogative and not an individual right.[6] Furthermore, there have been some legal disputes over whether Indian protection extends to OCIs in the same fashion as for NRIs. As late as 2010, the Delhi High Court stated that: "the gaining of the status of an OCI ... does not guarantee parity of treatment with Indian passport holders."[7] In the end, the nature and scope of protection of OCIs has depended on the political inclination of the Indian government.

The Indian government did not initially promote emigration nor did it create any special department or centralized agency to maintain ties with its community abroad. With the exception of NRIs, most overseas Indians became aliens like any foreigners and the Indian government restricted their rights in buying property and investing in their country of origin. As the High-Level Committee (HLC) on the Indian Diaspora (2001: xi) concluded in its report: "barring some high profile names in the Information Technology and entertainment sectors abroad, the Diaspora has been largely out of public sight and awareness." With the emergence of a successful Indian diaspora in the OECD economies, India gradually took a keen interest in providing services to both its NRIs as well as its larger diaspora, notably in order to attract its investments in India (see following section). In parallel, there was a gradual recognition by the Indian government of the vast resources and skills of its community abroad, which led it to introduce initiatives to leverage them for its own domestic development. Indian politicians and bureaucrats gradually moved away from an exclusively territorialized definition of Indians, but also away from the "brain drain" concern, as its community abroad increasingly got involved in India's rising information technology industry (Hunger 2004).

[6] United Nations General Assembly 55th Session, Summary record of the 19th Meeting of the Sixth Committee, "Agenda Item 159: Report of the International Law Commission on the Work of Its Fifty-Second Session," para. 40, p. 8, A/C.6/55/SR.19 (November 13, 2000), available at: https://undocs.org/en/A/C.6/55/SR.19 (accessed November 1, 2022).

[7] *Karm Kumar* v. *The Union of India*, 172(2010)DLT521, 2010(4)RCR(Civil)461, para. 23 (Delhi High Court August 03, 2010).

Since the early 2000s, India has engaged in systematic attempts to institutionalize its relationship with its community abroad, marking a distinct shift from its earlier policies of active dissociation with overseas Indians (Naujoks 2013; Kapur 2010; Varadarajan 2010). This growing engagement has also coincided with the rise to power of the Bharatiya Janata Party (BJP), which was the political party leading the ruling government coalition in 1998–2004, during which time several new diaspora policies were established. This new government believed "that the growing achievements of the vast Indian diaspora are a matter of pride and a source of strength for India" (Hegde 2018: 77). The deliberate attempt to co-opt India's community abroad started with the creation of the HLC on Indian diaspora which delivered in 2001 a comprehensive report to the Indian government on the strengths and weaknesses of the global Indian diaspora.

Responding to a long-standing request from the community abroad for dual citizenship, and within the government of India's economic outreach strategy to the diaspora, the HLC recommended introducing the OCI card.[8] The OCI was implemented in 2005 and did not offer official dual citizenship, given existing constitutional statutes and the Citizenship Act of 1955 prohibiting Indians from holding more than one nationality. However, the OCI card offered other benefits for overseas Indians, such as: multipurpose lifelong visas to visit India; exemption from reporting to police authorities for any length of stay in India; and parity with NRIs in financial, economic, and educational fields except in the acquisition of agricultural or plantation properties. By 2017, 3.2 million persons of Indian origin had obtained the OCI card, about half in the US and Canada, and 20 percent in the UK (Naujoks 2020). In addition, while only Indian diplomats were allowed to cast their votes in elections back home, a 2010 amendment of the Representation of the People Act of 1951 allowed NRIs to be included in voter rolls on the condition that they physically returned to India on election day to cast their votes.

Following another recommendation of the HLC, the Indian government – similarly to Egypt, Pakistan, and the Philippines in this volume – established a new, separate, and dedicated cabinet ministry in 2004, the Ministry of Overseas Indian Affairs (MOIA), to provide information and partnerships for all matters related to overseas Indians (Naujoks 2013). Through this reform, the Indian government transferred the emigration and protection authorities from the Ministry of Labor to the new MOIA.

[8] In 1999, the Indian government launched the PIO card, and legislation on the Overseas Citizenship of India (OCI) was adopted in 2003 and operationalized in 2005 as another membership category. For more details, see Naujoks (2020).

The MOIA has had different joint secretaries and divisions to cater to different categories of overseas Indians, and its annual reports on emigration clearances provided key data on the size and demographics of India's overseas population. However, the MOIA was discontinued and integrated into India's MEA in 2016, in a publicized effort to streamline migration governance (*Times of India* 2016). Within this new structure, the diaspora infrastructure is housed in the Overseas Indian Affairs division of the MEA that includes the Protector of Emigrants, which focuses on (mostly temporary and low-skilled) labor emigration, as discussed further on.[9] The MEA is also assisted in services offered to the diaspora by several independent or semi-independent bodies, including the India Center for Migration (ICM). The ICM was created in 2008 to act as a think tank to analyze trends in international labor markets to inform MEA policy-making on issues of emigration and overseas Indians.[10] The MEA also runs the Indian Workers Resource Centers (IWRC) in the UAE, Saudi Arabia, and Malaysia, which provide 24/7 helpdesks for both intending migrants and overseas Indians.

Furthermore, in 2003, the Indian government created an annual diaspora conference as an informal consultative channel between India and overseas Indians. One of the objectives of this conference has been to consult with the diaspora and emigrant workers. The Pravasi Bharatiya Divas (Non-Resident Indian Day) was decided to be held on January 9 (the day Mahatma Gandhi, the first *Pravasi* (expatriate), returned to India from South Africa). During this event, the Indian government also honors successful diasporic individuals with a prestigious Pravasi Bharatiya Samman Award (Non-Resident Indian Honor Award). However, there have been limits to this co-opting strategy targeted at NRIs in the OECD countries as low-skilled emigrants in the GCC countries have argued that their socioeconomic situation and problems in destination countries have not even acknowledged or addressed by such initiatives (Kumar and Rajan 2014: 38).

The Indian government has also increasingly worked with and relied on nongovernmental overseas Indian organizations, which are very diverse in nature and scope in their goals: these can be community-based associations (uniting overseas Indians through national, subnational, linguistic, caste, or religious affiliations) or associations with the objective to facilitate trade and investments with their country of origin (chambers of commerce, business associations, development associations, among others).

[9] Until the creation of the MOIA in 2004, the Protector of Emigrants was housed in the Ministry of Labor.

[10] For more details, see: https://icm.gov.in/.

The philanthropic and welfare contributions of these associations was highlighted by the HLC report and these associations have been increasingly involved in the Pravasi Bharatiya Divas conference (Bhat 2018).

Beyond the typical consular services, Indian missions and posts abroad have also been monitoring incidents threatening the physical security of overseas Indians, notably in the case of conflict- or catastrophe-affected regions or hostage situations (PTI 2019). However, the diplomatic missions do not take direct action but make sure that "such incidents are immediately taken up with the concerned authorities of the host country to ensure that these cases are properly investigated and perpetrators are punished" (ANI 2022b). The legal protection and physical security of these overseas Indians is guaranteed through regular negotiations, and at times the signing of agreements of memorandums of understandings, with foreign governments of countries where there is a sizable Indian population. India has signed bilateral social security agreements or labor agreements with twenty countries to protect the interest of expatriate workers and the companies on a reciprocal basis (Hameed 2021).[11] India and the EU also signed the Common Agenda for Migration and Mobility agreement to cooperate on migration management, with the objective of facilitating the contribution of migrants to the economies of destination countries as well as countries of origin, to secure a cost-effective flow of remittances and their development effect, and to support diaspora networks.[12]

Given some limitations of India's central governmental structure to provide assistance to all overseas Indians, and similarly to Mexico and Indonesia (see Chapters 3 and 9), there have also been subnational institutional and regulatory frameworks to support diaspora and migrant populations. For instance, the states of Kerala, Punjab, and Gujarat have pursued active policies relating to their expatriate populations. Kerala has had a proactive approach to ensure the welfare of emigrants from its state, notably diaspora organizations and returnee associations. Kerala has the largest emigrant population and its economy has greatly benefited from remittances from overseas Keralites based in the GCCs. It was the first Indian state to set up specialized agencies to deal with the governance of its emigrants such as the Non-Resident Keralites Affairs (NORKA) in 1996 (Kumar and Rajan 2014).

In 1996, the NRI Sabha (assembly) of Punjab, was also founded as a nongovernmental organization whose primary object has been to

[11] For a complete list, see: www.mea.gov.in/bilateraldocuments.htm?dtl/26465/Social_Security Agreements.

[12] For more details, see: www.icmpd.org/euindia.

strengthen ties between the Punjabi diaspora and the people and culture of their home state, and to help with their grievances, especially those concerning property issues. Despite an NGO set-up, the NRI Sabha is chaired by the state government's Commissioner for NRI Affairs. Since 1998, the Gujarat government has maintained a separate Department for Non-Resident Gujaratis (NRGs) under which an autonomous Gujarat State Non-Resident Gujaratis Foundation has aimed to promote social, cultural, and linguistic bonds, and explore the possibility of how NRIs and NRGs can play a vital role in the development of the state and identify the areas in which the state government can be of assistance to NRIs and NRGs. Other states have established NRI departments that aim at providing information and build partnerships with regional emigrant, diaspora, and returnee communities. To build on these initiatives and reinforce coordination with central governmental initiatives, the MEA has initiated an outreach program in 2017, Videsh Sampark, in collaboration with various states governments in India to collect more information about the connections between nationals abroad and India's regions (*The Hindu* 2017a).

Economic and Social Dimension

India's growing recognition and co-optation of the economic success of its larger diaspora has led to reforms long sought by nationals abroad, such as the OCI card or the creation of the MOIA. India has also developed a series of economic and social reforms to facilitate investments by overseas Indians and remittances, which have proven crucial to providing a vital balance-of-payments safety net for the country and to fund its economic growth. Moreover, India's economic activism towards its community abroad has simultaneously taken the form of welfare and social protection for low-skilled migrant laborers. This section looks at India's twofold economic outreach to nationals abroad: partnerships with NRI and PIOs in OECD countries and attempts to offer social protection for temporary NRI workers in the GCCs.

The first time any special agency designed to manage economic relations with overseas Indians was mentioned was in 1986, when a special approval committee was constituted within the Department of Industrial Development for the expeditious clearance of industrial proposals of NRIs. In 1987, an Indo-NRI Chamber of Commerce and Culture was set up to promote ties with overseas Indians (Singh and Rajan 2016: 31). During the 1990s, following the policy of economic liberalization in India, some other attempts were made to secure the involvement of affluent NRIs in setting up industries and to tide over foreign exchange crises through attractive financial schemes. India's policy of foreign noninvolvement slowly changed over the years to allow its nationals abroad to take part in the economic development of the country. However, the barriers remained high while the process remained slow.

It was then in the early 2000s, as the Indian authorities increasingly perceived NRIs, especially the Indian–American diaspora, as contributors to India's growth story that a number of new concessions were given to invest in the Indian industry, set up industrial ventures, and deposit foreign currency in Indian banks (Hunger 2004; Kapur 2010; Naujoks 2013). For instance, in order to attract foreign direct investment, the Indian government facilitated NRI investment in real estate and industry, and the existing investment ceiling for NRIs of 5 percent into the capital of a listed Indian company was raised to 24 percent under some provisions. The government of India also established a chief commissioner for NRIs and exempted NRIs from the Foreign Exchange Regulation Act on various issues (Naujoks 2018). These investments by Indians abroad were a major source of capital inflows during the 1990s and helped boost India's hard currency reserves. When the Indian economy was in urgent need of foreign exchange following the balance of payment crisis of 1991, India issued three foreign-currency diaspora bond schemes in order to receive $11.3 billion in foreign exchange. This financial support was also key when India endured sanctions imposed by the US. and World Bank in response to it carrying out nuclear tests in 1998 (Ketkar and Ratha 2010).

Conscious of their growing agency vis-à-vis their home country, NRIs also placed more demands to protect their investments and the question of dual citizenship was brought up to further facilitate investment in India. This led to the creation of the OCI card with new rights for PIOs. The Indian transnational diaspora organizations also became more active in promoting social and economic development in India (Agarwala 2018). However, given the existence of the Foreign Contribution Regulation Act of 1976, the role and contributions of these organizations has been strictly regulated (Naujoks 2018). Various partnerships with the Indian diaspora have therefore led to new economic institutions, policies, and engagement strategies in India. These developments are likely to increase, but diaspora FDI is only a fraction of the total FDI flows for India, and much of India's focus has been on opening investment opportunities for all foreign investors, while also employing an NRI-specific rhetoric and narrative, notably to convey to overseas Indians that their investments are appreciated (Naujoks 2018).

Along with the growing co-optation of India's high-skilled workers in OECD countries, India is also one of the largest sending countries of low-skilled labor migrants, many of whom reside in countries where migrants have limited access to host country social protection schemes. As a result, India has put into place a considerable number of schemes to provide transnational support for its citizens abroad. Many of these are restricted to Indian nationals residing in specific countries, chiefly the GCC countries. The present policy for these citizens has often been criticized as paternalist protection "under a 20th-century law inspired by a 19th-century mindset' (Kumar and Rajan 2014: xvii), given the legacies of British colonial policies designed to regulate Indian indentured migration. In 1966, the Supreme Court established the "right to travel" as a fundamental right under the Indian Constitution, following which the Indian Parliament enacted the Passports Act of 1967, which still contained several provisions to refuse the issuance of a passport if the government thinks this would not be in the "public interest" (Natarajan 2022).

A new Emigration Act was then enacted by the Ministry of Labor in 1983 to deal mainly with the massive emigration of Indian workers for overseas employment on a contractual basis, notably to the Gulf States since the 1970s, and to better safeguard the emigrants' interests and welfare (Jain 2005). The Emigration Act of 1983 clarified the institutional support provided by the central government through "emigration authorities." With this new legislation, India sought to reinforce its control over recruiting agencies and to allow for the setting of minimum standards for foreign work contracts. Seven field Protectors of Emigrants (PoEs) in six Indian states and Union Territories were set up to implement new regulatory procedures of the Act.

Further, under the Emigration Act of 1983, only registered recruiting agents became able to conduct the business of recruitment for overseas employment after obtaining a Registration Certificate from the Protector General of Emigrants (PGE) and taking into account the recruiting agent's financial guarantees, trustworthiness, and experience in the field of handling manpower export (Jain 2005: 63–66). The 1983 Act made it explicit that both intending and actual emigrants would be entitled to protection and advice but, in both Acts, the terms "protect(ion)," "aid," and "advice" were never clearly defined. In practice, the Indian government and specifically its Ministry of Labor have mainly concentrated on preventive services such as the issuing of emigration clearance and did not offer additional protection services, especially for low-skilled migrant laborers (Kumar and Rajan 2014: 106–108).

This repressive state monitoring of emigration of low-skilled workers is a practice which we still observe today in Indian migration policies with a socioeconomic discrimination between Emigration Clearance Required (ECR) and Emigration Clearance Not Required (ECNR) categories determined by the office of the Protector of Emigrants (POE), which distinguishes categories of emigrants according to levels of education, work skills, and gender to determine emigration clearance (Walton-Roberts and Rajan 2013; Mongia 2018: 2). While India envisaged in its Passports Act of 1967 one single type of ordinary passport, in practice two types of ordinary passports, namely ECR and ECNR, have been used in India based on the education and skill levels of the holders of these passports (Natarajan 2022).

This type of distinction between two types of passports meant that some Indian citizens required state authorization of their juridical labor contract before emigrating (Mongia 2018). In parallel to the creation of the supervisory role of the state over these contractual arrangements, there was the formation of a significant bureaucracy, including the PGE and POEs, which developed standard procedures to efficiently manage and monitor migration (Mongia 2018: 54–55). Until 2014, the POE was part of the Ministry of Labor and was then redeployed to become an integral part of the newly created MOIA in 2015.

The Indian state provided a series of welfare and social protection policies for Indians abroad. As the GCC countries host half of the Indian NRIs, most of these policies have had a strong emphasis on migrants to this part of the world. For instance, the MEA established Indian Workers Resource Centers in the UAE and Saudi Arabia (but also Malaysia) which provide 24/7 helpdesks for both intending migrants and overseas Indians and an electronic platform attends to queries in eleven Indian languages. Other key initiatives have included the Mahatma Gandhi Pravasi Suraksha Yojana (Non-Resident Indian Protection Scheme) for NRIs (now defunct) and the Indian Community Welfare Fund (ICWF), which is a fund established in 2009 to be tapped into by embassies to assist Indian (especially ECR) citizens abroad in situations of distress and emergency in the "most deserving cases" on a "means tested basis" (Bhaskar 2016). The funds have generally been limited to Indian citizens who have entered the host country legally and are raised by Indian consulates by levying a Service Charge on Consular Services, as well as through voluntary contributions by the Indian community and budgetary support from the government.

The stated target groups of these funds are "overseas Indian workers duped by unscrupulous intermediaries in the host countries, runaway house maids, those who become victim of accidents, deserted spouses of Overseas Indians or undocumented Overseas Indian workers in need of emergency assistance."[13] The ICWF can also help consulates to pay for the transportation of mortal remains of deceased Indian nationals to India or local cremation/burial of deceased. In the period 2009–2016, Indian consulates have provided support for 80,000 beneficiaries, notably in the context of the large-scale evacuations of more than 6,200 Indians from Iraq, 3,600 from Libya, and 6,700 from Yemen (Naujoks 2020). There are also subnational pension schemes such as the Non-Resident Keralites' Welfare Fund Act of 2008.

After 2014, the new Narendra Modi government tried to further co-opt its community abroad to facilitate India's economic and political interests overseas, notably through an aggressive public diplomacy reconnecting ethnonational links with its national community abroad, broadly defined as both citizens and persons of Indian origin, as well as publicizing a series of measures the Indian state put in place to safeguard the interests of overseas Indians in destination countries (Sahoo and Soome 2020). While implemented under the Modi government, these were measures or actions which evolved from a longer pattern of actions over the last two decades to try to improve India's reputation in the management of emigration and protection of emigrant welfare abroad. For instance, the Modi government set up the Madad (Help) online portal to address grievances related to existing consular services offered by Indian missions abroad on a priority basis by tracking online their redressal process until the final resolution.

One other key initiative to streamline the recruitment of certain categories of labor migrants abroad was the centralization since May 2015 of the migrant recruitment process through an online e-Migrate system. The e-Migrate online system was intended to replace the in-house System Automation Initiative platform and to reduce administrative and financial costs of the migration process. Like in Indonesia, digitization was directly framed as a response to criticisms of the existing long, costly, and burdensome administrative process of emigration clearance. The e-Migrate platform was launched with the promise that it would ensure a certain respect for basic labor standards, such as minimum referral wages in various sectors, and to foster a transparent process for recruitment and employment in the destination country. For instance, by requiring all prospective workers to the Gulf States holding ECR passports to be employed directly by a foreign employer, with both employees and employers submitting all necessary documents for emigration clearance, the e-Migrate platform intended to regularize and protect labor migrants deemed most vulnerable (Sasikumar and Sharma 2016).

[13] For more on the ICWF mission, see: https://indianembassynetherlands.gov.in/page/icwf/.

Security Dimension

Given India's increasing economic and political engagement with its national community abroad, and the growing recognition of the protection of Indians abroad as a key national interest, the government has also developed more incentives to track and protect its citizens overseas but also, if necessary, to evacuate Indians caught up in crisis situations where their immediate physical security is at risk. In public statements to the communities abroad, Prime Minister Modi has often publicized evacuation operations as evidence of India's support for the security and welfare of overseas Indians (*The Mint* 2022). However, India has never formalized any specific doctrine or standard procedures initiating the use of military force for the protection of Indians abroad.

The absence of a clear policy is due partly to the significant challenges India has faced in deploying its diplomatic and military assets abroad to protect its community overseas, notably due to its initial nonaligned stance and reluctance to get involved in conflict zones but also in the internal affairs of other states. In the initial post-independence years, India very consciously adopted a policy of distancing itself from emigrant communities spread across the globe during the colonial-era waves of migration. In 1952, an Indian government report instructed all diplomatic missions abroad that the "first objective in regard to Indian overseas communities should be to help them to assimilate themselves to local conditions and to identify themselves as closely as possible with the interests of the indigenous population."[14] Then, in an important statement to the Indian Parliament in 1957, Prime Minister Jawaharlal Nehru acknowledged that people of Indian origin were facing discrimination in different parts of the world,[15] but he spelled out the Indian government's post-independence policy towards migrants in terms of a choice that had to be made by the Indians abroad themselves. Nehru's decision to encourage Indians abroad to integrate within their host countries was both linked to the acknowledgment that independent India did not have the material resources to support or repatriate millions of overseas Indians, and to a realization that diplomatic partners in East Africa, but with Malaysia, Burma (Myanmar), and Ceylon (Sri Lanka), had

[14] Commonwealth Secretary Badruddin Tyabji, Burma–Hindu Muslim Relations on Burma (Ministry of External Affairs document at the National Archives of India, B/52/1335/4), 35.

[15] In a sporadic fashion, the Indian government attempted to mediate when Indians were targeted by discriminatory policies in Ceylon (Sri Lanka), Burma (Myanmar), or East African countries. See, for instance, India's intervention in the case of stateless Indians suffering discrimination in Ceylon (Sri Lanka). For more, see Phadnis (1967).

concerns that their Indian minority populations could be a channel for external influence (Phadnis 1967; Egreteau 2014).

The absence of any formal doctrine on the use of military force to protect Indian citizens abroad has not kept India from engaging in more than thirty missions across Asia and Africa since 1947 (Xavier 2016). India's evacuation of civilians from Kuwait during the 1990–1991 Gulf War still remains the world's largest evacuation exercise of civilians by air (170,000) and involved successful logistical coordination between private airline companies and air force support on one end and with regional actors in the Middle-East to facilitate the operations on the other end. This was also the first time that the Indian government recognized its responsibility to take care of the security of overseas Indian citizens in distress and actually arranged such a mass return of its overseas citizenry to safety. In other major evacuation operations in Lebanon (2006), Libya (2011), Nepal (2015), Yemen (2015), Afghanistan (2021), Ukraine (2022), and Sudan (2023), three conditions have generally been met to prompt Indian military intervention: (1) an imminent threat to Indian citizens; (2) the inability of the host state to protect them; and (3) India's intervention was strictly confined to protecting its citizens. In addition, the Indian Navy has publicized in its 2007 maritime strategy "actions to assist the Indian diaspora and Indian interests abroad" as a "likely scenario" for the use of military force. Yet, besides listing "support for the diaspora" as a key driver for maritime cooperation, few additional operational details were specified (Xavier 2016).

As visible during the Ukraine–Russia War and India's conduct of Operation Ganga, the success of India's evacuation of 18,000 citizens relied heavily on New Delhi's ability to collaborate with Central and Eastern European governments, social media strategies to collect information and provide hotlines for stranded citizens and collaboration with diaspora organizations. Furthermore, repatriation efforts have not been limited to conflict zones but have also covered Indians impacted by economic downturns and rising unemployment, notably in Gulf States. Also, in the context of the Covid-19 crisis, the Indian government undertook the Vande Bharat Mission to repatriate over 6 million Indians abroad, the majority of the requests coming from temporary NRIs in Gulf countries, through its then state-owned carrier, Air India, as well as military transport planes, and naval ships (*Hindustan Times* 2021).

Given the absence of formal doctrines or dedicated instruments to deal with repatriation operations, it is therefore unclear how these ad hoc operations are funded. In 1990, there were reservations and debates in the V. P. Singh government about the Kuwait evacuation operation given the dramatic costs, especially as India was then experiencing an important foreign exchange crisis. The repatriation of thousands of Indian NRIs from the GCCs through operation Vande Bharat have also raised the policy challenges of dealing with returnees. Evacuation operations, while publicized as an essential responsibility to support Indians abroad, have also complicated the socioeconomic situation of some states like Kerala, which have had to abruptly absorb hundreds of thousands of returning migrants while concurrently missing the regular and indispensable inflow of remittances. Given that the Indian community abroad, including its tourist population, is expanding and becoming more mobile, these evacuation operations are likely to become more frequent and will pose growing challenges. Noting that these diverse security and health crises have had implications on the security of an increasing number of Indians abroad, a parliamentary panel has called in March 2022 on the MEA to prepare an updated database of all Indians abroad and to formulate a clear set of official standard operating procedures for such emergency operations (ANI 2022a).

Another security dimension has been New Delhi's concerns over the support for separatist politics among Indians abroad. Through its embassies and foreign intelligence agency, the Research and Analysis Wing (RAW), India has been closely monitoring Indians abroad who question its territorial integrity or criticize its treatment of ethnic minorities (Singh 2023). One important example of these transnational dynamics has been the Khalistan movement, which has been a source of tension in Canada–India relations, especially as Sikhism in Canada has nearly 800,000 adherents who account for 2.1 percent of Canada's population as of 2021 (Bharath 2023). The demand for an independent Khalistan, a separate homeland for Sikhs, who are a religious minority that makes up 2 percent of India's population, peaked in India in the 1980s with an armed insurgency in the Indian state of Punjab. Since the late 1980s, the separatist movement has receded in India but has remained salient in Canada, the United States, and the UK as diaspora groups reacted to the events unfolding in India.

Recently, the Modi government has accused the UK and especially Canada of not doing enough to quell Sikh protests and "anti-India" activities. The rift between India and Canada further escalated in September 2023 as Canada publicly accused the Indian government of being linked to the murder on Canadian soil of a Canadian citizen and Sikh leader, Hardeep Singh Nijjar, who was wanted under India's Terrorist Act (Yousif 2023). Australia, the UK, and the US, which all host important Indian communities, have issued statements of concern over Canadian prime minister Justin Trudeau's recent allegations, and in November 2023 federal prosecutors in the US have also accused an employee from the government of India of arranging the murder of a prominent Sikh American activist, Gurpatwant Singh Pannun, who was living in New York City and had been a longtime associate of Nijjar (Hong 2023). While India has denied any implication in the murder in Canada, the government of India has called the US allegations a "matter of concern" and assured the US that it would cooperate in an investigation, arguing also that any sting operation was contrary to "Indian government policy" (Cohen, Mason & Brunnstrom 2023). It is true, however, that India has taken steps to identify Khalistani terrorists residing in the US., UK, Canada, and Australia, notably in order to confiscate their properties in India and cancel their OCI cards (*India Today* 2023). By taking these actions, the Indian government has developed a new set of repressive tools against Indians abroad, which it considers to be a threat to its national sovereignty and integrity.

Conclusion

From 1947 to the late 1980s, India very consciously adopted a policy of distancing itself from Indians abroad due to its limited material capacity to support a large and diverse overseas community. India was also reluctant to be perceived as interfering in the internal affairs of the host states. By contrast, since the early 1990s, in reaction to the emergence of an increasingly rich and influential Indian diaspora in the OECD countries, and as India's own material capacities grew, India deliberately sought to co-opt its national community abroad by providing more consular services and by redesigning its diaspora policies and institutions, notably through the creation of the Ministry of Overseas Indian Affairs and of the Overseas Citizenship of India status, which were long-term requests from Indians abroad.

The priority for the re-engagement of Indian nationals abroad has been the co-optation of NRIs in OECD countries to assist its economic growth through their investments and political influence in their host countries. Over the last decade, Prime Minister Modi has, for instance, traveled in the US, UK, and Australia to organize a series of outreach events to co-opt the diaspora through emotional appeals to reconnect with the homeland (Hegde 2018). This has also led Indians based in OECD economies to gradually place more demands on the Indian state, such as for dual citizenship and schemes to facilitate investments in India. In addition, beyond the engagement of India's high-skilled workers in OECD countries, the expansion of India's consular support services has also been driven by the need to ensure stable remittances from low-skilled migrants in the GCCs. This has led to a specific set of policy initiatives to regulate and manage temporary low-skilled worker emigration, often building on bureaucratic legacies from the British Indian period.

As a result, the Indian diplomatic and consular system has pursued, similarly to other countries discussed in this volume, a differentiated approach by focusing on providing important social and economic support for its temporary and low-skilled emigrant population in the GCCs, developing transactional economic partnerships with the richer diaspora communities in OECD countries, and operating costly ad hoc evacuation operations to support Indians abroad in distress.

For now, India's policies have been partly successful as the Indian community abroad contributes more each year than foreign direct remittances to India's economic growth and development policies. Since 2003, India has been the world's largest recipient of remittances, at least in absolute terms, moving from remittances valued at a modest $2.1 billion in 1991 to an estimated $83 billion in 2020. This is far more than any other country in absolute numbers and a full 64 percent higher than the $53 billion remittances sent to China and Mexico, the next largest remittance receivers (Ratha et al. 2021).

However, by deliberately expanding the conceptualization of its national community abroad over time, India has also expanded the definition of its national interests and priorities. If we go by the official Indian definition of overseas Indians, which includes both NRIs and PIOs, the Indian diaspora is estimated to be more than 30 million spread over 206 countries across the world (MEA 2019). Modi's government has also regularly assured Indian tourists, NRIs, and PIOs of proactive consular support from Indian missions abroad, broadcasting the evacuation and repatriation operations facilitated by the Indian government during the Covid-19 crisis and in conflict situations like the Ukraine crisis (*The Mint* 2022). Modi also asserted at the Pravasi Bharatiya Divas convention of 2017 that India did not look at the "color of the passport but only the blood relationship" (*The Hindu* 2017b). However, India is also still a country with a large domestic population and severe developmental challenges at home. Compared to other countries discussed in this volume, India's diaspora policies are not as institutionalized and are rather small in scale. The Indian rhetoric has therefore implications for the scope of situations and instruments through which India aims to provide protection to its overseas Indians, leading thereby to a possible gap between public rhetoric and actual policy and material tools available to adequately support all its nationals abroad.

References

Agarwala, Rina (2018) Transnational Diaspora Organizations and India's Development. In Radha Hegde and Ajaya K. Sahoo (eds.), *Routledge Handbook of the Indian Diaspora*. London: Routledge, 104–116.

Asian New International (ANI) (2022a) Parliamentary Panel Asks MEA to Prepare Database of Indians Abroad, Commends Role during Ukraine Evacuation. March 23. Available at: www.aninews.in/news/world/asia/parliamentary-panel-asks-mea-to-prepare-database-of-indians-abroad-commends-role-during-ukraine-evacuation20220323233850/.

Asian New International (ANI) (2022b) Govt Attaches Highest Priority to Safety of Indians Abroad, Including Those in Foreign Jails: V Muraleedharan in RS. February 11. Available at: www.aninews.in/news/national/general-news/govt-attaches-highest-priority-to-safety-of-indians-abroad-including-those-in-foreign-jails-v-muraleedharan-in-rs20220211181137/.

Bharath, Deepa (2023) India–Canada Tensions Highlight the Complexities of Sikh Activism. *Time*. September 23. Available at: https://time.com/6316936/india-canada-tensions-sikh-activism/.

Bhaskar, T. L. S. (2016) Protection of Labour Migrants at Destination Countries: A Note on the Indian Community Welfare Fund. In S. Idurayan Rajan (ed.), *Indian Migration Report 2016*. New Delhi: Routledge, 133–145.

Bhat, Chandrashekhar (2018): Indian Diaspora and Global Organizations: Communities and Contested Boundaries. In Elfriede Hermann and Antonie Fuhse (eds.), *India Beyond India: Dilemmas of Belonging*. Göttingen: Göttingen University Press, 27–48.

Cohen, Luc, Jeff Mason, and David Brunnstrom (2023) US Links Indian Official to Murder Plot That India Calls 'Contrary to Policy'. *Reuters*, December 1. Available at: www.reuters.com/world/us/us-charges-indian-national-with-conspiracy-assassinate-sikh-advocate-2023-11-29/.

Egreteau, Renaud (2014) The Idealization of a Lost Paradise: Narratives of Nostalgia and Traumatic Return among Indian Repatriates from Burma since the 1960s. *Journal of Burma Studies* 18(1): 137–180.

Ennis, Crystal A., and Nicolas Blarel (2022) *The South Asia to Gulf Migration Governance Complex*. Bristol: Bristol University Press.

Hameed, Sameena (2021) India's Labour Agreements with the Gulf Cooperation Council Countries: An Assessment. *International Studies 58*(4): 442–465.

Hegde, Radha S. (2018) Renewing Diasporic Bonds and the Global Branding of India. In Radha Hegde and Ajaya K. Sahoo (eds.), *Routledge Handbook of the Indian Diaspora*. London: Routledge, 269–281.

High Level Committee on the Indian Diaspora (2001) *Report of the High Level Committee on the Indian Diaspora*. New Delhi: Indian Council of World Affairs.

Hindustan Times (2021) India Repatriates over 6 Million under Vande Bharat Mission: Civil Aviation Minister Hardeep Singh Puri. *Hindustan Times*, March 2, 2021. Available at: www.hindustantimes.com/india-news/india-repatriates-over-6-million-under-vande-bharat-mission-hardeep-singh-puri-101614659365140.html.

Hong, Nicole (2023) How a Suspected Indian Murder-for-Hire Plot on U.S. Soil Was Foiled. *New York Times*, December 2. Available at: www.nytimes.com/2023/12/02/nyregion/india-sikh-assassination-attempt.html.

Hunger, Uwe (2004) Indian IT-Entrepreneurs in the US and India: An Illustration of the "Brain Gain Hypothesis." *Journal of Comparative Policy-Analysis* 6(2): 99–109.

India Today (2023) Indian Government Identifies Properties of Khalistani Terrorists Abroad, Revokes OCI Cards. September 24. Available at: www.indiatodayne.in/national/story/indian-government-identifies-properties-of-khalistani-terrorists-abroad-revokes-oci-cards-683472-2023-09-24.

Jain, Prakash C. (2005) Indian Migration to the Gulf Countries: Past and Present. *India Quarterly* 61(2): 50–81.

Jayal, Niraja Gopal (2016) Citizenship. In Sujit Choudhry, Madhav Khosla, and Pratap Bhanu Mehta (eds.), *The Oxford Handbook of the Indian Constitution*. New Delhi: Oxford University Press, 163–179.

Kapur, Devesh (2010) *Diaspora, Development, and Democracy: The Domestic Impact of International Migration from India*. Princeton, NJ: Princeton University Press.

Ketkar, Suhas, and Dilip Ratha (2010) Diaspora Bonds: Tapping the Diaspora during Difficult Times. *Journal of International Commerce, Economics and Policy 1*(2): 251–263.

Kumar, S. Krishna, and S. Iduraya Rajan (2014) *Emigration in 21st-Century India: Governance, Legislation, Institutions*. New Delhi: Routledge.

Lall, Marie (2003) Mother India's Forgotten Children. In Eva Qstergaard Nielsen (ed.), *International Migration and Sending Countries: Perceptions, Policies and Transnational Relations*. New York: Palgrave Macmillan, 121–139.

McAuliffe, Marie, and Anna Triandafyllidou (eds.) (2021) *World Migration Report 2022*. Geneva: International Organization for Migration. Available at: https://publications.iom.int/books/world-migration-report-2022.

McCarty, Niall (2020) This Chart Shows Where the World's Highly Educated Migrants Come From. *World Economic Forum*, December 2, 2020. Available at: www.weforum.org/agenda/2020/12/where-do-highly-educated-migrants-come-from/.

Ministry of External Affairs (2019) Question No.2885 Number of Overseas Indians Abroad. Media release, July 18, 2019. Available at: https://mea.gov.in/rajya-sabha.htm?dtl/31625/question+no2885+number+of+overseas+indians+abroad.

Mongia, Radhika (2018) *Indian Migration and Empire: A Colonial Genealogy of the Modern State*. Durham, NC and London: Duke University Press.

Narayan, K. Laxmi (2008). A Brief History of Indian Emigration during Ancient and Medieval Period. In Ajaya Kumar Sahoo and K. Laxmi Narayan (eds.), *Indian Diaspora: Trends and Issues*. New Delhi: Serials Publication, 1–6.

Natarajan, Kalathmika (2022) The Privilege of the Indian Passport (1947–1967): Caste, Class, and the Afterlives of Indenture in Indian Diplomacy. *Modern Asian Studies*: 1–30, doi:10.1017/S0026749X22000063.

Naujoks, Daniel (2013) *Migration, Citizenship, and Development: Diasporic Membership Policies and Overseas Indians in the United States*. New York: Oxford University Press.

Naujoks, Daniel (2018) Paradigms, Policies, and Patterns of Indian Diaspora Investments. In Radha Sarma Hegde and Ajaya Kumar Sahoo (eds.), *Routledge Handbook of the Indian Diaspora*. New York: Routledge.

Naujoks, Daniel (2020) Diaspora Policies, Consular Services and Social Protection for Indian Citizens Abroad. In Jean-Michel Lafleur and Daniela Vintila (eds.), *Migration and Social Protection in Europe and Beyond (Volume 3)*. Cham, Switzerland: Springer.

Pande, Amba (2013) Conceptualising Indian Diaspora: Diversities within a Common Identity. *Economic & Political Weekly* 48(49): 59–65.

Phadnis, Urmila (1967) The Indo-Ceylon Pact and the 'Stateless' Indians in Ceylon. *Asian Survey* 7(4): 226–36.

Press Trust of India (PTI) (2019). 65 Indians Taken Hostage in Various Countries during 2017–19. November 27. Available at: http://timesofindia.indiatimes.com/articleshow/72263099.cms?utm_source=contentofinterest&utm_medium=text&utm_campaign=cppst.

Ratha, Dilip, Eung Ju Kim, Sonia Plaza, Ganesh Seshan, Elliott J Riordan, and Vandana Chandra (2021) *Migration and Development Brief 35: Recovery: COVID-19 Crisis through a Migration Lens*. Washington, DC: KNOMAD-World Bank, 2021. Available at: www.knomad.org/sites/default/files/2021-11/Migration_Brief%2035_1.pdf.

Reserve Bank of India (2021) *Fifth Round of the Survey on Remittances*. New Delhi: Government of India. Available at: www.rbi.org.in/scripts/FS_PressRelease.aspx?prid=54044&fn=2759.

Sahoo, Ajaya K., and Anindita Shome (2020) Diaspora and Transnationalism: The Changing Contours of Ethnonational Identity of Indian Diaspora. *Perspectives on Global Development and Technology* 19: 383–402.

Sasikumar, S.K., and Seeta Sharma (2016) *Minimum Referral Wages for International Migrant Workers from India: An Assessment*. New Delhi: International Labour Organization. Available online: www.ilo.org/wcmsp5/groups/public/---asia/---ro-bangkok/---sro-new_delhi/documents/ publication/wcms_538168.pdf.

Singh, A. Didar, and S. Iduraya Rajan (2016) *Politics of Migration: Indian Emigration in a Globalized World*. New Delhi: Routledge.

Singh, Sushant (2023) Rift with Canada Puts Spotlight on India's Security Services. September 22. Available at: https://foreignpolicy.com/2023/09/22/india-canada-trudeau-accusations-nijjar-sikh-separatism-security-intelligence/.

Thandi, Shinder S. (2015) Punjabi Migration, Settlement and Experience in the UK. In S. Irudaya Rajan, V. J. Varghese and Aswini Kumar Nanda (eds.), *Migration, Mobility and Multiple Affiliations: Punjabis in a Transnational World*. Cambridge: Cambridge University Press, 105–130.

The Hindu (2017a) Telangana to Host First Videsh Sampark. May 12, 2017. Available at: www.thehindu.com/news/cities/Hyderabad/telangana-to-host-first-videsh-sampark/article18429726.ece.

The Hindu (2017b) Blood Ties Matter, Not Colour of Passport, Modi Tells Global Indians. January 9, 2017. Available at: www.thehindu.com/news/national/Blood-ties-matter-not-colour-of-passport-Modi-tells-global-Indians/article17009798.ece.

The Mint (2022) Jaishankar Highlights 'Vande Bharat Mission' in Saudi Arabia. September 11, 2022. Available at: www.livemint.com/news/india/jaishankar-highlights-vande-bharat-mission-in-saudi-arabia-11662871494095.html.

Times of India (2016) Government to Merge Overseas Indian Affairs Ministry with MEA. January 8, 2016. Available at: http://timesofindia.indiatimes.com/articleshow/50491031.cms?utm_source=contentofinterest&utm_medium=text&utm_campaign=cppst.

Times of India (2021) India, World's Largest Recipient of Remittances, Received $87 Billion in 2021: World Bank. November 18, 2021, Available at: http://timesofindia.indiatimes.com/articleshow/87772872.cms?utm_source=contentofinterest&utm_medium=text&utm_campaign=cppst.

Tinker, Hugh (1974) *A New System of Slavery: The Import of Indian Labour Overseas 1830–1920*. London: Oxford University Press.

Tinker, Hugh (1977) *The Banyan Tree: Overseas Emigrants from India, Pakistan, and Bangladesh*. Oxford: Oxford University Press.

Varadarajan, Latha (2010) *The Domestic Abroad: Diasporas in International Relations*. New York: Oxford University Press.

Walton-Roberts, Margaret, and S. Iduraya Rajan (2013) Nurse Emigration from Kerala: 'Brain Circulation' or 'Trap'. In S. Irudaya Rajan (ed.), *Global Financial Crisis, Migration and Remittances: India Migration Report*. New Delhi: Routledge, 206–223.

Weiner, Myron (1978) *Sons of the Soil: Migration and Ethic Conflict in India*. Bombay: Oxford University Press.

World Bank (2021) Defying Predictions, Remittance Fows Remain Strong during COVID-19 Crisis. Press release, May 12. Available at www.worldbank.org/en/news/press-release/2021/05/12/defying-predictions-remittance-fows-remain-strong-during-covid-19-crisis.

Xavier, Constantino (2016) India's Expatriate Evacuation Operations: Bringing the Diaspora Home. Washington, DC: Carnegie Endowment for International Peace. Available at: https://carnegieendowment.org/files/CP_299_Xavier_India_Diaspora_Final.pdf.

Yousif, Nadine (2023) Who Was Canadian Sikh Leader Hardeep Singh Nijjar? September 21. Available at: www.bbc.com/news/world-us-canada-66860510.

3 Mexico

Consular Protection as a Foreign Policy Priority

Daniel Hernández Joseph and Jorge A. Schiavon

Introduction

Mexico has developed a unique consular diplomacy to protect its citizens' rights around the world. Given that 97 percent of Mexicans living abroad are in the United States, its consular protection policies and strategies are almost entirely designed thinking of the conditions and challenges those Mexican nationals living in the territory of their northern neighbor face. In fact, Mexico's tradition for protecting its nationals abroad was borne out of the history of its bilateral relations with the US. In the aftermath of the 1846–1848 Mexican–American War, Mexicans who remained in the lost territories suffered discrimination and abuse. As a response, Mexico refocused its consular services from trade promotion to consular protection, and this consular assistance moved from advancing the nation's trade interests to looking after the vulnerable Mexican nationals living in the US. The onset of this activity in the mid nineteenth century was part of an effort to consolidate the nation after the territorial losses. Mexico lost Texas in 1836 and more than half of its remaining territory because of the Mexican–American War of 1846–1848 (55% of it, which accounts for more than 2.1 million km^2 and comprises the current states of Arizona, California, Nevada, Utah, and New Mexico, and parts of Colorado, Wyoming, Kansas, and Oklahoma). In directing its activity toward assisting those who remained in the lost territories, Mexico was recognizing them as part of the Mexican nation. Ever since, with growing migration flows, Mexico slowly developed its consular diplomacy, characterized by partnerships, proximity, flexibility, federal issues at the consular level, and high-visibility consular cases. No other foreign service has as strong a consular concentration nor is as centered in a single other country as is the Mexican Foreign Service and its consular network in the US (Hernández Joseph 2012).

This concentration, together with the overall complexity of the bilateral relationship, has given Mexican consular diplomacy a central role in Mexico's foreign policy. Maaiko Okano-Heijmans (2011: 21) defines consular diplomacy as "international negotiations on a consular (legal) framework and individual consular cases that attract substantial attention from the media, public and politicians." In its essence, consular diplomacy is also public diplomacy because it deals with foreign audiences such as visa solicitors and local authorities and a wide array of domestic publics, from citizens in distress overseas to diaspora communities and agencies involved in its consular services. For Mexico, addressing US citizens and authorities to promote a positive image of the Mexican communities living there, thus contributing to their social integration, is a major public diplomacy aspect of consular work.

In this chapter, we give an overview of the current scenario for Mexican citizens living abroad. We also analyze the Mexican consular and diplomatic work at a global level and its concentration in the US, as well as the economic, social, and military activities carried out by the Mexican state through its diplomatic missions. Because of its almost total concentration in a single country, its inception as an activity directed at particularly poor and vulnerable populations, and the domestic political sensibility of the issue because of the size of the populations living in the US, Mexico's policy for protecting its nationals abroad is multifaceted and goes well beyond traditional consular protection and into the realm of bilateral and multilateral political relations and public diplomacy.

Thus, beyond the direct motivation of affecting the lives of its citizens in the US, this very proactive policy was linked to the assertion of national identity and attempting to strengthen its clout in managing its bilateral relations with its northern neighbor. Consequently, the main motivation is one of support and, to a lesser degree, one of co-optation in that it seeks to include the Mexican population in the US as part of the Mexican nation. There is no motivation to repress simply because the Mexican state has nothing to gain from it.

Overview of the Mexican Community Abroad

According to the Institute for Mexicans Abroad (IME by its Spanish acronym), an office within the nation's Secretariat of Foreign Affairs (SRE by its Spanish acronym), 97 percent of Mexicans living abroad reside in the US (Instituto de los Mexicanos en el Exterior 2022). The regional distribution of Mexicans worldwide in 2020 is presented in Table 3.1. It is important to note that these figures do not include an additional more than 25 million people of Mexican origin (second and third generation) living in the US, who are also subject to Mexico's foreign policy, and whom several academics and activists believe should furthermore be considered part of the Mexican nation (Guillén López 2022).

Table 3.1 *Mexicans living abroad*

Worldwide	Millions	%
United States	11,750,000	96.94
Worldwide, minus United States	370,633	3.06
Latin America and Caribbean	201,896	1.67
Europe	140,820	1.16
Asia	17,323	0.14
Africa	1,083	0.01
Oceania	9,511	0.08
Total	12,120,633	100

Source: Data for 2020, "Población Mexicana en el Mundo," Instituto de los Mexicanos en el Exterior, Secretaría de Relaciones Exteriores. Available at: www.gob.mx/ime/acciones-y-programas/mexicanos-en-el-mundo.

Consequently, when addressing the subject of its nationals abroad, Mexico often equates it to the subject of its nationals in a single other country, the US. To offer a wider perspective requires, ironically, to "zoom in on the rest of the world." The SRE's strategies and policies for the protection of its citizens abroad are designed based on the goal of tending to Mexicans in the US (Hernández Joseph 2015). Furthermore, since Mexico's global protection policies are designed with thinking about the US, they are intimately connected to the history of US–Mexico relations and are strongly influenced by these bilateral relations and immigration trends (Hernández Joseph 2012). Therefore, understanding Mexico's policies, strategies, and practice for protecting its citizens abroad requires at least a basic understanding of this history and the context of this specific bilateral relation.

In reading this history, it is important also to keep in mind the fact that starting in the late nineteenth century, Mexico's protection policies centered on vulnerable populations such as undocumented immigrants, the poor, and the disenfranchised. This approach is taken because most Mexicans abroad are more vulnerable than the rest of the population and therefore need special social and legal protection (Hernandez Joseph 2015).

After the Mexican–American War of 1846–1848, the two countries signed the Guadalupe–Hidalgo Treaty on February 2, 1848. Suddenly, at a pen's stroke, around 75,000 Mexicans who lived in Upper California and New Mexico became foreigners (Morales cited in Gómez Arnau 1990: 131). Most Mexicans who stayed in the US lost their property and suffered from widespread discrimination and abuses, as well as other violent situations that required their home government's assistance (Moyano

Pahissa 1989). This situation, together with the growing emigration of workers to the US[1] and the anti-Mexican sentiments that existed in border states, pushed Mexico's government into developing, very early on, a specific type of consular protection focused on the defense against the unjust treatment of its citizens north of the border, rather than promoting trade and business as most other countries did (Hernández Joseph 2015: 50). Even though many Mexicans in the US had lived there since the late 1870s, from 1990 to 2009, 9.6 million additional Mexicans emigrated to the US (Israel and Batalova 2020).

Before the 1990s, the Mexican population clustered in the four border states (California, Arizona, New Mexico, and Texas), Illinois, and small pockets in other parts of the US. The economic expansion during that decade in the US and financial struggles in Mexico enabled Mexicans to move to every state, particularly in the South, Northeast, Northwest, and the West (Batalova 2008). As the needs and demands of Mexicans north of the border changed with the ups and downs of the US economy, so did the consular services offered by the most extensive network of consular offices in a host country, with a network of fifty-two Mexican consulates in the US, the largest consular network in the world that a state has in another country.

Nowadays, Mexico has a significant global presence with more than 150 diplomatic representations worldwide: 80 embassies, 67 consulates, 7 permanent missions to international world organizations, and 3 liaison offices (Secretaría de Relaciones Exteriores, 2022a and 2022c). There are close to 11.7 million people born in Mexico living in the US (Instituto de los Mexicanos en el Exterior 2022), accounting for approximately 9 percent of Mexico's total population. In addition, there are approximately 25.4 million people in the US who consider themselves of Mexican origin (Noe-Bustamante, Flores, and Shah 2019). Mexicans accounted for 24 percent of the 45 million foreign-born persons living in the US, making it the top country of origin. Of a population of 57 million Hispanics/Latinos in the US, 63 percent are of Mexican origin. In 2018, according to the Current Population Survey, there were 38.5 million people residing in the US of Mexican origin. The most important thing about the phenomenon is the concentration of migrants in this country;

[1] At different times in history, the United States, formally or informally, has been a labor magnet for Mexican nationals. Some US immigration policies have served to promote Mexican migration to the United States. The Chinese Exclusion Act of 1882 increased the hiring of Mexican labor; Mexican laborers were invited formally as temporary workers in 1917, as well as during the Bracero programs that spanned from 1942 to 1964, thus contributing to the establishment of a migration network from Mexico to certain states of the United States, especially California, Illinois, and Texas.

this is a feature that differentiates Mexico from other high-emigration countries such as China, India, and the Philippines: nearly 97.2 percent of the Mexicans abroad live in just one country, the US (Instituto de los Mexicanos en el Exterior 2022).[2]

For Mexican diplomacy, the resulting challenge goes way beyond the traditional one of providing consular services, which is already a monumental task given the 11.7 million Mexican nationals living in the US, of which approximately 55 percent are there without proper immigration documents. Consular services extend to fostering and administering the connection with a diaspora of an additional 25 million people of Mexican descent who are citizens of the US, but because of the close geographic proximity, maintain cultural and family links with Mexico, thus forming what could arguably be the largest transnational community in the world.

The 370,000 Mexicans living abroad outside of the US represent a sizable population. However, when it comes to policy, evidence suggests that it is all a matter of perception. Since they represent only 3 percent of the total population living abroad and the socioeconomic profile differs from the profile of "poor, vulnerable and constantly mistreated," they receive substantially less attention. This is not to say that their needs for consular protection are ignored, but the programs for that purpose tend to be adaptations of those established for the US case or ad hoc actions in response to specific events due to natural disasters or political upheaval (Hernandez Joseph 2015). An analysis of the country's statistical information regarding the economic activity of the Mexican population outside the US provided by IME shows a predominantly middle-class population, living legally in their countries of destination. They are also more integrated than the Mexican nationals living in the US (Instituto de los Mexicanos en el Exterior 2022).

Diplomatic and Consular Dimension

The mere size and complexity of the Mexican community in the US means that the diplomatic challenge has impacts on the political bilateral relations, the definition of Mexican positions in certain multilateral fora, public diplomacy, traditional consular services, and the efforts to

[2] Most immigrants in the United States normally plan to stay for the rest of their lives as they cannot go back to their home countries for several reasons, including fear of persecution and the cost of travel. In the case of Mexico, even with higher enforcement and costs of migrating, it is easier and less expensive to go back to Mexico since it is a neighboring country.

provide social protection for the diaspora of close to 36 million people of Mexican origin living abroad, almost all of them in the US (Hernández Joseph 2012).

The close connections with the diaspora raise several questions about the direction and consequence of state–diaspora relations in the Mexican case. Perceptions in this regard are twofold. On the one hand, there is the impact on political participation of the diaspora in Mexico as its country of origin and, on the other, there is the empowerment of the diaspora, as well as a venue for public diplomacy in the US. The debate on these issues is extremely complex and beyond the scope of this chapter. However, it is important to recognize that it does have an impact on the consular work described here. One of the most salient results of this state–diaspora relationship has been establishing the right to vote abroad in presidential and some state elections (Durand and Schiavon 2014).

Some political actors see this relationship as an opportunity for co-opting people of Mexican origin in the US as supporters of their side in Mexican domestic politics or as natural supporters of Mexico's interests in bilateral relations matters, through supporting public diplomacy efforts, lobbying or through their electoral support in US elections. These opinions, however, are far from constituting governmental, let alone state policy or motivation.

Because it is a truly binational community, it is both socially and politically connected with Mexico and the US. The Mexican diaspora in the US is centered on its own reality and has developed what can clearly be identified as its own agenda as a migrant community in the US, established because of an economic exodus from Mexico given the attraction created by the complementarities and asymmetry of the two economies. This means that their agenda is not always in line with the diplomatic bilateral agenda of Mexico, and in that sense, the diaspora is not necessarily a venue of public diplomacy. There are other circumstances, however, in which interests meet, and it could be argued that the Mexican diaspora serves to promote many of the positive aspects of Mexican culture and the migrants' contribution to development in the US (Gzesh and Schiavon 2018).

Consular Assistance Programs

Mexico has developed a wide array of consular assistance programs that include traditional consular protection and documentation services as well as innovative health, education, and legal defense schemes to take care of the needs of an increasingly complex and diverse Mexican community in the US. Implementing these efforts transformed the routine activities of the Mexican consular network in the US into consular diplomacy and consequently Mexico's global consular policy, as it is based on the US experience.

The subject of diplomatic and consular assistance for this population has gained increasing importance in the domestic political agenda in Mexico. Political parties, governors, mayors, human rights organizations, and civil society organizations routinely demand an energetic and aggressive foreign policy in defense and protection of Mexican nationals abroad, particularly those in the US. This is a generalized social and political demand that no public official can afford to ignore. The pressure of this demand falls mainly on the Mexican Foreign Service. In 2019, 75 percent of the Mexican public believed that protecting the interests of Mexicans abroad was very important and among the highest priorities of Mexican foreign policy (Maldonado et al. 2020).

Consequently, the services provided by the fifty-two Mexican consular offices in the US have no parallel. Over 825,000 passports and approximately 900,000 consular identification cards are issued annually by consulates in the US. Every year, close to 50,000 births of Mexicans born abroad are registered. In total, Mexican consulates in the US issue approximately 3.75 million documents per year. The SRE established in 2006 the MEXITEL call center, which provides information about the requirements to obtain consular documents and schedule appointments for documentation services at the nearest consulate (SRE 2019a). From 2012 to 2018, the service scheduled 15.6 million appointments (SRE 2019b: 92).

It is a monumental task to issue these documents while maintaining the highest standards of document security and quality of service. In addition, over US$4 million are spent annually in partial or full financial support for the transfer to Mexico of the bodily remains of Mexican nationals who died abroad. Additionally, US$14.7 million have been budgeted for the 2021–2024 period specifically for the legal defense of Mexican nationals in the US. This means almost US$5 million annually to which US$4.8 million are added specifically for cases related to the death penalty as described further on. Special programs are in place requiring additional funds for combating human trafficking and providing special attention to particularly vulnerable groups such as victims of domestic violence, underage migrants traveling alone, injured or severely ill people, and non-Spanish -speaking migrants from indigenous communities in Mexico, to name a few (S. G. Reyes y Castro, DGPE, personal communication, November 25, 2022). The amount of nonrefundable money invested in these consular assistance services is steadily increasing each year. In 2017, the Mexican peso equivalent of about US$29 million were budgeted for consular protection programs alone, in addition to the cost of human and material resources (Langner 2016).

Over the last few decades, the Mexican consular network had developed innovative mechanisms to provide consular services. For example, proactive programs are in place to regularly visit the more than 100,000 nationals who are imprisoned. Also, the consular network has been able to develop several additional specialized services that respond to demands that are expressed in the domestic arena. One of them has to do with Mexican nationals facing the death penalty in other countries, particularly in the US (Hernández Joseph 2015).

Partnering with attorneys and organizations that are opposed to the death penalty, the Mexican consular network has paid special attention to ensuring due process and proper legal representation for its nationals facing a trial that could result in a death sentence. Through an investment of US$4.8 million a year in legal services, over fifty Mexican nationals are excluded annually from the death penalty, with full respect and adhesion to the local legal system (S. G. Reyes y Castro, DGPE, personal communication, November 25, 2022). Excluding someone from the death sentence means either obtaining a different sentence through early legal intervention or legal intervention after first-instance sentencing to reverse the sentence for a prison term. It is not a matter of prejudging innocence or culpability, but rather one of assuring proper legal representation and due process (Hernández Joseph 2015).

Another area of special consular attention is human rights. The traditional decades-old debate over US–Mexico migration revolves around the axis of respect for the law and law enforcement from the US side and human rights arguments from the Mexican side. Thus, the domestic demand is strong in Mexico for its government's involvement in protecting the human rights of its citizens abroad and denouncing and prosecuting those who violate them. The perception of the migrant as a vulnerable, low-income, hardworking victim of his/her social condition further feeds this demand. This has led the consular network to maintain very close communications with the US governmental agencies responsible for the enforcement and protections of civil right as well as with the organized civil society involved in human rights (Gzesh and Schiavon 2018).

Some examples of institutionalized mechanisms for bilateral governmental communications have been the border liaison mechanisms and interior mechanisms between Mexican consuls and US immigration authorities established in the 1990s. Also, the regular meetings between the Embassy of Mexico in Washington and US law enforcement federal authorities under the Mechanism for High Visibility Cases, in which they jointly review Mexican consular protection cases that have interested public opinion as evidence by discussion of them in media. These joint reviews serve to follow up on judicial proceedings and to insure detailed vigilance on due process in each specific case (Hernández Joseph 2012: 233).

Labor rights also receive very specific attention in consular services. The diplomatic activity of the Mexican Embassy in Washington has led to partnerships between the Mexican consulates and offices of the Department of Labor throughout the US.[3] Mexican consulates organize labor fairs in partnership with the U.S. Department of Labor and labor organizations and unions to keep the community of Mexican origin informed of the laws and regulations regarding labor and the resources available to them. Part of the consular assistance program involves very active monitoring of the respect for the labor rights of Mexican nationals as established by local laws and regulations (Schiavon and Cárdenas 2014).

Consulates also display specific programs aimed at tending to particularly vulnerable populations. In coordination with local authorities, they are most actively involved in the prevention of human trafficking and international cooperation in detecting and prosecuting it when it takes place. Another especially vulnerable population is formed by the indigenous communities. Nearly 12 million Mexican nationals come from ethnic communities of very different cultures and the approximately sixty native languages that are still in use in Mexico, mostly in rural areas. Many people from these communities, whose first language is not Spanish but rather Náhuatl, Maya, Tzeltal, Mixteco, Tsotsil, Zapoteco, Otomí, Totonaco, Chol, or Mazateco, to name a few, have also migrated to the US. The consular network established a program based on requesting those who are fully bilingual or multilingual to become volunteers at the consulates as interpreters, to help consular officials with cultural understanding in providing services to the indigenous population. The program has 760 volunteers speaking thirty indigenous languages (Hernández Joseph 2015).

Mexico has also declared all its consular offices in the world as "safe-zones" for the LGBTQ+ population. In addition to performing egalitarian marriages and issuing documents that recognize the gender identity

[3] The agreements at the local level between federal authorities (Mexican consulate and local office of the U.S. Department of Labor) are based on the Agreement made by the Central Government Authorities at the national level. The most recent renewal of these agreements was completed by the U.S. Secretary of Labor and the Ambassador of Mexico, available at: www.dol.gov/sites/dolgov/files/OPA/newsreleases/2021/09/ILAB20211614.pdf. Similarly, see the U.S. Equal Rights Commission signed and Memorandum of Understanding (MOU) on workers' rights with the Government of Mexico, available at www.eeoc.gov/memorandum-understanding-between-united-states-america-equal-employment-opportunity-commission-and.

of the trans population, this program established a discrimination-free environment that should make the LGBTQ+ population feel at ease in approaching their consulate for services (Instituto de los Mexicanos en el Exterior 2022).

Mexico's consular assistance program is unique in that no other country pays millions of dollars in legal defense of its citizens abroad while also spending millions in the repatriation of human remains, providing translation services for national minorities like the indigenous population and repatriation of such vulnerable groups as children and the sick. It is at once a massive and highly personalized service.

Relations with the Diaspora

In addition to these traditional consular services, the government of Mexico has developed through its consular network a complex mechanism to maintain, foster, and administer its relations with the diaspora. Most notably, in 1989, it started the Program for Mexican Communities Abroad, and in 2003, the Program gave way to the IME. Operated mostly through its consular network, IME is supervised by a board formed by eleven cabinet-level agencies of the federal government. It puts forth programs in education, health, community organization, community development, and social participation in Mexico and in the US, thus strengthening ties with the diaspora and a veritable transnational community.[4]

This complex network of services and consular assistance in connection with the diaspora was constructed over many decades and has at least a century-old tradition. Providing these services has also fed into social expectations for even more services and a wider commitment on behalf of the government toward Mexican nationals abroad, particularly those in the US.

At least one in every four Mexicans has a close relative living in the US. Consequently, the well-being of the Mexican community in the US has become an increasingly salient subject in the domestic political agenda in Mexico. Increasingly, political subdivisions of Mexico such as states and municipalities are searching for formulas to undertake programs that service those born in their region or state and living in the US. Many municipal governments devise their own manner of engaging with their diaspora. Generally, with the help of the consulates, they establish clubs in the communities of destination and then

[4] Ample information about its legal constitution, structure and programs is available at its website (Spanish only) at: www.gob.mx/ime.

municipal governments negotiate with the clubs how the municipality may help the diaspora and how the diaspora, in turn, may help improve conditions at home for their relatives left behind (González Gutiérrez 2006a and 2006b). In the section on economic activities, we share more information on the linkages between these clubs and local governments in Mexico. The establishment of programs aimed at involving the migrants in development projects in their communities of origin can be read as a co-optation motivation of the states and municipalities in engaging the diaspora. However, it should be noted that the programs, which began decades ago into the proactive state engagement of diasporas, were borne out of the initiative of some of the diasporas themselves, particularly from the state of Zacatecas, who approached the government for matching funds to community programs they decided to undertake.

Conversely, Mexico's consular diplomacy in the US highlights the destination state's role. Græger and Leira (2019: 3) point out the level of consular assistance that a government offers to its citizens in difficulties abroad, as a variable of the sensitivity of the host country. In the Mexican case, the US's fragmented and autonomous political system has given an advantage for the consular work, which would be different if it were a centralized country (Schiavon 2020).

In fact, the SRE recognizes that the implementation of its policies will vary according to the local and state contexts. There is a big difference between states like California and Texas, and urban areas and rural districts (González Gutiérrez 2018). Therefore, consulates have the flexibility to execute policies according to their specific circumstances. It is very different working in a border city in a rural area such as Douglas, Arizona, or Presidio, Texas, to providing services out of a consular office in Chicago, Illinois, or Los Angeles, California.

This flexibility has also allowed experimentation of different approaches that have later developed into nationwide or even global programs. For example, one of the top consular schemes, the Health Windows (Ventanillas de Salud), began in California in 2003 (Rangel Gomez et al. 2015). Later it was expanded to all consulates and, in 2017, received the "Inter-American Award on Innovation for Effective Public Policy" of the Organization of American States (OEA 2017). For many years, the IME published *Lazos*, an electronic newsletter that included a summary of news relating to immigration issues in Mexico, Canada, and the US. Nowadays, IME issues a monthly digital magazine called *Casa de México* (IME 2024). These publications contribute to the diaspora's own efforts to connect nationwide in the US, establishing links that strengthen its integration and self-reliance capabilities.

The restriction of movement for most Mexicans due to different reasons, including irregular immigration status, lack of drivers' license, cost of traveling, or just fear of going out, have encouraged the government of Mexico to open consulates where there is a high concentration of Mexicans. The result was the establishment of an extended consular network across the country, which is sometimes spatially re-arranged in response to variations in population flows. For example, in 2009, Mexico inaugurated a consulate in Anchorage, Alaska, which closed in 2015, while opening a new one in Milwaukee, Wisconsin, in 2016 (Laveaga 2018: 234–235).

Mexico's outreach efforts to serve a dispersed community with many mobility challenges is not limited to the number and size of consulates. There is a mobile consulate program which has four different variants: Mobile Consulate, Consulate on Wheels, Saturday, Sundays, or Holidays opening hours, and Documentation Services during the week outside the consular office (SRE 2014). The objective is to bring consular services to communities away from the host consular city and to offer options to a community mostly composed of workers. The consulates of Mexico in the US issued 418,412 documents as part of the mobile consulate program from December 1, 2018, to July 31, 2019 (SRE 2019c: 141). Besides physical proximity, there has also been a push to get closer to the Mexican community via telephone, with the establishment and enlargement of the Information and Assistance Center for Mexicans (Centro de Información y Asistencia a Mexicanos, CIAM), a consular assistance-focus hotline call center, and via MiConsulmex, a consular services smartphone application. Additionally, social media (Twitter, Facebook, YouTube, Instagram, and Tik-Tok) have played a growing role in consular outreach efforts, like sharing information on new local regulations or changes to the law that have an impact on the migrant communities.

Coordination with Local Authorities

In many countries, high-visibility cases tend to become political, thus generating tensions that affect bilateral relations. In Mexico's case, Héctor Cárdenas Suárez (2019: 1080) indicates that "due to its technical nature, the [Mexican] consular policy partially maintains its isolation from strictly political decisions and in those tend to dominate specialized criteria." Therefore, they are mostly solved without affecting the overall relationship. This is achieved through bilateral dialogue. Both countries jointly determine which consular cases affecting Mexican nationals in the US have reached such high public visibility to warrant including them in the bilateral agenda. To attend to these cases, both governments have established mechanisms aimed at resolving them and reducing the tensions that may arise because of them. Generally, such cases result from alleged abuses by US authorities. This practice evidences the benefit, and therefore the foreign policy motivation of the state in its consular and diplomatic protection policies, as they may help avoid, reduce, or, in a worst case scenario, manage bilateral tensions resulting from bilateral migration.

Occasionally, they do have an impact on the bilateral relationship. One example was the cancellation of a visit to the US in 2002 by President Vicente Fox in protest at the execution of a Mexican sentenced to the death in Texas ("Mexico's Fox Cancels Texas Trip," 2002). To reduce the possibility of affecting the bilateral relations, the US Department of Justice and the Mexican Embassy in Washington have the previously mentioned a standing working group that meets regularly to jointly review high-visibility and special cases of alleged human rights violations by US authorities (Hernández Joseph 2012: 233). This demonstrates both countries' commitment to jointly address politically sensitive incidents involving human rights of their respective diasporas.

In addition, in 2014, both governments established the Border Violence Prevention Council which "promotes initiatives aimed at preventing incidents of border violence through collaborative efforts, joint public engagement campaigns, increased transparency and information exchange, and the sharing of best practices" (Secretaría de Relaciones Exteriores and the Department of Homeland Security 2018). Both processes have helped reduce the tension of high-visibility consular cases that involve possible abuses by US law enforcement agencies, including DHS officials at the border. It is a significant achievement of Mexico's consular diplomacy.

There is hardly another case in the world of cooperation between a pair of sending and receiving countries in international human migration as is the case for Mexico and the US. They share a 3,000-kilometer border that is the stage for about 1 million legal human crossings per day.[5] Administering the human flow between the two countries, both documented and undocumented, requires at least permanent communication and, at best, high levels of intensive cooperation.

Another dimension of consular diplomacy "involves the negotiation of preventive, practical arrangements of consular assistance between

[5] This mobility was largely curtailed due to the COVID-19 pandemic and it is speedily recovering its pre-pandemic dynamism.

states" (Okano-Heijmans 2011: 40). Considering both the size of the US and the significant autonomy of its authorities, there is a need to involve the consulates as part of Mexico's diplomatic effort in that country. The Mexican consular network in the US regularly initiates, implements, and even negotiates agreements about federal issues at the consular level. There are three examples of this. First, the establishment of a consular coordination scheme in the US between Mexico and the Northern Triangle of Central America's countries (El Salvador, Guatemala, and Honduras), called TRICAMEX. It began in McAllen, Texas, in December 2015, and later evolved into fourteen additional schemes in the cities where the four countries have consular representations (Schiavon and Ordorica 2018). TRICAMEX served as a mechanism of coordination between these Central American countries with Mexico to jointly negotiate with US local authorities to defend and protect the interests of their nationals in their constituencies.

Second, the Local Repatriation Arrangements. These twenty-six agreements, established in the late 1990s, were renewed in 2016–2017 by all the consulates of Mexico with the regional offices of the US Department of Homeland Security (DHS) agencies. The arrangements define schedules, ports-of-entry, and conditions for the return of the hundreds of thousands of Mexican nationals detained annually by US immigration authorities. Special attention was given to the care of children, those needing medical attention, and, in general, the most vulnerable populations. They include follow-up meetings and solving specific challenges at the local level. By establishing schedules, these agreements ensure that unaccompanied children and other vulnerable populations are not returned to the border at nighttime or other inconvenient times. It also guarantees that unaccompanied children are returned not just to the streets on the other side of the border, but rather directly to the Mexican child protection social services. Similarly, this coordination allows for medical attention when needed during repatriations. The scheduling further facilitates the work of Mexican authorities that assist those migrants who do not have the resources to return to their hometowns hundreds of kilometers away (SRE 2018: 192).

Third, and finally, is the area of labor collaboration. In the early 2000s, there was an impulse for greater cooperation on labor issues. Therefore, in 2004, the SRE and the U.S. Department of Labor signed a joint declaration that opened the door for joining forces with the local and regional offices of the Wage and Hour Division and the Occupational Safety and Health Administration (Bada and Gleeson 2015: 34). These agreements allowed the consulates to further collaborate with workforce state agencies and other organizations and unions that supported Mexican workers, particularly in the framework of the Labor Rights Week that started in 2009 (Márquez Lartigue 2021). As previously mentioned, these agreements have been regularly ratified and remain in effect.

The development over time of these consular protection practices in the US led to a generalized policy in all countries where the same practices were possible. Embassies are instructed to maintain regular communication with law enforcement authorities, social workers at public hospitals, officials at detention centers, and immigration authorities among others. Thus, the practice is not to wait until an incident requires finding out which authority the consular staff must approach in each country, but rather, to have preventively learned the functioning of the offices which they may need to address to assist a compatriot (Hernández Joseph 2015).

Consular Protection and Assistance

For over half a century, Mexican consulates in the US have retained pro-bono attorneys to provide initial legal advice and assistance in consular protection cases. This practice has been extended to other countries, so that most embassies have "consulting attorneys" they can activate immediately when needed. Similarly, the experience of collaborating with organizations of the Mexican communities in the US has led to promoting embassies to foster the creation of organizations among the diaspora, which in turn may help in disseminating information among the Mexican community in that country. This mostly helps in what Mexico calls "preventative consular protection": the actions that consular and diplomatic officers may undertake to reduce incidents that could derive in the need for consular assistance. It means that if people in the Mexican community in any country know where to go and who to address when confronted with specific challenges, ranging from dealing with crimes against them to the workings of the local financial system, consular authorities and organizations together may help their national avoid situations that require consular protection (Hernández Joseph 2015).

For example, since 1974 in Canada, Mexico has an ongoing program for temporary seasonal agricultural workers who are employed in several of the country's provinces. The protection of these workers represents the only systematic, long-standing consular assistance and protection program Mexico has in any other country besides the US This program includes the joint participation of three Mexican ministries in the annual negotiation of the operative terms of the program: SRE, Labor, and Interior (which oversees Mexico's immigration agenda). These terms foresee the Mexican consuls' oversight of the labor conditions and, under specific conditions, a role in mediating labor conflicts. As many of the workers return every year for the seasonal work, they may obtain retirement and other labor benefits foreseen in Canadian law. Consulates help to keep the workers fully informed of these rights and assist them in filing the appropriate claims (Hernández Joseph 2015).

As discussed before, bilateral communication and even collaboration, together with consular and public diplomacy are essential to Mexico's policy towards its citizens abroad, especially in the US. The experiences of negotiating and passing the North American Free Trade Agreement (NAFTA) in the early 1990s and establishing collaboration mechanisms conferred on the Mexican authorities a greater understanding of the US political system. This new knowledge and experience translated into a new interpretation of the "nonintervention" foreign policy principle and the end of delinking of the different issues of the bilateral agenda (Délano 2009: 765). Particularly relevant was the awareness of the vast possibilities of collaborating with different actors, including local and state authorities and nongovernmental organizations.

Private actors are also important for consulate activities. One of the key elements for Mexico is its proven capacity to establish strategic alliances with local and state authorities, as well as civil society organizations, with the goal of expanding the consular services that it provides to the Mexican community. The collaboration with agencies that do not even coincide with the vision of the contributions of immigrants to the development of the US and its society is a clear testimony of this ability to forge alliances. Topics like human trafficking and gender-based violence have allowed cooperation with these types of agencies and local authorities (Schiavon 2020).

In this sense, a contribution from Mexican practice to the concept of consular diplomacy is the importance of converting consular representations into relevant actors in the society in which they live. Its objectives are to be heard as part of the local decision-making process and to act as a bridge between the Mexican community and the host society. These functions typically cannot be developed by an embassy but consulates can do them.

Consulates establish regular communication with social workers in hospitals to remind them that consulates are a source to aid internal and out-patient Mexican nationals. Also, consulates must maintain constant communication with Mexican community and general civil society organizations to add resources by entering joint ventures of cooperation directed at providing such services as legal assistance, health, and education. Working in coordination with organized civil society has proven to have a very positive multiplier effect on consular resources, while also serving to involve the organizations in responding to their own demands. Some of the most long-standing collaborations with civil society organizations throughout the US happened with the Mexican–American Legal Defense and Educational Fund (MALDEF), the League of United Latin American Citizens, and the Southern Poverty Law Center, among others. In California, there is also a long-standing collaboration with the Coalition for Humane Immigrant Rights as also in Texas with Texas Rural Legal Aid. Consulates throughout the US collaborate with similar state or local organizations.

As mentioned previously, the number of Mexicans living in the US outstrips the human and financial resources of the consular network of Mexico. Therefore, out of necessity, there has been a push for establishing and expanding partnerships with all kinds of allies to provide services for them. From churches hosting mobile consulates to national Hispanic, labor, and health organizations and authorities, and from alliances with the consulates of Central America to lawyers and educational institutions, the number of official partnerships is staggering. In the field of consular protection alone, there are 1,050 agreements and informal collaboration schemes, as can be seen in Tables 3.2 and 3.3.

The IME and the Office of Consular Services also have multiple arrangements and other types of official collaborations with different groups.

Table 3.2 *Consular assistance agreements between the Mexican Consular network and US organizations and authorities*

Subject of the collaboration	Number of MOUs
Labor	312[a]
Legal Assistance (PALE)	349[b]
Local Repatriation Arrangements	26[c]
Children's Issues	37
TRICAMEX	15[d]
Total	**739**

Notes: [a] Signed with different labor authorities from 2012 to 2018. [b] Contract signed for the 2015–2018 program. [c] Signed with DHS agencies' regional offices. [d] Consular cooperation scheme with Honduras, El Salvador, and Guatemala consulates, also known as TRICAMEX.

Sources: Secretaría de Relaciones Exteriores (2018 and 2019b).

Table 3.3 *Consular assistance informal collaboration schemes between the Mexican consular network and US organizations and authorities*

Subject of the collaboration	Number of informal cooperation schemes
Mexican Civil Rights Advisory Groups (one national and nine regional groupings)	58[a]
Domestic violence and human trafficking	104[b]
Abogados Consultores (Consultant Lawyers)	149[c]
Total	**311**

Notes: [a]Around 13 civil rights organizations are members of the National Advisory Group, plus a minimum of 5 per each of nine regional groups. [b]Includes task forces, strategic alliances, and memoranda of understanding. [c]Certificates of designation issued by the Undersecretary for North American Affairs.
Sources: Secretaría de Relaciones Exteriores (2018 and 2019c).

Economic and Social Dimension

As we described above, Mexico's fifty-two consulates in the US constitute a network that aims at protecting the diaspora's basic rights as well as access to health, education, and an array of additional resources. The network is also the active arm for the implementation of programs to improve the economic condition of migrants and of their families at home.

For example, the 3x1 Program executes joint co-financing ventures at the home communities of migrants. The migrants from a specific community establish a club and register it through their consulate. The club submits projects to the 3x1 Program. The projects could be for infrastructure, community services, education, or productive endeavors. When approved, the funds gathered by the club for the project are matched once by the federal government and another time by the state government, thus tripling the funds gathered by the community club. The club, through the migrants' relatives at home, plays an active role in overseeing the implementation of the program and the proper use of funds. This program is administered by the Ministry of Wellbeing (Secretaría del Bienestar) in close coordination with IME at the SRE (Secretaría del Bienestar 2017).

The only governmental efforts directly linked to remittances have been those directed at reducing the costs of sending them home. These include arrangements with financial institutions that operate the remittances. However, in recent years, most migrants use electronic means to send funds, so the arrangements are no longer needed. Mexico is among the five countries with the highest levels of remittances in the world. According to Mexico's Central Bank, remittances have reached record levels and have grown at an impressive pace, from US$40 billion in 2020, to US$51.5 billion in 2021 and, in 2022 they totaled US$58.5 billion. Thus, remittances are the second source of foreign currency in Mexico. The first is the automotive industry (*El Economista* 2021).

Understanding the overall economic impact of remittances is a complex task beyond the scope of this chapter. Yet, it may be useful to identify some of the main data to establish a general idea of their economic significance to the country. Remittances had reached a peak of over US$20 billion in 2006, equivalent to 2.6 percent of GDP. They declined to 1.7 percent of GDP in 2013 and since 2016 have been rising steadily to over US$58 billion in 2022, equivalent to nearly 4 percent of GDP. The increase in the number of remittances is combined with an increase in the percentage of available income that the Mexican diaspora in the US is sending home (Ortiz 2019). The territorial distribution of remittances is uneven, with some states accounting close to 11 percent of their GDP to remittances (like Guanajuato, Michoacán, and Zacatecas), while others are much less dependent on this source of income.

The IME also implements the Financial Inclusion Program, with the goal of strengthening the financial skill of diaspora members. The program provides guidance on subjects ranging from management of personal finances to entrepreneurship on how to start a business in the host country. It includes advice on financial management for families that wish to return to Mexico. Each consulate identifies experts on personal financial management, preferably someone from the Mexican community itself and organizes presentations at the consular offices that are advertised among the Mexican community. Many consulates have also established "*ventanillas financieras*" (financial advice windows), whereby on certain days of the week individuals may receive information and advice on managing personal finances in the location where they live (IME n.d.). They also provide advice to returning migrants to Mexico on how to transfer their financial assets from the US to Mexico.

The number of Mexican migrants and their descendants in the US are large, but the flow has slowed considerably since 2010 to a fraction of its 2003 peak (Hernández López 2022). Concurrently, the flow of migrants returning to Mexico saw a boom in the period between 2008 and 2015 (Canales 2018). Thus, the net migration from Mexico to the US has slowed to near net zero. In this context, the economic-oriented programs are aimed neither at promoting nor at disincentivizing migration in either direction. Rather, they are directed at assisting a vulnerable and disadvantaged population in its efforts to improve its economic condition and perspectives.

Historically, Mexican consular services and specifically those directed at improving the quality of life of the diaspora respond to migration patterns and the resulting characteristics of the Mexican-born population living in the US. The slowing down of migration flows has resulted in a more established population. Even the undocumented have been living in the US, on average, for over a decade. Thus, the services and programs are oriented toward an established population as opposed to those of the 1990s and early 2000s that were oriented toward recent arrivals, most of them undocumented. Today, consular services are concentrating in providing medical and financial advice to Mexican nationals, as well as courses on Mexican culture and Spanish language. Anecdotal observation and some recent data seem to suggest a possible increment in 2022 and 2023 in the undocumented flow of migrants due to increasing insecurity and economic crisis in Mexico. If this trend is in fact taking place and extends for a longer period, adjustments in the consular services are sure to follow. This is the most notable benefit of the flexibility of Mexico's consular protection services.

Through Mexico's embassies and consulates worldwide, the IME, in collaboration with the Ministry of Economy and the National Council on Science and Technology, has developed the "Red Global" (Global Net), a network of organizations of high- and medium-skill Mexican professionals abroad. Red Global has chapters in thirty-four countries (Red Global n.d.). Several chapters have their own webpages or can be found in LinkedIn, Twitter, Instagram, or Facebook. For example, "Red Global Mx Capítulo España" shares on LinkedIn a broadcast like a podcast on a variety of political, social, and scientific subjects, called *Colloquiorgmx*, as well as a YouTube channel on Mexican culture. The UK chapter has a program to give visibility to Mexican essential workers in the UK (Red Global Mx United Kingdom 2020). These efforts have served to connect high- and medium-skilled Mexicans abroad, not only with each other within one country, but regionally and globally. Whereas it aims at empowering them abroad, it also connects them with Mexico's own efforts in technological development and innovation. Rather than regretting the brain drain, it turns it into an asset. The global network also has chapters in the US, but it clearly serves to point out the different dominant socioeconomic profiles of the Mexican population in this country compared to that in the rest of the world.

Security Dimension

Mexican military personnel can only be found abroad under any of three conditions: for participation in training programs, participation in international military relations (attaches and ad hoc gatherings), and to participate in rescue and assistance activities to other nations during natural disasters. Thus, Mexico's military does not participate in activities or defense of protection of Mexican nationals abroad.

The only recorded case of military participation in a consular protection situation occurred during the 2010 earthquake in Haiti. It was an extraordinary situation, since the Mexican Navy had established an "air bridge" to constantly take aid to Haiti. This meant that one or more navy planes flew daily to Haiti transporting needed goods. Since the planes were mostly returning empty to Mexico, they were also used for the evacuation of the Mexican population affected by the earthquake.

Conclusion

Mexican consular practice has had an atypical development due to the different historical conditions, particularly in its concentration in a single country, due to the need to provide consular protection to Mexicans who remained in the territories annexed to the US and, later, to the Mexican workers who emigrated to that country. Unlike other nations that sought the national interest of commercial expansion and the defense of their merchants through their consulates, Mexico had to plead for its nationals who faced serious disadvantages just for being foreigners. According to the concept of consular diplomacy presented by Okano-Heijmans (2011), it can be argued that, in Mexico's case, its consular practice already included some of the characteristics that define consular diplomacy, as is the media, public, and political attention since the 1850s.

The Mexican experience expands the conceptualization of consular diplomacy, bringing a new perspective from the Global South, which should be considered in studies about the consular institution. It is difficult to think of Mexican consular diplomacy in a context different from that of the US and its vulnerable community, which can be seen in the challenges that have arisen when expanding some of the practices outside of that country. Even Mexico's consular experience in Canada is very different. Nevertheless, there are successful cases such as the MX Global Network (Red Global MX) and the Mental Health Desks (Ventanillas de Salud Mental) established in Europe.

These specific characteristics of Mexico's consular protection show that the support and co-optation motivations of the Mexican State rest upon a foreign policy motivation via-à-vis the US. It is connected to the definition of a national identity that includes the diaspora because of the loss of half of the national territory to the US and currently with the huge presence of people of Mexican origin in that country. There is no benefit to the Mexican state from the repression and consequently it does not figure as a policy motivator in this case.

Among the challenges that Mexico's current consular diplomacy faces, the change in the US' position regarding migrants stands out, particularly towards those of Mesoamerican origin (which, apart from Mexico, includes Central American countries). Although at a federal level the impasse between pro-immigrant and opposing forces is maintained, at a state and local level there are pronounced differences in the implementation of politics, which range from welcome actions for these communities to plain rejection and even persecution.

It is foreseeable that Mexico's consular services will continue to grow as the nation's domestic social and political arenas assume the paradigm that their government is responsible not only for the traditional consular protection of its citizens abroad, but also for their social well-being. Health, education, and access to social justice and political participation, both in their country of origin and in their place of residence, will increasingly be a matter of consular and diplomatic concern.

A fact that deserves further research is the relationship that currently exists in the fight for civil rights of the Hispanic population and the defense of undocumented immigrants' rights, who, for the most part come from Latin America. As Hernández Joseph (2012: 228–229) points out, migration policy on Mexican families that have members with different migratory categories, from citizens to undocumented, do not distinguish between them. Thus, the migratory issue significantly impacts everything they do, including their income and educational levels. This same phenomenon has wide repercussions in the links with the diaspora that lives in the host country, which should also be a topic of further analysis from the perspective of consular diplomacy.

References

Alanis Enciso, and Fernando Saúl (2006) Que vayan y se queden allá: la política mexicana hacia la migración a Estados Unidos. In Jorge A. Schiavon, Daniela Spenser, and Mario Vázquez (eds.), *En busca de una nación soberana: relaciones internacionales de México, siglos XIX y XX*. Ciudad de México: Centro de Investigación y Docencia Económicas (CIDE) /Secretaría de Relaciones Exteriores, 351–384.

Banco de México. Reporte Analítico (October 3, 2022) Available at: www.banxico.org.mx/publicaciones-y-prensa/remesas/%7B19F19A0F-0438-36FC-2E1E-E80C3D463366%7D.pdf (last accessed November 24, 2022)

Barcelo Durazo, Rafael (2007) *Restricciones institucionales en la implementación de la política de protección consular*. MA, thesis, Center for Research and Teaching in Economics (CIDE), Ciudad de México.

Batalova, J. (2008) *Mexican Immigrants in the United States*. Migration Policy Institute. 23 April. Available at: www.migrationpolicy.org/article/mexican-immigrants-united-states-2006.

Canales, Alejandro I. and Sofía Meza (2018) Tendencias y Patrones de la migración de retorno a México. *Migración y Desarrollo* 16(30), 123–55.

Cárdenas Suárez, H. (2019). Consular Policy in the United States: Protection, Documentation and Connection with Mexican Communities Abroad. *Foro Internacional* LIX (3–4), 1077–1113.

Cervantes González, Jesús A., and Rodolfo Ostolaza (2022) Inmigrantes mexicanos en Estados Unidos: solidarios con sus parientes en México. *El Economista, Revista IMEF*, March 29. Available at: www.eleconomista.com.mx/revistaimef/Inmigrantes-mexicanos-en-Estados-Unidos-solidarios-con-sus-parientes-en-Mexico-20220329-0054.html (last accessed May 9, 2022).

Consulado de Carrera de México en Fresno (2022) Pena Capital. Asistencia Jurídica a casos de pena capital en EUA. Available at: http://consulmex.sre.gob.mx/fresno/index.php/asistencia-y-proteccion-consular/59 (last accessed May 9, 2022).

Délano, A. (2009). From Limited to Active Engagement: Mexico's Emigration Policies from a Foreign Policy Perspective. *International Migration Review*, 43(4), 764–814.

Durand, Jorge, and Jorge A. Schiavon (eds.) (2014) *Perspectivas migratorias III: Los derechos políticos de los mexicanos en el exterior*. Ciudad de México: CIDE.

El Economista (2021) Las remesas son la segunda fuente de divisas; los autos, la primera. February 4, 2021. Available at: www.eleconomista.com.mx/economia/Las-remesas-son-la-segunda-fuente-de-divisas-los-autos-la-primera-20210204-0062.html (last accessed November 24, 2022).

Gómez Arnau, Remedios (1990) *México y la protección de sus nacionales en Estados Unidos*. Ciudad de México: Centro de Investigaciones sobre Estados Unidos de América-UNAM.

Gómez-Robledo Verduzco, Alonso (2003) Derecho Internacional y Nueva Ley de Nacionalidad Mexicana. *Temas selectos de Derecho Internacional*. Ciudad de México: UNAM.

González Gutiérrez, Carlos (2006a) Introducción: De estados y diásporas. In Carlos González Gutiérrez (ed.), *Relaciones Estado-diáspora: Aproximaciones desde cuatro continents (Volume I)*. Ciudad de México: IME-SRE/Universidad Autónoma de Zacatecas (UAZ)/Asociación Nacional de Universidades e Instituciones de Educación Superior (ANUIES)/Miguel Ángel Porrúa.

González Gutiérrez, Carlos (2006b) Introducción: El papel de los gobiernos. In Carlos González Gutiérrez (ed.), *Relaciones Estado-diáspora: Aproximaciones desde cuatro continents (Volume II)*. Ciudad de México: IME-SRE/UAZ/ANUIES/Miguel Ángel Porrúa.

González Gutiérrez, Carlos (2018). El significado de una relación especial: las relaciones de México con Texas a la luz de su experiencia en California. In R. Fernández de Castro (coord), *La Diplomacia Consular Mexicana en tiempos de Trump*. Tijuana: El Colegio de la Frontera Norte & El Colegio de San Luis, 253–269.

González, Guadalupe, Jorge A. Schiavon, Gerardo Maldonado, Rodrigo Morales Castillo, and David Crow (2013) *México, las Américas y el Mundo 2012–2013. Política exterior: opinión pública y líderes*. Ciudad de Mexico: CIDE.

González-Barrera, Ana, and Mark Hugo López (2013) *A Demographic Portrait of Mexican-Origin Hispanics in the United States*. Pew Hispanic Center. Available at: www.pewhispanic.org/2013/05/01/a-demographic-portrait-of-mexican-origin-hispanics-in-the-united-states/ (last accessed April 17, 2022).

Græger, N., and H. Leira (2019) Introduction: The Duty of Care in International Relations. In N. Græger and L. Halvard (eds.), *The Duty of Care in International Relations: Protecting Citizens beyond the Border*. New York: Routledge, 1–15.

Guillén López, Tonatiúh (2022) La mejor política exterior es ... exterior. *Proceso* 20403, 54–55.

Gzesh, Susan, and Jorge A. Schiavon (2018) *La protección consular mexicana ante la administración Trump: Recomendaciones de acción inmediata*. Ciudad de Mexico: CIDE and CIDE-MIG.

Hernández Joseph, Daniel (2012) Mexico's Concentration on Consular Services in the United States. *The Hague Journal of Diplomacy* 7(2), 227.

Hernández Joseph, Daniel (2015) *Protección Consular Mexicana*. Ciudad de México: Ed. Miguel Ángel Porrúa.

Hernández López, and Ana Gabriela (2022) ¿Ha disminuido la migración de mexicanos hacia Estados Unidos? *Nexos*, Observatorio Migrante, May 4. Available at: https://migracion.nexos.com.mx/2022/05/ha-disminuido-la-migracion-de-mexicanos-hacia-estados-unidos/ (last accessed November 17, 2022).

Instituto de los Mexicanos en el Exterior (IME) (n.d.) ¿Qué hacemos? Available at: www.gob.mx/ime/que-hacemos (last accessed June 26, 2022).

Instituto de los Mexicanos en el Exterior (IME) (2022) Estadística de la población mexicana en el mundo 2012. Available at: www.ime.gob.mx/es/resto-del-mundo (last accessed November 17, 2022).

Instituto de los Mexicanos en el Exterior (IME) (2024) Revista Casa de México. Available at: https://ime.red/casa-de-mexico/ (last accessed May 24, 2024).

Israel, E., and J. Batalova (2020). *Mexican Immigrants in the United States*. Migration Policy Institute. 5 November. Available at: www.migrationpolicy.org/article/mexican-immigrants-united-states-2019.

Langner, Ana (2016) La protección consular, prioridad en S.R.E. *El Economista*, September 9. Available at: www.eleconomista.com.mx/politica/Proteccion-consular-prioridad-en-SRE-20160909-0033.html last accessed November 24, 2022).

Laveaga Rendón, R. (2018) Mantenerse a la Vanguardia: Desafío para los Consulados de México en Estados Unidos. In R. Fernández de Castro (coord), *La Diplomacia Consular Mexicana en tiempos de Trump*. Tijuana: El Colegio de la Frontera Norte & El Colegio de San Luis, 231–251.

Ley Orgánica de la Administración Pública Federal (LOAPF) art. 28, fraction II. Available at: www.diputados.gob.mx/LeyesBiblio/pdf/153.pdf (last accessed April 16, 2022).

Maldonado, Gerardo et al. (2020) *México, las Américas y el Mundo, 2018–2019: Opinión pública y política exterior*. Ciudad de México: CIDE.

Márquez Lartigue, Rodrigo (2021) Public-Consular Diplomacy That Works: Mexico's Labor Rights Week in the U.S. *CPD Blog*. 6 October. Available at: https://uscpublicdiplomacy.org/blog/public-consular-diplomacy-works-mexicos-labor-rights-week-us (last accessed April 16, 2022).

Márquez Lartigue, Rodrigo (2022) *The Development of Mexico's Consular Diplomacy: Broadening the Perspective of the World's Consular Affairs*. Paper presented at the International Studies Association Convention 2022, Nashville, TN.

Márquez López, Fernando (2011) *Guía estratégica para el aprendizaje autodirigido: Derecho consular*. Ciudad de México: Facultad de Estudios Superiores de Acatlán-UNAM.

Mexico's Fox cancels Texas Trip. (2002) *BBC News*. 15 August. Available at: http://news.bbc.co.uk/2/hi/americas/2194566.stm (last accessed April 16, 2023).

Motel, Seth, and Eileen Patten (2012) *Hispanics of Mexican Origin in the United States, 2010*. Pew Hispanic Center. Available at: www.pewhispanic.org/2012/06/27/hispanics-of-mexican-origin-in-the-united-states-2010/ (last accessed April 17, 2022).

Moyano Pahissa, A. (1989) *Antología Protección Consular a Mexicanos en los Estados Unidos 1849-1900*. Ciudad de México: Archivo Histórico Diplomático Mexicano, Secretaría de Relaciones Exteriores.

Okano-Heijmans, M. (2011) Conceptualizing Economic Diplomacy: The Crossroads of International Relations, Economics, IPE and Diplomatic Studies. *The Hague Journal of Diplomacy* 6(1–2), 7–36.

Organización de Estados Americanos (OEA) (2017) *V Premio Interamericano a la Innovación para la Gestión Pública Efectiva – 2017 Acta Final de Evaluación*. 29 September. Available at http://portal.oas.org/LinkClick.aspx?fileticket=PrGVA5zsAL0%3D&tabid=1826 (last accessed April 17, 2022).

Ortiz, Angel (2019) Alta dependencia de remesas en México, tema de preocupación. *El Economista*, September 23. Available at: www.eleconomista.com.mx/sectorfinanciero/Alta-dependencia-de-remesas-en-Mexico-tema-de-preocupacion-20190923-0029.html (last accessed May 24, 2024).

Rangel Gomez, M. G., J. Tonda, G. R. Zapata, M. Flynn, F. Gany, J. Lara, I. Shapiro, and C. Ballesteros Rosales (2017) Ventanillas de Salud: A Collaborative and Binational Health Access and Preventive Care Program. *Frontiers in Public Health* 5 (30 June). Available at: doi.org/10.3389/fpubh.2017.00151 (last accessed May 24, 2024).

Red Global, Emprendimiento Europa (n.d.) Available at: www.redglobalmx.eu/ (last accessed November 24, 2022).

Red Global Mx, United Kingdom (2020) Available at: https://redglobalmx.uk/ (last accessed November 24, 2022).

Reglamento de la Ley del Servicio Exterior Mexicano. Available at: www.diputados.gob.mx/LeyesBiblio/regley/Reg_LSEM.pdf (last accessed May 9, 2022).

Schiavon, Jorge A. (2020) La diplomacia multinivel de México en Estados Unidos. *Foreign Affairs Latinoamérica* 20(3), 65–68.

Schiavon, Jorge A., and Nuty Cárdenas (2014) La protección consular de la diáspora Mexicana. *Revista Mexicana de Política Exterior* 101, 43–67.

Schiavon, Jorge A., and Gabriela Díaz Prieto (2011) Introducción. In Jorge A. Schiavon and G. Díaz Prieto (eds.), *Los derechos humanos de las personas migrantes en México: estudios de casos para promover su respeto y defense*. Ciudad de México: CIDE.

Schiavon, Jorge A., and R. Guillermo Ordorica (2018) Las sinergias con otras comunidades: El caso de Tricamex. In Rafael Fernández de Castro (coordinator), *La Diplomacia consular mexicana en tiempos de Trump*. Tijuana: El Colegio de la Frontera Norte & El Colegio de San Luis, 185–203.

Secretaría de Relaciones Exteriores (2012) Evaluación y desarrollo del Servicio Exterior Mexicano de Carrera (2006–2012): Memoria documental. Available at: https://sre.gob.mx/images/stories/doctransparencia/rdc/memodoc/12mdd gserhsem.pdf (last accessed November 15, 2018).

Secretaría de Relaciones Exteriores (2014). Normas para la realización del programa de Consulados Moviles en sus modalidades "Consulados Moviles", Jornadas Sabatinas, Dominicales o en días inhábiles", "Consulados sobre Ruedas" y "Actividades de documentacion entre semana fuera de la oficina consular". https://sre.gob.mx/images/stories/docnormateca/dgsc/2014/norm2801.pdf (last accessed April 17, 2022).

Secretaría de Relaciones Exteriores (2018) Lineamientos de las Ventanillas de Salud (VDS). Available at: https://sre.gob.mx/component/phocadownload/category/7-normateca-interna?download=639:lineamientos-de-las-ventanillas-de-salud-vds (last accessed November 15, 2018).

Secretaría de Relaciones Exteriores (2019a) Realiza tu cita en Mexitel. *CIAM Blog*. 8 January. Available at: www.gob.mx/ciam/articulos/mexitel (last accessed April 17, 2022).

Secretaría de Relaciones Exteriores (2019b) *Fortalecimiento de la Atención a Mexicanos en el Exterior, Libro Blanco 2012-2018*. 10 January. Available at: www.gob.mx/sre/documentos/libro-blanco-sobre-el-fortalecimiento-de-la-atencion-a-mexicanos-en-el-exterior-2012-2018 (last accessed April 17, 2022).

Secretaría de Relaciones Exteriores (2019c) *Primer Informe de Labores 2018-2019*. 1 September. Available at: www.gob.mx/sre/documentos/primer-informe-de-labores-2018-2019 (last accessed April 17, 2022).

Secretaría de Relaciones Exteriores (2022a) Consulados de México en el Exterior. Available at: https://portales.sre.gob.mx/directorio/consulados-de-mexico-en-el-exterior (last accessed November 13, 2022).

Secretaría de Relaciones Exteriores (2022b) Zona segura. May 25. Available at: www.gob.mx/ciam/articulos/zona-segura (last accessed November 23, 2022).

Secretaría de Relaciones Exteriores (2022c) Embajadas de México en el Exterior. Available at: https://portales.sre.gob.mx/directorio/embajadas-de-mexico-en-el-exterior (last accessed November 13, 2022).

Secretaría de Relaciones Exteriores and the Department of Homeland Security (2018). *Border Violence Prevention Council Factsheet*. December. Available at: www.gob.mx/cms/uploads/attachment/file/430226/Border_Violence_Prevention_Council_espa_ol_-_ingl_s.pdf (last accessed November 13, 2022).

Secretaría del Bienestar (2017) Programa 3X1 para Migrantes. Available at: www.gob.mx/bienestar/acciones-y-programas/programa-3x1-para-migrantes (last accessed November 13, 2022).

4 Russia
Empire's Echo

Ethan Larson

Introduction

On September 30, 2022, President Vladimir Putin of Russia announced the annexation of four provinces of Ukraine. As members of the diaspora, Putin asserted, they had faced "genocide"; now annexation had ensured their "safety." Here was an explanation for an offensive war seemingly plucked from the annals of pre-Second World War diplomacy. Yet Putin claimed no desire to "return to the past" (Putin 2022) or to recreate the boundaries of the Soviet Union. Putin had something else in mind: a vision of Russia based not just on its historical territory, but on "the determination of millions of people who … consider themselves part of Russia, whose ancestors lived in a single country for centuries" (Putin 2022). By mobilizing the diaspora, the reasoning went, Russia could recover its status as a global power – albeit of a different sort than its Soviet forebear.

Russia is not the first – or only – country to stretch the skin of nationhood over the framework of diaspora (e.g., Choate 2008). But Russia aspires to be not merely what Glick and Levitt (2004: 1023) term a "transnational nation-state" (a state that treats the diaspora as part of the national body), but a transnational *empire*. The legacy of empire defines who Russia considers "its" people, and "defense" of that diaspora is often an imperial act. Pursuing these aims, the Russian state cultivates, co-opts, and, at times, even creates compatriots whom it can "defend," prioritizing people living in the countries that once were part of the Soviet Union, rather than those millions of Russians living overseas or in Western Europe. Assistance takes various forms, ranging from legal aid, cultural outreach, and linguistic support to outright military intervention.

Overview of the Russian Community Abroad

Counting a diaspora – an inherently fluid and voluntaristic category – is always fraught. Going by citizenship, there were 10.7 million Russians

Table 4.1 *Russians living abroad, 2020*

Region	Number of Russian citizens	Top countries	Number of Russian citizens
World	10,756,697	Ukraine	3,330,576
Europe/North America (excluding Russia)	6,657,423	Kazakhstan	2,476,018
North Africa/Western Asia	252,431	Germany	1,198,831
Central and Southern Asia	3,766,915	Uzbekistan	871,047
East and Southeastern Asia	20,456	Belarus	672,481
Latin America/Caribbean	12,947	United States	397,061
Australia/New Zealand	37,411	Tajikistan	234,998
North Africa/Western Asia	252,431	Estonia	119,097
Sub-Saharan Africa	9,056	Latvia	116,071

Source: United Nations (2020) Population Division, International Migrant Stock. Available at: www.un.org/development/desa/pd/content/international-migrant-stock (last accessed April 3, 2022).

abroad in 2020 – largely in Western Europe, North America, and Central Asia (United Nations 2020) (Table 4.1).

However, the Russian Federation, like many countries in this volume, does not limit its definition of diaspora to citizenship. More unusually, ethnicity is also an imprecise frame; Russia has been a multiethnic empire for nearly 500 years, and neither citizenship nor culture wholly encompass the group that Russia considers to be "its" diaspora. Rather, the Russian government uses a complex and ambiguous conceptual framework surrounding the term "compatriot," or *sootechestvennik* in Russian (Grigas 2016: 73–89; United Nations 2020).

In brief, a "compatriot" is someone who has "historical, ethnic, cultural, linguistic, and spiritual ties with Russia." Furthermore, a compatriot needs "to maintain contacts and cooperation with Russia" (KPRFSR 2001). Additionally, a compatriot may be someone who once possessed Soviet citizenship or belongs to any of the 185 constituent nationalities of the erstwhile Tsarist or Soviet empires – so long as they live outside their titular nation-state (if they have one). Thus, a Kazakh in Belarus is a compatriot, but a Kazakh in Kazakhstan in not. Compatriots are not required to speak Russian, though Russian is counted as a "linguistic" connection with Russia and ethnic Russians living abroad are considered compatriots by default. Non-Russians may qualify as a compatriot by joining a compatriot organization, a network loosely overseen by the Russian foreign ministry. This counts as a "maintaining ties" with Russia. The primary criterion, however, seems to be linguistic: the number of compatriots claimed by Kremlin spokespeople – 35 million – roughly coincides with the number of Russophones worldwide (Zevelev 2001: 94Grigas 2016: 73–89).

Russian "compatriots" are heterogeneous. Indeed, Russians emigrated at different times, under different circumstances, for different reasons, and settled in different places. The first major wave of emigration occurred between 1890 and 1920. During this period, 2.5 million people left the Tsarist empire, seeking work and (if they were Jewish) fleeing persecution. Most ended up in the United States – especially in New York (Massey 1995). The second wave of emigration occurred during and after the Russian Revolution of 1918. Unlike the first wave, this was primarily a political emigration – mainly of the intelligentsia. The 1.5 million people of the second wave went to Paris, Berlin, Belgrade, or Prague, though they did not always remain there (Andreyev and Savicky 2004: xi–xviii, 160–192). The third major wave began during the 1980s, following the relaxation of Soviet restrictions on emigration, and accelerated during the chaotic collapse of the USSR. The exodus continued into the early 2000s. The total outflow was 4.2 million people. These emigrants were typically young and well-educated. Their main destinations were the US, Germany, and Israel (Aleshkovski, Grebenyuk, and Vorobyeva 2018).

For our purposes, however, the most important wave of migration was internal to the Soviet Union. Russians, typically skilled industrial workers, moved to the new factory towns in the non-Russian Soviet Social Republics (SSRs). When the Soviet Union collapsed, they became "emigrants" overnight. Although Russians settled in all the SSRs, the 25 million "stranded" Russians were especially concentrated in Ukraine (11 million), Belarus (1.3 million), the Baltic States (1.6 million), and Northern Kazakhstan (6.1 million) (Golovakha, Panina, and Churilov 1994; Gudkov 1994; Chinn and Kaiser 1996: 7, 94, 129, 164). That said, since the collapse, the number of "stranded" Russians has sharply declined in every former SSR (Table 4.2).

The Russians in Ukraine, Kazakhstan, and Estonia are especially significant, since they are present in a compact territorial unit that abuts the Russian Federation. For this reason, there is potential for separatism. Elsewhere in the former Soviet Union, Russians are typically concentrated only in urban islands far from the Russian border, and thus cannot not realistically aspire to independence or annexation to Russia (Zevelev 2001).

As we will see, protection of the "stranded" Russians is the Russian Federation's priority. There are three practical reasons for this. First, when the Soviet Union collapsed in 1991, there were 25 million "stranded" Russians, several times the size of the other waves. Second,

Table 4.2 *Ethnic Russians in the former Soviet Union*

Country	Number of Russians 1,000s (1989)[1]	Number of Russians 1,000s most recent census (year)
Ukraine	11,355	8,334 (2001)[2]
Kazakhstan	6,227	2,982 (2021)[3]
Uzbekistan	1,653	720 (2021)[4]
Belarus	1,342	707 (2019)[5]
Kyrgyzstan	916	341 (2021)[6]
Latvia	905	454 (2022)[7]
Moldova*	562	112 (2014)[8]
Estonia	475	315 (2021)[9]
Azerbaijan	392	119 (2009)[10]
Tajikistan	388	35 (2010)[11]
Lithuania	344	141 (2022)[12]
Georgia*	341	26 (2014)[13]
Turkmenistan	334	242 (2012)[14]
Armenia	51	12 (2011)[15]

Note: All countries are called by their current names. Thus, Belarus instead of Byelorussian SSR, Kyrgyzstan instead of Kirghiz SSR, etc.
* During their most recent census, these countries did not fully control their de jure territory. Any Russians in Transnistria, Abkhazia, and South Ossetia likely went uncounted.
Sources 1–15: See the list at the end of the chapter under "Table 4.2 Sources."

Russia has more diplomatic leverage over its neighbors than Germany or the US. And third, this cohort of the diaspora faced the greatest threats, especially during the 1990s, when Russians were faced with the loss of citizenship rights, jobs, and cultural dominance. The "stranded" Russians have three demographic characteristics that structure the Russian state's approach to "protection."

The first quirk of the "stranded" Russians is that most did not speak the local language when the USSR collapsed. On one extreme, less than one percent of the 6.1 million Russians who settled in Kazakhstan spoke Kazakh. Russians in the other Central Asian SSRs were similarly linguistically limited. Local language proficiency was (somewhat) better in the Baltic States (37.4% for Lithuania, 22.4% for Latvia, and 15% for Estonia) and in Ukraine (34.3%) (Gaidys 1994: 97). As such, the "stranded" Russians were vulnerable to laws that made the indigenous language the sole, or dominant, language of administration, education, and media. Moreover, such language laws proliferated after the Soviet Union collapsed, though their severity varied. In Estonia, Tajikistan, Kyrgyzstan, Uzbekistan, Ukraine, and Turkmenistan, Russian enclaves were permitted to use Russian for most administrative tasks. No such allowances, however, were made in Latvia and Lithuania (Payin 1994: 26–27). Belarus, conversely, made Russian an official language in 1995 (Zeller and Sitchinava 2019: 108).

In the years since, Russians have grown more proficient in the local language, at least in some countries. By the early 2000s, for instance, 58% of Russians in Lithuania spoke Lithuanian, a 20% increase. This pattern held across the Baltic states (Goble 2001; Hogan-Brun and Ramonienė 2004). In Kazakhstan, however the number of Russians who spoke Kazakh had risen only marginally, to 3.6% (Smagulova 2008: 462). In general, Russians in Central Asia have preferred to emigrate rather than acculturate (Zevelev 2001: 107).

The second quirk of this diaspora is that remittances are low – this is true for the entire diaspora, not just the stranded portion. In aggregate, remittances are a negligible portion of the Russian GDP, averaging around 0.5% over the last decade (World Bank 2022a). This is remarkably low for a diaspora as large and affluent as Russia's. For comparison, remittances constitute around 4% of Mexico's GDP, a country where roughly 12 million of its 130 million citizens live and work abroad (World Bank 2022b). In short, Mexico (12 million) and Russia (10.7 million) have comparable numbers of citizens residing abroad, but Mexico's citizens contribute about eight times as much relative to GDP. Russia's GDP is only about 50% higher than Mexico's – not enough to explain this discrepancy. It remains unclear why Russians abroad prefer not to send money "home," though polling indicates that Russians abroad tend to identify more with their country of residence than with Russia (Barrington, Herron, and Silver 2003). Regardless, remittances – the quintessential incentive for a state to engage with its diaspora – are much less of a factor for Russia.

The third peculiarity of the "stranded Russians" is their organizational fragmentation. The paucity of umbrella organizations linking the various diaspora groups has made it difficult for them to act as a political lobby. Yet this fact has also presented an opportunity to the Russian state, which has filled the vacuum with its own set of "coordinating councils" and compatriot "congresses" (Chinn and Kaiser 1996: 10; Byford 2012; Fonseca and Rouvinski 2018; PKDSR 2018).

The combination of these three traits – low indigenous language competence, low remittances, and low levels of organization – present different challenges and opportunities to the Russian state. The potential windfalls from "co-opting" this diaspora are geopolitical, not financial. The Russian diaspora can be a source of diplomatic pressure on neighboring states, a reserve source of population, and even a convenient *casus belli*.

Diplomatic and Consular Dimension

Russia maintains consular offices around the world, even in countries without large Russian populations. However, the distribution of consulates does not always correspond to the distribution of Russians. In the US, for example, the closest consulate to the large Russophone community in California is in Texas. In Canada, meanwhile, consulates are situated in Ontario and Quebec, even though many "compatriots" live in the prairie provinces of Alberta, Manitoba, and Saskatchewan. For some Russian "compatriots," consular services are thousands of miles away. This sets Russia apart from countries like Mexico or Germany, whose consular networks are a tighter fit to the contours of their respective diasporas. When it comes to the "stranded" Russians, however, there is much less of a disconnect. The 3.7 million Russians in Kazakhstan, for instance, are served by four consulates, of which three are in areas where Russians are numerically predominant. Russians in Estonia and Ukraine had equally good consular coverage – at least until the 2022 war in Ukraine forced the closure of several consulates (Ministry of Foreign Affairs 2022a).

As one might expect, Russian embassies and consulates support Russian compatriots by helping them obtain passports and travel documents. When it suits the Kremlin, consulates can be helpful indeed; mass grants of passports through an expedited process gives the Kremlin a (quasi)-legal pretext to "defend" a group of compatriots who are thus made into citizens – blurring the lines between support and co-optation of compatriot communities. This tactic of granting passports *en masse* is conventionally called "passportization" (e.g., Mühlfried 2010: 8–9; Bebler 2015:194–195; Grigas 2016: 9–10; 41–43). On three occasions – South Ossetia, Crimea, and in Eastern Ukraine – passportization preceded military intervention. Yet passportization is not invariably an omen of war; it can also be an economic lifeline, giving the bearer an opportunity to work in the Russian Federation. In depressed areas or for stateless peoples, like the Ossetians, this can be appealing. Moreover, in some cases, a concomitant of a Russian passport is access to Russian state pensions (Mühlfried 2010: 8–9; Bebler 2015: 194–198; Grigas 2016: 76, 105, 112).

The Russian Foreign Ministry also seeks to co-opt emigrant civil society organizations. Concretely, they host conferences, encourage smaller organizations to consolidate into larger ones, and link these together via transregional "coordinating councils" (Byford 2012: 727–730; Fonseka and Rouvinski 2018: 84; PKDSR 2018). This approach has yielded some dividends. In the 2011 and 2018 Latvian elections, for instance, a pro-Russian party (the center-left Harmony Center) received the most votes (Saari 2014). Nonetheless, Harmony Center has never been included within a governing coalition – being perceived as a "tool" of Putin remains a liability (Higgins 2018).

Co-optation does not always succeed; compatriots have agency as well. In some instances, such as with the Coordinating Council of Russian Compatriots in Britain, the competition for state support worsened the rivalry between two diaspora organizations: Obshchina and Eurolog (Byford 2012: 728–730). Additionally, diaspora friendliness toward Putin can vary from country to country, limiting the effectiveness of coordinating councils (Morgunova and Byford 2018). The coordinating council in Estonia, for instance, has struggled to get compatriot organizations to send delegates to its conferences, and those that do chafe at their lack of autonomy – voting in the coordination council must be pre-approved by the Russian embassy (Kallas 2016: 10–11).

Another form of support is legal. Russian diplomats, for instance, may seek the release of Russian nationals who are arrested overseas. This has sometimes taken the form of hostage diplomacy – almost invariably with the US. When Russia sought the release of Viktor Bout, an arms dealer, from US custody, it traded him for Brittany Griner, an American basketball player arrested in early 2022 in Russia on drug charges (Crowley 2022; Shear and Baker 2022). Prisoner exchanges have also been proposed for Konstantin Yaroshenko, Roman Seleznev, and Alexei Burkov. All are alleged to have committed serious offenses, ranging from smuggling drugs to fraud and credit card theft, and all were in US custody at the time (Periroth 2017; Roth 2019; Shear and Nechepurenko 2022).

Russia does not always intervene to support compatriots in legal trouble, however. On March 8, 2022, the US Department of Justice charged Elena Branson, the chairman of the Russian Community Council of the US, with being an unregistered foreign agent (presumably in retaliation for the invasion of Ukraine). Branson fled abroad. The Russian Foreign Service denounced the "persecution and discrimination" facing Russian compatriots, but otherwise took no concrete action, such as attempting to negotiate an end to Branson's legal peril (Oladipo 2022; Zakharova 2022). As the Russian ambassador to the US later admitted in an interview, the embassy has had few opportunities to meet with the White House since February 2022 (Ministry of Foreign Affairs 2022e). When diplomatic relations break down, there are limits to what can be accomplished.

If the legal hot water is less scalding, the assistance is more passive and indirect. A suborganization of the Foreign Ministry, the Foundation for the Support and Defense of the Rights of Compatriots (FPZPS), provides legal advice to compatriots (Russian Federation 2014: 11; FPZPS 2022). Concretely, the Foundation collaborates with lawyers, legal experts, and universities to research local legal regimes. Then, the Foreign Ministry converts these into digestible guidelines and distributes them through information centers. The bulk of these centers are in the former Soviet Union – as noted, the "stranded" diaspora remains the priority. Besides providing information, the Foreign Ministry also helps Russians living abroad find Russian-speaking lawyers (PKDSR 2018: 5–7).

The Foreign Ministry also handles repatriation, an initiative aimed at combating population decline – Russia lost some 10 million people during the 1990s. In 2006, the Russian state began to encourage the "stranded" diaspora to move to Russia. However, this resettlement program targeted Siberia and the Far East, areas experiencing the severest population decline, rather than Moscow or St. Petersburg. Conditions can be much less congenial in Siberia, especially in rural areas. Not surprisingly, few "compatriots" opted for resettlement. Though Russia planned to accept 100,000 per year, the best that could be achieved was 32,500, in 2011 (Zeigler 2006; Grigas 2016: 84). Russians in Kazakhstan accounted for about a third of the resettlement (Laruelle, Royce and Beyssembayev 2019: 221). In Estonia, however, a mere 1,355 Russians emigrated to Russia between 2008 and 2012. According to those interviewed, wages, healthcare, housing, and other amenities were better in Estonia, which made people reluctant to leave (Kallas 2016: 14).

Nonetheless, the invasion of Ukraine has changed the math on resettlement. Millions of people have been displaced, and a substantial portion have gone to Russia. It is possible that this was a secondary goal of the invasion. Suggestively, in 2020, Putin directed the foreign ministry to redouble their resettlement efforts (Putin 2020) – roughly contemporaneously to the beginning of passportization in the Donbas (Arutunyan 2019; Burkhardt 2020). Advance preparation has yielded results. In April alone, sources report that around 100,000 people were "voluntarily resettled" to Siberia (Sharma 2022; Russkiy Vek 2022a). Resettlement was not voluntary, according to participants interviewed by the *New York Times* (Ostrovsky, Tiefenthaler, and Pavone 2022). By October 2022, Russian sources reported that around 4.6 million people had arrived in Russia from Ukraine (Russkiy Vek 2022b). These numbers are probably exaggerated; the UNHCR (2023) estimates that a roughly 6 million people have been displaced since the start of the war, a substantial portion of which have gone west, not east. They put the number of refugees in Russia at 1.2 million. Regardless, this is still far more than the resettlement programs of the 2000s and 2010s.

Economic and Social Dimension

Many states seek to ensure that "their" diaspora does not acculturate to their host countries, a pattern to which Russia is no exception (Waterbury 2014: 39). In 2005, Putin declared that "preserving a Russian-speaking territory" was a priority for his government (Grigas 2016: 86). Though this may seem paradoxical, given that Russians abroad had not typically learned the language of their host countries, bilingualism *was* increasing in the Baltic states (Hogan-Brun and Ramonienė 2004).

Currently, two government agencies handle cultural and educational work: Russkiy Mir (Russian World) and Rossotrudnichestvo. At the time of writing, Rossotrudnichestvo is overseen by Evgenii Primakov Jr., who holds a rank analogous to deputy minister and reports to the head of the Ministry of Foreign Affairs, Sergei Lavrov (Ministry of Foreign Affairs 2022f). Russkiy Mir, on the other hand, is overseen by a board of trustees who are appointed by Putin (Putin 2007). This board contains representatives from various ministries, the legislature, and even the Russian Orthodox Church (Putin 2021). When an initiative requires it, both Rossotrudnichestvo and Russkiy Mir collaborate with the Ministry of Education, the Federal Agency for the Press, the Ministry of Sport, the Ministry of Science, and/or the Ministry of Culture (PKDSR 2018).

Cultural support takes various forms. Russkiy Mir, for instance, operates Russian centers abroad that promote Russian language and culture: e.g., the Russian Center at Kazakhstan's Al-Farabi University (Laruelle et al. 2019: 230), Rossotrudnichestvo, meanwhile, disseminates Russian language media and textbooks among emigrant communities, primarily those in the former Soviet Union (Saari 2014: 60–61). Nonetheless, the Russian state does not fund language retention as heavily as other countries. Each year, Germany's Goethe Institute receives ten times the funding that its Russian counterparts received between 2011 and 2015 (Grigas 2016: 86).

Both Russkiy Mir and Rossotrudnichestvo use the internet to distribute materials, though the (post-Ukraine War) block on Russkiy Mir's web address in the US and the European Union (EU) curtailed its reach, though only somewhat – Kazakhstan and (paradoxically) Russia accounted for most of Russkiy Mir's web traffic (Laruelle et al. 2019: 230). Moreover, Rossotrudnichestvo's website on VKontakte, a Russian social network, remains accessible everywhere (PKDSR 2018: 9).

Besides supporting language retention, Russia also encourages its diaspora to celebrate patriotic holidays. As with language retention, this task is split between government agencies. Rossotrudnichestvo, for instance, handles "Russian Language Day" and the birthdays of famous ethnic

Russians – cultural figures and writers, mainly. The Foreign Ministry, however, handles Victory Day and Russia Day, holidays with a higher profile (PKDSR 2018: 4, 8–10). The Russian state may also prioritize these holidays since they dovetail with the Russian state's nonethnic definition of "compatriot." After all, the Second World War (which Victory Day commemorates), was experienced and remembered by all Soviet citizens and remains a rich vein of symbolic capital (Hosking 2002).

Perhaps for that reason, the Russian Foreign Ministry has prioritized preserving Soviet-era military monuments that are now abroad. This is handled through bilateral agreements with the monuments' "host country" (Ministry of Foreign Affairs 2022b). Though seemingly unrelated to "compatriot" issues, monuments are not treated as such by the Foreign Ministry. To take a recent example, the "preservation of common historical memory" was one of the six goals discussed at the 7th World Congress of Compatriots, which was held in 2021 (VKSRS 2021). Moreover, threats to monuments are often mentioned in the same breath as threats to compatriots in official pronouncements (Ministry of Foreign Affairs 2022c).

The 2007 riots in Tallinn, Estonia are illustrative. Following an attempt by the Estonian government to relocate a Soviet-era war monument, Russians in Tallinn rioted for nearly a month. This was accompanied by cyberattacks on Estonian government websites that some analysts speculated that were directed by Moscow. Whether true or not, the Russian Foreign ministry issued protests, accusing Estonia of violating the rights of its Russian minority (Herzog 2011). In short, monument protection and compatriot protection have become linked issues.

Security Dimension

The Russian Federation has also become known for its willingness to use military force to defend compatriots. Moreover, unlike many of the countries discussed in this volume, where armed force is typically used to facilitate evacuations, Russian interventions aim not at moving compatriots, but keeping them where they are. This can entail the extension of regional hegemony or even annexation of territory. Though the 2022 invasion of Ukraine threw this issue into sharp relief, this pattern of behavior began in the 1990s. Under Yeltsin, when Russia was still a democratic country (at least nominally), military interventions were improvised responses to ethnic violence in the former Soviet Union. Following Putin's authoritarian transformation of Russia in the early 2000s, however, sending in soldiers to defend compatriots has become a way for a resurgent Russia to project power. These later interventions, moreover, have tended to follow a formula: passportization creates compatriots, mistreatment of those compatriots is then alleged, then Russia invades, creating or consolidating client states that ostensibly defend those compatriots.

The First Interventions

The first military intervention occurred in 1992 in a breakaway region of Moldova called Transnistria. A thin strip of land next to the Dniester River, Transnistria is populated by a mix of Russians (29.1%) and Ukrainians (22.9%), who together slightly outnumber the non-Slavic Moldovans. Following the secession of Moldova from the USSR in 1991 and the passage of a discriminatory language law in the newly independent republic, Transnistria declared independence from Moldova. This escalated into a brief armed conflict between the separatists and Moldova in 1992. The Russian 14th Army then intervened on the separatist side, allowing the Transnistrians to fend off the Moldovan army (Miarka 2020).

That same year, civil war broke out in Tajikistan. No ethnic group was entirely insulated from the escalating violence, and over 300,000 Russians fled. Russia intervened in 1993, forcing an end to the fighting and brokering a ceasefire in 1997 (United Nations 2004; Nourzhanov and Bleuer 2013: 323–335; Grigas 2016: 178).

Russian soldiers have remained in both Transnistria and Tajikistan ever since, serving as peacekeepers (Grigas 2016: 193; Putz 2021; Miarka 2020). Both Transnistria and Tajikistan, moreover remain politically and economically close with Russia. Tajikistan, for instance, provides its Russian population with language schools and opportunities for dual citizenship, something few other post-Soviet states allow (Grigas 2016: 73; Ministry of Foreign Affairs 2022d). Transnistria, meanwhile, depends on Russian subsidies to pay pensions and meet its energy needs, and is arguably a client state of Russia (Sprague 2016).

These early interventions, though ad hoc, taught an important lesson to policy-makers – intervening to "protect" Russians abroad was a way to project power (German and Block 2006; Crandall 2012). Transnistria, for instance, has helped keep Moldova out of the EU, which tries to avoid incorporating states with ongoing border disputes (Sprague 2016). The first to observe the potential in protecting compatriots was the academic Sergei Karaganov in 1992. Karaganov went on to become an advisor to Putin, though he later complained that the "Karaganov Doctrine" (as it is now known) did not stipulate the use of military force (Pieper 2020: 764). Regardless, the leverage Russia gets from protecting migrants has limits; overreach is possible. On June 23, 2022, the European Council agreed to grant candidate status to Moldova, an implicit rebuke of Russia for the invasion of Ukraine (European Council 2022).

Georgia

The third major intervention to "defend" compatriots came in 2008. This intervention, the Russo-Georgian War, was both the first to occur under Putin's watch and the first instance where the "defense" of compatriots was pro-active, rather than purely reactive.

The compatriots in question lived within two unrecognized states within Georgia's de-jure territory: South Ossetia and Abkhazia, both of which were (and are) protected by Russian peacekeepers. Like Transnistria, they seceded during the 1990s. In 2002, Russia permitted the Abkhaz and Ossetians (who are not Slavic) to swap their Soviet passports for Russian ones. By 2008, the Ossetians and Abkhaz overwhelmingly possessed Russian citizenship – between 80–90 percent (Grigas 2016: 83). When Mikheil Saakashvili was elected president of Georgia in 2004, he aimed to reassert Georgian control over Abkhazia and South Ossetia. Even more provocatively, Saakashvili wanted Georgia to become part of NATO (IIFFMCG 2009: 14–15). On April 3, 2008, in Bucharest, NATO members declared that they would welcome Georgia (and Ukraine's) accession to NATO (North Atlantic Council 2008). Less than a month later, Putin called for assistance – consular, economic, educational, and cultural – to Russian compatriots in Georgia (Grigas 2016: 117).

On August 7–8, Georgian forces began shelling Tskhinvali, a town in South Ossetia (IIFFMCG 2009: 22–23). Claiming that these (newly minted) Russian citizens faced "genocide," the Russian army overran Georgia in five days. A subsequent investigation conducted by the EU did not substantiate the Russian claim of genocide; the number of civilian deaths was later found to be 162 (IIFFMCG 2009: 20–27, 408). Nonetheless, the pattern was clear: real or fabricated threats to Russia's compatriots gave Russia a pretext to keep its neighbors in its "sphere of influence."

Ukraine

Russia has also twice intervened to "defend compatriots" in Ukraine. The first intervention, John Mearsheimer (2014) argues, was precipitated by the 2008 Bucharest declaration – Russia would not permit Ukraine, a country it saw as belonging to its sphere of influence, to become a

NATO member. Though Mearsheimer's assertion drew heated criticism at the time (McFaul 2014; Sestanovich 2014) – it remains true that Russia began passportization in Crimea immediately after the Bucharest declaration (Bebler 2015: 194–195).

No intervention, however, occurred until 2014, when the pro-Russian president of Ukraine, Victor Yanukovych, was overthrown in the Euromaidan uprising, thereby foreclosing Ukraine's prospective membership in the Eurasian Economic Union (International Crisis Group 2019: 2). The Russian media presented this as a "fascist" takeover that threatened Russians in Ukraine, citing (and exaggerating) the role that Right Sector, a Ukrainian ultranationalist organization, had played in the Maidan protests (Shekhovtsov 2015). Nonetheless, many Russians in Ukraine *did* feel threatened. Following Maidan, the Ukrainian parliament nearly passed a law that would have abrogated legal protections for Russian speakers. One Russian publication called it a "war on the Russian language" (Newsru 2014). The parliament later backtracked, but the damage was done.

Anti-Kyiv sentiment was particularly sharp in Crimea, where a Russian separatist movement had long existed. In 1991, for instance, 93 percent of Crimeans had voted to secede from Ukraine, which proceeded to placate the separatists with autonomy (Chinn and Kaiser 1996: 149). On February 27, 2014, armed groups, probably from Russia, seized control of strategic locations throughout the peninsula. On March 16, Crimea held a referendum on annexation to Russia. Although the result (a 96% "yes" vote) indicated rigging, there was significant grassroots support for annexation to Russia (Bebler 2015: 194–198). Regardless, Crimea was another milestone in the evolution of Russia's policy toward diaspora "protection": the first instance where "protection" has meant territorial annexation.

Russia's annexation of Crimea energized anti-Kyiv protesters in Ukraine's south and east, a region known as the Donbas. In March and April 2014, Russian nationalists seized government buildings in Donetsk, Luhansk, and Kharkhiv, declaring their intent to secede from Ukraine and join Russia. In other places, the separatists did less well. In Odesa, for instance, Ukrainian counterprotesters set fire to a building containing Russian protesters, killing thirty. Right Sector was implicated (Amos and Salem 2014). Putin gave the separatists verbal support, and volunteers, funds, and weapons flooded over the border (International Crisis Group 2019: 2–5).

Russian assistance proved insufficient. By mid-2014, the separatists had lost control of all but the cities of Donetsk and Luhansk and their hinterlands (International Crisis Group 2019: 6; UNHCHR 2014). In lieu of annexation, a stream of under-the-table aid – military and financial – kept the statelets afloat. The Kremlin also sought to negotiate a stable ceasefire. None of the ceasefires held, and the eventual diplomatic settlement, the Minsk II agreement, was a dead letter (International Crisis Croup 2019: 8–16; Koshiw 2022).

A second phase of passportization – this time targeting the Donbas – began in April 2019, following the election of Volodymyr Zelensky (Arutunyan 2019). True to pattern, Russia invaded Ukraine on February 22, 2022. The decision to intervene militarily, as Putin described it, emerged from "the situation in the Donbas," and "the genocide of the millions of people living there" (Fisher 2022). This claim of "genocide" was not corroborated by a UN Human Rights Commission investigation conducted just prior to the invasion. The investigation did find, however, that pro-Russian parties faced political repression, including beatings and death threats. Three pro-Russian TV stations were also shut down (OHCHR 2021: 4–8).

Although Ukraine is not wholly innocent of the charge of mistreating Russians, the Russian intervention in Ukraine has been a calamity for the very compatriots Russia sought to "defend" (OHCHR 2022: 11–13). By 2023, over 6 million people had been forced to flee Ukraine, many from the Russian-speaking east of Ukraine (UNHCR (2023). In the longer term, this intervention is certain to poison, perhaps permanently, Russo-Ukrainian relations and could manifest in internal anti-Russianism. In March 2022, for instance, Zelensky banned 11 political parties on Ukraine's left, alleging they had ties to Russia (Shapero 2022). As of writing, however, the war is far from over.

Estonia and Kazakhstan: The Noninterventions

Russia has not always intervened to protect "compatriots." During the 1990s, observers predicted that ethnic tensions in Estonia and Kazakhstan would escalate into armed secessionism, which would then draw in Russia. However, they did not. Simply put, Russia was either unable or unwilling to intervene, and both Estonia and Kazakhstan found ways to neutralize the unrest before matters escalated into armed conflict.

For a period during the 1990s, however, the situation in Estonia looked dire. For context, Russians are concentrated along the Russo-Estonian border and make up about a third of Estonia's total population (Grigas 2016: 156). This notwithstanding, in 1990, Estonia's government decided that Russians who had emigrated or resettled in Estonia during the Soviet period (which was most of the Russians there – some

500,000 people) would not become citizens (Chinn and Kaiser 1996: 94–99). This was one of the most discriminatory citizenship laws of the post-Soviet states. Non-citizens had trouble finding housing and employment, and could not own land, join political parties, carry weapons, or be guaranteed re-entry if they left the country (Payin 1994: 28–29). Matters escalated further in 1993, when the Estonian parliament required non-citizens to reapply for residency at five-year intervals. In response, Russians in Estonia's northeast threatened secession (Chinn and Kaiser 1996: 101).

As one scholar at the time wrote, "many tangible factors seemed to push Estonia in 1991–1993 towards ethnic violence" (Park 1994: 69). Russians in Estonia had become radicalized – by 1994, 42,000 Russians in Estonia took Russian citizenship, the highest number of any former SSR at that time. In the 1993 Russian election, 59 percent of the votes coming from Russians in Estonia were for Vladimir Zhirinovsky, an ultranationalist (Chinn and Kaiser 1996: 107). However, a "Donbas scenario" in Estonia did not materialize. This cannot solely be attributed to NATO and the EU, since Estonia only joined both organizations in 2004.

Some credit goes to Estonia's government, which softened the requirement for non-citizens to apply for residence permits and permitted non-citizens the right to vote. This channeled Russian unrest into electoral politics rather than armed uprising (Chinn and Kaiser 1996: 101). Moreover, annexation to Russia was economically unappealing; many Russians in Estonia believed that Estonia, for reasons of geography and history, would attain a Western European level of prosperity quicker than Russia (Park 1994: 70). Estonia's Russian separatists also received little support from the Russian state. Scholars have argued that any such effort would have been hamstrung by a weak army, an economic crisis, and pervasive corruption within Russia (Zevelev 2001: 153–154).

Regardless, the danger of an Estonian Donbas now seems remote; separatism has become a fringe position in Estonia. Polling indicates broad skepticism of Russian claims to "protect" compatriots (Grigas 2016: 140–142). Moreover, the perks of EU membership, such as the right to travel and work in the Schengen Area, have proven attractive to many Russians in Estonia (Cheskin and Kachuyevski 2019: 13). The political will to create another Donbas in Estonia no longer exists, if it ever did.

Another noteworthy exception is Kazakhstan, where 6.2 million Russians were "stranded" following the collapse of the Soviet Union. Much like in Ukraine, Russians in Kazakhstan were concentrated in a set of provinces that abut Russia. They were also, as previously noted, particularly vulnerable to language laws; less than one percent of Russians in Kazakhstan spoke Kazakh. Following independence, Kazakhstan required academics and national-level officials to be proficient in Kazakh. In response, Russian nationalist organizations demanded autonomy and even independence. Hundreds of thousands of Russians emigrated, and Kazakhs were settled in Russian-dominated areas, provoking further tensions. The Russian foreign minister issued protests, prompting an angry reply from Kazakhstan's president, Nursultan Nazarbayev, who compared these pronouncements to Hitler's "defense" of Sudeten Germans (Chinn and Kaiser 1996: 190–199; Peyrouse 2007).

Examining this situation, Chinn and Kaiser (1996: 185) concluded that Kazakhstan was "on the verge of an international crisis between Russians and Kazakhs that has the potential to become an interstate conflict between Russia and Kazakhstan." So why did a "Donbas scenario" not materialize in Kazakhstan?

Part of the answer is repression. Beginning in 1995, President Nazarbayev began to crack down on Russian nationalist parties. Those nationalists also received little support from Moscow. In 2000, Putin informed them that he would neither support secession nor pressure Kazakhstan for Russian cultural autonomy. Instead, Putin urged them to repatriate to Russia (Peyrouse 2007: 483–495). This meeting roughly coincided with the formation of the Eurasian Economic Community; Kazakhstan was a founding member. As one scholar has argued, the close economic and political relations between Russia and Kazakhstan outweighs "protection" of Kazakhstan's Russians (Zeigler 2006: 103).

Conclusion

To summarize, the Russian Federation seeks to support and co-opt the "stranded" portion of its diaspora to reassert hegemony over its neighbors. In so doing, Russia has resorted to military force on five occasions: Moldova, Tajikistan, Georgia, and twice in Ukraine. Military interventions typically follow grants of passports, something that, in the Kremlin's eyes, gives a legal pretext to defend a (newly minted) diaspora from mistreatment. Interventions are not necessarily precipitated by mistreatment, as the cases of Estonia and Kazakhstan show, but by geopolitical calculation. These cases of Russia *not* intervening, however, both took place in the 1990s or early 2000s, when Russian state capacity was weaker. The trend from 2000 to 2020 has been toward the proactive, rather than reactive, use of force, and for the pursuit of expanded goals, such as the acquisition of territory.

Whether this trend will continue is difficult to say. At the time of writing, the Ukraine–Russia War has become a bloody stalemate, something that might prompt Putin to reaccess his growing reliance on military methods. Yet leaders do not always behave rationally. A safer course is to prognosticate not what Russia *will* do, but *can* do. In that vein, it seems clear that Russia's ability to co-opt "compatriots" has been weakened, though not irreparably, by the global response to the 2022 invasion of Ukraine. Russia's emigrant outreach efforts have faced official pushback in the US, Japan, Australia, and every European country except Serbia, Bosnia, Hungary, Türkiye, and Belarus. In the US, emigrant outreach activities were forced to cease altogether (Ministry of Foreign Affairs 2022c). Russian media organizations, like RT, and websites like that of Russkiy Mir were also blocked in the US and the EU (Schechner 2022). Though it may seem that the Russian foreign ministry has far fewer tools at its disposal, it merits reiterating that the bulk of the Russian diaspora live in states of the former Soviet Union – of which only three (Estonia, Latvia, and Lithuania) are EU members.

There is also ample (albeit anecdotal) evidence that compatriots – from New York to Transnistria – were repulsed and appalled by the invasion of Ukraine (Fasman 2022; Gettleman 2022; Jordan 2022; Satzewich 2022; Walker 2022). It seems likely that many will distance themselves from Kremlin-controlled emigrant organizations. A greater obstacle to Russia's attempts to use its diaspora against its neighbors may be the compatriots themselves.

Table 4.2 Sources

[1] All-Union Population Census of 1989, Working Archive of the State Statistics Committee of Russia (1989). Table 9c. Distribution of the Population by Nationality and Native Language. Available at: www.demoscope.ru/weekly/ssp/sng_nac_89.php?reg=1 (last accessed June 11, 2022).

[2] State Statistics Committee of Ukraine, 2001 Census Results. Available at: http://2001.ukrcensus.gov.ua/eng/results/nationality_population/nationality_1/s5/?botton=cens_db&box=5.1W&k_t=00&p=75&rz=1_1&rz_b=2_1%20%20%20&n_page=4 (last accessed December 3, 2022).

[3] Statistics Committee of Kazakhstan, Chislenost' Naseleniia Respubliki Kazakhstan po Otdelnym Etnosam. Available at: www.stat.gov.kz/api/getFile/?docId=ESTAT355258 (last accessed December 4, 2022).

[4] State Committee of the Republic of Uzbekistan on Statistics, Permanent Population by National and/or Ethnic Group, Urban/Rural Place of Residence. Available at: www.stat.gov.kz/api/getFile/?docId=ESTAT355258 (last accessed December 4, 2022).

[5] National Statistics Committee of the Republic of Belarus, Perepis' Naseleniia 2019. Available at: www.belstat.gov.by/ofitsialnaya-statistika/makroekonomika-i-okruzhayushchaya-sreda/perepis-naseleniya/perepis-naseleniya-2019/ (last accessed December 4, 2022).

[6] National Statistics Committee of the Kyrgyz Republic, Nationalnyi Sostav Naseleniia. Available at: www.stat.kg/ru/opendata/category/312/ (last accessed December 4, 2022).

[7] Official Statistics of Latvia, Population by Ethnicity. Available at: https://data.stat.gov.lv/pxweb/en/OSP_PUB/START__POP__IR__IRE/IRE010/ (last accessed December 4, 2022).

[8] National Bureau of Statistics of the Republic of Moldova, The Population of the Republic of Moldova. Available at: https://statistica.gov.md/en/the-population-of-the-republic-of-moldova-at-the-time-12_896.html (last accessed December 4, 2022).

[9] Statistics Estonia, Population by Ethnic Nationality, December 2021. Available at: https://andmed.stat.ee/en/stat/rahvaloendus__rel2021__rahvastiku-demograafilised-ja-etno-kultuurilised-naitajad__rahvus-emakeel/RL21429 (last accessed December 4, 2022).

[10] Ethnic Composition of Azerbaijan 2009. Available at: http://pop-stat.mashke.org/azerbaijan-ethnic2009.htm (last accessed December 4, 2022).

[11] Tajstat, Nationalyi Sostav, Vladenie Iazykami i Grazhdanstvo Naseleniia Respubliki Tadzhikistan. Available at: https://web.archive.org/web/20131014054442/http:/www.stat.tj/ru/img/526b8592e834fcaaccec26a22965ea2b_1355501132.pdf (last accessed December 4, 2022).

[12] Official Statistics Portal, 2014 General Population Census. Available at: https://osp.stat.gov.lt/gyventoju-ir-bustu-surasymai1 (last accessed December 4, 2022).

[13] National Statistics Office of Georgia, Population by Ethnicity. Available at: http://census.ge/files/results/Census_release_ENG.pdf (last accessed December 4, 2022).

[14] The Results of Census in Turkmenistan, Chronicles of Turkmenistan, March 2, 2015. Available at: https://web.archive.org/web/20161006054812/http://www.chrono-tm.org/en/2015/02/the-results-of-census-in-turkmenistan/ (last accessed December 4, 2022).

[15] Armstat, Perepis' Naselennia, Naseleniia po Natsional'nosti, polu, i vozrastu. Available at: www.armstat.am/file/doc/99484883.pdf (last accessed December 4, 2022).

References

Aleshkovski, Ivan, Alexander Grebenyuk, and Olga Vorobyeva (2018) The Evolution of Russian Emigration in the Post-Soviet Period. *Social Evolution and History* 17(2), 140–155.

Amos, Howard, and Harriet Salem (2014) Ukraine Clashes: Dozens Dead after Odessa Building Fire. *The Guardian*, May 2. Available at: www.theguardian.com/world/2014/may/02/ukraine-dead-odessa-building-fire (last accessed April 18, 2022).

Andreyev, Catherine, and Ivan Savicky (2004) *Russia Abroad: Prague and the Russian Diaspora*, 1918–1938. New Haven, CT: Yale University Press, 2004.

Arutunyan, Anna (2019) Is Russia Changing the Calculus in Eastern Ukraine? *International Crisis Group*, 11, June. Available at: www.crisisgroup.org/europe-central-asia/eastern-europe/ukraine/russia-changing-its-calculus-eastern-ukraine (last accessed May 25, 2024).

Barrington, Lowell, Erik Herron and Brian Silver (2003) The Motherland is Calling: Views of Homeland among Russians in the near Abroad. *World Politics* 55(2), 219–313.

Bebler, Anton (2015) Crimea and the Ukrainian/Russia conflict. In Anton Bebler (ed.), *Frozen Conflicts in Europe*. Leverkusen: Leverkusen Verlag, 189–208.

Burkhardt, Fabian (2020) Russia's "Passportisation" of the Donbas. *SWP Comment* 41. Berlin: Stiftung Wissenschaft und Politik.

Byford, Andy (2012) The Russian Diaspora in International Relations: 'Compatriots' in Britain. *Europe-Asia Studies* 64(4), 715–35.

Cheskin, Ammon and Angela Kachuyevski (2019) The Russian-Speaking Populations in the Post-Soviet Space: Language, Politics, and Identity. *Europe-Asia Studies* 71(1), 1–23.

Chinn, Jeff and Robert Kaiser (1996) *Russians as the New Minority: Ethnicity and Nationalism in the Soviet Successor States.* New York: Routledge.

Choate, Mark (2008) *Emigrant Nation: The Making of Italy Abroad.* Cambridge, MA: Harvard University Press.

Crandall, Matthew (2012) Hierarchy in Moldova–Russia Relations: The Transnistrian Effect. *Studies of Transition States and Societies* 4(1), 3–15.

Crowley, Michael (2022) Russia Hints at Linking Griner's Case to Fate of 'Merchant of Death.' *New York Times,* 1 July, 2022. Available at: www.nytimes.com/2022/07/01/us/politics/brittney-griner-trial-russia.html (last accessed July 17, 2022).

European Council (2022) EU Relations with the Republic of Moldova. Available at: www.consilium.europa.eu/en/policies/eastern-partnership/moldova/ (last accessed November 13, 2022).

Fasman, Jon (2022) Grief, Rage, Anxiety: Voices from Brighton Beach, New York's 'Russian' Neighborhood. *The Economist,* March 3. Available at: www.economist.com/1843/2022/03/03/grief-rage-anxiety-voices-from-brighton-beach-new-yorks-russian-neighbourhood (last accessed October 1, 2022).

Fisher, Max (2022) Putin's Case for War, Annotated. *New York Times,* 24 February. Available at: www.nytimes.com/2022/02/24/world/europe/putin-ukraine-speech.html (last accessed August 14, 2022).

Fonseca, Brian and Vladimir Rouvinski (2018) The Russians of Latin America. *Military Review,* 80–88.

FPZPS (Fond Podderzhki i Zashchity Prav Sootechestvennikov) (2022) O Fonde. Available at: https://pravfond.ru/about/ (last accessed July 4, 2022).

Gaidys, Vladis (1994) Russians in Lithuania. In Vladimir Shlapentokh, Munir Sendich, and Emil Payin (eds.), *The New Russian Diaspora: Russian Minorities in the Former Soviet Republics.* New York: M. E. Sharpe, 91–106.

German, Tracey and Benjamin Block (2006) The South Ossetia Conflict: Collision of Georgian and Russian Interests. *Politique Étrangère* 1, 51–64.

Gettleman, Jeffrey (2022) A Mini-Russia Gets Squeezed by War. *New York Times,* 15 May, 2022. Available at: www.nytimes.com/2022/05/15/world/europe/transnistria-moldova-russia-ukraine.html (last accessed October 10, 2022).

Glick, Nina and Peggy Levitt (2004) Conceptualizing Simultaneity: A Transnational Social Field Perspective on Society. *International Migration Review* 38(3): 1002–1039.

Goble, Paul (2001) Bilingualism in Latvia. *The Baltic Times,* April 26. Available at: www.balticimes.com/news/articles/4893/ (last accessed November 6, 2022).

Golovakha, Evgenii, Natalia Panina, and Nikolai Churilov (1994) Russians in Ukraine. In Vladimir Shlapentokh, Munir Sendich, and Emil Payin (eds.), *The New Russian Diaspora: Russian Minorities in the Former Soviet Republics.* New York: M. E. Sharpe, 59–71.

Grigas, Agnia (2016) *Beyond Crimea: The New Russian Empire.* New Haven, CT: Yale University Press.

Gudkov, Lev (1994) The Structure and Character of Migration of Russians from the Former Republics of the USSR. In Vladimir Shlapentokh, Munir Sendich, and Emil Payin (eds.), *The New Russian Diaspora*. New York: M. E. Sharpe, 169–182.

Herzog, Stephen (2011) Revisiting the Estonian Cyberattacks: Digital Threats and Multinational Responses. *Journal of Strategic Security* 4(2), 49–60.

Higgins, Andrew (2018) Populist Wave Hits Latvia, Lifting Pro-Russia Party in Election. *New York Times,* 8 October, 2018. Available at: www.nytimes.com/2018/10/07/world/europe/latvia-election-russia.html?searchResultPosition=3 (last accessed November 12, 2022).

Hogan-Brun, Gabriel and Meilutė Ramonienė (2004) Changing Levels of Bilingualism across the Baltic. *International Journal of Bilingual Education and Bilingualism* 7(1), 62–77.

Hosking, Geoffrey (2002) The Second World War and Russian National Consciousness. *Past and Present* 175(1), 162–187.

IIFFMCG (Independent International Fact-Finding Mission on the Conflict in Georgia) (2009) Report. Vol. 1. Available at: www.mpil.de/en/pub/publications/archive/independent_international_fact.cfm (last accessed October 10, 2022).

International Crisis Group (2019) Report No. 254. *Rebels without a Cause: Russia's Proxies in Eastern Ukraine*. Available at: https://icg-prod.s3.amazonaws.com/254-rebels-without-a-cause%20%281%29.pdf (last accessed October 10, 2022).

Jordan, Miriam (2022) 'I Don't Want to Be Called Russian Anymore': Anxious Soviet Diaspora Rethinks Identity. *New York Times,* March 4. Available at: www.nytimes.com/2022/03/04/us/immigrant-identity-russia-ukraine.html (last accessed October 1, 2022).

Kallas, Kristina (2016) Claiming the Diaspora: Russia's Compatriot Policy and Its Reception by the Estonian–Russian Population. *Journal of Ethnopolitics and Minority Issues in Europe* 15(3), 1–25.

Koshiw, Isobel (2022) Everyone Is Talking about Minsk but What Does It Mean for Ukraine? *Open Democracy,* February 4. Available at: www.opendemocracy.net/en/odr/russia-ukraine-what-are-the-minsk-agreements/ (last accessed October 1, 2022).

KPRFSR (Kontseptsiia Podderzhki Rossiiskoi Federatsiei Sootechestvennikov za Rubezhom na Sovvremennom Etape) (2001). Available at: http://ksors.ru/koncepciya-podderzhki-rossijskoj-federaciej-sootechestvennikov-za-rubezhom/ (last accessed June 11, 2022).

Laruelle, Marlene, Dylan Royce, and Serik Beyssembayev (2019) Untangling the Puzzle of 'Russia's Influence' in Kazakhstan. *Eurasian Geography and Economics* 60(2), 211–243.

Massey, Douglass (1995) The New Immigration and Ethnicity in the United States. *Population and Development Review* 21(3), 631–652.

McFaul, Michael (2014) Moscow's Choice. *Foreign Affairs,* November/December, 167–171.

Mearsheimer, John (2014) Why the Ukraine Crisis Is the West's Fault. *Foreign Affairs,* September/October. Available at: www.ianfeinhandler.com/iaclub/articles/Russia_Ukraine_West_Fault.pdf (last accessed September 9, 2022).

Miarka, Agnieszka (2020) Para-states as an Instrument for Strengthening Russia's Position: The Case of Transnistria. *Journal of Strategic Security* 13(2), 1–18.

Ministry of Foreign Affairs (2022a) Consular Information Portal. Available at: www.kdmid.ru/docs/ (last accessed September 11, 2022).

Ministry of Foreign Affairs (2022b) Istoricheskaia Spravka. Available at: www.kdmid.ru/war-memorials/historical-reference/ (last accessed September 18, 2022).

Ministry of Foreign Affairs (2022c) O Narushenniiakh Prav Rossiiskikh Grazhdan i Sootechestvennikov v Zarubezhnykh Stranakh. Available at: https://mid.ru/ru/foreign_policy/humanitarian_cooperation/1815559/ (last accessed October 10, 2022).

Ministry of Foreign Affairs (2022d) O 30-y Godovshchine Ustanovleniia Diplomatichesikh Otnosheniy mezhdu Rossiiskoi Federatsiey i Respublikoi Tadzhikistan. April 7. Available at: www.mid.ru/ru/foreign_policy/news/1808507/ (last accessed April 17, 2022).

Ministry of Foreign Affairs (2022e) Interv'iu Posla Rossii v SShA A. I. Antonova 'Rossiiskoi Gazete.' September 5. Available at: www.mid.ru/ru/foreign_policy/news/1828648/ (last accessed October 10, 2022).

Ministry of Foreign Affairs (2022f) *Structure*, Central Office. Available at: https://mid.ru/ru/about/structure/central_office/ (last accessed November 12, 2022).

Morgunova, Oksana and Andy Byford (2018) Between Neo-nationalizing Russia and Brexit Britain: The Dilemma of Russian Migrants Political Mobilizations. *Revue d'études comparatives Est-Ouest* 49(4), 129–162.

Mühlfried, Florian (2010) Citizenship at War: Passports and Nationality in the 2008 Russian–Georgia Conflict. *Anthropology Today* 26(2), 8–13.

Newsru (2014) "Na Ukraine Protistiruiut Protiv Nachatoi Novymi Vlastiami Bor'by s Russkim Iazykom." February 26. Available at: www.newsru.com/world/26feb2014/ukr_russian.html (last accessed October 10, 2022).

North Atlantic Council (2008) Bucharest Summit Declaration. North Atlantic Treaty Organization, April 3. Available at: www.nato.int/cps/en/natolive/official_texts_8443.htm (last accessed April 17, 2022).

Nourzhanov, Kirill and Christian Bleuer (2013) *Tajikistan: A Political and Social History*. Canberra: ANU Press.

OHCHR (Office of the High Commissioner for Human Rights) (2021) Civic Space and Fundamental Freedoms in Ukraine, 1 November 2019–31 October 2021. Available at: www.ohchr.org/sites/default/files/2021-12/UkraineCivicSpace2021-EN.pdf (last accessed October 10, 2022).

OHCHR (Office of the High Commissioner for Human Rights) (2022) Situation of Human Rights in Ukraine in the Context of the Armed Attack by the Russian Federation, 24 February–15 May 2022. Available at: www.ohchr.org/sites/default/files/documents/countries/ua/2022-06-29/2022-06-UkraineArmedAttack-EN.pdf (last accessed October 10, 2022).

Oladipo, Gloria (2022) Woman Who Ran Russia Propaganda Center in New York Charged as Foreign Agent. *The Guardian*, May 9. Available at: www.theguardian.com/us-news/2022/mar/09/elena-branson-russia-propaganda-center-new-york-charged (last accessed March 13, 2022).

Ostrovsky, Simon, Ainara Tiefenthaler, and Alessandro Pavone (2022) Hear the Stories of Ukrainians Who Were Forcibly Resettled to Russia and Escaped.

New York Times, 20 June, 2022. Available at: www.nytimes.com/2022/06/20/world/europe/hear-the-stories-of-ukrainians-who-were-forcibly-resettled-to-russia-and-escaped.html (last accessed September 18, 2022).

Park, Andrus (1994) Ethnicity and Independence: The Case of Estonia in Comparative Perspective. *Europe-Asia Studies* 46(1), 69–87.

Payin, Emil (1994) The Disintegration of the Empire and the Fate of the 'Imperial Minority.' In Vladimir Shlapentokh, Munir Sendich, and Emil Payin (eds.), *The New Russian Diaspora*. New York: M. E. Sharpe, 21–36.

Periroth, Nicole (2017) Russian Hacker Sentenced to 27 Years in Credit Card Case. *New York Times*, 21 April, 2017. Available at: www.nytimes.com/2017/04/21/technology/russian-hacker-sentenced.html (last accessed July 17, 2022).

Peyrouse, Sebastien (2007) Nationhood and the Minority Question in Central Asia. *Europe–Asia Studies* 59(3), 486–492.

Pieper, Moritz (2020) Russkiy Mir: The Geopolitics of Russian Compatriots Abroad. *Geopolitics* 25(3), 756–779.

PKDSR Pravitel'stvennaia Komissiia po Delam Sootechestvennikov za Rubezhom (2018) Kompleksnyi Plan Osnovnykh Meropriiatii po Realizatsii Gosudarstvennoi Politiki Rossiiskoi Federatsii v Otnoshenii Sootechestvennikov, Prozhivaiushchikh za Rubezhom, na 2018–2020 gody. Available at: https://ruvek.mid.ru/documents/ (last accessed June 3, 2022).

Putin, Vladimir (2007) Ukaz no. 976: O Sozdanii Fonda Russkiy Mir. June 21, 2007. Available at: www.intelros.ru/subject/ross_rasput/834-ukaz_796_o_sozdanii_fonda_russkijj_mir.html (last accessed December 11, 2022).

Putin, Vladimir (2020) Ukaz no. 322: O Nekotorykh Voprosakh Realizatsii Gosudarstvennoi Programmy po Okazaniiu Sodeistviia Dobrovol'nomu Pereseleniiu v Rossiiskoi Federatsiiu Sootechestvennikov, Prozhivaiushchikh za Rubezhom. May 12.

Putin, Vladimir (2021) Ukaz no. 215: O Nekotorykh Voprosakh Fonda 'Russkiy Mir.' April 12. Available at: http://publication.pravo.gov.ru/Document/View/0001202104120042?rangeSize=1 (last accessed December 11, 2022).

Putin, Vladimir (2022) "Signing of Treaties on Accession of Donetsk and Lugansk People's Republics and Zaporozhye and Kherson Regions to Russia." Moscow, September 30. Speech. Available at: http://en.kremlin.ru/events/president/news/69465 (last accessed October 2, 2022).

Putz, Catherine (2021) Russia to Hold Military Drills Near Afghan Border in Tajikistan, Uzbekistan. *The Diplomat*, July 21. Available at: https://thediplomat.com/2021/07/russia-to-hold-military-drills-near-afghan-border-in-tajikistan-uzbekistan/ (last accessed April 17, 2022).

Roth, Andrew (2019) Russia Accused of Hostage Diplomacy over Jailed Foreigners. *The Guardian*, November 18. Available at: www.theguardian.com/world/2019/nov/18/russia-accused-of-hostage-diplomacy-over-jailed-foreigners (last accessed July 17, 2022).

Russian Federation (2014) Programma Raboty s Sootechestvennikom, Prozhivaiushchimi za Rubezhom, na 2015–2017 gody. Available at: https://ruvek.mid.ru/document/compatriots/programma_raboty_s_sootechestvennikami_prozhivayushchimi_za_rubezhom_na_2015_2017_gody_956/ (last accessed July 4, 2022).

Russkiy Vek (2022a) Na Dal'niy Vostok: Pereselentsam s Ukrainy Pomogut s Trudoustroistvom i Material'no. April 4. Available at: https://ruvek.mid.ru/publications/na_dalniy_vostok_pereselentsam_s_ukrainy_pomogut_s_trudoustroystvom_i_materialno/ (last accessed September 18, 2022).

Russkiy Vek (2022b) Tol'ko 0,9% iz 4,6 mln Bezhentsev s Ukrainy i Donbassa Nakhodiatsia v Punktakh Razmeshcheniia. October 31. Available at: https://ruvek.mid.ru/news/tolko_0_9_iz_4_6_mln_bezhentsev_s_ukrainy_i_donbassa_nakhodyatsya_v_punktakh_razmeshcheniya/ (last accessed September 2, 2023).

Saari, Sinikukka (2014) Russia's Post-Orange Revolution Strategies to Increase Its Influence in Former Soviet Republics: Public Diplomacy *po Russkii*. *Europe–Asia Studies* 66(1), 50–66.

Satzewich, Vic (2022) The Russian Diaspora Isn't Showing Much Support for Russia's Invasion of Ukraine. *The Independent*, March 17. Available at: https://theconversation.com/the-russian-diaspora-isnt-showing-much-support-for-russias-invasion-of-ukraine-178623 (last accessed October 1, 2022).

Schechner, Sam (2022) EU Orders Removal of Russian State-Owned Media from Search Results, Social Media Reshares. *Wall Street Journal*, March 10. Available at: www.wsj.com/livecoverage/russia-ukraine-latest-news-2022-03-09/card/eu-orders-removal-of-russian-state-owned-media-from-search-results-social-media-reshares-Nxb4WXbCaQnCUMmL9Mvk (last accessed July 10, 2022).

Sestanovich, Stephan (2014) How the West Has Won. *Foreign Affairs*, November/December, 171–175.

Shapero, Julia (2022) Zelensky Has Announced Ban on 11 Political Parties with Ties to Russia. *Axios*, March 20. Available at: www.axios.com/2022/03/20/ukraine-ban-political-parties-russian-ties (last accessed September 3, 2022).

Sharma, Shweta (2022) Putin 'Resettling Ukrainians 5,500 Miles Away in Siberia and Far East Russia,' Report Claims. *Independent*, April 12. Available at: www.independent.co.uk/news/world/europe/russia-ukraine-resettling-siberia-putin-b2056054.html (last accessed September 18, 2022).

Shear, Michael, and Peter Baker (2022) Brittney Griner Is Freed in a Prisoner Swap with Russia. *New York Times*, December 8. Available at: www.nytimes.com/live/2022/12/08/world/brittney-griner-russia-ukraine-news (last accessed December 10, 2022).

Shear, Michael, and Ivan Nechepurenko (2022) Russia Releases Former U.S. Marine in Prisoner Swap. *New York Times*, April 27. Available at: www.nytimes.com/2022/04/27/world/europe/trevor-reed-russia-prisoner-swap.html (last accessed July 17, 2022).

Shekhovstov, Anton (2015) The Spectre of Ukrainian Fascism: Information Wars, Political Manipulation, and Reality. In Andrew Wilson (ed.), *What Does Ukraine Think*. [No place stated]: European Council on Foreign Relations, 80–87.

Smagulova, Juldyz (2008) Language Policies of Kazakhization and Their Influence on Language Attitudes and Use. *International Journal of Bilingual Education and Bilingualism* 11(3), 440–475.

Sprague, Andrew (2016) Russian Meddling in Its Near Abroad. Institut Barcelona d'Estudis Internacionals. *Student Paper Series* 28, 1–24. Available at: www.ibei.org/ibei_studentpaper28_71440.pdf (last accessed May 25, 2024).

UNHCHR (United Nations High Commissioner for Human Rights) (2014) Report on the Human Rights Situation in Ukraine, August 17. Available at: www.ohchr.org/sites/default/files/Documents/Countries/UA/UkraineReport28August2014.pdf (last accessed October 10, 2022).

UNHCR (United Nations High Commissioner for Refugees) (2023) Operational Data Portal: Ukraine Refugee Situation. Available at: https://data.unhcr.org/en/situations/ukraine (last accessed September 2, 2023).

United Nations (2004) Minorities at Risk Project, Chronology for Russians in Tajikistan. Available at: www.refworld.org/docid/469f38e51e.html (last accessed April 17, 2022).

United Nations (2020) Population Division, International Migrant Stock. Available at: www.un.org/development/desa/pd/content/international-migrant-stock (last accessed April 3, 2022).

VKSRS (Vsemirnyi Koordinatsionnyi Sovet Rossiiskikh Sootechestvennikov, Prozhivaiushchikh za Rubezhom) (2021) VII Vsemirnyi Kongress, October 15. Available at: https://vksrs.com/events/vii-vsemirnyy-kongress/ (last accessed September 18, 2022).

Walker, Shaun (2022) 'Beyond Understanding': Odesa Braced to See If Putin Attacks City of Such Resonance for Russians. *The Guardian*, March 7. Available at: www.theguardian.com/world/2022/mar/07/beyond-understanding-odesa-braced-to-see-if-putin-attacks-city-of-such-resonance-for-russians (last accessed: 10/1/2022).

Waterbury, Myra (2014) Making Citizens beyond the Border: Non-resident Ethnic Citizenship in Post-communist Europe. *Problems of Post-Communism* 61(4), 36–49.

World Bank (2022a) Personal Remittances Received (% of GDP)-Russian Federation. Available at: https://data.worldbank.org/indicator/BX.TRF.PWKR.DT.GD.ZS?locations=RU (last accessed April 3, 2022).

World Bank (2022b) Personal Remittances Received (% of GDP)-Mexico. Available at: https://data.worldbank.org/indicator/BX.TRF.PWKR.DT.GD.ZS?locations=MX (last accessed April 3, 2022).

Zakharova, M. V. (2022) Kommentarii Ofitsial'nogo Predstavleniia MID Rossii M. V. Zakharovoi o Prediavlenii Obvinenii Predsedateliu Koordinatsionnogo Soveta Organizatsii Rossiiskikh Sootechestvennikov SShA Elene Brenson, March 3. www.mid.ru/ru/foreign_policy/news/1803439/ (last accessed March 13, 2022).

Zeigler, Charles (2006) The Russian Diaspora in Central Asia: Russian compatriots and Moscow's Foreign Policy. *Demokratizatsiya* 14(1), 103–126.

Zeller, Jan and Dmitri Sitchinava (2019) The Russian Language in Belarus and Ukraine. In Arto Mustajoki, Ekaterina Protassova, Maria Yelenevskaya (eds.), *The Soft Power of the Russian Language*. London: Routledge, 108–122.

Zevelev, Igor (2001) *Russia and Its New Diasporas*. Washington, DC: United States Institute of Peace Press.

5 China

Focusing on Low-Cost and Low-Key Administrative and Diplomatic Initiatives

Andrea Ghiselli

Introduction

During one of his very first meetings with a foreign leader visiting China since the outbreak of the Covid-19 pandemic, Chinese President Xi Jinping, mentioned "his great concern about the safety of Chinese nationals in Pakistan, and conveyed his hope that Pakistan will provide a reliable and safe environment for Chinese institutions and personnel working on cooperation projects there" to Pakistani Prime Minister, Muhammad Shehbaz Sharif (PRC Ministry of Foreign Affairs 2022). Delivered to the leader of a country wherein Chinese nationals have often been victims of attacks, Xi's message is an important reminder of how much the Chinese government today pays attention to the protection of its nationals in foreign countries as part of its efforts to protect what policy documents call "overseas interests," or 海外利益 (*Hǎiwài lìyì*) in Chinese.

As shown in this chapter, China has made significant efforts to fulfil that mission as well as achieve and balance a variety of goals, from co-opting well-educated citizens to capturing wanted fugitives, related to the management of Chinese nationals overseas. It has mostly employed a great variety of low-cost and low-key administrative and diplomatic initiatives. Despite much discussion among Western policy-makers about the possibility that China's efforts to protect its citizens and companies overseas will involve a significant use of military means, that has not happened so far.

Against this background, the first section of the chapter provides an overview of the presence of Chinese nationals overseas, where they are mostly located, and the factor that shapes their presence. Hence, I analyze the main regulatory diplomatic efforts made by the Chinese state to protect them. Then, I focus on the policies adopted by the Chinese government to support and manage the Chinese diaspora, as well as to lure back those highly educated nationals who are seen as an important source of innovation for the Chinese economy. After that, I show the evolution of China's military activities aimed at protecting

Chinese citizens overseas. In the last section, I discuss how the situation might evolve in the future.

Overview of the Chinese Community Abroad

Although there is no official statistics regarding the total number of Chinese nationals overseas, World Bank (2022) data show that the number of departures that Chinese citizens made from China to any other country for any purpose other than a remunerated activity in the country visited peaked at around 154.5 million in 2019, steadily growing from 4.5 million in 1990. At the same time, although the precise number of people who can be considered as belonging to Chinese diaspora varies depending on who estimates it, recent studies refer to more than 40 million individuals (Song 2019). This is the result of a combination of diverse factors, from escaping the country during one of its turbulent moments in the twentieth century to greater wealth at the disposal of Chinese citizens to pay for study and tourism overseas as well as the growing footprint of Chinese companies in foreign countries. The data of the United Nations Department of Economic and Social Affairs also show a similar trend, with over 10 million Chinese nationals overseas in mid-2020 (Figure 5.1). Among them are the 700,000 Chinese students going to overseas universities every year (*China Daily* 2022). Yet, while the protection of tourists and students is undoubtedly an important task for the Chinese foreign and security policy machine, Chinese workers overseas have long been the main source of concerns

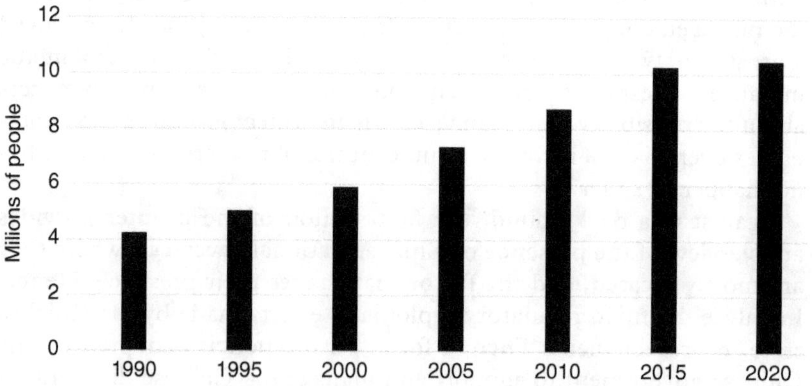

Figure 5.1 Chinese nationals overseas (mid-year stock)
Source: Own depiction based on data from United Nations Department of Economic and Social Affairs – Population Division (2020).

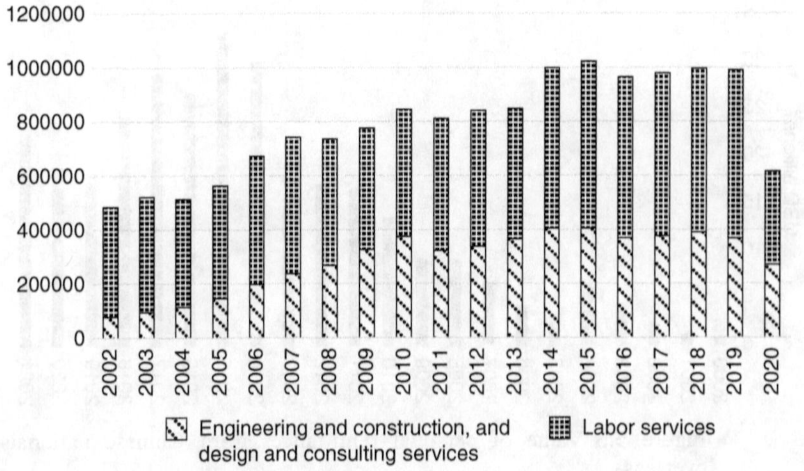

Figure 5.2 Chinese workers overseas
Source: Own depiction based on data from the China Trade and External Economic Statistical Yearbook (various editions).

for Chinese officials (discussed below). Hence, it is important to look at where Chinese construction workers and citizens employed for labor services overseas are located.

According to the data annually released by the National Bureau of Statistics of China, the number of Chinese workers overseas peaked at slightly more than 1 million in 2015 and remained close to that number until 2020. Covid-19 is likely the main cause of the drastic reduction of Chinese workers overseas from 990,000 in 2019 to almost 615,000 in 2020 (Figure 5.2). These data include workers in one of either three types of contracts: labor services contracts, engineering and construction services, and design and consulting services. Although the bureau does not provide information regarding the employer of these workers, it is extremely likely that they work for centrally owned state-owned companies (SOEs), that is, companies directly managed by the state-owned Assets Supervision and Administration Commission of the State Council. There are two main reasons behind this hypothesis. The first is that communication between state organs and state-owned entities is surely easier than between state organs and private enterprises (Corkin 2011). The second reason is that it is large central SOEs that usually play a leading role in overseas projects, often financed through loans and grants from Chinese financial institutions.

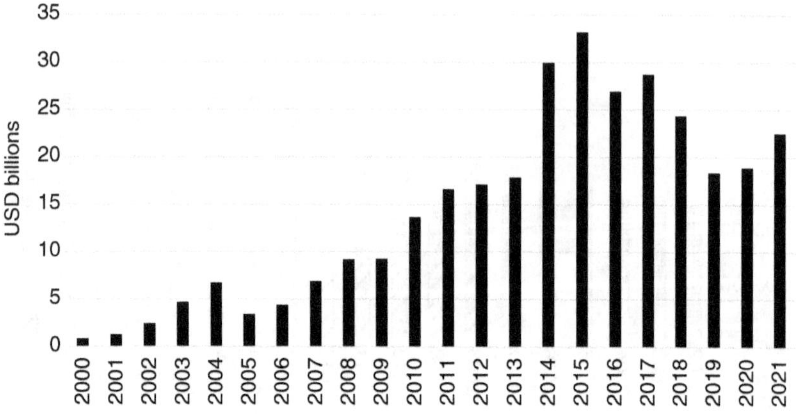

Figure 5.3 Value of personal remittances from Chinese nationals overseas
Source: Own depiction based on data from the World Bank.

This latter point is important as scholars have found that construction companies whose headquarters are in provinces in China where there is frequent unrest caused by economic slowdown and unemployment are often selected by the Chinese government to carry out construction projects overseas (Mueller 2022). The workers so mobilized, as well as those who voluntarily choose to work on projects overseas are an important source of remittances (Figure 5.3). For many, this is the only way to earn enough money to buy a house and get married, or, in the case of older workers, to help sons buy a house with an eye to enhancing their marriage prospects (Driessen 2021).

Geographically speaking, East and Southeast Asian countries are by far the most important destinations for those workers (Ghiselli and Morgan 2021a). Indeed, the top host economies are in fact Japan's (with an average of almost 143,000 workers present at the end of each year between 2002 and 2019) and Singapore's (with an average of just over 87,600). The data also show substantial numbers of Chinese workers in South Korea (almost 32,000 on average) and Saudi Arabia (22,000 on average). As to the factors that shape the number of those workers overseas, the only two existing studies on this topic identifies several variables (Ghiselli and Morgan 2021b, 2022). One of them is the regime type of the host country. All things being equal, less democratic countries allow Chinese companies to bring more workers. This is because authoritarian regimes prefer avoiding extracting capital and labor from the local population that could otherwise question how those resources are spent and/or ask for political representation (Bueno De Mesquita and Smith 2010; Wright, Frantz, and Geddes 2015). Moreover, those regimes are also less sensitive to popular concerns regarding the fact that Chinese and foreign workers in general take on jobs that their local counterparts could also do.[1]

Another important factor that has a significant effect on the number of Chinese workers overseas is instability in the host country. The intervening mechanism that connects violent events and the number of workers is particularly important. Statistical analysis strongly suggests that Chinese companies ignore the warnings issued by the Chinese embassies and consulates, even when they recommend leaving the country (Ghiselli and Morgan 2021b). On the contrary, they reduce the number of their employees only after large violent events, including when civil, ethnic, communal, and genocidal violence and warfare take place.

Though more research on this issue is necessary, the same articles on the subject suggest that there is a unsurprisingly positive correlation between the number of Chinese workers and the aggregate financial value of Chinese contracts in host states (Ghiselli and Morgan 2021b, 2022). The level of globalization of a country's economy, too, plays a positive role. Instead, local unemployment and a large population in the host country negatively influence the number of Chinese workers.

Diplomatic and Consular Dimension

The activities that the Chinese state today carries out to protect its citizens overseas must be seen as products of a process of growing securitization of nontraditional security issues overseas that pushed the Chinese definition of national security beyond the narrow survival of the regime and the state to also include the safety of common citizens. This became particularly evident when Hu Jintao became the top Chinese leader in the early 2000s (Xia 2021). His emphasis on "putting the people first" (以人为本, *Yĭ rén wéi běn*) prompted a deep change in the understanding of security in China, from one centered on the survival of the state to another more people-focused one (Zhang 2004; Men 2009).

The Defense White Paper published in 2004 introduced the idea of "comprehensive national security" (综合安全观, *Zònghé ānquán guān*).

[1] It is important to emphasize that the accusation that Chinese construction workers "steal" jobs from local labor is not always true. Sometimes, the jobs created by Chinese companies are not appealing to the local population, even when the level of unemployment is high (Alden and Aggad-Clerx 2021). Sometimes, concerns about the impact of Chinese labor on the local job market are exaggerated by the fact that the project in which they work are highly visible (Iacoella et al. 2021).

According to the white paper, "China sticks to keeping its development in pace with its security and makes great efforts to enhance its national strategic capabilities by using multiple security means to cope with both traditional and nontraditional security threats so as to seek a comprehensive national security in the political, economic, military, and social areas" (PRC Information Office of the State Council 2004). Hence, a new set of "historic missions" was bestowed on the People's Liberation Army (PLA) that included protecting the rule of the Party and China's national security, sovereignty, territorial integrity, and – most importantly for the subject of this chapter – development interests. The term "security" is largely associated with China's economic expansion abroad, including its citizens sent overseas.[2] This was the first time that their security became part of China's understanding of national security.

Against this background, the idea that the military had to play a more active role vis-à-vis nontraditional security issues in foreign policy gained traction. In particular, nontraditional security dominated the Defense White Paper issued in January 2009 (PRC Information Office of the State Council 2009). The white paper also officially enshrined the concept of Military Operations Other Than War (MOOTW) in Chinese defense policy, a set of missions that today includes the protection of Chinese nationals overseas.

In late 2012, in the aftermath of the evacuation of about 36,000 Chinese nationals, mostly construction workers, from Libya the year before, the rhetorical link between nontraditional security and the role of the PLA abroad grew stronger and the PLA was then expressly required to play a more active role in peacetime foreign policy while continuing to improve the level of war readiness (*Xinhua* 2012). The Defense White Paper issued in 2013 fully reflected Hu's point of view and called for an even greater PLA engagement in foreign policy during times of peace (PRC Information Office of the State Council 2013). Crucially important, that document called for the first time for strengthening of "overseas operational capabilities such as emergency response and rescue, merchant vessel protection at sea and evacuation of Chinese nationals, and provide reliable security support for China's interests overseas." This was the first time that a Chinese Defense White Paper explicitly mentioned Chinese nationals overseas, rather than using the more general term "development interests." Since then, the protection of Chinese citizens and legal persons overseas started to appear regularly in the

[2] The original set of "historic missions" bestowed upon the Chinese military by previous Chinese leaders include promoting China's modernization, completing the reunification with Taiwan, and promoting world peace.

Defense White Papers and annual government reports as an important foreign and defense policy priority.

The development of the Chinese consular protection system has taken place in this context. Although China had to evacuate some of its citizens from foreign countries like Somalia in the 1990s, it was in the mid 2000s that it started to develop a systematic approach to protect its citizens and economic assets overseas. During those years, a number of critical developments took place, including the publication of first *Guide to Consular Protection and Services Outside Chinese Territory*, the establishment of the Consular Protection Division under the Department of Consular Affairs of the Ministry of Foreign Affairs (MFA), and the issuing of an inter-ministerial note to clarify the foreign policy aspects of the State Council-approved National Overseas Emergency Response Plan (Xiang 2017). The Deputy Director of the MFA Department of Consular Affairs at the time, Zhang Weiwei, stated that these efforts were based on the idea that "prevention is the main goal, though preventing and dealing with problems in an effective way are equally important" (Li 2012: 108).

Since then, this regulatory and institutional framework has continued to develop following the same logic, especially with the ministries of commerce and foreign affairs working together to develop a series of regulations and services aimed at helping Chinese companies to avoid risks overseas, on the one hand, and disincentivize them from investing or taking on projects in unstable countries, on the other (Ghiselli 2021). In 2014, the MFA also created an account on the Twitter-like Chinese social media Weibo and in the messaging app WeChat to communicate with Chinese nationals overseas. It furthermore created a special 24-hour emergency response hotline in the same year.

It is against this background that China built the largest diplomatic network around the world, with more than 170 embassies and over 90 consulates in foreign countries (Lowy Institute 2022), surpassing the United States in 2019. Undoubtedly, such a vast diplomatic presence has been fueled by Beijing's growing diplomatic ambitions as well as the quick expansion of China's human and economic footprint overseas. However, it is difficult to say whether the consular protection system has kept up with this expansion. It is difficult to find recent data but the available information shows that the system came under significant stress in the past, at least. The consular protection system has had its own budget since 2005. A diplomat declared that it was less than RMB30 million (around US$4.3 million) in 2015 (Xia 2016: 18). Embassies and consulates abroad have their own small emergency budget, too. The MFA used almost its entire annual emergency budget in 2011 on the Libya evacuation (see further for details) and, as a Chinese scholar pointed out, that event revealed the excessively overstretched state of China's consular protection system (Li 2016: 14).

Moreover, there is a limit on the number of diplomats assigned to deal with overseas emergencies. The number of officers working in the Consular Protection Center is between fifteen and twenty and, even when the top leadership gave the order to evacuate Chinese citizens from Libya, the number never surpassed thirty (Xia 2016: 21). As of 2013, fewer than 300 diplomats overseas were in charge of dealing with problems encountered by Chinese nationals, which may vary from being robbed or detained to having to be quickly evacuated from war zones. This task of theirs has to be carried out in addition to carrying out a number of others, such as issuing passports and other documents (Yang 2013: 18). In 2011, the number of diplomats in charge of consular affairs abroad was the same as in 1994, but the number of Chinese nationals going abroad every year was ten times higher while the number of cases handled by the consular affairs offices was seventy times higher (Lai 2012). China was among the few countries not pushing their nationals to evacuate from Ukraine in early 2022, despite the many signs of an imminent Russian attack, thereby showing that its consular protection system also risks being marginalized when policy-makers face a complex international environment.

Meanwhile, China has been strengthening cooperation with other countries. While it signed many bilateral consular conventions in the past, diplomatic efforts have intensified in recent years under the form of agreements that, in practice, outsource the protection of Chinese projects and citizens to local security and law-enforcement agencies. The most prominent case is the protection of the projects that are part of the China–Pakistan Economic Corridor. After several incidents and terrorist attacks against Chinese nationals in 2016 and 2017, the Pakistani military and security forces have adopted a set of unprecedented measures to protect Chinese workers and projects, including the creation of a 1,000-strong police protection force. China has offered its strong support for the strengthening of law-enforcement and antiterrorism cooperation to boost the security of the China–Pakistan Economic Corridor (The News 2020), as it has done also in other parts of the world (Benabdallah 2020). Indeed, the protection of Belt-and-Road Initiative-related projects is part of law-enforcement cooperation between China and other countries like Myanmar, Uzbekistan, Tajikistan, Ethiopia, and Serbia (*Xinhua* 2018, 2020a, 2020b, 2021; PRC State Council 2020). The 2015 Antiterrorism Law (revised in 2018), which explicitly allows Chinese national security and law-enforcement agencies to send teams to investigate attacks against Chinese nationals and companies overseas in cooperation with their local counterparts (PRC National People's Congress 2018), played a key role boosting and normalizing these practices. Security-force assistance to boost the capacity and quality of the recipient state's coercive institutions is another important part of China's diplomatic efforts to improve the protection of its citizens and companies overseas (Carrozza and Marsh 2022). China has also pushed for this kind of cooperation at the multilateral level through, for example, the China–Arab States Cooperation Forum and the Forum on China–Africa Cooperation (Murphy 2022).

In comparison to these diplomatic and administrative measures, it is important to point out that China has also been extremely cautious regarding the development of its own private security industry (Ghiselli 2020). While private security companies have long discussed a possible compromise that would allow Chinese companies overseas to improve their protection without requiring a direct intervention from the state, concerns regarding diplomatic incidents created by those companies have undermined attempts to reform that industry, especially regarding the possibility to carry firearms. As such, Chinese private security companies mostly provide consulting services while their foreign, usually Western, counterparts offer high-end armed protection to rich customers like the Chinese state-owned oil companies.

Economic and Social Dimension

Outside the grounds of embassies and consulates, though often supported by them, there are also "overseas Chinese service centers." According to some (e.g., Daum 2022), they are often made up of videoconferencing rooms established in chambers of commerce and other community areas, advertising the facilitation of activities such as various kinds of formal mediation with parties in China, license applications, and even remote physicals required for bureaucratic and employment purposes. They are heavily represented in countries with large numbers of long-term resident Chinese nationals and tourists. That said, while they all usually provide the same basic services as those just mentioned, if and how those stations carry out other activities is likely to be influenced by their connection with different Chinese institutions back home.

For example, some centers are affiliated with province-level public security authorities in China, though they are not staffed by policy officers and do not carry out investigation-related activities (Daum 2022). Others appear to be, in most cases, preexisting organizations that were later given a service center designation by the PRC State Council Overseas Chinese Affairs Office (merged into the Chinese Communist

Party's United Front Work Department in 2019) with the goal of ensuring that the Chinese diaspora overseas supports the policies adopted by the government on key issues like the reunification with Taiwan. The difficulty of fully categorizing the nature of those centers – official Chinese government organizations or private/semi-private initiatives? – and of their activities can be seen in the fact that, as in the South African case (Schrader 2019), they are often led by prominent members of the local Chinese community, such as established businessmen, while coordinating with or working on behalf of a variety of Chinese official institutions and organizations. This fact is also reflected in the significant variety of reactions that the work of these centers prompted from foreigners: while some foreign governments praised them for supporting the development of good relations between the Chinese diaspora and the local population, they have also come under fire for allegedly providing cover to attempts to repatriate Chinese citizens wanted by the government without the host country's authorization. Despite much indignation from politicians in Western countries, investigations carried out by authorities in Italy and the United Kingdom, for example, have been rather inclusive about the existence or actual activities of those centers (Foschini 2022; *The Guardian* 2023).

What is certain, however, is that China does have a program to bring back Chinese citizens accused of financial crimes and corruption. Various ministries are involved in the so-called "Operation Fox Hunt" and "Operation Sky Net," that have been recently consolidated together. Reportedly, high-level government officials and high-ranking party members who fled abroad are the priority of these actions, which are usually led by the Ministry of State Security and/or the Ministry of Public Security (Huang 2015), though the actual targets might include a more diverse group of people. In 2015, the Chinese authorities published a list of 100 of the most wanted suspects accused of corruption who had been targeted by an Interpol red notice, many of whom are living in the US, Canada, and Australia (Blanchard 2017). While sometimes these wanted citizens are extradited back to China in cooperation with the local government (Timmons 2015), many are also "persuaded" to return in ways that are often seen as illegal by the host country (Rotella and Berg 2021). The American authorities have often complained that their Chinese counterparts do not provide information about whom they are looking for and why, thereby fueling suspicions about China's actions.

In comparison, China's policies toward those who studied abroad, especially in the West, and are seen as possessing critical skills to support the development of the Chinese economy are far easier to understand. Figure 5.4 shows the flow of outgoing and returning Chinese students.

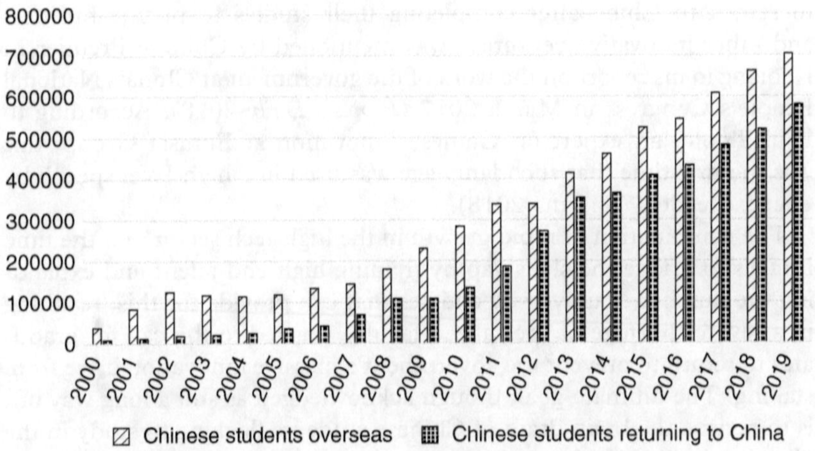

Figure 5.4 Chinese students overseas: coming and going
Source: Own depiction based on data from the National Bureau of Statistics of China.

David Zweig (2006) traces the origin of today's policies to bring Chinese nationals with foreign degrees and/or experience of working abroad up to March 1992, when the Ministry of Personnel announced a strategy to entice returnees back under the slogan of "improving services for returned students." The new policy included job introduction centers for returned students in Shenzhen, Shanghai and Fujian (five other cities had already established their own centers), as well as "preferential policies" like giving returnees more living space and higher professional titles, letting family members move to new cities where returnees found jobs, permitting students who had signed two- or three-year contracts with their research centers to switch jobs once their agreements expired, establishing a national association of returned students, and increasing support for scientific research.

Since then, Chinese leaders have affirmed on various occasions their support for Chinese students to travel overseas and, no less important, return to contribute to China's development. Attracting Chinese students back from abroad has become policy at the highest level of the Chinese government in a bid for world-class talent to fuel an innovation boom in the country as it moves away from reliance on manufacturing as its main engine of economic growth. This is a goal that often appears in Chinese official documents. For example, the intention to strengthen existing measures and new ones to "encourage overseas Chinese students to return to China after completing their studies to pursue business and other innovative ventures" was mentioned by Chinese Premier Li Keqiang in his report on the work of the government at China's National People's Congress in March 2017 (*People's Daily* 2018). According to Paul Triolo, an expert on Chinese innovation at Eurasia Group, this was the first time that such language was used in a high-level speech by Chinese leaders (Sharma 2018).

The combination of rapid growth in the high-tech sector and the time it takes to bridge the skills gap by training high-end talent and expanding the number of university courses that can provide for this, resulting in a severe shortage of specialized faculty, has led to the call for graduates to return to prevent the government's massive innovation drive from stalling. The ultimate goal, though acknowledged as still a long way off, is to reverse the brain drain of Chinese students flocking to study in the West, embodied by the many Chinese doctoral candidates who still prefer trying to build a career overseas than going back home.

The most important program established by the Chinese government to lure highly educated Chinese nationals back to China is the Thousand Talents Plan, which was established in 2008. Although the program also recognizes a small number of elite foreign-born experts with skills that are critical to China's international competitiveness in science and innovation, it primarily targets Chinese citizens who were educated in elite programs overseas and who have been successful as entrepreneurs, professionals, and researchers. Alongside this program, the Chinese government also created the Junior Thousand Talent Plan to attract faculty members under the age of forty who have carried out high-impact research at one of the world's top universities. Usually, the scholars who have been attracted back on this basis end up working in one of the so-called C9 universities in China – Fudan University, Harbin Institute of Technology, Nanjing University, Peking University, Shanghai Jiao Tong University, Tsinghua University, University of Science and Technology of China, Xi'an Jiaotong University, and Zhejiang University. As of 2011, these universities alone produced 20 percent of the nation's academic publications and 30 percent of total citations (Times Higher Education 2011). Such efforts have produced at least some results in terms of increased volume of publications by those scholars (Marini and Yang 2021), though issues remain as many of them prefer retaining their overseas affiliations and/or staying in China for short periods.

Beyond prestigious titles and large-scale research funding at top universities, the Chinese government has long been committed to incentivizing the entrepreneurship of the returnees through intellectual property-backed loans for start-up financing, a simpler process for trademark registration, optimized application procedures for export qualification, and support for the commercialization of R&D findings (*China Daily* 2018). At the local level, various cities and provinces in China have also long had their own individual policies such as providing subsidies and simpler immigration processes to attract Chinese nationals with foreign degrees or experience of working overseas (*People's Daily* 2022).

It is important to mention that other policies adopted by the Chinese government contribute indirectly to the return of Chinese students and experts from overseas as well. This is especially true in the case of Chinese nationals specialized in science, technology, engineering, and math-(STEM) related subjects (Bloomberg 2018), rather than the humanities (Fan 2017). Indeed, the government has long provided strong support for companies operating in sectors of the economy deemed of strategic interest. There is no doubt that the support has allowed them to offer above-average pay and packages, as well as better career prospects than those available to them in other countries (Thorne and Codd 2018). For example, as of 2018, team leaders in the Artificial Intelligence sector with three to five years of experience can earn over $237,000 annually (Qiu and Glenn 2018).

Security Dimension

When it comes to the use of the armed forces to protect Chinese nationals overseas, the first key development took place in late December 2008, when the first Chinese naval task force – two destroyers and one auxiliary ship – left Sanya in Hainan, South China, to join the international efforts against pirates in the Gulf of Aden. This was an especially important event for two reasons. Primarily, it represented the first Chinese military action specifically aimed at deterring threats to its interests overseas. Second, the rotation of the naval escorts is planned so as to guarantee a constant presence in a strategic part of the world where Chinese energy and economic interests and human presence are significant (Figures 5.5 and 5.6). Since the warships carry helicopters and special forces operators, Chinese policy-makers have the option to project limited military power on land. Nonetheless, it is important to emphasize that the Chinese warships' focus remains on deterring threats rather than actively seeking to neutralize them, despite the growing availability of modern warships, the accumulated experience, and the improved coordination with foreign navies over the years. They still do not enter Somali waters, as their Western counterparts do, and follow very restricted rules of engagement (Erickson and Strange 2015).

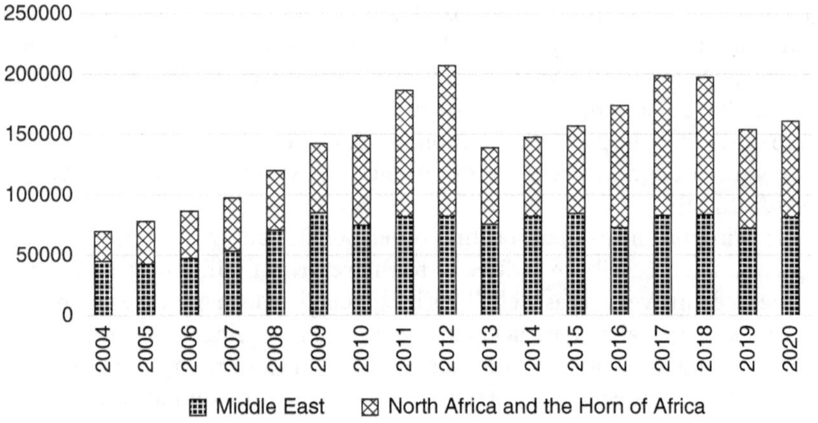

Figure 5.5 Number of Chinese workers in the Middle East, North Africa, and the Horn of Africa
Source: Own depiction based on data from the China Trade and External Economic Statistical Yearbook (various editions).

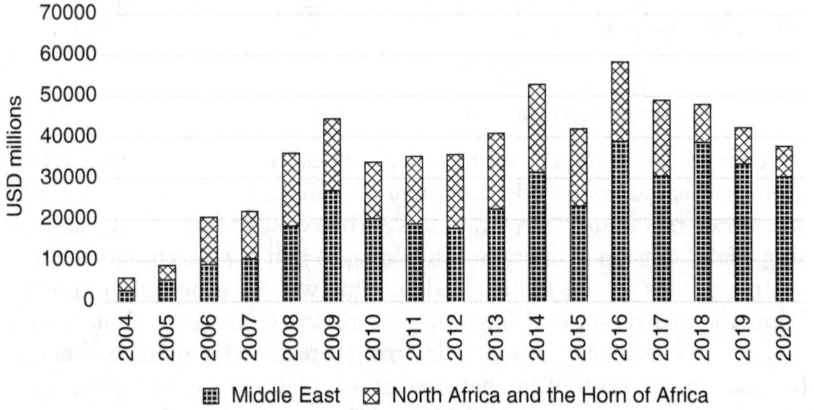

Figure 5.6 Value of the contracts won by Chinese construction and labor service companies in the Middle East, North Africa, and the Horn of Africa
Source: Own depiction based on data from the China Trade and External Economic Statistical Yearbook (various editions).

In 2011, the warships part of the antipiracy taskforce also supported the efforts to evacuate 36,000 Chinese nationals, mostly construction workers, from Libya. Many scholars identify that event as the main cause behind the acceleration in the securitization process that I described earlier in this chapter (Zerba 2014; Parello-Plesner and Duchâtel 2015; Ghiselli 2021). That event was indeed seen as a shock in China, with the newspaper of the PLA declaring that the Libyan crisis showed for the first time that China's "interest frontiers" (利益边疆, *Lìyì biānjiāng*) expanded well beyond Asia (Huang 2011). This is not surprising. Chinese companies were totally unprepared to face a crisis like this, despite the warnings and regulations of the ministries of commerce and foreign affairs, as pointed out by senior Chinese diplomats (Southern News Network 2011). The PLA managed to send the frigate *Xuzhou* to the Mediterranean in a timely manner simply because that ship coincidently had just completed replenishment in the Gulf of Aden when the orders arrived (Phoenix 2011). Moreover, the warship had no information about the situation onshore, as later admitted by its captain (Global Times 2017). The number of evacuees was six times more than the whole of the previous ten years. Moreover, the Chinese media reported that the companies involved in the crisis not only lost contracts worth US$18.8 billion in total, but also suffered losses of up to US$1.5 billion in machinery and facilities destroyed or damaged during the clashes and Western air raids (Southern News Network 2011).

The warships operating in the Gulf of Aden also played a more direct role in 2015 to evacuate Chinese nationals from Yemen by directly picking up evacuees. Yet, mirroring the Chinese government's great cautiousness in employing military means, they did so during a brief ceasefire, and Chinese soldiers simply established a small security perimeter on the wharf where the warships were docked.

Military efforts indirectly related to the protection of overseas interests took place between 2013 and 2015, when combat troops were deployed as part of the UN-led peacekeeping missions in Mali and South Sudan. On the one hand, those troops contribute to stabilizing countries in which China has economic interests or are bordering other countries where Chinese economic interests are significant. It is likely that China's offer to send combat troops to South Sudan played a role in the negotiations in 2014 that led to the inclusion of oil fields, mostly owned by Chinese companies, among the facilities protected by the peacekeeping mission (Lynch 2014). On the other hand, at least in South Sudan, Chinese peacekeepers coordinate with the Chinese embassy to provide medical services and protection for Chinese companies (*Xinhua* 2014). It is important to mention the fact that these actions were taken against the background of a growing emphasis in the Chinese Defense White Papers on the necessity for the military to play a more active role in the protection of the country's interests overseas. Indeed, while the 2013 white paper explicitly exhorted the military to "provide reliable security support for China's interests overseas" (PRC Information Office of the State Council 2013), the 2015 white paper listed the protection of China's interests overseas as one of the strategic tasks of the People's Liberation Army (PLA) (PRC Information Office of the State Council 2015). Moreover, the protection of the interests overseas has gained prominence in Chinese military doctrine as result of renewed emphasis on Military Operations Other Than War (MOOTW) since the publication of the 2013 edition of the authoritative *The Science of Military Science* (PLA Academy of Military Science – Strategic Research Department 2013).

However, the direct contribution of the peacekeepers to the protection of Chinese nationals and assets is extremely limited because they provide assistance only in case of emergency and within short distances from their base. For example, no soldier from the Chinese peacekeeping contingent was sent to help when seven Chinese nationals were kidnapped in Bamako, Mali, by jihadist groups in 2015 (*The Observer* 2015). Chinese peacekeepers in Sudan were forbidden to join the efforts to rescue twenty-nine Sinohydro employees from their kidnappers in 2012 (Cui and Wu 2012). Moreover, while South Sudanese Chinese-invested oil fields might be safer, they are not guarded by Chinese soldiers.

China opened its first and only military base overseas in Djibouti in 2017. When the Chinese government made the plans to open it public in 2015, the MFA spokesperson stated that the base would provide logistic support to the Chinese antipiracy and peacekeeping missions, previously mentioned (PRC Ministry of Foreign Affairs 2015). Yet, at the time of writing, no Chinese or foreign media has reported on whether any activity related to those missions has ever taken place.

In general, as outlined by experts, concerns about international reputation and the rising competition with the US have jointly contributed to make the extensive use of the military an unattractive option for policymakers in Beijing (Fung 2019; Ghiselli 2021; Kardon 2022), despite the growing capability of the PLA to project power in regions far away from China. This is also consistent with the cautious Chinese approach to private security companies mentioned earlier in this chapter.

Conclusion

This chapter analyzed the efforts made by the Chinese government to manage its many and diverse groups of citizens overseas. Over the past twenty years, the importance of protecting them has grown significantly as the Chinese definition of national security relaxed from a solely state-centric one to include the safety of the common citizens. Among the many Chinese traveling and living abroad, those working on construction projects have attracted special attention from their government, though it is impossible to discount the scale of the efforts made to lure back those citizens with skills and experience deemed of strategic importance for the Chinese economy. Similarly, the Chinese government has increasingly invested in finding new ways to bring back those citizens who are wanted by judicial and party disciplinary organs.

As shown, the drivers of Chinese actions and the priority accorded to them by the government have changed significantly over time. This is a natural outcome of the changes in Chinese economic development and domestic priorities, on the one hand, and the international situation, on the other. For example, the intensifying competition with the US undoubtedly shapes China's attempt to bring back educated elites who can help close the technological gap that separates it from its American rival. At the same time, China does not want to provoke the American military superpower and, thus, it is very cautious about its moves to protect its citizens (and economic interests) overseas. The features of its domestic political system also play a key role in shaping Chinese goals and the choices about the means to pursue them, as well as how other countries react to them. For example, while China's general approach to catch wanted citizens overseas surely mirrors the rule-by-law model that exists within its borders, the malign element of its intentions is certainly highlighted in its depictions in Western media and political debates.

Generally speaking, China's policies toward its citizens overseas are largely characterized by continuity. The quantity of resources devoted to them is what really changes. For example, when it comes to protecting Chinese nationals abroad, the authorities have continuously focused on crisis prevention, despite accidents in which Chinese nationals were among the victims and the growing number of economic, diplomatic, and military resources that could have been mobilized. Indeed, while the PLA is considered one of the actors that must contribute to the protection of Chinese nationals, its role is still secondary in comparison to China's law enforcement and security cooperation with other countries, as well as its efforts to improve its consular protection system. This approach has largely proven to be successful as China managed to evacuate its citizens from countries like Yemen, Iraq, and Ethiopia in an orderly manner. No Libya-like crisis has happened since 2011. Similarly, over time, the Chinese government has consistently invested in facilities to lure back elite citizens to support the economic and technological development of the country. These efforts have long been deemed essential and will continue to be seen as such.

That said, the Chinese approach is not perfect and is thus not immune to failure. As mentioned earlier, studies have shown that the warnings issued by the Chinese MFA and its embassies and consulates overseas usually fail to have any effect on the number of Chinese workers in foreign countries. This is something that has not changed even after the 2011 Libya crisis. Moreover, the consular protection system can also fail to act quickly enough, as shown in Ukraine in 2022, in the aftermath of the Russian attack (Ni 2022). The MFA has long been struggling to take care of all the cases of Chinese nationals in danger abroad. Were these problems to cause another massive crisis, a possible change in China's behavior might occur, perhaps as reform in the private security industry or, less likely, through a more active use of its security forces overseas.

As of time of writing, the number of Chinese tourists abroad is still recovering after the dramatic Covid-19 period (Girma 2024), and economic and geopolitical concerns have started to affect the interest and capability of Chinese youth to go abroad to study (Lin 2024). At the same time, the Chinese government's decreasing appetite for expensive project overseas might lead to a more permanent reduction in the number of Chinese workers abroad, especially in unstable regions of the world, thereby also leading to a decreasing demand for protection. In that scenario, China's policy is far less likely to change.

References

Alden, Chris, and Faten Aggad-Clerx (2021) *Chinese Investments and Employment Creation in Algeria and Egypt*. African Development Bank. Available at: www.afdb.org/fileadmin/uploads/afdb/Documents/Publications/Brochure%20China%20Anglais.pdf.

Benabdallah, Lina (2020) *Shaping the Future of Power: Knowledge Production and Network-Building in China-Africa Relations*. Ann Arbor, MI: University of Michigan Press.

Blanchard, Ben (2017) China Says Three of Most Wanted Graft Suspects Let Off. *Reuters*. May 11. Available at: www.reuters.com/article/china-corruption-idINKBN18705A.

Bloomberg (2018) Chinese Workers Abandon Silicon Valley for Riches Back Home. January 11. Available at: www.bloomberg.com/news/articles/2018-01-10/chinese-workers-abandon-silicon-valley-for-riches-back-home?leadSource=uverify%20wall.

Bueno De Mesquita, Bruce, and Alastair Smith (2010) Leader Survival, Revolutions, and the Nature of Government Finance. *American Journal of Political Science* 54(4), 936–950.

Carrozza, Ilaria, and Nicholas J. Marsh (2022) Great Power Competition and China's Security Assistance to Africa: Arms, Training, and Influence. *Journal of Global Security Studies* 7(4). Available at: https://doi.org/10.1093/jogss/ogac027.

China Daily (2007) 胡锦涛在党的十七大上的报告 (Hu Jintao's Report to the 17th National Congress of the CCP). October 25. Available at: www.chinadaily.com.cn/hqzg/2007-10/25/content_6205616_9.htm (in Chinese).

China Daily (2018) China Will Intensify Efforts to Encourage Return of Overseas Talent. April 4. Available at: https://global.chinadaily.com.cn/a/201804/04/WS5ac4e4e2a3105cdcf6516563.html.

China Daily (2022) Overseas Students Returning Home in Search of Better Career Prospects. September 6. Available at: https://global.chinadaily.com.cn/a/202209/06/WS63169212a310fd2b29e761ac.html.

Corkin, Lucy (2011) Redefining Foreign Policy Impulses toward Africa: The Roles of the MFA, the MOFCOM and China Exim Bank. *Journal of Current Chinese Affairs* 40(1), 61–90.

Daum, Jeremy (2022) "Overseas Police Stations?": A Clearer Look. China Law Translate. November 3. Available at: www.chinalawtranslate.com/overseas-police-stations-a-clearer-look/#_edn7.

Department of Trade and External Economic Relations Statistics; National Bureau Statistics (various years) 中国贸易外经统计年鉴 (*China Trade and External Economic Statistical Yearbook*). Beijing: China Statistics Press.

Department of Trade and External Economic Relations Statistics, National Bureau of Statistics (2008) *China Trade and Economic Statistical Yearbook*. Beijing: China Statistics Press.

Driessen, Miriam (2021) Chinese Workers in Ethiopia Caught between Remaining and Returning. *Pacific Affairs* 92(2), 329–346.

Erickson, Andrew S., and Austin M. Strange (2015) *Six Years at Sea … and Counting: Gulf of Aden Anti-piracy and China's Maritime Commons Presence*. Washington, DC: Jamestown Foundation.

Fan, Yiying (2017) Chinese Grads Return Home with Degrees and Disillusionment. *Sixth Tone*. November 10. Available at: www.sixthtone.com/news/1001154/chinese-grads-return-home-with-degrees-and-disillusionment.

Foschini, Giuliano (2022) Le stazioni di polizia cinesi in Italia sono fuori legge, Piantedosi: "Pronto a sanzionarli" (Chinese Police Stations Are Illegal, Piantendosi: "We Are Ready to Punish Them"). *La Repubblica*. December 7. Available at: www.repubblica.it/cronaca/2022/12/07/news/le_stazioni_di_polizia_cinesi_in_italia_sono_fuori_legge_piantedosi_pronto_a_sanzionarli-377967845/.

Fung, Courtney (2019) *China and Intervention at the UN Security Council: Reconciling Status*. Oxford: Oxford University Press.

Ghiselli, Andrea (2020) Market Opportunities and Political Responsibilities: The Difficult Development of Chinese Private Security Companies Abroad. *Armed Forces & Society* 46(1), 25–45.

Ghiselli, Andrea (2021) *Protecting China's Interests Overseas: Securitization and Foreign Policy*. Oxford: Oxford University Press.

Ghiselli, Andrea, and Pippa Morgan (2021a) A Turbulent Silk Road: China's Vulnerable Foreign Policy in the Middle East and North Africa. *China Quarterly* 247, 641–661.

Ghiselli, Andrea, and Pippa Morgan (2021b) Built by China: China's Global Economic and Human Presence beyond Aid and Investment. Unpublished manuscript.

Ghiselli, Andrea, and Pippa Morgan (2022) Building Legitimacy? The Role of Chinese Contract Workers in Foreign Regimes' Political Strategies. *Review of International Political Economy*. Latest articles. Available at: www.tandfonline.com/doi/abs/10.1080/09692290.2022.2127833?journalCode=rrip20.

Girma, Lebawit Lili (2024) Chinese Tourists Are Again Embracing International Travel. *Bloomberg*, April 24. Available at: www.bloomberg.com/news/articles/2024-04-24/chinese-tourists-are-again-embracing-international-travel-in-2024.

Global Times (2017) 利比亚撤侨舰长谈利比亚撤侨舰长谈《战狼2》:'中国海军不会像电影中那样反应迟缓！(The Captain That Participated in the Evacuation from Libya Discusses "Wolf Warrior 2": "The Navy Would Not React So Slowly Like in the Movie!), November 30. Available at: https://world.huanqiu.com/article/9CaKrnK4xU2 (in Chinese).

Huang, Keira Lu (2015) China Ramps Up Global Manhunt for Corrupt Officials with Operation 'Skynet'. *South China Morning Post*. March 26. Available at: www.scmp.com/news/article/1748113/china-ramps-global-manhunt-fugitive-corrupt-officials-skynet.

Huang, Kunlun (2011) 全球化时代的国家利益观 (Outlook on the National Interests in a Globalized Era). *PLA Daily*. March 15. Available at: http://mil.news.sina.com.cn/2011-03-15/0330637667.html (in Chinese).

Iacoella, Francesco, Bruno Martorano, Laura Metzger, and Marco Sanfilippo (2021) Chinese Official Finance and Political Participation in Africa. *European Economic Review* 136, doi.org/10.1016/j.euroecorev.2021.103741.

Kardon, Isaac (2022) China's Global Maritime Access: Alternatives to Overseas Military Bases in the Twenty-First Century. *Security Studies.*, doi.org/10.1080/09636412.2022.2137429.

Lai, Jingchao (2012) 外交部副司长：部分海外公民对政府提无理要求 (Deputy Director of the MFA: Some Overseas Citizens Make Unreasonable Demands on the Government). *Chinanews.com*. Available at: www.chinanews.com/gn/2012/04–25/3843849.shtml (in Chinese).

Li, Haibo (2012) 海外中国公民领事保护问题研究 *(1978–2011)* (*Research on China's Consular Protection (1979–2011)*). Guangzhou: Jinan University Press.

Li, Haipi (2016) 中国领事保护持续发展探析 (An Analysis of the Sustainable Development of China's Consular Protection). *Contemporary International Relations* 6, 9–14.

Lin, Ulrica (2024) China's International Students under Pressure as Economic Uncertainty Looms. *CNBC*, May 14. Available at: www.cnbc.com/2024/05/15/chinas-overseas-students-under-pressure-amid-economic-uncertainty.html.

Lowy Institute (2022) Global Diplomatic Index. Available at: https://globaldiplomacyindex.lowyinstitute.org/country_rank.html.

Lynch, Colum (2014) U.N. Peacekeepers to Protect China's Oil Interests in South Sudan. *Foreign Policy*. Available at: https://foreignpolicy.com/2014/06/16/u-n-peacekeepers-to-protect-chinas-oil-interests-in-south-sudan/.

Marini, Giulio, and Lili Yang (2021) Globally Bred Chinese Talents Returning Home: An Analysis of a Reverse Brain-Drain Flagship Policy. *Science and Public Policy* 4(48), 541–552.

Men, Honghua (2009) 要加强对中国海外利益的研究 (It Is Necessary to Boost the Research on China's Overseas Interests). *Study Times*. June 15. Available at: http://theory.people.com.cn/GB/136457/9472800.html (in Chinese).

Mueller, Joris (2022) China's Foreign Aid: Political Determinants and Economic Effects. *Working Paper*. Available at: www.jorismueller.com/files/chinaaid_latest_draft.pdf.

Murphy, Dawn C. (2022) *China's Rise in the Global South: The Middle East, Africa, and Beijing's Alternative World Order*. Stanford, CA: Stanford University Press.

National Bureau of Statistics of China. Available at: www.stats.gov.cn/tjsj/ndsj/2021/indexeh.htm.

Ni, Vincent (2022) 'It Came Too Late': Chinese Students Who Fled Ukraine Criticise Embassy Response. *The Guardian*. March 8. Available at: www.theguardian.com/world/2022/mar/08/chinese-students-fled-ukraine-condemn-embassy-response.

Parello-Plesner, Jonas, and Mathieu Duchâtel (2015) *China's Strong Arm: Protecting Citizens and Assets Abroad*. New York: Routledge.

People's Daily (2010) 戴秉国：所谓的中国的战略意图不想有些人想得那么复杂 (Dai Bingguo: The So-Called China's Strategy Is Not as Complex as Some People Think). December 7. Available at: http://politics.people.com.cn/GB/1026/13417139.html (in Chinese).

People's Daily (2018) Full Text: Report on the Work of the Government (2). April 3. Available at: http://en.people.cn/n3/2018/0403/c90000-9445262-2.html.

People's Daily (2022) China's Shenzhen Draws Returned Overseas Chinese Talent. April 14. Available at: http://en.people.cn/n3/2022/0414/c90000-10083785.html.

Phoenix (2011) 大撤侨也凸显中国软肋：徐州号上阵存在偶然因素 (The Evacuation Exposes China's Weakness: It Was Only by Chance That the *Xuzhou* Warship Was There), July 3. Available at: http://news.ifeng.com/mil/4/detail_2011_03/07/5012988_0.shtml (in Chinese).

PLA Academy of Military Science, Strategic Research Department (2013) 战略学 (*The Science of Military Strategy*). Beijing: Military Science Press.

PRC Information Office of the State Council (2004) China's National Defense in 2004. Available at: www.china.org.cn/e-white/20041227/I.htm.

PRC Information Office of the State Council (2008) China's National Defense in 2008. Available at: http://news.xinhuanet.com/english/2009-01/20/content_10688124.htm.

PRC Information Office of the State Council (2011) China's Peaceful Development. Available at: http://english1.english.gov.cn/official/2011-09/06/content_1941354.htm.

PRC Information Office of the State Council (2013) The Diversified Employment of China's Armed Forces. Available at: http://news.xinhuanet.com/english/china/2013-04/16/c_132312681.htm.

PRC Ministry of Commerce (2008) 对外承包工程管理条例 (Administrative Regulation on Contracting Foreign Projects). Available at: www.mofcom.gov.cn/article/swfg/swfgbi/201101/20110107352097.shtml (in Chinese).

PRC Ministry of Foreign Affairs (2002) China's Position Paper on the New Security Concept, 2002. Available at: www.fmprc.gov.cn/mfa_eng/wjb_663304/zzjg_663340/gjs_665170/gjzzyhy_665174/2612_665212/2614_665216/t15319.shtml.

PRC Ministry of Foreign Affairs (2015) Foreign Ministry Spokesperson Hong Lei's Regular Press Conference on November 11, 2015. November 11. Available at: www.mfa.gov.cn/ce/cohk//eng/xwdt/wjbt/t1313996.htm.

PRC Ministry of Foreign Affairs (2022) President Xi Jinping Meets with Pakistani Prime Minister Muhammad Shehbaz Sharif. November 2. Available at: www.fmprc.gov.cn/mfa_eng/zxxx_662805/202211/t20221102_10797417.html.

PRC National People's Congress (2018) 中华人民共和国反恐怖主义法 (PRC Antiterrorism Law). December 6. Available at: www.npc.gov.cn/zgrdw/npc/xinwen/2018-06/12/content_2055871.htm (in Chinese).

PRC State Council (2020) China, Tajikistan to Improve Security, Law Enforcement Cooperation. Available at: http://english.www.gov.cn/statecouncil/zhaokezhi/202009/18/content_WS5f63e7b7c6d0f7257693c274.html.

Qiu, Stella, and Elias Glenn (2018) Chinese Tech Firms Narrowing Pay Gap with Silicon Valley as State Pours Money into IT, Surveillance. *Japan Times*. January 25. Available at: www.japantimes.co.jp/news/2018/01/25/business/tech/chinese-tech-firms-narrowing-pay-gap-silicon-valley-state-pours-money-surveillance.

Rotella, Sebastian, and Kirsten Berg (2021) "Operation Fox Hunt: How China Exports Repression Using a Network of Spies Hidden in Plain Sight. *ProPublica*. July 22. Available at: www.propublica.org/article/operation-fox-hunt-how-china-exports-repression-using-a-network-of-spies-hidden-in-plain-sight.

Schrader, Matt (2019) "Chinese Assistance Centers" Grow United Front Work Department Global Presence. *China Brief* 19(1), 1–5.

Sharma, Yojama (2018) Luring Back Talent Is Top Priority to Fuel Innovation. *University World News*. March 8. Available at: www.universityworldnews.com/post.php?story=20180308174428919.

Song, Zhifang (2019) Global Chinese Diaspora. In Steven Ratuva (ed.), *The Palgrave Handbook of Ethnicity*. London: Palgrave Macmillan, 1167–1183.

Southern News Network (2011) 中国企业在利比亚资产达188亿美元 损失难估量 (Chinese Companies Lost Contracts Worth USD 18 Billion, It Is Difficult to Assess the Damage). April 24. Available at: http://finance.huanqiu.com/roll/2011-03/1584398.html (in Chinese).

The Guardian (2023) China Has Closed Unofficial 'Police Stations' in Britain, UK Minister Says. June 6. Available at: www.theguardian.com/world/2023/jun/07/china-has-closed-unofficial-police-stations-in-britain-uk-minister-says#:~:text=3%20months%20old-,China%20has%20closed%20unofficial%20'police%20stations,in%20Britain%2C%20UK%20minister%20says&text=The%20UK%20security%20minister%2C%20Tom,Chinese%20state%20at%20these%20sites.

The News (2020) Law Enforcement: China Ready to Boost Cooperation with Pakistan. September 9. Available at: www.thenews.com.pk/print/712293-law-enforcement-china-ready-to-boost-cooperation-with-pakistan.

The Observer (2015) 马里恐袭3名中国人遇害 中国维和部队为什么不去救? (Three Chinese Killed during a Terrorist Attack in Mali, Why Did the Chinese Peacekeepers Not Go to Save Them?). November 21. Available at: www.guancha.cn/Third-World/2015_11_21_342088.shtml (in Chinese).

Thorne, Sharon, and Emma Cod (2018) How China Is Winning Back More Graduates from Foreign Universities Than Ever Before. *Forbes*. January

25. Available at: www.forbes.com/sites/ljkelly/2018/01/25/how-china-is-winning-back-more-graduates-from-foreign-universities-than-ever-before/?sh=659aba875c1e.

Times Higher Education (2011) Eastern Stars: Universities of China's C9 League Excel in Select Fields. February 17. Available at: www.timeshighereducation.com/news/eastern-stars-universities-of-chinas-c9-league-excel-in-select-fields/415193.article?storyCode=415193&sectioncode=26.

Timmons, Heather (2015) China's "Operation Fox Hunt" Just Bagged a Trophy in Italy. *Quartz*. February 4. Available at: https://qz.com/338634/chinas-operation-fox-hunt-just-bagged-an-economic-fugitive-in-italy.

United Nations Department of Economic and Social Affairs – Population Division (2020) *International Migrant Stock*. Available at: www.un.org/development/desa/pd/content/international-migrant-stock.

World Bank (2022) International Tourism, Number of Departures – China. Available at: https://data.worldbank.org/indicator/ST.INT.DPRT?locations=CN.

Wright, Joseph, Erica Frantz, and Barbara Geddes (2015) Oil and Autocratic Regime Survival. *British Journal of Political Science* 45(2), 287–306.

Wu, Wenbin, and Tongchen Cui (2012) 中国驻苏维和部队官兵辩证看待华工被劫事件 (Chinese Peacekeepers in Sudan Look at the Kidnapping of Chinese Workers Dialectically). *Jiangsu Daily*. February 6. Available at: http://js.people.com.cn/html/2012/02/06/75416.html (in Chinese).

Xia, Liping (2016) 中国领事保护需求与外交投入的矛盾及解决方式 (On the Contradiction of the Chinese Consular Protection Service and Diplomatic Input and Its Solutions). *Journal of International Studies* 4, 10–25.

Xia, Liping (2021) Consular Protection with Chinese Characteristics: Challenges and Solutions. *The Hague Journal of Diplomacy* 16(2–3), 253–276.

Xiang, Wenhui (2017) 中国的海外公民保护 – 战略实施、制约因素及策略应对 (The Protection of Chinese Citizens Abroad: Strategic Measures, Constraints, and Policy Responses). *Global Review* 4, 87–103.

Xinhua (2012) 十八大报告 (Report to the 18th National Congress of the CCP). November 8. Available at: www.xj.xinhuanet.com/2012-11/19/c_113722546.htm (in Chinese).

Xinhua (2014) 中国维和部队积极应对南苏丹紧张局势履 行维和义务 (Chinese Peacekeepers Actively Respond to Tensions in South Sudan Fulfilling Their Duty). January 3. Available at: www.gov.cn/jrzg/2014-01/03/content_2559512.htm (in Chinese).

Xinhua (2018) China to Enhance Cooperation on Law Enforcement Security with Other SCO Countries, May 22. Available at: www.xinhuanet.com/english/2018-05/22/c_137195896.htm.

Xinhua (2020a) China, Serbia to Enhance Cooperation on Law Enforcement, Security. May 21.

Xinhua (2020b) Senior Officials of China, Myanmar Meet on Law-Enforcement Cooperation. May 8. Available at: www.xinhuanet.com/english/2018-05/09/c_137164815.htm.

Xinhua (2021) China, Ethiopia Ink Accord on Establishing Security Safeguarding Mechanism for Major Projects under BRI. March 7. Available at: www.xinhuanet.com/english/2021-03/07/c_139792150.htm.

Yang, Yang (2013) 中国领事保护中存在的问题及对策 (The Problems of China's Consular Protection System and Solutions). *Journal of International Studies* 2, 17–29 [in Chinese].

Zerba, Shaio H. (2014) China's Libya Evacuation Operation: A New Diplomatic Imperative – Overseas Citizen Protection. *Journal of Contemporary China* 23(90), 1093–1112.

Zhang, Lantao (2004) 关于"和平崛起"与新安全观的理论思考 (Thoughts about "Peaceful Rise" and the New Security Concept). *Journal of the University of International Relations* 5, 6–9.

Zweig, David (2006) Competing for Talent: China's Strategies to Reverse the Brain Drain. *International Labor Review* 145(1–2), 65–90.

6 Pakistan

Tapping into Its Diasporas' Economic Potential

Sahar Khan

Introduction

As Pakistanis move all over the world and diaspora communities continue to grow and flourish, the Pakistani government sees an opportunity to enhance its public image and further its foreign policy goals. Pakistan's foreign policy interests are centered around having stronger bilateral relations with Saudi Arabia, the United Arab Emirates, the United Kingdom, the United States, and Canada, which are also consequently the countries with the largest Pakistani diasporas.

Pakistani governments have always played an active role in protecting its citizens abroad, but technological advancements, democratization, and a politically active public are compelling the current government to do more. The best example of this was former prime minister Imran Khan's quest to make online voting accessible, where overseas Pakistanis no longer have to fly to Pakistan to cast their vote in any election but instead can vote via different apps. While still an emerging – and very contentious – domain (Atlantic Council 2022), for the first time, those living outside of Pakistan have power and the potential to actively participate in domestic politics without having to live in the country.

As this chapter highlights, Pakistan is undergoing a brain drain despite Pakistanis facing a variety of visa restrictions worldwide. Not to lose out completely, the Pakistani government has been engaged in various diplomatic, consular, economic, and social activities to harness the potential of its citizens abroad. Pakistan supports its national community abroad by creating avenues by which the state can export manpower overseas and engages in co-optation strategies that allow the state to harness the economic potential of those living outside the country. While repression of religious minorities, especially the Ahmadiyya Muslim community, is a grim reality within Pakistan (Thames 2021), the state's reach of repression is limited.

This chapter has three important findings. The first is that the activities carried out by the Pakistani government for its overseas citizens is essentially a civilian project where the military has been minimally involved. Second, remittances have become increasingly important for Pakistan's economy, shaping how political parties think – and consequently prioritize – their overseas citizens. And third, while there have been no instances where the Pakistani military has engaged in military activities to protect its citizens abroad, the armed forces media wing, Inter Services Public Relations (ISPR), has been concentrating on changing the image of the military for both the domestic public and diaspora communities (ISPR n.d.). This chapter highlights why ISPR's increasing focus on the national community abroad is a natural outcome and important for understanding the Pakistani military's nuanced role in the country's economy and politics. Overseas Pakistanis have become an essential economic bloc that the country relies on and is impacting the country's democratization, foreign relations, and economy.

Overview of the Pakistani Community Abroad

The United Nations International Migration Stock is obtained from national statistics, mainly population censuses, and estimated that in 2020, over 6 million Pakistanis lived abroad (the exact number is 6,328,400). According to the Pakistan's Ministry of Overseas Pakistanis and Human Resource Development *Year Book 2020–2021*, 8.4 million Pakistanis were living outside the country (MOPHRD 2021: 10). Pakistan conducted its last census in 2017, which is what the UN International Migration Stock relies on, but the MOPHRD *Year Book* (2020–2021) collects data from Pakistan's diplomatic missions abroad through the Ministry of Foreign Affairs, and hence, is likely to be more accurate. Furthermore, Pakistan's 2017 census did not include overseas Pakistanis and received criticism for not doing so (Gul 2017; *Dawn* 2017). As of this writing, there is no discussion on when the next census will be and whether or not it will include overseas Pakistanis. The number of overseas Pakistanis is expected to grow as the global economy tries to recover from the negative economic impact of the Covid-19 pandemic (International Labour Organization 2022). As the world's fifth-most populous country with 229.5 million people, 3.5–4 percent of its population is currently abroad.

According to the Migrant Resource Center, Pakistanis live in 115 countries (Migrant Resource Center 2022a). The "Net Migration" World Bank data shows Pakistan had a net migration of −1,574,581 in 2017, −1,647,986 in 2012, −563,471 in 2007, −834,546 in 2002, 151,546 in 1997, and −1,320,633 in 1992 (World Bank 2022a). The top five countries where Pakistanis are living abroad is as shown in Table 6.1.

Table 6.1 *Top destination countries of Pakistani migrants*

Country of migration	Number of overseas Pakistanis
Saudi Arabia	2,300,000
United Arab Emirates	1,600,000
United States	1,200,000
United Kingdom	1,175,000
Canada	223,000

Source: Government of Pakistan Ministry of Overseas Pakistanis and Human Resource Development *Year Book 2020–2021* (MOPHRD 2021: 57).

In 2021, there were 2.3 million Pakistani expatriates living in Saudi Arabia. This number does not include Pakistani military officers and cadets who are stationed in Saudi Arabia. Pakistan and Saudi Arabia have a strong defense and security relationship, where Pakistani military officers, like the Pakistan Air Force pilots, train their Saudi counterparts. In essence, the Saudi military would have serious capacity issues without the training support of the Pakistani military (Hincks 2019). While this particular angle lies outside the scope of this chapter, the presence of the Pakistani military in Saudi Arabia has some broader impacts on Pakistani migrant workers and other overseas Pakistanis, which is discussed later in the chapter.

Over the years, the Kingdom has consistently been the largest market for unskilled Pakistani workers, especially in construction (Global Media Insight 2022). Migration from South Asia has been consistent even before the Partition of India in 1947, where small communities existed and facilitated trade between the subcontinent and East Africa. About a decade after Partition, Pakistanis began migrating to Saudi Arabia to work for oil companies like Aramco. By 1956, 7 percent of Aramco's workers were from Pakistan, and by 1972, approximately 40,000 Pakistanis were employed in Gulf countries (Addleton 1981: 321). After the UAE was formed in 1972, the oil boom made it an attractive destination for Pakistanis and before the Covid-19 pandemic, there were 1.2 million Pakistanis working in construction, banking, waste management, and universities there (De Bel-Air 2018). In the last two decades, many Pakistani men with higher education than the national average have been going to Saudi Arabia and the UAE on fixed-term contracts, typically of two to four years, and returning after four to five years (Erdal 2015), though the UAE, especially Dubai, is the preferred destination of migration for many Pakistanis (Errichiello and Nyhagen 2021). The Pakistani government, however, has restricted the migration of female workers due to accounts of harassment and abuse (Mahdavi 2011; Zahra 2019).

Pakistani diaspora communities in the US, the UK, and Canada consist of both unskilled and skilled workers. The US census numbers show 550,000 Pakistanis living in the US, but informal estimates go up to over a million (Budiman 2021). The diaspora community is concentrated in major population centers like New York City, Washington, Houston, Chicago, Dallas, Los Angeles, San Francisco, Baltimore, Philadelphia, and Atlanta, with the largest numbers in the states of New York, Texas, and California. Pakistani migration to the US remained low until the introduction of the 1965 U.S. Immigration and Naturalization Act (Chaudhary et al. 2021).

According to the 2021 census of the UK, Pakistanis are 2.7 percent of England and Wales population (Office of National Statistics 2022). But Pakistani migration to the UK is a direct result of British colonial rule, and hence impacts the social, cultural, and economic roots of migration there (Harris and Shaw 2007; BBC 2014). Since Pakistan was part of the Commonwealth, the barriers to entry were considerably low but the Commonwealth Immigration Act of 1962 and 1968 and the Immigration Act of 1971 restricted any primary immigration to the UK, though family members of already settled immigrants were allowed to join their relatives (The National Archives). However, the Pakistani diaspora in the UK is an integral part of British society, especially in the National Health Service, where Pakistanis currently make up the third largest group of doctors (after the UK and India) (Baker 2022).

For Pakistanis, immigrating to Canada has been less complicated than trying to enter into the US and the UK. Even though Canada ranks fifth on the list of overseas Pakistanis, it is home to some of the largest Pakistani diaspora communities, especially inside and outside of Toronto (Heritage Toronto 2012). High-skilled Pakistani professionals are attracted to Canada because the country's Express Entry Program has streamlined the immigration process (Husain 2022). However, with respect to remittances, Canada is not amongst the top five.

The growth of Pakistani diasporas has led to two important developments. The first is a brain drain (Farooq and Ahmad 2017; Laila and Faiz 2018). As a developing country, Pakistan is no stranger to brain drain, but as the country's population grows and lives through its youth bulge (e.g., it is the fifth most populous country in the world, and 55 percent of Pakistanis are under the age of 25) (United States Institute of Peace 2018), the brain drain greatly impacts the country's economic

Table 6.2 *Top countries sending remittances to Pakistan*

Country of migration	Amount of remittances (million US$)
Saudi Arabia	7667
United Arab Emirates	6114
United Kingdom	4067.1
Other Gulf Cooperation Council countries	3309.9
United States	2754.2

Source: Government of Pakistan Ministry of Overseas Pakistanis and Human Resource Development *Year Book 2020–2021* (MOPHRD 2021). "Other Gulf Cooperation Council countries" consist of Bahrain, Kuwait, Qatar, and Oman.

growth (Rehman 2022; Ahmed 2022). The second factor is that as the number of overseas Pakistanis have grown, so has the size of their remittances – and its impact. For Pakistan, according to MOPHRD *Year Book 2017–2018*, remittances were the second largest source of national foreign exchange after exports (MOPHRD 2018: 13). In the MOPHRD *Year Book 2020–2021*, remittances are recorded as the largest source of national foreign exchange (MOPHRD 2021: 14).

The World Bank's "Personal Remittances, Received" data indicates that Pakistan has experienced an increase in remittances every year since 2004, and in 2021, Pakistan received $31.31 billion in remittances. According to the Pew Research Center's "Remittance Flows Worldwide in 2017" interaction, Pakistan received $19.66 billion in remittances from other countries in 2017 (Pakistan to India and India to Pakistan is not available). The top countries sending remittances are presented in Table 6.2.

In the fiscal year 2020–2021, Pakistan received $29.4 billion in remittances compared to $23.3 billion in the fiscal year 2019–2020, showing an increase during the Covid-19 pandemic. For example, during March–July 2021, Pakistan experienced a 26 percent growth in remittances when compared to March–July 2020 (Ministry of Planning, Development and Special Initiatives 2021). The additional money during the pandemic pulled the country from the brink of a balance-of-payment crisis, though it is important to note that Pakistan's economy remains weak and is facing several problems. While remittances fell by 6.6 percent in November 2021, they grew by almost 10 percent in the four-month period preceding it (Haider 2021). However, in 2022, remittances fell substantially.

According to the State Bank of Pakistan, during July–October 2022, remittances from Saudi Arabia, the UAE, and the UK fell by 11.7, 9.2, and 8.3 percent, respectively. This decline is due to three reasons. First, the number of expatriate Pakistanis working in Saudi Arabia, from where

Pakistan receives the most remittances, has declined because expatriate workers from other countries, especially India, are outnumbering them in professional and managerial jobs. Second, Covid-19 restrictions made it difficult for Pakistani citizens to get visas in all three countries, hampering their ability to travel, earn, and send remittances back home. And third, Pakistan's financial investment environment is not as attractive or stable as the environments of Saudi Arabia, the UAE, and the UK (Aazim 2022).

The Pakistani government has always been aware of the ongoing impact of brain drain on the country's economy. The civilian government has taken several measures to address this downward trend by developing various diplomatic and consular activities that are centered around economic incentives and social programs.

Diplomatic and Consular Dimension

The Ministry of Overseas Pakistanis and Human Resource Development (MOPHRD) was established in 2013 to meet the needs of the national community abroad worldwide. It was formed by the merger of the Ministry of Human Resource Development and the Ministry of Overseas Pakistanis. The MOPHRD was set up to "deal with all matters and affairs of the overseas Pakistanis; attending to their needs and problems, initiating schemes and projects for their welfare and working for the resolution of their problems and issues" (MOPHRD 2021: 1). One of the ministry's main goals is to promote export of Pakistani manpower abroad and elevate the living conditions of the working class through better protection and decent working conditions for them.

The MOPHRD has been designed to create an atmosphere of transparency, efficiency, and innovation for improved services for overseas Pakistanis and has articulated thirteen objectives centered around these principles. It also concentrates on the rehabilitation and reintegration of returning overseas Pakistanis and taking measures for the protection of their investments, along with securing emigration for workers and ensuring the provision of social protection and decent working conditions. Finally, the MOPHRD includes the preparation of special incentives for the Pakistani diasporas to participate in national development and growth. As such, the official vision on the ministry's website is: "Prosperous Human Resource; Prosperous Pakistan," while its mission is stated as: "Efforts to enhance employment opportunities abroad and to ensure their welfare; provide decent working conditions and social protection to workers in Pakistan."

The MOPHRD also oversees the welfare of overseas Pakistanis and their dependents in Pakistan and conducts a periodic assessment, review, and analysis of manpower resources and employment requirements abroad. The ministry, therefore, plays a central role in the creation of national policy, planning, and coordination of "manpower development" and "employment promotion of overseas workers." For example, the inaugural "National Emigration Welfare Policy for Overseas Pakistanis," which was initiated in 2013, included major policy objectives such as addressing irregularities in the emigration process and exploitation of overseas Pakistanis and key in prospective migrants in order to promote safe, orderly, and regular emigration; monitor labor demand, skills, and competency; facilitate the use of remittance; and facilitate reintegration for returnees (International Labour Organization 2013).

The Pakistan government's diplomatic activities related to protecting its citizens abroad has also included a variety of agreements, such as bilateral memoranda of understanding (Ministry of Foreign Affairs 2022), signing recruitments agreements, establishing protectorate offices abroad, streamlining the issue of licenses, creating task forces to troubleshoot challenges facing overseas Pakistanis (including but limited to imprisonment), participating in seminars, and so on.

The MOPHRD is in the process of establishing two new "Protectorate Offices" at Abbottabad and Sukkur under the Ehsaas ("feeling") Program to enhance the geographical outreach of "Protectorates of Emigrants Offices" (MOPHRD 2021: 16). The Ehsaas program is a social safety and poverty alleviation program that was launched in March 2019 under Pakistan's Tehrik-e-Insaf's government to alleviate poverty. The program was one of the campaign promises made by Prime Minister Khan. It provides a set of services such as targeted subsidies, increased health coverage, and unlimited cash transfers, which are especially beneficial to Pakistanis living abroad who want to send large sums of money back home (Barber and Shahzad 2022). Since many Pakistanis from rural areas go to Gulf States to earn a better living and hence send remittances, these offices are being developed to streamline the process.

Setting up protectorate offices has facilitated the issuing of Overseas Employment Promoter Licenses. An Overseas Employment Promoter (OEP) "is one who desires to engage, or to assist or to recruit any person to emigrate shall apply for a license to the Federal Government and shall with his application furnish such information and documents, pay security and fee, and at such time and in such manner as may be prescribed" (Bureau of Emigration and Overseas Employment 2022). These promotors play a vital role in connecting the private and public sectors and in ensuring that countries that have a high demand for manpower, such as Gulf states, hire Pakistanis. According to the MOPHRD, 2,314 valid license-holder OEPs are currently operational, and from July 2020 to June 2021, 139 new licenses were given (MOPHRD 2021: 16). The MOPHRD will also set up special courts to process these licenses quickly (*Express Tribune* 2022). OEPs, however, are frustrated with the current licensing process and have identified the weak regulation of recruiters and companies and the lack of political will of both the Pakistani and Saudi governments to address and mediate problems between companies and the migrants they hire (Babar 2020). The Inter-Ministerial Taskforce on Overseas Employment and Welfare of Overseas Pakistanis has also been constituted by Economic Coordination Committee to facilitate overseas employment, provide relief to overseas workers and organize the system of Pakistani schools abroad for the welfare of the overseas Pakistanis.

Another important diplomatic dimension has been prisoner exchanges. In 2019, the Justice Project Pakistan reported that 11,000 Pakistanis are suffering in foreign jails and 3,309 are jailed in Saudi Arabia. The report highlighted gaps that are exploited by unauthorized intermediaries and recruiters who operate illegally alongside OEPs and called on the Pakistani government to improve the coordination between state authorities, provide consular assistance to Pakistanis who are languishing in foreign jails, and actively work toward preventing the over-criminalization of migrant workers and other overseas Pakistanis (Justice Peace Project 2019). In 2022, research indicated that 12,000 Pakistanis were in jail, most of them in Saudi Arabia and the US (Gishkori 2022). Pakistan has prisoner-exchange agreements with several countries, including the top five countries where overseas Pakistanis reside: Saudi Arabia, the UAE, the US, UK, and Canada.

Prisoner-exchange agreements and treaties are handled by both the Ministry of Foreign Affairs and the Ministry of Overseas Pakistanis and Human Resource Development and debated in the Senate (Senate Standing Committee on Overseas Pakistanis and Human Resource Development 2019). However, most exchanges are done piecemeal. For example, in 2019, the Kingdom released 200 prisoners and in 2019, 2,000 were released (*Dawn* 2021). The terms of the release/exchange are rarely stated, which adds to the lack of transparency when it comes to studying migrant workers and the challenges they face. Sometimes, prisoner-exchange agreements are stalled, as is the current case with the UK, where the British government wants Pakistanis convicted in British courts to serve their sentences when transferred to Pakistan. Instead, Pakistanis from the UK are transferred to Thailand, where drug convictions are inflexible (Kamal 2019).

The MOPHRD is also engaged in a variety of consular activities. Under Section 7 of Emigration Ordinance 1979, the Federal

Government of Pakistan may appoint a Labor Attaché, also called a Community Welfare Attaché, in a place outside Pakistan and may define his or her duties. The main goals of the Community Welfare Attaché involve the safeguarding of the interests of emigrants and promoting overseas employment. There are 24 posts of Community Welfare Attachés in 16 countries at 18 Pakistan Missions abroad, including recently created posts of Community Welfare Attachés along with supporting staff, each one at Riyadh, Jeddah, Doha, Pretoria, and Tokyo. These attachés are posted for three years (MOPHRD 2021: 50–53, 58).

The complaint department is led by the Deputy Secretary of Administration and falls under the administrative wing of the MOPHRD. The Deputy Secretary of Administration works with the Joint Secretary of the Ministry when it comes to complaints and they report to the Secretary of the Ministry, who is appointed by Parliament. After receiving a complaint from a migrant or a family member in Pakistan, the grievances are taken up by the appropriate Community Welfare Attachés or directly by the Overseas Pakistani Foundation, which is overseen by the MOPHRD. During the 2017–2018 fiscal year, the Community Welfare Attachés received 450 complaints, forwarded 286 to the Overseas Pakistani Foundation, and resolved 115, but 355 still remained pending, stuck in the resolution process. In the fiscal year 2020–2021, 5,103 complaints were received and all were resolved (MOPHRD 2021: 9).

The Special Assistant to the Prime Minister on Overseas Pakistanis and Human Resource Development has ordered that the Overseas Pakistani Advisory Council – made up of fifty Pakistani volunteers living overseas – be reactivated to address the needs of expatriates. The council comprises of Pakistanis who have contributed substantially to the cause of Pakistan and overseas Pakistanis, such as philanthropists, technocrats, social workers, businessmen, and so on. The members are tasked with communicating Pakistani diaspora needs in the host country to the relevant boards in Pakistan. They also submit policy proposals and suggestions regarding the welfare of overseas citizens (Migrant Resource Center 2022).

The ongoing war in Ukraine following Russia's invasion of the country is a good illustration of how the Pakistani government dealt with its citizens facing a precarious turn of events via social media. When Russia invaded Ukraine on February 24, 2022, approximately 3,000 Pakistani students were residing there. The Pakistan Embassy in Ukraine used social media (Pakistan Embassy Ukraine 2022), especially Twitter, to make announcements about evacuations, which routes were safe to use, and when and from where the embassy would be operating from as the war intensified. The Pakistan Embassy in Ukraine also coordinated with its neighboring counterparts in Hungary, Romania, and Poland to safely evacuate its citizens and embassy staff (*Express Tribune* 2022b; AP News 2022). As the war continues, Pakistani students studying in Ukraine feel stranded, with several stating that the government should try to assist them in continuing their studies, either in Pakistan by urging local universities to provide special admissions or by facilitating their travel elsewhere. For now, the government maintains that there is not much it can do for the students (Khan 2022). It is important to note that the Pakistani military was not involved in the evacuations. Instead, the government used Pakistan International Airlines to airlift Pakistanis out of Ukraine (Aaj News 2022). At the time of writing, there is insufficient research on whether or not social media has impacted consular services.

It is important to note that while Pakistan has been notorious for sponsoring militant groups and has struggled with holding known militant groups operating within its borders accountable, there is no open-source information on whether or not the government has ever outsourced certain activities related to the physical security of overseas Pakistanis. In other words, the Pakistani government claims sole responsibility for protecting its citizens abroad. This lack of "outsourcing" may prove to be a positive development for Pakistan and its national community abroad as it allows the state to learn from how other countries deal with citizens abroad as the number of overseas Pakistanis increase. Pakistan's approach to diplomatic and consular support is still elementary, unlike India's or Egypt's (see Blarel and Norman, Chapters 2 and 11, respectively). Both India and Egypt have sizable diaspora communities, which have allowed both states to develop customized services. As Pakistan's national community abroad grows, it will need to do the same.

Economic and Social Dimension

Remittances have been a vital economic source for Pakistan. Prime Minister Imran Khan's administration identified Saudi Arabia, the UAE, Malaysia, Qatar, and Oman as priority countries and Kuwait, South Korea, Japan, Germany, and China as new countries for the diversification of manpower export and actively coordinating with relevant stakeholders to achieve the set targets. As such, the prime minister constituted the Economic Outreach Coordination Group to better coordinate relations with each state (Ahmed 2022). In line with this emphasis on "economic diplomacy," Pakistan has negotiated a bilateral memorandum of understanding with Kuwait that is focused on hiring skilled, semi-skilled, and unskilled Pakistani manpower in health, education, agriculture, and construction in Kuwait (PT Profit 2019). In 2020, similar agreements were signed with Malaysia (Khan 2019) and Turkey (Radio Pakistan 2022). Engagement with Malaysia has also included a technical meeting between MOPHRD and the Social Security Organization of the Government of Malaysia – the first of its kind between the two countries – that took place on May 25, 2021. It centers on increasing cooperation and promoting social security programs and activities for Pakistani citizens insured in Malaysia. Regarding relations with Japan, the MOPHRD organized a seminar titled, "Highlight Potential of Manpower Export to Japan in Information Technology Sector," on December 17, 2020, which was part of an initiative that began in 2016 (Embassy of Pakistan Tokyo 2016).

The majority of Pakistanis in Saudi Arabia and the UAE are considered unskilled workers and are commonly known as "migrant workers." Pakistani migrant workers face a host of challenges. For example, many migrants fall into debt when trying to migrate and their efforts to repay the costs of migration hinder their ability to send remittances back home (Khan, Tippu, and Ali 2021). They face a series of human rights abuses, especially those who are held in Saudi detention centers after the Kingdom conducts sweeps to vet undocumented workers (Human Rights Watch 2020). Thousands of Pakistani workers have died, but there is a serious lack of transparency when it comes to migrant worker deaths. A report by The Vital Signs Partnership (2022), a group of organizations that campaigns for the rights of low-paid migrant workers in the Gulf States, emphasized the lack of transparency when it comes to migrant workers. The report states that between 2008 and 2021, about 6,500 insurance claims for Pakistani migrant workers were filed by their families. Since insurance is mandatory for all workers, insurance claims are a feasible way to approximate the number of Pakistani migrant deaths in the Gulf. The data, however, does include claims made by pilgrims (to the holy sites in Saudi Arabia) and tourists, but is not broken down by country and is mainly provided by nongovernmental organizations (Vital Signs 2022: 17–18, 26).

Saudi Arabia is eager to attract – and eventually increase – skilled labor from Pakistan and the countries signed two agreements: The Agreement on Workers' Recruitment and The Agreement on Skills Verification. Pakistan's Ministry of Foreign Affairs (2021) described the Workers' Recruitment Agreement as "streamlining the process of export of workforce from Pakistan in diverse professions in the Kingdom while safeguarding their due rights and providing comprehensive legal protection to Pakistani workers employed in Saudi Arabia." It will also resolve contractual disputes and allow for legal action against recruitment offices, companies, or agencies that violate the agreement. The Skills Verification Agreement focuses on certification to "create opportunities for technical workforce in Pakistan to get internationally recognized trainings and certifications." These agreements paved the way for Pakistan to become one of the countries to secure the highest number of domestic worker recruitment contracts (Ahmed 2022). Both of these agreements are examples of co-optation, as they try to tap into citizens who can – and want to – leave Pakistan to earn more. Making it easier for migrant workers to work abroad allows the state to tap into this group's economic potential in a similar way that the governments of the Philippines and Indonesia have done. Ma. Divina Gracia Z. Roldan (Chapter 7) describes how the Philippines considers its migrant workers as foreign policy assets while Ann Maria Murphy and Amy Freedman (Chapter 9) explain how Indonesia tries to protect its citizens abroad through domestic reforms and international efforts.

Pakistan has also participated in the Colombo Process (Agunias and Aghazarm 2012). This is a dialogue forum of twelve Asian labor-sending countries, which provides a platform to cooperate on issues related to migrant workers. It has five Thematic Area Working Groups: Remittances (Pakistan is Chair), Skills Qualification and Recognition, Pre-departure Orientation, Ethical Recruitment, and Labor Market Analysis. The first meeting on remittances was on June 30, 2021. The Abu Dhabi Dialogue is a forum of seven labor-receiving countries of Asia (i.e., Bahrain, Kuwait, Malaysia, Oman, Qatar, Saudi Arabia, and UAE) and ten labor-sending countries of Asia (i.e., Afghanistan, Bangladesh, India, Indonesia, Nepal, Pakistan, Philippines, Sri Lanka, Thailand, and Vietnam), and Pakistan is an active participant. The Dialogue aims to ensure the protection of migrant workers, empower workers to fulfill their goals and aspirations, and provide workers the opportunity to benefit equitably from the outcomes of temporary labor migration. Pakistan was allocated the Chair of the Abu Dhabi Dialogue for 2022–2024. More research needs to be done to gauge the he actual impact of both of these forums.

Remittances, however, are declining and the Pakistani government has made it a high priority to address the issue. From the perspective of the State Bank of Pakistan, remittances are essential for macroeconomic stability. As such, the State Bank of Pakistan, Ministry of Overseas Pakistanis, and Ministry of Finance launched the joint Pakistan Remittance Initiative (PRI). The objectives of the initiative include: (1) facilitating and supporting faster, cheaper, and efficient flow of remittances, and (2) creating investment opportunities in Pakistan for overseas Pakistanis (Pakistan Remittance Initiative n.d.).

Each civilian government and the Central Bank have developed a number of initiatives to monitor, regulate, and take advantage of remittances. The Roshan (To Shine) Digital Account is a State Bank of Pakistan initiative and provides digital onboarding and banking solutions for millions of Non-Resident Pakistanis (NRPs), and Pakistanis with wealth declared abroad seeking to undertake banking, payment, and investment activities in Pakistan. The Naya Pakistan Certificates / Islamic Naya Pakistan Certificates are investment instruments offered by the State Bank of Pakistan for non-resident Pakistanis and Pakistanis with wealth declared abroad. These certificates offer customers attractive returns over various tenures and currencies. Roshan Apna Ghar (Brighten Your House) is a home finance facility only available to Non-Resident Pakistanis living in Malaysia, Singapore, Bahrain, and the UAE. Roshan Samaaji Khidmat (Roshan Social Services) is an online tool for charity where any Pakistanis with online bank accounts can donate to their preferred charities online.

Gul and Mahmud (2012) studied remittances from Saudi Arabia and surveyed 542 Saudi migrant households and analyzed individual, household, and community determinants of remittances in a combined framework. They found that the education level of the migrant is the most important factor affecting the level of remittances to Pakistan from Saudi Arabia. They also found that the Pakistani government has not simply designed and implemented various remittance policies and strategies but also plays a role in influencing the level of economic development across districts.

Educational Programs and Opportunities

Pakistanis, especially the youth, are hungry for education, specifically specialized, higher education. The Pakistan Institute of Development Economics (PIDE) (2022) found that 37 percent of Pakistanis would go overseas if they could, with the biggest reason for wanting to leave being economic stability. From 1971 to June 2020, over 11.2 million Pakistanis sought work in 52 countries, according to the Pakistan Bureau of Immigration and Overseas Employment (Samaa Web Desk 2022). Pakistanis prefer to study abroad in the US, Canada, the UK, and Australia, but China and Germany are also emerging as new preferred destinations.

US-funded educational exchanges play a special part in the US–Pakistan bilateral relationship. Educational and cultural programs seem to be resilient and somewhat immune to foreign policy tensions and disagreements. The number of Pakistani students did decline by about 45 percent after the September 11, 2001 attacks o the Twin Towers in New York. This decline was mainly driven by immigration procedures and fears of discrimination, but today Pakistan ranks sixteenth in the world for international students in the US (Open Doors 2022). This uptick began in 2005, when 75 percent of participants in US-funded educational programs came from Pakistan. In fact, since 1951, over 8,000 Pakistanis and 935 Americans have participated in educational and cultural exchanges, including the Fulbright Program that is supported by the US Educational Foundation in Pakistan (USEFP) (South Asia Investor Review 2011; ICEF Monitor 2014). In 2021, Pakistan signed a memorandum of understanding with the US to expand the number of doctoral students funded by the Fulbright Program (USEFP Gazette). Pakistanis remain the highest recipients of the Fulbright scholarship, making the program one of the most successful ones designed to "win hearts and minds."

In order to streamline the process of studying abroad, the MOPHRD and the Department of Labour Punjab have set up the Migrant Resource Centers (MRCs). These centers operate all over Pakistan and provide information and counseling services in overseas employment, rights and protection of migrants, skills development and vocational trainings in Pakistani, and access to education systems in other countries like China, Australia, and Germany. For example, an MRC study guide for Pakistani students includes information on the best universities to apply to, the breakdown of tuition fees, accommodation, living expenses, and visa requirements, and information about various scholarship programs available to Pakistani students (Migrant Resource Centre 2022b). The China Pakistan Economic Corridor (CPEC) has also provided a number of opportunities for Pakistanis seeking educational opportunities, with China also striving to attract Pakistani students. For example, studying in China is less expensive than studying in the US, Canada, or the UK. In 2019, over 28,000 Pakistani students studied in China, making them the third largest student population in the host country (Safdar 2021). The biggest barrier for Pakistanis studying in China is language. Since at least 2018, even families of limited means are taking their chances on paying for Mandarin lessons (Hadid 2018; Toppa 2018).

Returning Pakistanis

Pakistan also has bilateral agreements with states regarding returns and readmissions for those residing legally in various countries, which are good examples of co-optation. For example, in August 2022, Pakistan and the UK signed an agreement regarding the rules about readmitting persons with authorization to the UK. This new agreement was necessary due to the UK exiting the European Union (Pakistan High Commission London 2022). Similarly, Pakistan has an agreement with the European Union that is focused on how to safely return illegal persons back to Pakistan (Council of the European Union 2010). The Covid-19 pandemic added further restrictions to agreements regarding reentry, where some countries like the US have urged those coming back to be vaccinated.

Deportations are handled by the MOPHRD and the Federal Investigation Agency. Deportations occur for a variety of reasons, such as overstaying on expired visas, having no visas (in other words, illegal entry), being involved in nefarious activities like trading in narcotics or human trafficking, or other offenses. In 2020 it was reported that about 285,980 Pakistanis were deported from Saudi Arabia between 2015 and 2019 (*Dawn* 2020). In 2022, Türkiye deported 4,224 Pakistanis (*Pakistan Today* 2022). Zahid Gishkori (2021) report that since 2015, 283 Pakistanis are deported each day.

Returning Pakistani migrants often return through the "Voluntary Assisted Return" program of the International Organization for Migration. The program is for migrants who have exhausted their appeals process to remain in a host country and serves as a last resort before deportation. In 2013, nearly half of the 5,000 migrants in Greece who took advantage of the program returned to Pakistan, and 8,000 Pakistanis were deported from EU countries. The United Nations Office on Drugs and Crime (UNODC) estimates that 400,000 Pakistanis were deported between 2007 and 2013. Iran, Oman, Türkiye, Greece, and Spain are the top five countries to deport Pakistani migrants (Erdal 2015).

Most Pakistanis who return of their own free will are motivated by a desire for a lifestyle change, such as retirement or a career break. These returnees are able to do so because of their dual citizenship. Pakistan has dual citizenship agreements that serve as co-optation tools. It has such agreements with 21 countries, where citizens of these countries do not have to renounce their nationality when acquiring their Pakistani citizenship (Ministry of Interior 2022). Most of these returnees are more temporary in nature than forced returnees. Care work, usually for elderly parents or in-laws, also plays a large role. A relatively unusual circumstance is of some migrants returning with children born overseas – typically a mother returning to Pakistan with children while the father remains in the host country to send money home. Many Pakistanis return (either temporarily or permanently) to assist in development as well (Erdal 2015). Those who wish to assist in development from other parts of Europe or North America will often not have the option to return to their host country because of additional citizenship hurdles.

Security Dimension

There have been no instances where the Pakistan Army has engaged in military activities to protect its citizens abroad. There also have been no incidents where military measures could have been expected but were not undertaken. These are mainly related to a lack of opportunities or the need to engage in this way. Since most overseas Pakistanis are in countries that have been stable and are not experiencing war within their borders – Saudi Arabia, UAE, UK, and the US – there has also been no need for the military to be involved in activities like flying its citizens out of warzones.

In the case of Saudi Arabia, for example, the presence of Pakistani military officers and cadets who are tasked with training their Saudi counterparts also ensures consistent, reliable, and trustworthy lines of communication where if the need to evacuate Pakistanis from Saudi Arabia ever arose, it could be fulfilled relatively quickly. The Pakistani military has been an active player in Gulf security since the 1960s and Pakistani troops have been stationed in the Kingdom since the 1980s (Weinbaum and Khurram 2014; Tharoor 2015; Freeman and Khan 2017; Karim 2018). The growing strength of military ties between Pakistan and Saudi Arabia may not be directly linked to protecting overseas Pakistanis but it is logical to conclude that if the need for emergency evacuation occurred, it could be done smoothly due to strong military-to-military ties.

It is an established fact that Pakistan's military plays an active role in its political, economic, and social life. As Pakistan's economy faces its nth crisis, Uzair Younus, the director of the Pakistan Initiative at the Atlantic Council's South Asia Center, makes a case for accepting the military's role in the economy: "It is time to accept that rather than trying to cut this empire down to size, it may be more fruitful to develop Military Inc. 2.0: a corporate empire that is globally competitive" (Younus 2022). What this means is that the Pakistani military will always be linked to diaspora communities, especially as the government focuses on reviving remittances. Yet, the relationship between the Pakistani military and citizens living abroad is not so transparent.

In the past, there have been reports on how Pakistan (and it really means the Pakistani establishment or military in this context) spies on its diasporas. The *New York Times* had reported in 2011 that the military, especially the Inter-Services Intelligence (Pakistan's premier intelligence agency) likes to keep tabs on the diaspora. Pakistan's sponsorship of militant groups (Khan 2018) and troubles with regulating anti-terrorism financing and money laundering (Peshimam 2022) have also created tensions but mainly at the state-to-state level and not at the diaspora-to-state level. And while the Pakistani military is wary of Imran Khan, who continues to enjoy a great deal of support in the diaspora worldwide, there is no evidence indicating that the military has interfered in any diaspora activity related to Khan or the PTI (Ibrahim 2022).

In order to win over the diaspora and maintain support, the ISPR has been focused more on its image and reputation. It is in the military's interest to ensure that the diaspora communities worldwide view the institution favorably, despite Pakistan's civil–military imbalance that continues to privilege the military. To that effect, the military's media wing and public relations branch, ISPR, produces dramas, songs with music videos, and documentaries focused on the military's meritocracy and patriotism (ISPR Productions 2022). These dramas are usually available on YouTube and can be watched by overseas Pakistanis on Pakistani channels by VPNs. The military also has a monthly bilingual magazine called *Hilal* (Crescent) and prides itself on being a credible source of information on Pakistan. There is also a video game that can be downloaded by interested gamers called *Glorious Resolve* which is centered around anti-terrorist operations conducted by Pakistan Armed Forces and law enforcement agencies. ISPR is also active on social media, and the goal seems to be to make the army accessible and also assure the diaspora that it is a credible source of information.

As remittances gain even more economic power, the Pakistani military's engagement with the diaspora will likely increase but in creative ways. This interaction provides a useful avenue for scholars and policy analysts alike to observe the evolution of Pakistan's armed forces.

Conclusion

As this chapter highlights, the Pakistan government has been actively protecting its citizens abroad through diplomatic relationships, consular engagements, and economic activities. Overseas Pakistanis continue to grow in number, expanding the national community abroad. The three main challenges that exist for the Pakistani government in protecting its citizens abroad are interconnected and have to do with maintaining remittances, increasing educational opportunities, and potentially loosening visa restrictions that hamper the ability of Pakistanis to travel and interact with other countries economically.

To ensure a steady flow of remittances, the Pakistani government has signed various agreements related to "manpower employment" with friendly states to ensure that Pakistanis continue to take advantage of labor opportunities. Educational opportunities have also been a positive development. As a country that has one of the world's largest youth populations, young Pakistanis are eager to go abroad for higher education. Education programs are also lucrative for host countries. The main hurdle, of course, has been the cost of education, which is only allowing Pakistanis with the means to be able to go abroad for education. Visa restrictions, however, continue to remain an obstacle. Pakistanis need a visa to enter almost any country in the world, which has been limiting. The government is motivated by support and co-optation as it focuses on working around visa restrictions by having exceptions in place for workers, since they are the main source of remittances. And in order to do so, the state targets migrant and low-skilled workers, students, and diasporas.

One of the most interesting revelations about Pakistan's quest to protect its citizens abroad is the lack of direct military involvement. Allegations of spying on the diaspora and the Pakistan Army being wary of Khan are certainly valid, but there have not been any instances where Pakistan has wanted to engage in military action to protect its citizens abroad – however, it must be noted that this author does not have access to any classified information and the analysis presented in the chapter is based on open-source data. Instead, the Pakistani military is focused on its image and approval rating and is striving for the acceptance of diaspora communities.

Overseas Pakistanis and their quest to work, integrate, and create lives for themselves outside Pakistan while remaining tied to the homeland is a unique opportunity for the government. For the past two decades especially, Pakistan has been in the limelight for terrorism-related activities, from sponsoring Kashmir-based militant groups to supporting the Taliban in Afghanistan to battling the Tehrik-i-Taliban Pakistan within its borders. While the world has focused on security, mainly evaluating Pakistan from an Afghanistan-focused lens as US and NATO forces remained in the country till August 2021, Pakistanis have been busy seizing opportunities for themselves and their families, indicating a high level of agency. The Pakistani government is motivated by its diaspora's agency and self-identity needs and welcomes engagement. This movement has now resulted in remittances becoming Pakistan's largest source of national foreign exchange. In order to maintain remittances, the Pakistani government's activities in regard to overseas Pakistanis are likely to intensify over time.

References

Aaj News (2022) PIA Starts Operation to Airlift Pakistanis Stranded in Ukraine. March 8. Available here: www.aajenglish.tv/news/30280568/ (last accessed January 17, 2023).

Aazim, Mohiuddin (2022) Why Are Remittances Falling? *Dawn*. November, 21. Available at: www.dawn.com/news/1722232 (last accessed November 30, 2022).

Abu Dhabi Dialogue. Available at: http://abudhabidialogue.org.ae/about-abu-dhabi-dialogue.

Addleton, Jonathan (1981) The Role of Migration in Development: Pakistan and the Gulf. *The Fletcher Forum* 5(2) (Summer), 319–332.

Agunias, Dovelyn Rannveig, and Christine Aghazarm (2012) Labour Migration from Colombo Process Countries: Good Practices, Challenges and Ways Forward. Available at: www.migrationpolicy.org/pubs/ColomboProcessBrief.pdf (last accessed January 17, 2023).

Ahmed, Ali (2022) Economic Diplomacy: Govt Sets Up Economic Outreach Apex Committee. *Business Recorder*. October 7. Available at: www.brecorder.com/news/40024242 (last accessed December 16, 2022).

Ahmed, Khurshid (2022) Pakistan Secures Second Highest Domestic Worker Contracts in Saudi Arabia in Dec. 2021. *Arab News*. February 13. Available at: www.arabnews.pk/node/2023881/pakistan (last accessed December 16, 2022).

Ahmed, Waqas (2022) Country's Brain Drain Situation Accelerated in 2022. *Express Tribune*. December 12. Available at: https://tribune.com.pk/story/2390704/countrys-brain-drain-situation-accelerated-in-2022 (last accessed January 17, 2023).

AP News (2022) Hundreds of Pakistani Students Stuck in Ukraine since Attack. February 26. Available at: https://apnews.com/article/russia-ukraine-kyiv-science-europe-karachi-0df872ad9680b9fbf87cd8f4bebd2a5b (last accessed January 17, 2023).

Atlantic Council (2022) Event. Should Overseas Pakistanis Have a Vote in Pakistan? August 10. Available at: www.atlanticcouncil.org/commentary/event-recap/event-recap-should-overseas-pakistanis-have-a-vote-in-pakistan/ (last accessed January 17, 2023).

Babar, Zahra (2020) Purveyors of Dreams: Labour Recruiters in the Pakistan to Saudi Arabia Migration Corridor. *Migration and Development* 10(1), 68–85.

Baker, Carl (2022) NHS Staff from Overseas: Statistics. Research Briefing. November 22. Available at: https://commonslibrary.parliament.uk/research-briefings/cbp-7783/ (last accessed January 17, 2023).

Barber, Sir Michael, and Muqueet Shahzad (2022) Frameworks for a Developmental Welfare State: Lessonf rom Pakistan's Ehsaas Programme. June. CDDRL Working Papers. Stanford University. Available at: https://fsi9-prod

.s3.us-west-1.amazonaws.com/s3fs-public/ffdws_ehaas_20220602_0.pdf (last accessed January 17, 2023).

BBC (2014) The Pakistani Community. September 24. Available at: www.bbc.co.uk/gloucestershire/untold_stories/asian/pakistani_community.shtml (last accessed January 17, 2023).

Budiman, Abby (2021) Pakistanis in the U.S. Fact Sheet. Pew Research Center. Available at: www.pewresearch.org/social-trends/fact-sheet/asian-americans-pakistanis-in-the-u-s/#pakistani-population-in-the-u-s-2000-2019 (last accessed January 9, 2023).

Bureau of Emigration and Overseas Employment (2022) Government of Pakistan. Roles and Functions of Overseas Employment Promotors. Available at: https://beoe.gov.pk/roles-and-functions-of-oeps (last accessed January 17, 2023).

Chaudhary, Shamila N., Faraz Ansari, Jason Grill, Nainika Paul, Jonathan Pearl, and Zoya Sattar (2021) The Ties That Bind: A Study of Pakistani American Connectivity & Giving to Pakistan. January. https://static1.squarespace.com/static/5d3664e0f88abf00019016dc/t/600b037c82889a1bf20ce1a5/1611334532287/APF+Ties+That+Bind+Report+Final.pdf (last accessed January 17, 2023).

Council of the European Union (2010) EU-Pakistan Readmission Agreement. Available at: https://eur-lex.europa.eu/legal-content/EN/ALL/?uri=celex:22010A1104(02) (last accessed January 17, 2023).

Dawn (2017) JI K-P Demands Inclusion of Overseas Pakistanis in Census. Available at: https://tribune.com.pk/story/1380882/ji-k-p-demands-inclusion-overseas-pakistanis-census (last accessed January 9, 2023).

Dawn (2020) Saudi Arabia Deported 285,980 Pakistanis in Last Five Years, Senate Told. January 31. Available at: www.dawn.com/news/1531682 (last accessed January 17, 2023).

Dawn (2021) Pakistan, Saudi Arabia Sign Prisoner Transfer Deal. May 11. Available at: www.dawn.com/news/1623183 (last accessed January 17, 2023).

De Bel-Air, F. (2018) Asian Migration to the Gulf States in the Twenty-First Century. In Mehdi Chowdhury and S. Irudaya Rajan (eds.), *South Asian Migration in the Gulf: Causes and Consequences*. London: Palgrave Macmillan, 7–34.

Embassy of Pakistan Tokyo (2016) Event. 2016. Available at: www.pakistanembassytokyo.com/content/embassy-launches-its-drive-promote-it-industry-pakistan-japan (last accessed January 17, 2023).

Erdal, Marta Bivand (2015) Pakistan as a Return Migration Destination. PRIO Policy Brief 13. Available at: https://migration.prio.org/utility/DownloadFile.ashx?id=62&type=publicationfile (last accessed January 17, 2023).

Errichiello, Gennaro, and Line Nyhagen (2021) "Dubai Is a Transit Lounge": Migration, Temporariness and Belonging among Pakistani Middle-Class Migrants. *Asian and Pacific Migration Journal*, *30*(2), 119–142.

Express Tribune (2022a) Govt Targets Exporting Manpower. Available at: https://tribune.com.pk/story/2389837/govt-targets-exporting-manpower (last accessed December 16, 2022).

Express Tribune (2022b) Large Numbers of Pakistanis Evacuated from War-Hit Ukraine. February 26. Available at: https://tribune.com.pk/story/2345362/large-number-of-pakistanis-evacuated-from-war-hit-ukraine (last accessed January 17, 2023).

Farooq, Samina, and Eatzaz Ahmad (2017) Brain Drain from Pakistan: An Empirical Analysis. *Forman Journal of Economic Studies* 13, 55–81.

Freeman, Colin, and Taimur Khan (2017) Pakistan in Talks with Saudi Arabia to Send Combat Troops to Protect the Kingdom. *N World*. March 12. Available at: www.thenationalnews.com/world/pakistan-in-talks-with-saudi-arabia-to-send-combat-troops-to-protect-the-kingdom-1.44396 (last accessed January 17, 2023).

Gishkori, Zahid (2021) 283 Pakistanis Being Deported Every Day since 2015. June 24. *The News*. Available at: www.thenews.com.pk/print/854253-283-pakistanis-being-deported-every-day-since-2015 (last accessed January 17, 2023).

Gishkori, Zahid (2022) Jailed Up Abroad: Most Pakistanis Held Captive in Middle East. October. *Samaa*. Available at: www.samaaenglish.tv/news/40019604 (last accessed January 17, 2023).

Global Media Insight (2022) Saudi Arabia Population Statistics 2022. December 26. Available at: www.globalmediainsight.com/blog/saudi-arabia-population-statistics/ (last accessed January 17, 2023).

Gul, Asha, and Mahreen Mahmud (Winter 2012) Remittances from Saudi Arabia: A Community Phenomenon. *Pakistan Development Review* 51 (4), 245–258.

Gul, Ayaz (2017) Pakistan Set to Conduct First Census in 19 Years. *Dawn*. Available at: www.voanews.com/a/pakistan-census/3762227.html (last accessed January 9, 2023).

Hadid, Diaa (2018) In Pakistan, Learning Chinese is Cool – And Seen As a Path to Prosperity. *NPR Online*. October 9. Available at: www.npr.org/2018/10/09/638987483/in-pakistan-learning-chinese-is-cool-and-seen-as-a-path-to-prosperity (last accessed January 17, 2023).

Haider, Mehtab Haider (2021) Foreign Remittances Fall by 6.6pc in Nov 2021. *The News*. December 23. Available at: www.thenews.com.pk/print/919060-foreign-remittances-fall-by-6-6pc-in-nov-2021 (last accessed January 19, 2022).

Harris, Kaveri, and Alison Shaw (2007) Kinship Obligations, Gender and the Life Course: Re-writing Migration from Pakistan to Britain. In Virinder S. Kalra (ed.), *Pakistani Diasporas: Culture, Conflict, and Change*. Oxford: Oxford University Press, 125–153.

Heritage Toronto (2012) Faith and Family: Pakistani Heritage in Toronto. Available at: www.heritagetoronto.org/explore-learn/diversity-story-pakistani-community/ (last accessed January 17, 2023).

Hincks, Joseph (2019) Saudi Arabia Is Investing $20 Billion in Pakistan. Here's What It's Getting in Return. *Time*. February 19. Available at: https://time.com/5531724/saudi-arabia-pakistan-mbs-imran-khan/ (last accessed January 17, 2023).

Human Rights Watch (2020) Saudi Arabia: Migrants Held in Inhuman, Degrading Conditions. December 15. Available at: www.hrw.org/news/2020/12/15/saudi-arabia-migrants-held-inhuman-degrading-conditions (last accessed January 17, 2023).

Husain, Khadija (2022) Moving to Canada: An Insider's View on Whether the Grass Is Actually Greener. *Business Recorder*. August 30. Available at: www.brecorder.com/news/40194679 (last accessed January 17, 2023).

Ibrahim, Azeem (2022) Pakistan's Military Is Africa of Imran Khan. Foreign Policy. November 4. Available at: https://foreignpolicy.com/2022/11/04/pakistan-military-imran-khan-assassination/ (last accessed January 17, 2023).

ICEF Monitor (2014) Demand for Education and Skills Building in Pakistan. April 8. Available at: https://monitor.icef.com/2014/04/demand-for-education-and-skills-building-in-pakistan/ (last accessed January 17, 2023).

Inter Services Public Relations (ISPR) (n.d.) Press Releases. Available at: https://ispr.gov.pk/ (last accessed January 17, 2023).

International Labour Organization (2013) National Policy for Overseas Pakistanis. February 20. Press Release. Available at: www.ilo.org/islamabad/info/public/pr/WCMS_205280/lang--en/index.htm (last accessed January 17, 2023).

International Labour Organization (2022) World Employment and Social Outlook Trends 2022. Geneva. Available at: www.ilo.org/wcmsp5/groups/public/---dgreports/---dcomm/---publ/documents/publication/wcms_834081.pdf (last accessed January 17, 2023).

Irfan, Maheen (2022) PTI and the Diaspora. T-Magazine. *Express Tribune*. April 17. Available at: https://tribune.com.pk/story/2352895/pti-and-the-diaspora (last accessed January 17, 2023).

ISPR Productions (2022) Available at: https://ispr.gov.pk/index-new-02.php#ispr_productions (last accessed January 17, 2023).

Junaidi, Ikram (2022) No Convictions in 96pc of Journalists Killings in Pakistan: Report. *Dawn*. October 28. Available at: www.dawn.com/news/1717278 (last accessed January 17, 2023).

Justice Project Pakistan (2019) Through the Cracks: The Exploitation of Pakistani Migrant Workers in the Gulf Recruitment Regime. Available at: https://data.jpp.org.pk/api/files/15722450651400x13lyqkk98.pdf (last accessed January 17, 2023).

Kamal, Shahid (2019) UK Suspends Agreement with Pakistan for Exchange of Prisoners. *Dawn*, November 21. Available at: www.dawn.com/news/1517929 (last accessed May 26, 2024).

Karim, Umer (2018) Why Pakistan Has Troops in Saudi Arabia – And What It Means for the Middle East. *The Conversation*. March 6. Available at: https://theconversation.com/why-pakistan-has-troops-in-saudi-arabia-and-what-it-means-for-the-middle-east-92613 (last accessed January 17, 2023).

Khan, Abdullah., Tippu, Khadija, Saffi Ur Rehman, and Muhammad Ali (2021) Determinants of Remittances by Unskilled Pakistani Migrant Workers. *Asian and Pacific Migration Journal* 30(3), 338–356.

Khan, S. (2022) Repatriated Pakistanis Worry for Their Future. *DW News*. May 17. Available here: www.dw.com/en/ukraine-war-repatriated-pakistani-students-worry-for-their-future/a-61827198 (last accessed January 17, 2023).

Khan, Sahar (2018) Double Game: Why Pakistan Supports Militants and Resists U.S. Pressure to Stop. *Policy Analysis* No. 849. Cato Institute. Available at: www.cato.org/policy-analysis/double-game-why-pakistan-supports-militants-resists-us-pressure-stop (last accessed January 17, 2023).

Khan, Sanaullah (2019) Pakistan, Malaysia Sign Agreements for 5 'Big Projects.' *Dawn*. March 22. Available at: www.dawn.com/news/1471200 (last accessed December 16, 2022).

Laila, Shah Ume, and Muhammad Farhan Fiaz (2018) Impact of Brain Drain on Economic Growth in Pakistan. *Business and Management Review* 9(4), 548–552.

Mahdavi, P (2011) *Gridlock: Labor, Migration, and Human Trafficking in Dubai*. Stanford, CA: Stanford University Press.

Mangi, Faseeh (2021) Funding of Pakistani Startups Crosses $300 Million This Year. *Bloomberg*. December 9. Available at: www.bloomberg.com/news/articles/2021-12-09/funding-of-pakistani-startups-crosses-300-million-this-year (last accessed November 30, 2022).

Mazzetti, Mark, Eric Schmitt, and Charlie Savage (2011) Pakistan Spies on Its Diaspora, Spreading Fear. *New York Times*. July 23. Available at: www.nytimes.com/2011/07/24/world/asia/24isi.html (last accessed January 17, 2023).

Migrant Resource Center (2022a) Pakistani Diaspora. Available at: www.mrc.org.pk/en/migration-network/pakistani-diaspora (last accessed January 30, 2022.)

Migrant Resource Centre (2022b) Study in China: A Guide for Pakistani Students. Available at: www.mrc.org.pk/en/information hub/study-abroad/study-in-china-a-guide-for-pakistani-students (last accessed January 17, 2023).

Ministry of Foreign Affairs (2022) List of Memorandum of Understandings Ratified by the Government of Pakistan. Available at: https://mofa.gov.pk/mous-agreements/ (last accessed January 17, 2023).

Ministry of the Interior (2022) Directorate General of Immigration and Passports. Government of Pakistan. Available at: https://dgip.gov.pk/immigration/dual_nationality.php#:~:text=Government%20of%20Pakistan%20has%20dual,nationality%20while%20acquiring%20Pakistani%20Citizenship (last accessed December 29, 2022).

Ministry of Planning, Development and Special Initiatives (2021) Government of Pakistan. Planning Commission. Available at: www.pc.gov.pk/uploads/report/Workers_Remmit_Jul-Mar_FY21.pdf (last accessed January 17, 2023).

(MOPHRD) Ministry of Overseas Pakistanis and Human Resource Development (n.d.) Home. Available at: www.ophrd.gov.pk/ (last accessed January 17, 2023).

(MOPHRD) Ministry of Overseas Pakistanis and Human Resource Development (2018) Government of Pakistan. *Year Book 2017–2018*. Available at: https://web.archive.org/web/20190829202243/http://callsarzameen.ophrd.gov.pk/web/wp-content/uploads/2019/07/Year-Book-2017-18.pdf (last accessed February 15, 2022).

(MOPHRD) Ministry of Overseas Pakistanis and Human Resource Development (2021) Government of Pakistan. *Year Book 2020–2021*. Available at: www

.ophrd.gov.pk/SiteImage/Misc/files/Year%20Book%202020-21.pdf (last accessed December 31, 2022).

Office of National Statistics (2022) Ethnic Group, England and Wales: Census 2021. November 2021. Available at: www.ons.gov.uk/peoplepopulationandcommunity/culturalidentity/ethnicity/bulletins/ethnicgroupenglandandwales/census2021 (last accessed January 17, 2023).

Open Doors (2022) Pakistan Fact Sheet. Available at: https://opendoorsdata.org/fact_sheets/pakistan/ (last accessed January 17, 2023).

Pakistan Embassy Ukraine (2022) Tweet. February 28. Available here: https://twitter.com/pakinukraine/status/1498266375231520770 (last accessed January 17, 2023).

Pakistan High Commission London (2022) Press Release. Available at: www.phclondon.org/pressrelease/pakistan-uk-agreement-on-returns-and-readmissions (last accessed January 17, 2023).

Pakistan Institute of Development Economics (2022) Desire to Live in Pakistan: Stay or Leave? Available at: https://pide.org.pk/research/desire-to-live-in-pakistan-stay-or-leave/ (last accessed January 17, 2023).

Pakistan Remittance Initiative (n.d). About PRI. Available at: www.pri.gov.pk/ (last accessed January 17, 2023).

Pakistan Today (2022) Pakistanis among Irregular Migrants Deported from Turkiye So Far This Year. November 13. Available at: www.pakistantoday.com.pk/2022/11/13/pakistanis-among-irregular-migrants-deported-from-turkiye-so-far-this-year/ (last accessed January 17, 2023).

Peshimam, Gibran Naiyyar (2022) Pakistan Taken Off Global Watchdog's 'Grey' List for Terrorism Financing. *Reuters*. October 21. Available at: www.reuters.com/world/asia-pacific/pakistan-taken-off-global-watchdogs-grey-list-terrorism-financing-2022-10-21/ (last accessed January 17, 2023).

PT Profit (2019) Kuwait to Sign MoU for Pakistani Manpower's Import. October 18. Available at: https://profit.pakistantoday.com.pk/2019/10/18/kuwait-to-sign-mou-for-pakistani-manpowers-import/#:~:text=Kuwait%20has%20decided%20in%20principle,%2C%20education%2C%20agriculture%20and%20construction (last accessed December 16, 2022).

Radio Pakistan (2022) Pakistan, Turkey Ink Agreements, MOUs to Enhance Cooperation. June 1. Available at: www.radio.gov.pk/01-06-2022/pakistan-turkey-sign-various-agreements-mous-to-enhance-cooperation#:~:text=Pakistan%20and%20Turkey%20have%20signed,communication%2C%20environment%2C%20and%20housing (last accessed December 16, 2022).

Rehman, Mujeeb ur (2022) Brain Drain: A Threat to Pakistan? *Global Village Space*. October 4. Available at: www.globalvillagespace.com/brain-drain-a-threat-to-pakistan/ (last accessed January 17, 2023).

Safdar, Muhammad Tayyab (2021) The Local Roots of Chinese Engagement in Pakistan. June 2. Carnegie Endowment for International Peace. Available at: https://carnegieendowment.org/2021/06/02/local-roots-of-chinese-engagement-in-pakistan-pub-84668 (last accessed January 17, 2023).

Samaa Web Desk (2022) Survey Reveals Nearly Half of Pakistanis Will Leave Country If Given Chance. December 8. Available at: www.samaaenglish.tv/news/40022950 (last accessed January 17, 2023).

Senate Standing Committee on Overseas Pakistanis and Human Resource Development (2019) Available at: https://senate.gov.pk/com/pressreleasedetail.php?id=143&pressid=3357 (last accessed January 17, 2023).

South Asia Investor Review (2011) Pakistan's Growing Education Market. October 21. Available at: www.southasiainvestor.com/2011/10/pakistans-growing-education-market.html (last accessed January 17, 2023).

Thames, Knox (2021) The Perils of Being Ahmadi in Pakistan. June 4. Available at: https://inkstickmedia.com/the-perils-of-being-ahmadi-in-pakistan/ (last assessed: July 20, 2023).

Tharoor, Ishaan (2015) Pakistan's Long History of Fighting Saudi Arabia's Wars. *The Washington Post*. March 27. Available at: www.washingtonpost.com/news/worldviews/wp/2015/03/27/pakistans-long-history-of-fighting-saudi-arabias-wars/ (last accessed January 17, 2023).

The National Archives. Commonwealth Immigration Control and Legislation. Available at: www.nationalarchives.gov.uk/cabinetpapers/themes/commonwealth-immigration-control-legislation.htm (last accessed January 17, 2023).

The Vital Signs Project (2022) The Deaths of Migrants in the Gulf. Available at: https://media.business-humanrights.org/media/documents/Vital_Signs_Report_1_2022_OHNTDZz.pdf (last accessed December 28, 2022).

Toppa, Sabrina (2018) Why Young Pakistanis Are Learning Chinese. *Pulitzer Center*. November 14. Available at: https://pulitzercenter.org/stories/why-young-pakistanis-are-learning-chinese (last accessed January 17, 2023).

United Nations International Migration Stock (2020) Available at: www.un.org/development/desa/pd/content/international-migrant-stock (last accessed January 17, 2023).

United States Institute of Peace (2018) Will Pakistan's Youth Be a Boom or a Bust for Its Democracy? Event. July 18. Available at: www.usip.org/events/will-pakistans-youth-be-boom-or-bust-its-democracy (last accessed January 17, 2023).

USEFP Gazette (2022) USEFP, HEC Agreement Aims to Increase Pakistani PhD Students in the United States, July 6. Available at: http://newsletter.usefp.org/2021/07/usefp-hec-agreement-aims-to-increase-pakistani-phd-students-in-the-united-states/ (last accessed August 28, 2022).

Weinbaum, Marvin G., and Abudullah B. Khurram (2014) Pakistan and Saudi Arabia: Defense, Dependence, and Deterrence. *Middle East Journal* 68(2), 211–228.

World Bank (2022a) Net Migration – Pakistan. Available at: https://data.worldbank.org/indicator/SM.POP.NETM?end=2017&locations=PK&start=1962&view=chart (last accessed February 10, 2022).

World Bank (2022b) Personal Remittances, Received (Current US$) – Pakistan. Available at: https://data.worldbank.org/indicator/BX.TRF.PWKR.CD.DT?end=2021&locations=PK&start=1976&view=chart (last accessed May 20, 2022).

Younus, Uzair (2022) Pakistan's Military-Run Enterprises Need Upgrade to Revive Economy. *Nikkei Asia*. July 21. Available at: https://asia.nikkei.com/Opinion/Pakistan-s-military-run-enterprises-need-upgrade-to-revive-economy (last accessed January 17, 2023).

Zahra, Maysaa (2019) *The Legal Framework of the Sponsorship System of the Gulf Cooperation Council Countries: A Comparative Examination.* Explanatory Note, GLMM – EN – No. 4/2019. Gulf Labour Market and Migration (GLMM) programme of the Migration Policy Center (MPC) and the Gulf Research Center (GRC). Available at: http://gulfmigration.org/media/pubs/exno/GLMM_EN_2019_04.pdf (last accessed January 17, 2023).

7 Philippines

Valuing Human Assets

Ma. Divina Gracia Z. Roldan

Introduction

The Philippines is known for having one of the largest diaspora populations in the world and is a major labor-exporting country globally. Its culture of migration has been evolving from the early twentieth century to the present, with millions of Filipinos emigrating and seeking jobs overseas amidst the uncertainties they face in their host countries. This phenomenon "has been greatly aided by migration's institutionalization" (Asis 2006), as government institutions and mechanisms have been formalized to facilitate and regulate migration-related activities.

Given this, the protection of citizens overseas has been a principal task of the government conducted mainly through diplomacy albeit at times, supported by activities of the military. The increase in the number of Filipinos migrating to various parts of the world has shaped the Philippine government's policy and program to support and protect its migrant population. Various Philippine administrations have undertaken a sustained policy to support the migration of Filipinos while seeking ways to improve efforts to protect them. Moreover, changes in the regimes (from then President Ferdinand Marcos in the 1970s to the present administration of his son Ferdinand Marcos Jr.) indicate fine-tuning this policy as domestic and external developments unfolded.

Overseas Filipinos (OFs) and Overseas Filipino workers (OFWs), with the latter touted as the "new heroes" by the Philippine government, have significantly contributed to the Philippine economy through their remittances, which account for 9.6 percent of the country's gross domestic product (World Bank 2020). They are considered by the Philippine government as valuable assets to the country and need the utmost support and protection.

Recognizing their role in the Philippine economy's growth and development, laws and programs have been put in place to safeguard their rights and welfare. The effective implementation of these initiatives is an ongoing process. Challenges remain, such as the continued demand for assistance to Filipinos in distress and Filipino migrant workers whose welfare is compromised. However, mechanisms are put in place to address the needs and concerns of Filipinos who live and work abroad.

The Philippine state's motivation in interacting with its national community abroad is mainly to support, with special emphasis placed on overseas Filipino workers who bring in remittances that keep the economy afloat. The state's support activities are in the form of ensuring the legal recruitment of Filipino migrant workers, securing their protection and fair treatment through bilateral agreements, providing legal and livelihood assistance to distressed OFWs, as well as delivering repatriation and integration services. To some extent, co-optation happens by enrolling the national community abroad into the development agenda of Philippine administrations by means of diaspora philanthropy, which brings in donations and allows the state to tap into the skills and expertise of overseas Filipinos.

Overview of the Filipino Community Abroad

Under President Ferdinand Marcos, the Philippine government embarked on a policy to send Filipino contract workers in the 1970s to the Middle East to meet infrastructure demands in these petroleum-rich countries, while at the same time, addressing domestic unemployment and balance-of-payment requirements. The strategy was supposed to be temporary but as the domestic labor market shrank and the economy became more dependent on remittances, what was supposed to be a stop-gap measure became a permanent one. Moreover, the worsening political conditions in the country at the time were rife for the exodus of Filipinos belonging to the middle class and the political opposition to other countries as Martial Law was imposed in 1972, officially lasting up to 1981.

After the Marcos regime was toppled by People Power in 1986, former President Corazon Aquino (1986–1992) continued the policy to promote the safety and welfare of Filipinos overseas and started an awards system to give recognition to overseas Filipino individuals and private voluntary groups for their exemplary contributions to the Filipino migrant community and the home country's development. This policy was followed by then-President Fidel Ramos (1992–1998), who instituted "The Migrant Workers and Overseas Filipinos Act of 1995" (Republic Act 8042), setting "a higher standard of protection and the promotion of the welfare of migrant Filipino workers, their families, and distressed

Filipinos abroad" (*Official Gazette* 1995). This was further reinforced by the Rodrigo Duterte administration (2016–2022) by carrying out programs to shield overseas Filipinos and overseas Filipino workers from abuses. Strong measures were implemented to convict illegal recruiters, provide legal assistance to distressed OFWs, and order the banning of Filipino household service workers to leave for Kuwait because of the high incidence of abuse.

The policy to protect Filipino citizens abroad remains a priority under the current administration of President Ferdinand "Bongbong" Marcos Jr., as he announced in his State of the Nation Address on July 25, 2022. As a result, the One Repatriation Command Center (ORCC) was set up as an emergency hub for distressed overseas Filipino workers needing immediate assistance for rescue and repatriation. The ORCC, now named One-Repat DMW, is under the newly formed Department of Migrant Workers (DMW). Individuals who have requests for assistance can go to the office of the Command Center located at the DMW. Family members of overseas Filipino citizens in distress can report their concerns via email or through the One-Repat DMW hotline. This initiative aims to attend to the needs of overseas Filipinos in emergency situations and to further improve the government's response to saving Filipino nationals abroad who are in grave danger.

Overseas Filipinos are defined under the Philippine Republic Act 10022 (Amending the Migrant Workers and Overseas Filipinos Act of 1995) as encompassing "migrant workers, other Filipino nationals and their dependents abroad" or all Filipinos working and living overseas, whether permanently or temporarily (Commission on Filipinos Overseas 2015b). Overseas Filipinos (OFs) is a general term that refers mainly to those who have migrated and acquired permanent residency or citizenship in other countries. Those who have acquired foreign citizenship through naturalization lose their Philippine citizenship and are no longer the responsibility of the Philippine government. As such, their rights and privileges are taken care of by their host countries. However, they can apply for and reacquire Philippine citizenship by taking the oath of allegiance to the Republic under Republic Act (RA) No. 9225 or the Citizenship Retention and Reacquisition Act (Embassy of the Philippines Singapore n.d.). Temporary migrants, particularly Filipino migrant workers, are more vulnerable and require assistance and protection from the Philippine government as nationals.

According to United Nations data, in 2020, there were 6,094,307 overseas Filipinos worldwide (United Nations 2020). However, the Philippine government's numbers are much higher given that a national survey of overseas Filipinos is conducted every year yielding more

Table 7.1 *Top destination countries of overseas Filipinos*

Country	Number of Filipinos
USA	3,535,676
Saudi Arabia	1,028,802
United Arab Emirates (UAE)	822,410
Malaysia	793,580
Canada	721,578
Australia	397,982
Italy	271,946
United Kingdom	218,126
Qatar	204, 550
Singapore	203, 243

Source: Commission on Filipinos Overseas Stock Estimate (2013).

updated data. There are an estimated 10.2 million Filipinos[1] working and living in more than 200 countries (Commission on Filipinos Overseas 2015b: 9). Of them, 48 percent are permanent residents (emigrants who have been naturalized in other countries, hold dual citizenship, and are Filipino spouses and other partners of foreign nationals), 41 percent are temporary migrants (land-based and sea-based Filipino workers, and others whose stay abroad for six months or more, and their accompanying dependents), and 11 percent are irregular migrants (undocumented Filipinos without valid residence or work permits, or who may be overstaying in a foreign country) (Commission on Filipinos Overseas 2015b: 9).

Of the 10.2 million overseas Filipinos, about 4.3 million are in the Americas and Trust territories, 2.4 million are in West Asia or the Middle East, 1.6 million are in East and Southeast Asia, 866,000 are in Europe, and 59,000 are in Africa. The top ten destination countries of registered Filipino emigrants are the USA, Saudi Arabia, Canada, UAE, Malaysia, Canada, Italy, the United Kingdom, Qatar, and Singapore (Table 7.1).

Some 1.34 million OFWs left the country to work during the first two quarters of 2021, 11.5% higher than the number in the same period in 2020. Saudi Arabia is the most preferred destination of OFWs (22.4%), followed by the UAE (13.2%), Hong Kong (7.5%), and Taiwan (6.7%).

[1] Data on the Philippines from the UN show a much lower number. See International Migrant Stock 2020: Destination and Origin: www.un.org/development/desa/pd/content/international-migrant-stock. The figures adopted here are from the Philippine government's stock estimate of overseas Filipinos as it integrates updated administrative data culled from different government agencies, recent national surveys, and foreign service post reports.

The largest proportion of OFWs are skilled workers (39.6%), 1.1% hold managerial positions, and 0.8% work in the agriculture, forestry, and fishery sectors (House of Representatives 2021).

It is important to note that the Philippines is a top provider of sea-based workers in the world. Around 30 percent of the total global shipping fleet is comprised of Filipino mariners, one third of whom work in foreign sea vessels from countries in Europe, Latin America, Asia, and the US. The rest of the Filipino seafarers work in Philippine-flagged ships (dataSpring Editors 2022).

Female OFWs made up 56 percent of the total number of workers deployed abroad in 2020. Connected to this is the fact that a large share of the Filipino diaspora, particularly in the United States, were women and were registered nurses. The feminization of migration is an important issue in the Philippines as it underscores the need to adopt an intersectional rights-based approach (Henderson 2021) in addressing this issue and prioritize safeguards against exploitation, especially in vulnerable occupations such as Filipina domestic workers, entertainers, and agriculture and factory workers (Center for Migrant Advocacy 2014).

Moreover, the Philippines ranks among the top ten global remittance receivers in the world, with an estimated total cash remittance amounting to $38 billion in 2022 (World Bank 2022). As of July 2022, remittances made through banks amounted to $2.9 billion, increasing by 2.3 percent from the same period in the previous year (Businessworld 2022). The top ten contributors of cash remittances from overseas Filipinos and overseas Filipino workers are the USA, Singapore, Saudi Arabia, Japan, the UK, UAE, Canada, Hong Kong, Qatar, and South Korea. Remittances from these countries make up more than 70 percent of the total remittances sent to the Philippines (Venzon 2022). The global economic slowdown arising from the Covid-19 pandemic has a significant effect on the number of remittances overseas Filipinos infuse into the economy. The Philippines is the most affected country in Southeast Asia, with its remittance falling over 20 percent in 2020. This has implications for poverty reduction and reducing inequality in the Philippines, as low-income households rely on money sent by OFW family members to meet their needs. Nevertheless, with the global economy slowly recovering as the end of the pandemic neared, remittance inflows to the Philippines increased by 3.9 percent to $37.2 billion in 2023 (Bangko Sentral ng Pilipinas 2024).

Diplomatic and Consular Dimension

The Philippine government has always utilized diplomacy in protecting its citizens abroad. Since it became a republic in 1946, the country has adhered to UN principles of peace and dialogue. Given its limitations in resources to beef up its military capability, the country's leaders believe that forging peaceful official ties with other members of the international community is the most effective means of safeguarding the welfare of its citizens overseas.

The Philippine Department of Foreign Affairs (DFA) is the main government agency tasked to implement the State's foreign policy enshrined in the 1987 Constitution. The Philippine Foreign Service Act of 1991 (Republic Act No. 7157) provides the mandate of the Department of Foreign Affairs to implement the three pillars of the Philippine foreign policy, namely: (1) to preserve and enhance national security; (2) promote economic security; and (3) protect the rights and welfare of Filipinos overseas (Department of Foreign Affairs n.d.). Its mission is to advance Philippine interests in the global community through diplomatic representation and consular work while providing advice and assistance to the president in planning, coordinating, and evaluating activities with respect to foreign relations (*Official Gazette* n.d.).

The Philippines has 63 embassies, 26 consulates-general, and 4 permanent missions to international organizations, as of January 2022. In countries where there are large concentrations of Filipinos such as the US, Canada, and Japan, among others, Philippine embassies are established in the capital and consulates in key cities. For example, in the US, the Philippine embassy is in Washington, DC, with consulates existing in the cities of Los Angeles, San Francisco, New York, Chicago, Miami, Portland, and Honolulu. In Canada, the Philippine embassy is in Ottawa, while there are also consulates in Toronto, Vancouver, Calgary, Edmonton, Winnipeg, and St. Johns.

The size of the Filipino population in foreign countries as well as trade and investment opportunities are factors considered in opening Philippine foreign service posts. For instance, the growing number of Filipinos in Sweden and in Morocco (about 14,443 and 4,603, respectively) led to the reopening of the Philippine embassy in Stockholm, Sweden, on May 15, 2020, after being closed for eight years due to economic constraints and the opening of the Philippine embassy in Rabat, Morocco, on March 17, 2022. New consulates were opened in 2020 in Istanbul, Türkiye, serving around 3,000 Filipinos; Melbourne, Australia, with a Filipino population of at least 68,000; and Nagoya, Japan, where an estimated 75,000 Filipinos live. The Cataluña region in Spain is where more than 15,000 Filipinos live. The reopening of the Philippine consulate in Barcelona on June 7, 2021 will be beneficial to them (Rocamora 2019).

Aside from the DFA, there are government agencies that are also involved in supporting Philippine labor migration. The Philippine

Overseas Employment Administration (POEA) under the Department of Labor and Employment (DOLE) is tasked with supervising the recruitment of Filipinos for overseas employment. Among its functions are licensing private recruitment and ship-manning agencies, setting minimum labor standards, facilitating the deployment of workers hired through government-to-government arrangements, conducting Pre-Deployment Orientation Seminars (PDOS) for hired workers, and providing repatriation and legal assistance to victims of illegal recruitment (Philippine Overseas Employment Administration n.d.).

The Overseas Workers Welfare Administration (OWWA) is another agency that caters to the interests of OFWs and their families through social security, education and training, repatriation, and reintegration services. It is funded by membership contributions from overseas workers and is supplemented by the national government budget (Overseas Welfare Administration n.d.).

The Commission of Filipinos Overseas (CFO), for its part, is the national agency under the Office of the President of the Philippines, which develops and implements programs for overseas Filipinos specifically catering to Filipino permanent migrants and their descendants, spouses of foreign nationals leaving the country, Filipino youth overseas, and Filipino Au Pair participants (Commission on Filipinos Overseas n.d.a.). The CFO retains its autonomy as an agency as it is excluded from RA 11641 which is discussed below.

The Department of Migrant Workers (DMW) was recently created when President Rodrigo Duterte signed into law Republic Act (RA) 11641, also known as "An Act Creating the Department of Migrant Workers," in December 2021. The new department assumes the functions of the Philippine Overseas Employment Administration (POEA), the National Reintegration Center for OFWs (NRCO), the National Maritime Polytechnic, the Department of Foreign Affairs Office of the Undersecretary for Migrant Workers' Affairs (OUMWA), the International Labor Affairs Bureau (ILAB), the Office of the Social Welfare Attache (OSWA), and all Philippine Overseas Labor Offices (POLO), which serve as "migrant workers" offices in 34 of the 94 Philippine foreign service posts around the world (Rocamora 2022d). The DMW is tasked with focusing on attending to documented and undocumented OFWs and serving as a one-stop-shop from pre-employment, and employment to reintegration. The creation of the department confirms the deployment of Filipino labor abroad as a permanent national policy and institutionalizes it.

The DMW is the newest agency dedicated to OFW concerns and is expected to formally operate in 2023 (Patinio 2022). Under the law, it is given a two-year transition period to organize. The agencies subsumed under the DMW continue their activities until such time that the DMW can harmonize the absorbed agencies' programs for OFWs. This is the reason why it does not have much of a role in this chapter because to date, it has had no significant accomplishments yet as a department.

Similar to Indonesia (see Murphy and Freedman, Chapter 9), the Philippine government has actively entered into bilateral labor agreements (BLAs) and social security agreements (SSAs) with countries that have high populations of Filipino migrant workers (Ignacio 2020). These instruments are aimed at establishing cooperation from the governments of destination countries in extending adequate protection to Filipino citizens overseas. They also pave the way for standardized employment contracts that ensure fair wages, work hours, rest periods, and other benefits to OFWs. It also safeguards against illegal and inhumane acts and practices by local employers such as withholding the passports of OFWs, inflicting physical harm, and other forms of abuse.

About seventy-one bilateral labor agreements were signed by the Philippine government with governments of countries hosting OFWs to provide them with safer and fairer work environments. These countries where large diaspora groups work and reside include Saudi Arabia, Kuwait, Jordan, Lebanon, Israel, South Korea, Germany, Switzerland, and the UK, among others.

The government has also pursued the portability of social security benefits for overseas Filipinos. Bilateral SSAs entitle them to pensions and insurance under the same conditions applicable to nationals of the host country. They can file their claim applications for retirement, disability, and death/survivor benefits with each country's designated liaison office. The Philippines has fourteen existing SSAs with countries where Filipinos emigrate namely, Austria, the UK, Northern Ireland, Spain, France, the Netherlands, Switzerland, Belgium, Denmark, Portugal, Germany, Japan, Sweden, and Luxembourg (Ignacio 2020).

The agreement entered into by the Philippines with the UAE in March 2021, for example, shows how guarantees on the protection of the rights and welfare of Filipino workers can lead to a resumption of labor deployment to these countries. In 2014, a suspension order was issued by the Philippine government to prevent Filipino household service workers from leaving the country for work in the UAE due to incessant reports of abuses and exploitation. Under the new agreement, a Unified Employment Contract shall be adopted that would hold UAE employers and Philippine recruitment agencies liable for any violations of the rights of Filipino domestic workers provided in the new accord, namely: (1) the right to keep one's passport; (2) the right to take a paid break at least one full day a week outside of the employer's residence; (3) the right to open one's own bank account for payment of salary; (4) the right to rest and take at least eight continuous hours of sleep every night; (5) the right to cook one's own food; and (6) the right to own communication devices (Department of Labor and Employment 2021).

In the case of the Philippines' agreement in November 2019 with South Korea on social security benefits, Filipino citizens living and working in Korea may remain under Korea's National Pension Service (NPS) and may opt to refund their NPS contributions at the end of their overseas employment contract. They may file claims with the liaison agencies of the Philippines and South Korea and are entitled to the Philippines' Social Security System (SSS) pension by becoming active members also of SSS (Social Security System 2019).

Overseas Filipinos are also a source of votes and can be considered a new constituency that has the potential of changing the political landscape. The Philippine government's policy to involve overseas Filipinos in the electoral process entailed hammering out legislation that came into effect in the early 2000s. Through the passage of the Overseas Absentee Voting Act (Republic Act 9189) in February 2003, Filipinos residing or working outside of the Philippines can already participate in elections. In 2003, another law the Citizenship Retention and Reacquisition Act (Republic Act 9225) allowed even Filipinos naturalized in other countries to re-acquire their Filipino citizenship thus enabling them to also take part in Philippine elections. Ten years later, the Overseas Voting Act of 2013 (Republic Act 10590) was passed by the Philippine Congress to address flaws in Republic Act 9189 which prevented overseas Filipinos from participating in the electoral exercise, removing the provision requiring overseas Filipinos to resume actual physical permanent residence in the Philippines three years from the approval of registration.

The DFA's Overseas Voting Secretariat (OVS) is instrumental in ensuring qualified Overseas Filipinos to register and vote during elections. Through its link to foreign posts, it serves as a repository of all data derived from Philippine embassies and consulates with regard to overseas voting. An uptick in the number of registered overseas voters can be noted during the period from 2004 to 2022. From 4.6 percent in 2004 of the 7.6 million total overseas population, the number of overseas registered voters reached 7 percent of the 10.4 million total overseas Filipino population in 2022. The highest percentage of overseas voter registration and voter turnout is in the Asia Pacific, North America, and

Europe. The uptick is probably the result of interventions from both government and migrant groups. Increased registration campaigns and voter education were conducted especially by NGOs that advocate for migrants' rights. The Center for Migrant Advocacy is an example of an NGO that works closely with the CFO. During the previous electoral periods, it produced studies on elections and informational materials such as posters and brochures on registration procedures that were distributed to overseas Filipino workers. It was also engaged in monitoring election results and lobbied for amendments to the law to strengthen the participation of overseas Filipinos during elections.

Overseas voter registration exceeded the 1 million target, with 1.69 million overseas voters registered for the 2022 national elections. The region with the highest total of registered voters was the Middle East and Africa (779,970), followed by Asia Pacific (435,022), the Americas (302,994), and Europe (104,996). The highest percentage of voter turnout was in Asia Pacific, with 51.70 percent of the total number of registered voters, followed by Europe at 45.48 percent, the Americas at 37.23 percent, and the Middle East and Africa at 30.91 percent (Commission on Elections 2022).

Different methods were employed to address factors that impede overseas Filipinos from participating in the electoral exercise. Automated voting was carried out in 30 overseas posts, postal voting in 20 posts, and personal voting in 26 posts. The registration and voting period were extended and field stations were deployed where overseas Filipinos could register and vote in aside from Philippine embassies and consulates, thereby helping increase voter registration and turnout.

There are existing Philippine laws aimed at protecting Filipino citizens overseas, namely the Migrant Workers and Overseas Filipinos Act of 1995 and the Anti-Human Trafficking of Persons Act. The Migrant Workers and Overseas Filipinos Act of 1995 (Republic Act 8042) and its amended version, the Republic Act 10022, are historic and significant legislation passed to promote the rights of Filipino migrant workers. It mandates government agencies to provide legal representation and assistance to distressed Filipinos abroad, deliver repatriation and reintegration services, and grant OFWs social, economic, and medical benefits. The assistance accorded to migrant workers is also extended to their families. This law is a basis for the DFA's assistance to nationals and OWWA's programs on livelihood assistance, social security benefits, repatriation, and reintegration catering to Filipino migrant workers.

The Anti-Human Trafficking in Persons Act of 2003 (Republic Act 9208) and Republic Act 10364, known as the Expanded Anti-Human

Trafficking in Persons Act of 2012, guard against illegal recruitment and human smuggling. They provide support for victims and impose severe penalties on those violating these laws. In the 2020 report of the Philippines' Inter-Agency Council Against Human Trafficking, a total of 27, 215 Filipinos overseas were assisted in countries in the Middle East such as Qatar, Saudi Arabia, Kuwait, and the UAE, and in Asia such as Malaysia and Hong Kong. The number of trafficking victims decreased by 16 percent from 2019 with 32,557 clients. This indicates the efficacy of these laws in providing support for cases of illegal recruitment and human trafficking among distressed overseas Filipinos.

Aside from the domestic legal framework that upholds the dignity of Filipino citizens abroad, the Philippines is also a signatory to international agreements that promote their welfare. Among these international instruments is the UN Global Compact for Migration, which seeks to mitigate the vulnerabilities of migrants; the International Convention on the Protection of the Rights of All Migrant Workers and Members of their Families, which guarantees the fundamental rights and freedoms of migrant workers; the Convention on the Elimination of All Forms of Discrimination Against Women protecting women domestic migrant workers; and the Maritime Law Convention of 2006 ensuring decent work for seafarers.

While overseas Filipinos are often viewed as purveyors of aid to their home country, their position has been reversed, making them recipients of government assistance instead during the Covid-19 pandemic and recent global tensions. Even prior to these developments, there have been incessant and disturbing cases of maltreatment and abuse of Filipino citizens, especially Filipino migrant workers abroad. These range from low salaries, late payment and non-payment of wages, contract substitution, and other human rights violations. Verbal, psychological, and physical abuse, including sexual harassment and rape, are noted among household service workers. It is common for domestic workers to be overworked and undernourished, with poor living and work conditions. Employers usually keep their passports and mobile phones, which curtails their mobility and communication with their families and other people, making it difficult for them to ask for help when needed. Some Filipino workers also lack medical care, health insurance, and access to justice when they are falsely accused of wrongdoing by their employers.

A turning point that shaped the re-evaluation of the DFA's work is the celebrated case of a Filipina domestic worker in Singapore, Flor Contemplacion, who in 1995 was convicted and executed for the killing of a fellow Filipina domestic worker and the three-year-old son of her employer. Singapore's rejection of the appeal of then-President Fidel Ramos caused a diplomatic row between the Philippines and Singapore. This event led to President Ramos working vigorously for the passage and eventual signing into law of the Migrant Workers and Overseas Filipinos Act of 1995. He further declared that the protection of nationals is an important pillar of Philippine foreign policy and that this should be a priority for diplomats and consular officers posted in foreign missions.

Another controversial case that sparked indignation in the Philippines was that of Joanna Demafelis, a Filipina domestic worker in Kuwait who was found dead in a freezer in 2018, two years after she went missing in 2016. She was tortured and murdered by her Lebanese employers and her body was placed in a freezer found in an abandoned apartment of the employers. This case and other reports of Filipino migrant workers' maltreatment caused a rupture in the bilateral relations between the Philippines and Kuwait. President Rodrigo Duterte thereafter ordered a ban on the deployment of Filipino household service workers to Kuwait until a new bilateral agreement was adopted by the Philippine and Kuwaiti governments giving more stringent provisions to safeguard the rights, welfare, and safety of Filipinos leaving for Kuwait to work.

As of 2020, there were 4,302 reported cases of maltreatment against overseas Filipino workers from the Middle East, 539 from Asia, and 86 from Europe and the Americas (Statista 2022a). Those who are undocumented are the most vulnerable because they do not have the legal status to stay in their countries of destination. As such, they are more prone to exploitation and harassment. In Malaysia, for example, a large number of undocumented Filipinos estimated at 400,000, live and work in Peninsular Malaysia and in the Sabah region. The Malaysian government's crackdown on illegal migrants in the past years has resulted in the imprisonment, caning, and deportation of thousands of undocumented Filipinos in Malaysia. This started the sending by the Department of Social Welfare and Development (DSWD) of its personnel to foreign posts to assist the Philippine embassy in attending to the needs of these Filipino nationals.

Moreover, as part of the measures taken to serve beleaguered citizens overseas, the Philippine Congress enacted on April 17, 2019, the Republic Act 11299, known as An Act Establishing the Office for Social Welfare Attaché, which institutionalizes the presence of social welfare attachés in Philippine foreign service posts. The social welfare attachés coming from the DSWD are to be fielded to Philippine embassies and consulates in countries where there is a high concentration of Filipino workers. Section 2e.i. of the law outlines their task, which is to "manage cases of OFWs and other overseas Filipinos in distress needing psychosocial services, such as victims of trafficking or illegal recruitment, rape or sexual abuse, maltreatment and other forms of physical and mental abuse, and cases of abandoned or neglected children" (*Official Gazette* 2019).

To date, there are only a few social welfare attachés assigned to Philippine foreign service posts. They are in Philippine missions in Malaysia, Hong Kong, Qatar, Riyadh, and Jeddah in Saudi Arabia, Dubai in UAE, Kuwait, and Jordan. Some 61,131 overseas Filipinos in distress were reportedly served between 2013 and 2017 (Senate of the Philippines 2019). The law paves the way for an increased number of social welfare attachés to be dispatched to Philippine embassies and consulates abroad, making them a more permanent part of the Philippine diplomatic mission. The provision of on-site psychosocial services to distressed Filipino nationals is a much needed intervention since this is a gap that Philippine foreign posts need to fill.

Since the outbreak of the Covid-19 pandemic in 2020, huge numbers of Filipinos abroad have lost their jobs and have returned home to join the unemployed. Repatriation started in January 2020 with thirty Filipinos from Wuhan, China, and later from Middle Eastern countries such as Bahrain, the Kingdom of Saudi Arabia, Kuwait, and Qatar. Some 2.24 million OFWs, 1.4 million of whom were land-based workers and roughly 808,000 who were sea-based, had been repatriated by the Department of Foreign Affairs (Statista 2022b).

During the start of the pandemic, a whole-of-government approach was adopted by providing relief assistance to affected OFWs. Foreign service posts and other concerned agencies, particularly the OWWA, in collaboration with recruitment agencies, were activated to help distribute food packs and hygiene kits, provide temporary shelter, and make flight arrangements for returning OFWs coming from Bahrain, Qatar, Kuwait, Saudi Arabia, Japan, Singapore, Greece, and Macau, among other places. The Department of Transportation was also tapped to provide free transport services for OFW returnees from the airports to their places of residence in the capital and other regions in the Philippines. Aside from this, the government through the OWWA, also provided stranded OFWs with cash assistance of PHP10,000 (equivalent to US$170) drawn from the OWWA Trust Fund and the DOLE-AKAP program.

Livelihood development assistance for OFW returnees was also provided through the Balik Pinas! BalikHanapbuhay! (literally translated into English as, “Return [to the] Philippines! Return [to] Livelihood!”) Program. This program provides a seed capital of PHP20,000 (equivalent to an estimated US$340) to returning Filipino migrant workers who would like to set up small businesses and are members of the OWWA, the government arm that handles matters concerning OFW welfare and benefits. The program is intended to provide immediate livelihood opportunities for returning displaced or distressed OFW members. An entrepreneurial development training seminar is provided to qualified OFWs to enable them to draw up a business plan and operate their microenterprises.

Long-term, comprehensive assistance to displaced and repatriated nationals should be part of the government’s post-Covid-19 recovery program (Roldan 2020a). Considering the substantial number of resources required to assist them, greater collaboration among the government, private sector, and civil society organizations is crucial to carrying out this enormous task.

The invasion of Ukraine by Russia in February 2022 is a critical global crisis that had severe repercussions for many Filipinos living, studying, and working in the war-torn country. Placing Ukraine at Alert Level 4 (mandatory evacuation), Philippine embassies in Warsaw, Poland, and Budapest, Hungary, have been directed by the home office to assist Filipino nationals from Ukraine who had to flee and seek refuge. Since the invasion in February 2022, the Philippine Department of Foreign Affairs (DFA) reported it had assisted 405 Filipinos, repatriated 342, and evacuated 63 to neighboring countries (Rocamora 2022c).

The controversial visit by US House Speaker Nancy Pelosi to Taiwan on August 2, 2022, showed heightened tensions in the Asia Pacific region, with China aggressively reacting to the visit by conducting military drills around Taiwan. This was a concern to the Philippine government as an estimated 200,000 Filipinos live and work in Taiwan, 8,000 of whom are undocumented. The Philippines officially recognizes the People’s Republic of China as the sole legitimate government of China under the One-China Policy. As such, the Philippine government considers Taiwan not as an independent state but as a province of China. However, the Philippines maintains economic and cultural ties with Taiwan. The Manila Economic Cultural Office in Taipei serves as a consular office tasked to protect and promote the rights and welfare of Filipinos in Taiwan, while overseeing business, tourism, and other exchanges between the Philippines and Taiwan. In the wake of the tensions following the Pelosi’s visit to Taiwan, the DFA announced that a contingency plan was put in place and would be implemented if necessary (Rocamora 2022b).

The unrest and crackdown on democracy activists following the February 2022 military coup in Myanmar called for the Philippine government to come to the aid of affected Filipino nationals there. Filipinos in Myanmar are employed in the manufacturing, media, and development sectors, with some working in international organizations such as the UN. As of July 2022, a total of 701 Filipinos from Myanmar have been repatriated by the DFA, which constitutes about 60 percent of the total number of overseas Filipinos in the country. Filipinos who are still in Myanmar are advised to restrict nonessential movements, avoid public places, and prepare for evacuation" (Rocamora 2022a). Given the increased violence in Myanmar, the Philippine government has retained the country's classification at Alert Level 4 (mandatory evacuation) and imposed a total ban on the deployment of Filipino workers to Myanmar.

Assistance was also provided by the Philippine government during recent regional tensions. The collapse of Sri Lanka's economy which led to political unrest also severely affected Filipino nationals living and working there. There are more than 600 Filipinos in Sri Lanka and many of them are spouses of Sri Lankan nationals. About 115 Filipino nationals expressed their desire to leave the country, driving the Foreign Affairs Home Office to take immediate action to assist Filipino nationals. The Philippine government prepared financial assistance of $300 for distressed Filipinos, covered plane fares of repatriated Filipinos, and banned the further deployment of Filipino contract workers in Sri Lanka. The DFA, through the Office of the Undersecretary for Migrant Workers Affairs, the Philippine Embassy in Bangladesh, and the Philippine Honorary Consulate General in Colombo, have consistently monitored the situation in Sri Lanka and the plight of affected Filipino nationals. Thirteen Filipinos were repatriated in July 2022, comprising the first batch of Filipino returnees. Repatriation efforts are expected to be completed once all 114 Filipinos in Sri Lanka return to the Philippines (Department of Foreign Affairs 2022).

The armed conflict in Sudan, which broke out in April 2023, has affected Filipinos working and living there. An estimated 700 Filipino OFWs are employed in Sudan as professionals and others as domestic workers. More than 400 OFWs were evacuated from Sudan's capital Khartoum to neighboring Egypt and Saudi Arabia and were provided with financial assistance. Repatriation started in April 2023 and is ongoing for Filipinos who voluntarily seek state assistance to return to the Philippines for reasons of safety.

Use of Social Media in Activities to Protect Citizens Abroad

Social media has become a widely used platform that allows people to directly communicate, share their views, and create content across national borders in a timely and cost-efficient manner. Among migrant Filipinos, Facebook and Twitter are commonly used to keep in touch with family and friends, and to obtain news and information from their host and home countries. Cases of OFWs in distress are known and reported on social media through posts made by the OFWs themselves or are shared by other people through videos or blogs. These reports of abuses and pleas for help become viral, catching the attention not only of netizens but of authorities as well. In response to this, the DFA has taken measures to adopt information and communications technologies to better attend to the needs of Filipino nationals abroad. Starting in 2011, it has adopted social media platforms to monitor the plight of OFWs and handle assistance to national cases. Since a majority of Filipino migrant workers use Facebook, the DFA maintains a Facebook OFW Help page where information on migrant-related concerns is communicated and exchanged (Katigbak and Roldan 2021). In host countries that are in political and economic turmoil, a crisis alert system was created to provide immediate assistance to OFWs. Overseas preparedness and response teams are formed under the direction of the DFA and DOLE in cases where evacuation and repatriation are needed.

Challenges to Migrant Protection

The issues that arose during the Covid-19 pandemic showed the limitations to what the government can do to address the needs of distressed Filipinos abroad because of limited funds and bureaucratic inefficiencies. The return of hundreds of thousands of OFWs and its economic impact on the country was unanticipated. Without a well-coordinated strategic plan to address such a global crisis, the government was hardly prepared to assist this many displaced Filipino migrant workers at the outset. Moreover, promoting the welfare of Filipino nationals in foreign countries goes beyond mere assistance to them while they are away from home during crisis situations. Assistance must be continued even up to the time they return to either remain in the country or find employment again overseas.

Repatriation and reintegration programs entail huge budgets. This includes costs shouldered by the government in the form of providing cash assistance and assuming payments for flights of OFW returnees. It also entails an organized system of procedures from the country of origin to arrival in the Philippines which involves not just the Philippine government and foreign governments but non-governmental organizations, migrant groups, the private sector, and concerned members of the community, as well. While government agencies and foreign service posts were quick to put in place an emergency repatriation plan during the pandemic, more time was required to systematically organize and coordinate.

Reliance on the cooperation of other countries is also a challenge. If there is resistance or a delay from the foreign government involved, it may derail a swift implementation of assistance. For example, in the case of Sri Lanka, approval from the Sri Lankan government for landing rights of a rescue flight was first needed to repatriate Filipinos who wanted to leave the country. There was also a challenge in sending cash relief to Filipinos stranded in Sri Lanka because of government regulations (Ismael and Cueto 2022).

Even with bilateral labor agreements, the Philippine government is dependent on foreign governments' cooperation. The Philippine government has yet to work on securing agreements with all countries where Filipino migrant workers are present. A memorandum of understanding does not have to undergo ratification, which is why it is preferred by the Philippine government. Nevertheless, the Philippine government has no control over the implementation of such agreements. The implementation still rests on foreign governments to hold employers in their countries accountable for the recruitment and treatment of Filipino migrant workers.

The DFA, being the lead agency in protecting the interests of OFWs, is also beset with organizational issues that must be attended to. It works within a limited budget that constrains its operations given its own infrastructure, human resources, and technology needs. For example, social media and different messaging apps are effective tools to obtain information directly from nationals needing help. This is especially useful in the case of domestic workers who have difficulty reaching foreign service posts for help due to employers' restrictions on mobility and geographic distance. However, the DFA still needs to craft and adopt a social media policy and strategy (Katigbak and Roldan 2021) that allows for an interactive exchange of information between the DFA and the nationals they serve abroad. Aside from having protocols, dedicated offices, and technically trained personnel, safeguards against security breaches and jeopardizing privacy in the transmission of online data have to be improved. The DFA also needs to ramp up the training of foreign service officers on crisis management and assistance-to-nationals (ATN) to better respond to the needs of Filipino migrant workers. In addition to this, the administrative bottlenecks for the processing of ATN cases need to be minimized.

Economic and Social Dimension

Migrant Engagement for Development

Overseas Filipinos are generally seen as contributors to Philippine national development. They serve as conduits for assets needed by the country for growth. It cannot be denied that in the case of the Philippines, overseas Filipinos have a role in the country's development process. They provide valuable resources to the country through their skills and networks. This is seen in their participation in diaspora philanthropy, especially in times of disasters.

The Philippine government, through the CFO, institutionalized a mode of economic diaspora activities aimed at improving development accomplishments in vital development sectors. It established the BalinkBayan[2] Overseas Filipinos One-Stop online portal for diaspora engagement to bring together 10.24 million Filipinos overseas onto an integrated and comprehensive platform that taps into their knowledge, expertise, skills, networks, material, and financial resources for the development of the Philippines. It links overseas Filipinos to development-oriented diaspora initiatives in the Philippines and provides options to use business and investment opportunities at the national level and in their respective hometowns, and to automated transaction processes at the local government level. BalinkBayan's long-term objective is to attain inclusive and sustainable growth, driven by the collective strength of overseas Filipinos that can have a catalytic effect on Philippine economic development (Commission on Filipinos Overseas 2015b: 22), although medium–long-term outcomes are yet to be determined.

Another long-standing program designed by the CFO is the Lingkod sa Kapwa Pilipino (LINKAPIL), or Link for Philippine Development program, which started in 1989 and was developed as a mechanism to tap resources from overseas Filipinos in the form of donations, grants, or subsidies to support education, health and welfare, livelihood, and small-infrastructure projects. The projects are documented and closely monitored by the CFO, providing transparency for the donors and beneficiaries involved. Since its founding, LINKAPIL has successfully channeled PHP2.5 billion from Filipino migrants around the world (Commission on Filipinos Overseas 2015a: 14) to 39 provinces in the Philippines, helping approximately 230,000 beneficiaries (Commission on Filipinos Overseas 2015a: 26). The majority of contributions (75%) have been connected to

[2] The term is a derivative of *balik* in Filipino, meaning "return" in English, "link" in English which means to connect, and *bayan* in Filipino which refers to "nation" in English.

health-related initiatives and medical missions, with the second-largest proportion of donations going to disaster relief (10%).

Aside from its economic and social policies toward its overseas population, the Philippine government also has symbolic policies to reinforce the links between overseas Filipinos and their home country. These include the celebration of the month of Overseas Filipinos by virtue of Proclamation No. 276, dated June 21, 1988, and the International Migrants' Day every December of the year based on the United Nations Resolution No. 55/93.

Another symbolic policy is the holding of diaspora conferences. The Commission on Filipinos Overseas (CFO), under the auspices of the Office of the President, has held biennial diaspora conferences since the agency launched the Diaspora to Development (D2D) program in 2011. The 1st Global Summit of Filipinos in the Diaspora conference "provided a framework for Filipino communities to interact and work together to address issues, encourage participation, empower migrants, and strengthen the Filipino diaspora's capacity to integrate with the host country and re-engage with the Motherland" (Commission on Filipinos Overseas n.d.b).

A system of recognition and awards for the outstanding contributions of Overseas Filipinos has also been institutionalized – the Presidential Awards for Filipino Individuals and Organizations (PAFIOO) – through Executive Order No. 498, issued by President Corazon Aquino in 1991. The PAFIOO, held biannually, awards overseas Filipino individuals who excel in their professions and organizations that outstandingly contribute to the progress of the country and promote the interests of Filipino communities abroad. Since then, about 541 individuals and organizations based in 55 countries were given these presidential awards (Presidential Awards for Filipino Individuals and Organizations Overseas n.d.).

Security Dimension

In cases where Filipinos overseas are in critical situations, the military helps in evacuation and repatriation efforts by the government to secure the safety of nationals in distress. The Philippine Army and Navy, in particular, have always been called upon to provide the necessary assistance in emergency situations.

During escalating tensions in the Middle East in January 2020, after the death of top Iranian general Qasem Soleimani from a US drone strike at an international airport in Baghdad, the AFP assisted in the repatriation of Filipino workers in Iraq and Iran as Alert Level 4, which called for the evacuation or mandatory repatriation, was issued by Philippine

Embassy in Iraq. Two battalions of soldiers, one from the army and one from the Marines, were sent not to engage in combat but to assist in the evacuation and repatriation of OFWs in Iraq and Iran where there were an estimated 1,600 and 1,000 documented Filipinos, respectively (Viray 2020). Among the logistical preparations of the military was the deployment of C-130 and C-295 planes for evacuation and two landing docks BRP Tarlac and BRP Davao del Sur (Viray 2020).

In June 2020, the AFP also successfully repatriated OFWs amongst 227 overseas Filipino workers (OFWs) from Algeria, 40 from Libya, and 20 from Tunisia who boarded chartered flights arranged by the DFA through the AFP's Joint Task Force Pag-Pauli (JTFP). The Navy also helped repatriate 30 Filipinos from India and Sri Lanka aboard naval vessels BRP Davao Del Sur and escorted by BRP Ramon Alcaraz (Nepomuceno 2020).

As a matter of policy, the AFP assists in bringing home safely overseas Filipinos in distress. In the process, the AFP seeks to preserve peace by strengthening ties with its foreign counterparts through military diplomacy. This is exemplified by Marine Colonel Noel Beleran, who engaged in talks with Rear Admiral Abdullah Bin Khasim Bin Abdullah Al Raisi, chief of the Royal Navy of Oman in February 2020 amid the repatriation of Filipinos in the Middle East (Nepomuceno 2020).

Also, an integral component of the Philippine military's activities to ensure the overall security of Filipinos is the participation in Joint Defense Cooperation Committee meetings such as the one held with Spain in November 2019 and with France in November 2022. The visit of Philippine officials from the Department of Defense and the Armed Forces of the Philippines (AFP) to Madrid in November 2019 resulted in the signing of the Memorandum of Agreement between the Philippines and Spain which facilitates the Philippine government's procurement of defense equipment from Spain in line with the modernization plan of the AFP (Embassy of the Philippines Madrid 2019). In addition to this, the talks between the French and Philippine military officials held in Manila in November 2022, paved the way for a cooperation agreement that will help build the Philippines' defense manufacturing capability, as well as acquire multirole aircraft and naval vessels which can be used for reconnaissance, carrying cargo, rescue, and evacuation (Sadongdong 2022).

Conclusion

Based on the foregoing discussion, it is clear that the motivations of the Philippine state that drive its activities toward Filipino communities overseas are support and co-optation. Support is embedded in the nature of the state as democratic, where governance principles of accountability and participation in nation-building, development, and the electoral process extend to its nationals abroad.

The Philippine state's support and co-optation activities, as discussed earlier, underscore the economic as well as political relevance of its national community abroad. The Philippine government has focused on Filipino migrant workers because of their economic relevance to the country, bringing in much needed remittances. They can also potentially bring in votes for political candidates who promise to give attention to their welfare, thereby gaining their favor during elections. Support is prioritized for them given their more vulnerable status compared to those who have attained citizenship in developed countries where they can obtain more stability and state protection. Overseas Filipinos who have immigrated abroad are targeted more for investments in development-related projects, donations, grants, and skills transfer as they are deemed more capable of doing so. Those who are highly skilled and have attained success in their professions in developed countries such as the US, Australia, Canada, New Zealand, among others are tapped to "give back" to the home country. An example of this is the Balik (Return)-Scientist program which seeks to reverse the effects of brain drain by enlisting Filipino scientists to share knowledge and expertise upon returning to the country. On the other hand, state action of support is more emphasized in countries where conditions are more volatile and with high concentrations of Filipino migrant workers such as in the Middle East. Assistance to nationals is more prominent in these areas.

There are numerous Filipino communities that are organized in different parts of the world, based on locality, occupation, and ethnic and regional origins. Their agency is seen in their proactive involvement in providing donations and technical and financial assistance to the home country, especially in times of need such as during natural disasters.

The task of protecting Filipino citizens abroad is a complex process that entails collaboration with foreign governments, national and local government agencies, and non-state actors such as civil society organizations and migrant groups. While the government plays a central role in this endeavor, non-government organizations as well as online communities are also important. They help monitor, access, and share vital information concerning OFWs. It is imperative that a comprehensive and inclusive multisectoral approach be adopted through which other stakeholders can provide inputs into decision-making. Migrant workers and advocacy groups can be consulted proactively on key issues that concern the safety and protection of OFWs.

Given the limitations of the government's capacity to carry out more intensive assistance during crisis situations, long-term preventive measures must be made beyond providing temporary relief and assistance in repatriation. The government can capitalize on alliances with other labor-sending countries like Indonesia and Vietnam, which are fellow ASEAN member countries, to obtain a better response from host countries that have more stringent regulatory environments. In this regard, in 2007, ASEAN heads of state adopted the ASEAN Declaration on the Protection and Promotion of the Rights of Migrant Workers and later in 2013 the ASEAN Declaration on Strengthening Social Protection. These two instruments are significant in that they assert that migrant workers have a substantial contribution to the economies of both their home and host countries and that they need social protection which is due to them. These ASEAN Declarations emphasize that cooperation between sending and receiving states is required to resolve cases and address the legitimate concerns of migrant workers from ASEAN member states.

With the creation of a separate new Department of Migrant Workers, it is expected that more vigorous government activities will be undertaken to promote the interest of OFWs. More streamlined and efficient ways of delivering services to OFWs are foreseen once the new department hurdles the transition period. It takes political will to effectively carry out a policy that promotes the safety and welfare of Filipino citizens in foreign lands. The success of this undertaking will depend on the government's commitment and concrete actions that support this policy under the direction of the national leadership.

With the continued significance of Philippine national communities abroad, the state's motivation to support and co-opt will remain. The long-standing policy to encourage labor migration is projected to continue in the next decade or so, given that the new DMW indicates the permanency of this policy. Therefore, current state activities towards its nationals abroad are projected to be strengthened, leaving room for innovation, given the changing global and domestic landscapes.

References

Asis, Maruja (2006) The Philippines' Culture of Migration. Available at: www.migrationpolicy.org/article/philippines-culture-migration (last accessed October 12, 2022).

Bangko Sentral ng Pilipinas (2024) Personal Remittances Set a New Record High in December 2023 at US$3.6 Billion; Full-Year Level of US$37.2 Billion Highest to Date. Available at: www.bsp.gov.ph/SitePages/MediaAndResearch/MediaDisp.aspx?ItemId=7005 (last accessed May 25, 2024).

Businessworld (2022) July Remittances Hit 7-Month High. Available at: www.bworldonline.com/top-stories/2022/09/16/475031/july-remittances-hit-7-month-high/ (last accessed October 12, 2022).

Center for Migrant Advocacy (n.d.) Bilateral Labor Agreements and Social Security Agreements. Available at: https://centerformigrantadvocacy.files.wordpress.com/2012/06/bilateral-labor-agreements-and-social-security-agreements.pdf (last accessed October 12, 2022).

Center for Migrant Advocacy (2014) The Feminization of Migration in the Philippines. Available at: https://centerformigrantadvocacy.files.wordpress.com/2014/04/feminization-of-migration-v-1-0-021315.pdf (last accessed October 12, 2022).

Commission on Elections (2022) Number and Turnout of Registered Voters for Overseas Automated and Manual Voting, per Country and Local Absentee Voting. Available at: https://comelec.gov.ph/?r=2022NLE/Statistics/2022OAVLAV (last accessed October 28, 2022).

Commission on Filipinos Overseas (n.d.a.) About Us. Available at: https://cfo.gov.ph/about-us/#:~:text=Established%20on%2016%20June%201980,their%20ties%20with%20the%20Motherland (last accessed December 17, 2022).

Commission on Filipinos Overseas (n.d.b) Global Summit on the Filipino Diaspora. Available at: https://mail.cfo.gov.ph/other-programs-initiatives/global-summit-of-filipinos-in-the-diaspora.html (last accessed October 28, 2022).

Commission on Filipinos Overseas (2015a) Annual Report. Manila.

Commission on Filipinos Overseas (2015b) CFO Primer. Manila.

Commission on Filipinos Overseas (2019) CFO Statistics on International Migration. Manila.

dataSpring Editors (2022) Filipino Seafarers, the Modern Foundation of the Maritime Industry, May 10. Available at: www.d8aspring.com/eye-on-asia/filipino-seafarers-the-modern-foundation-of-the-maritime-industry (last accessed December 16, 2022).

Department of Foreign Affairs (n.d.) Philippine Foreign Policy. Available at: https://dfa.gov.ph/about/phl-foreign-policy (last accessed December 16, 2022).

Department of Foreign Affairs (2022) DFA Brings Home First Batch of Filipinos from Sri Lanka, July 31. Available at: https://dfa.gov.ph/dfa-news/dfa-releasesupdate/30919-dfa-brings-home-first-batch-of-filipinos-from-sri-lanka (last accessed October 17, 2022).

Department of Labor and Employment (2021) PH-UAE Signs Historic, New Labor Accord; Deployment Resumes March 31, March 2. Available at: www.pressreader.com/philippines/sunstar-pampanga/20210305/281590948301862 (last accessed December 27, 2022).

Embassy of the Philippines Madrid (2019) Spain DND and AFP Officials Sign Bilateral Defense Cooperation Agreement with Spain, Hold 1st Joint Defense Cooperation Meeting, December 19. Available at: www.philembassymadrid.com/dnd-afp (last accessed December 26, 2022).

Embassy of the Philippines Singapore (n.d.) Reacquisition of Philippine Citizenship. Available at: www.philippine-embassy.org.sg/consular/citizenship/

retention-and-re-acquisition-of-philippine-citizenship/ (last accessed December 14, 2022).

Henderson, Sophie (2021) The Legal Protection of Women Migrant Domestic Workers from the Philippines and Sri Lanka: An Intersectional Rights-based Approach. *International Journal of Care and Caring* 5(1), 65–83.

House of Representatives Congressional Policy and Budget Research Department (House of Representatives) (2021) FF2021–05: Overseas Filipino Workers Profile. Available at: https://cpbrd.congress.gov.ph/2012-06-30-13-06-51/2012-06-30-13-36-50/1286-ff2021-05-overseas-filipino-workers-profile (last accessed December 16, 2022).

Ignacio, Aurora (2020) SSS Bilateral Agreements: Social Security Coverage for Overseas Filipinos, August 12. Available at: https://businessmirror.com.ph/2020/08/12/sss-bilateral-agreements-social-security-coverage-for-overseas-filipinos/ (last accessed October 13, 2022).

International Labor Organization (2012) Philippines Ratification Marks Global Milestone for Decent Work for Seafarers. Available at: www.ilo.org/global/standards/maritime-labour-convention/WCMS_187712/lang--en/index.htm (last accessed October 20, 2022).

Ismael, Javier Joe, and Cueto, Francis Earl (2022) Sweeper Flight Readied for Pinoys in Sri Lanka, July 23. Available at: www.manilatimes.net/2022/07/23/news/national/sweeper-flight-readied-for-pinoys-in-sri-lanka/1851907 (last accessed October 17, 2022).

Katigbak, Jovito, and Ma. Divina Gracia Roldan (2021) Protecting Filipino Migrant Workers in Distress through Social Media Platforms. *Asian and Pacific Migration Journal* 30(3), 357–369.

Loebach, Peter (2016) Space and a Damaged Place: Philippine Migrant Transnational Engagement Following the Guinsaugon Landslide Disaster. *Population, Space and Place* 22(6), 526–538.

Nepomuceno, Priam (2020) AFP Repatriates 299 Distressed Pinoys Abroad, June 25. Available at: www.pna.gov.ph/articles/1106981 (last accessed December 17, 2022).

Official Gazette (n.d.) Department of Foreign Affairs. Available at: www.dole.gov.ph/news/ph-uae-sign-historic-new-labor-accord-deployment-resumes-march-31/https://www.officialgazette.gov.ph/section/briefing-room/department-of-foreign-affairs-briefing-room/ (last accessed December 16, 2022).

Official Gazette (1995) Republic Act No. 8042: An Act to Institute the Policies of Overseas Employment and Establish a Higher Standard of Protection and Promotion of the Welfare of Migrant Workers, Their Families and Overseas Filipinos in Distress, and for Other Purposes, June 7. Available at: www.officialgazette.gov.ph/1995/06/07/republic-act-no-8042-2/ (last accessed December 28, 2022).

Official Gazette (2019) Republic Act No. 11299: An Act Establishing the Office for Social Welfare Attaché, April 17. Available at: www.officialgazette.gov.ph/2019/04/17/republic-act-no-11299/ (last accessed December 30, 2022).

Overseas Welfare Administration (n.d.). About OWWA. Available at: https://owwa.gov.ph/# (last accessed December 17, 2022).

Patinio, Ferdinand (2022) Department of Migrant Workers May Start by 2023: POEA, January 13. Available at: www.pna.gov.ph/articles/1165329 (last accessed December 12, 2022)

Philippine Overseas Employment Administration (n.d.) About POEA. Available at: www.dmw.gov.ph/archives/programs/programs&services.html (last accessed December 16, 2022)

Philippine Statistics Office (2019) Available at: https://psa.gov.ph/statistics/survey/labor-and-employment/survey-overseas-filipinos; https://psa.gov.ph/sites/default/files/2019%20Survey%20on%20Overseas%20Filipinos.pdf (last retrieved October 12, 2022).

Presidential Awards for Filipino Individuals and Organizations Overseas (n.d.) About the PAFIOO. Available at: https://presidentialawards.cfo.gov.ph/ (last accessed December 17, 2022).

Qaisrani, Ayesha (2020) Reaching Out, Inviting In: Pakistan's Approach to Diaspora Engagement. *Migration and Development* 11(3), 501–520.

Ragazzi, Francesco (2014) A Comparative Analysis of Diaspora Policies. *Political Geography* 41, 74–89.

Rocamora, Joyce Ann (2019) DFA to Open 6 New Embassies, PCGs. Available at: www.pna.gov.ph/articles/1085284 (last accessed December 16, 2022).

Rocamora, Joyce Ann (2022a) Alert Level 4 in Myanmar Remains; 701 Pinoys Repatriated So Far, July 27. Available at: www.pna.gov.ph/articles/1179962 (last accessed October 17, 2022).

Rocamora, Joyce Anne (2022b) Contingency Plan for OFWs in Taiwan Ready: DFA, August 11. Available at: www.pna.gov.ph/articles/1181108 (last accessed October 17, 2022).

Rocamora, Joyce Ann (2022c) Filipino Repatriates from War-Torn Ukraine. *Philippine News Agency*, March 23. Available at www.pna.gov.ph/articles/1170497 (last accessed October 17, 2022).

Rocamora, Joyce (2022d) OFW Dep't Law Takes Effect, Transition Underway, February 3. Available at www.pna.gov.ph/articles/1167006 (last accessed October 13, 2022).

Rocamora, Joyce Ann L. (2023) PH Evacuates First Batch of 50 Filipinos from Sudan. *Philippine News Agency*, April 25. Available at: www.rappler.com/nation/overseas-filipinos/philippines-plots-land-air-sea-exits-ofws-sudan/ (last accessed August 28, 2023).

Roldan, Ma. Divina Gracia (2020a) Reintegrating Overseas Filipino Workers Amidst the COVID-19 Pandemic. *De La Salle-Jesse M. Robredo Institute of Governance Policy Brief* 1(5). Available at: www.dlsu.edu.ph/research/covid-19-research-portal#pb (last accessed October 26, 2022).

Roldan, Ma. Divina (2020b) Reintegrating Returning Overseas Filipino Workers through Entrepreneurship. Paper presented at DLSU Research Congress 2020. Available at: www.dlsu.edu.ph/wp-content/uploads/pdf/conferences/research-congress-proceedings/2020/SEP-02.pdf (last accessed October 26, 2022).

Sadongdong, Martin (2022) PH, France Agree to Diversify Defense, Security Cooperation, November 12. Available at: https://mb.com.ph/2022/11/12/ph-france-agree-to-diversify-defense-security-cooperation/ (last accessed December 26, 2022).

Senate of the Philippines (2019) Senate Ratifies Measure Creating Social Welfare Attachés for Distressed OFWs, February 14. Available at: https://legacy.senate.gov.ph/press_release/2019/0214_prib1.asp (last accessed December 30, 2022).

Sinatti, Giulia, and Cindy Horst (2015) Migrants as Agents of Development: Diaspora Engagement Discourse and Practice in Europe. *Ethnicities* 15(1), 134–152.

Social Security System (2019) SSS Lauds Ph-SoKor Agreement on Social Security, December 2. Available at: www.sss.gov.ph/sss/appmanager/viewArticle.jsp?page=NR2019_063 (last accessed December 27, 2022).

Statista Research Department (2022a) Number of Reported Cases of Maltreatment against Overseas Filipino Workers (OFWs) in 2020, by Region of Employment. Available at: www.statista.com/statistics/1271337/philippines-abuse-incidents-against-ofws-by-region-of-employment/ (last accessed December 30, 2022).

Statista Research Department (2022b) Repatriated Overseas Filipino Workers (OFWs) during COVID-19 Pandemic 2022. Available at: www.statista.com/statistics/1243715/repatriated-overseas-workers-coronavirus-philippines/ (last accessed October 17, 2022).

Turner, Simon, and Nauja Kleist (2013) Introduction: Agents of Change? Staging and Governing Diasporas and the African State. *African Studies* 72(2), 192–206.

United Nations (2020) International Migrant Stock. Destination and Origin. Available at: www.un.org/development/desa/pd/content/international-migrant-stock (last accessed December 16, 2022).

Venzon, Cliff (2022) Philippines 'Modern-Day Heroes' Sent Record Remittances Last Year, February 15. Available at: https://asia.nikkei.com/Economy/Philippines-modern-day-heroes-sent-record-remittances-last-year (last accessed October 12, 2022).

Viray, Patricia (2020) Philippines to Send 2 Battalions to the Middle East for OFW Repatriation, January 8. Available at: www.philstar.com/headlines/2020/01/08/1983122/philippines-send-2-battalions-middle-east-ofw-repatriation (last accessed December 17, 2022).

World Bank (2020) Personal Remittances, Received (% of GDP) – Philippines. Available at: https://data.worldbank.org/indicator/BX.TRF.PWKR.DT.GD.ZS?locations=PH (last accessed December 12, 2022).

World Bank (2022) Remittances Brave Global Headwinds. *Migration and Development Brief 27*. Available at: www.knomad.org/sites/default/files/publication-doc/migration_and_development_brief_37_nov_2022.pdf. (last accessed December 27, 2022).

8 The United Kingdom

Good Information, Limited Liability, and a Powerful Safety Net

James Strong

Introduction

The United Kingdom generally tries to limit its liability for its nationals abroad. Adopting a broadly laissez-faire approach similar to those of China (Ghiselli, Chapter 5), Germany (Brummer and Oppermann, Chapter 10), and the US (Hogan and Krebs, Chapter 13), it focuses its support efforts on providing advice and offering basic consular services, primarily to tourists and other short-term travelers. Thanks to its relative wealth and nature as a liberal democracy, it rarely seeks to co-opt or suppress its nationals abroad. The main exceptions to this rule involve individuals whose status as British nationals is in some dispute.

Most UK nationals abroad are relatively wealthy by global standards, visiting or residing in stable, developed, often English-speaking states that might themselves be considered part of a greater UK diaspora as former colonies of the British Empire. They generally do not need the UK's help. Nor does the UK generally need them. Remittances play a minor part in its economy, while its popularity as a destination for inbound migration compensates for any loss of skilled labor caused by outbound migration. UK governments are under no legal obligation to support UK nationals abroad. Nor does the UK have a dedicated diaspora or migrant ministry.

In the absence of economic, legal or institutional pressures to do so, UK governments engage with UK nationals abroad when they feel moral or political pressure to do so. The two are often intertwined, with Parliament, the press, or the public demanding action on behalf of (or, more rarely, against) individuals with some sort of moral claim on the UK government's attention. This political dynamic makes the UK somewhat inconsistent and piecemeal in its approach, since government legitimacy derives less from consistency and more from compliance with prevailing political currents.

Overview of the British Community Abroad

A large number of UK nationals currently reside abroad. The UN Population Division (2020) estimates that 4.73 million *UK-born individuals* live permanently outside of the UK, while the UK's Office for National Statistics put the number of *UK citizens* abroad as high as 5.5 million – implying that the UK's overseas migrant population could be nearly 10 percent of the size of the UK resident population (Sriskandarajah and Drew 2006: viii–ix). This is a higher proportion even than India, the state with the largest migrant population abroad in absolute terms (Blarel, Chapter 2). If we look more widely, at people who might be eligible for a UK passport or consider themselves ethnically or culturally British despite not having been born (or possibly ever having lived) in the UK, the figure grows by another 50 million (Hampshire 2013: 307). Several hundred thousand UK nationals divide their time between the UK and a second home overseas, while British tourists make an estimated 50 million overseas trips every year (Schwarck 2016: 37).

During Britain's imperial period, its people migrated abroad at an extraordinary rate. Richards (2018) estimates that close to 19 million people migrated permanently from the British Isles between 1815 and 1930, more than a third of all European migrants during this period (Hampshire 2013: 304). By the early twentieth century, around 140 million people around the world claimed British descent. As is the case with Russia (Larson, Chapter 4), the UK's imperial past is a major driver of its contemporary diaspora and migration patterns. Unlike Russia, however, the UK does not pursue irredentist policies aimed at bringing these populations back under British rule. In part this is because Britain's imperial migrants moved to territories geographically far removed from the UK itself, like North America or Australia, rather than contiguous territories. In part it is because, at a certain point, most British migrants stopped thinking of themselves as British – becoming American, Australian, or Canadian instead. Although Victorian attempts to build a federal "Greater Britain" failed (Bell 2007, 2020), the British Empire still left behind large overseas populations who speak English and retain some cultural affinity with the UK. The so-called Commonwealth Realms[1] even share the UK head of state. This means that British migrants have obvious places to go; there is a British world beyond the UK's shores (Constantine 2003: 17).

[1] As well as being the King of the United Kingdom, Charles III is King of Antigua and Barbuda, Australia, The Bahamas, Belize, Canada, Grenada, Jamaica, New Zealand, Papua New Guinea, Saint Kitts and Nevis, Saint Lucia, Saint Vincent and the Grenadines, the Solomon Islands, and Tuvalu.

Table 8.1 *Locations of UK-born individuals resident outside of the UK, 1990–2020*

	1990 %	1995 %	2000 %	2005 %	2010 %	2015 %	2020 %
Settled	73.6	73.8	71.9	67.0	63.5	62.1	60.4
EU	12.0	12.5	13.1	17.5	20.5	20.8	22.2
British Isles	7.1	5.7	5.8	7.2	7.7	8.2	8.5
Colonized	3.2	3.7	4.1	3.4	3.3	3.4	3.2
Other	4.0	4.4	5.2	4.9	4.9	5.5	5.7
Total (millions)	**3.79 m**	**3.71 m**	**3.86 m**	**4.15 m**	**4.43 m**	**4.38 m**	**4.73 m**

Source: (UN Population Division 2020).

Between decolonization and the UK's membership of the EU, British emigration came to be matched, and then exceeded, by immigration (Sturge 2022: 19). This is the main reason why Britain pays little attention to emigration despite being "an emigrant nation *par excellence*" (Hampshire 2013: 303). Immigration is new and politically controversial. Emigration is old and uncontroversial.

As Table 8.1 shows, the distribution of British national communities abroad reflects the shape of the former British Empire, despite small increases in intra-EU migration after 2000. Some 62 percent of the 4.73 million UK-born people living overseas in 2019 lived in "settled" territories where European colonists had displaced indigenous peoples. A further 3.2 percent lived in formerly "colonized" territories – such as India, where Europeans took power but did not displace the indigenous population. Just 5.8 percent of the UK's overseas population in 2019 lived outside of the EU or the former British Empire, widely but thinly dispersed in over one hundred countries with a British population of at least 1,000 (Sriskandarajah and Drew 2006: ix).

As Table 8.2 shows, British migration patterns are remarkably stable and highly concentrated. In 2020, approximately 1.29 million British migrants lived in Australia, comprising 27.2 percent of the total migrant population, but just 34,195 in the Isle of Man, the tenth-ranked destination. The largest British populations outside of English-speaking or European nations were in Indonesia (32,911), Bangladesh (32,820), the United Arab Emirates (UAE) (29,191), and Türkiye (26,016).

When British migrants move to English-speaking countries, they generally integrate quickly. This precludes the formation of a "diaspora" identity, and makes it difficult to identify specific population clusters.

Table 8.2 *Top 10 Locations of UK-born individuals living outside of the UK by size of expatriate population, 1990–2020*

Rank	1990	1995	2000	2005	2010	2015	2020
1	Australia	Australia	Australia	Australia	Australia	Australia	Australia
2	Canada	USA	USA	Other EU	Other EU	Other EU	Other EU
3	USA	Canada	Canada	USA	USA	USA	USA
4	Other EU	Other EU	Other EU	Canada	Canada	Canada	Canada
5	New Zealand	New Zealand	New Zealand	New Zealand	New Zealand	Ireland	Ireland
6	Ireland	Ireland	Ireland	Ireland	Ireland	New Zealand	New Zealand
7	South Africa	South Africa	South Africa	South Africa	South Africa	South Africa	South Africa
8	Channel Islands	Channel Islands	Channel Islands	Channel Islands	Channel Islands	Channel Islands	Channel Islands
9	Isle of Man	Isle of Man	Isle of Man	Isle of Man	Isle of Man	Switzerland	Switzerland
10	Switzerland	Switzerland	Philippines	Switzerland	Switzerland	Isle of Man	Isle of Man

Source: (UN Population Division 2020).

Table 8.3 *Number of non-citizen UK passport holders by category*

Category	Number of passport holders
British Overseas Territories Citizens	63,391
British Overseas Citizens	12,192
British Subjects	32,418
British Nationals (Overseas)	314,779
British Protected Persons	1,252
Total	424,032

Source: (HM Passport Office 2020; HM Government 2022b).

When they move to non-English-speaking countries, things look different. British migrants in the UAE, for example, live in distinct expatriate communities near to employment centers and away from local populations (Coles and Walsh 2010: 1330–1331). The 300,000 or so British nationals who have retired to sunnier climates in Spain are notorious for forming English-speaking communities, socializing at English-speaking restaurants, and buying imported British products from English-speaking shops (Sriskandarajah and Drew 2006: ix). Even where UK nationals apparently integrate with non-English-speaking host populations, appearances can deceive. The UK imposes no restrictions on dual citizenship. According to the 2011 census, 488,467 British citizens resident in England and Wales also held a non-UK passport (Office for National Statistics 2021). The 2021 census, meanwhile, found that 5.9 million UK residents held citizenship of another country (Office for National Statistics 2022). In many cases, the UK nationals who live in non-English-speaking countries are also (and often originally) citizens of their "host" state.

A final complicating factor arises from the UK's unusual practice of granting British passports to people who are not British citizens. These people do not necessarily have the right to live and work in the UK, but are entitled to British consular assistance and diplomatic protection. Five such categories exist (see Table 8.3). In total, some 424,032 people hold a passport that does not grant them the right to live in the UK but does enable them to call on UK officials for assistance abroad.

Diplomatic and Consular Dimension

The UK has a large global diplomatic and consular network comprised of 283 embassies, consulates, high commissions, liaison offices, and trade missions (Foreign, Commonwealth and Development Office 2022a). There is no link between the distribution of the UK's overseas representations and the location of its national communities abroad, in part because the UK has some form of representation in most major population centers around the world whether it has nationals there or not, and in part because UK migrants can usually access support from local authorities.

The UK has no specific diaspora ministry: the Foreign, Commonwealth and Development Office (FCDO) is responsible for tourists, migrants, and (some) members of the diaspora (Tsinovoi and Adler-Nissen 2018: 15). Its efforts are mostly limited to "encouraging self-help, managing expectations and explaining the limits of its assistance" (House of Commons Foreign Affairs Committee 2014: 3). This approach developed during the nineteenth century, when governments disclaimed responsibility for their citizens' welfare at home as well as abroad, and when most British migrants moved to territories run by British colonial authorities. The occasional initiatives that *did* aim to support migrants, such as the creation of the Emigrant's Information Office in 1886 and the various forms of support for overseas settlers under the Empire Settlement Act of 1922, never coalesced into a coherent diaspora policy.

The FCDO produces detailed guidance for tourists, covering both general principles like the importance of proper insurance (HM Government 2022a), and country-specific information about visa requirements, local customs, and laws – an approach Hampshire (2013: 313) describes as "more advanced" than most other governments in terms of "pre-departure services." In extreme cases, this advice extends to specific instructions not to travel to particular states or territories, advice that generally voids travel insurance and triggers automatic refunds on organized tours. For migrants, the FCDO produces 138 "living in country guides" covering rules on residency, healthcare and benefits (Foreign, Commonwealth and Development Office 2022c). It also offers tailored advice for businesses and entrepreneurs looking to trade abroad (Consterdine 2020: 439–440).

The FCDO provides consular support to several hundred thousand British nationals every year. In 2019, for example, it assisted 22,000 British nationals, offered advice to a further 415,000, issued 30,000 emergency travel documents, and provided support in 3,000 cases of detention, 3,000 deaths, and 2,600 hospitalizations overseas (Raab 2021; Walker and Robinson 2021: 2). These services operate on a cost-neutral basis. Individuals pay for specific consular services such as issuing emergency travel documents, while a premium of £15.50 from the fee charged for each British passport goes towards funding the UK's consular operations (Walker and Robinson 2021: 2). Notwithstanding these numbers, UK nationals have no *legal* right to consular assistance (Brummer and Ganguly, Chapter 1; Geyer 2007). The government's position is that UK nationals should seek assistance from local authorities first, and can only expect diplomatic assistance where that is unreasonably withheld (Foreign, Commonwealth and Development Office 2022b).

The UK considers "the safety and security of British nationals overseas ... the responsibility of the country that these individuals are resident in" (Ministry of Defence 2021: 3). There are, however, circumstances when Parliament or the public demand more robust action, typically crises involving natural disasters, conflict or civil unrest, especially those that generate emotive media images at home of stranded British nationals. For this reason, every diplomatic post is expected to maintain a crisis management plan to "ensure the safety and security of the British community", including by developing a network of UK national "wardens" to assist in evacuations (Ministry of Defence 2021: 29). After the Bali bombings of 2002, the FCDO opened a new section, the Crisis Centre, designed to assist officials overseas in responding to major events affecting British nationals (Hague 2012). It also operates a dedicated Forced Marriages Unit (Charsley 2006: 1170; HM Government 2012).

The UK's most high-profile consular efforts involve supporting victims of terrorism abroad. Given their large numbers and wide geographic distribution, it is unsurprising that UK nationals have frequently been affected by major terrorist incidents overseas. The British Consul General in Istanbul was himself killed in a bombing in November 2003. The UK's most sensitive consular efforts involve UK nationals detained overseas on espionage charges. Iran regularly accuses dual UK–Iranian nationals – such as Nazanin Zaghari-Ratcliffe, detained between 2016 and 2022 – of spying, and demands diplomatic and economic concessions from the UK to secure their release. Although the FCDO refers to such detainees as "consular cases," the House of Commons Foreign Affairs Committee has suggested calling them "hostages," to reflect the fact that Iran often makes demands unrelated to the individual case as part of release negotiations (House of Commons Foreign Affairs Committee 2020b: 19–20). Although the UK government insists that it does not "accept dual British nationals being used as diplomatic leverage" (HM Government 2021: 7), it did agree to settle an outstanding debt due to the Iranian government immediately before Zaghari-Ratcliffe's release (House of Commons Foreign Affairs Committee 2020b: 22–23). Two general policy positions complicate how the UK handles these cases. First, the UK does not usually offer consular assistance to dual nationals in the state of their other nationality (Warbrick 1988: 1003). Second, even where it does offer consular assistance, its efforts are usually limited to ensuring that detainees are treated no worse than host state nationals.

The UK has embraced social media as a tool for disseminating information and communicating in crises (Tsinovoi and Adler-Nissen

2018: 13). In 2013, the FCDO discontinued the LOCATE database, its main mechanism for keeping track of nationals abroad, to focus on social media. Most embassies and consulates run Facebook pages for UK national migrants and tourists (Consterdine 2020: 441–442), while the FCDO Twitter account publishes both general and targeted travel advice (Foreign and Commonwealth Office 2013).

The UK sometimes collaborates with other states in order to share the burden of providing diplomatic and consular support to nationals abroad. During its period of EU membership, it participated in arrangements that allowed EU nationals to request consular assistance from other EU states' overseas missions. The UK also helped develop the Non-combatant Evacuation Operation Coordination Group (NEOCG), a multilateral partnership formed in 2000 to support coordination and collaboration in the rescue of nationals affected by conflict or disaster abroad. It is an informal association, primarily of EU and NATO member states, who agree to share best practice, information, and resources in the sort of crisis situations that warrant military rescue operations. Members meet twice annually, with the position of chair rotating amongst them. Its primary goal is to facilitate the rapid establishment of a "coordination cell" – a concept developed by UK emergency planners – in response to a crisis, to enable member states to pool resources to ensure evacuations are conducted efficiently and effectively (Sutherland 2012).

In some cases – such as through its support of the British Hajj Delegation (2011), which helps British Muslims undertaking the pilgrimage to Mecca – the UK collaborates with non-state actors to offer targeted consular assistance. Otherwise, it expects employers to take responsibility for their employees (Tsinovoi and Adler-Nissen 2018: 18) and travel companies for their customers. It advises small and medium-sized enterprises through its Overseas Business Risk service (Okano-Heijmans and Caesar-Gordon 2016: 433–437). The warden network also represents a form of privatization of consular activities, engaging volunteers to locate UK nationals in a crisis (Sutherland 2012: 15; Ministry of Defence 2021: 13). Although the UK military has not engaged with Private Security Companies to the same extent as its US counterpart, the FCDO does employ private security contractors (Cusumano 2015: 229). There have been cases of UK military personnel collaborating with private security contractors (especially former UK military personnel) in emergencies (Grimal and Melling 2011: 167).

The UK remains reluctantly willing to help tourists get home as a last resort, a stance most clearly illustrated during the early days of the Covid-19 pandemic. On March 23, 2020, as states began to close their borders, Foreign Secretary Dominic Raab (2020b) advised UK nationals to return home at once. Several thousand were stranded by flight cancellations and travel restrictions. Although the UK had used military aircraft to evacuate nationals from Hubei early in the pandemic, it shifted tack as Covid-19 spread. The FCDO focused on providing information to British travelers about how to access available flights, while also lobbying governments and airlines to keep commercial routes open. Only where these efforts failed did the government charter aircraft to 'rescue' stranded nationals. The House of Commons Foreign Affairs Committee (2020a: 5–7) criticized this approach as "too slow" and warned against "too much reliance on commercial providers", noting that other states offered faster, more comprehensive charter flight programs. It also noted that the UK's usual approach of providing information and expecting citizens to look after themselves fell short in uncertain, fast-moving circumstances, with consular staff forced to work from home without access to office phone lines, central helplines overwhelmed by unprecedented demand, and less social-media savvy travelers cut off from the most up-to-date sources of advice (House of Commons Foreign Affairs Committee 2020a: 11). The government rejected most of these criticisms, insisting that the benefits of keeping commercial air routes open vastly outweighed what could possibly have been achieved by chartering additional repatriation flights (HM Government 2020: 3). By May 2020, over 30,000 people had been repatriated from 27 countries (Foreign and Commonwealth Office 2020), while a further 1.3 million had returned independently via commercial routes (Raab 2020a: 12).

One interesting aspect of the UK's Covid-19 repatriation policy was its focus on tourists over migrants. With the exception of the initial round of evacuations from Hubei, British nationals permanently resident overseas generally did not qualify for repatriation (House of Commons Foreign Affairs Committee 2020a: 8). This policy led to criticism that the government was prioritizing (predominantly white) holidaymakers over (predominantly non-white) dual-residents (Bi 2020). In the end, however, the UK did repatriate nationals stuck in countries such as India, Pakistan, Nigeria, and Bangladesh (Ahmad 2020: 344).

Though the UK generally does not attempt to co-opt its national communities abroad using consular or diplomatic means, an exception to this rule occurred relatively recently. Under the Sino-British Joint Declaration of 1984 which set the terms for the return of sovereignty over Hong Kong, the Chinese government agreed not to restrict civil liberties in the territory until at least 2037. The UK regarded China's imposition on Hong Kong of a new National Security Law in 2020 as a major breach of this commitment. In response, it created a new visa route to enable BN(O) passport holders – Hong Kong nationals who retain their colonial-era right to access UK consular support outside of China – to relocate to the UK. Over 160,000 BN(O) visas were granted in the two years following the scheme's introduction in January 2021 (HM Government 2023a). Effectively, the UK co-opted these individuals into its diplomatic response to the National Security Law, signaling that it was willing and able to trigger a partial exodus of (relatively wealthy, high-skilled) Hong Kong citizens should China persist.

There is also one obvious exception to the rule that the UK does not repress its nationals abroad using diplomatic or consular tools: the case of Shamima Begum. Born in London to parents of Bangladeshi heritage, Begum was one of three 15-year-old British schoolgirls who traveled to Syria in 2015 to join Da'esh. Although her case attracted considerable attention at the time, UK authorities were unable to locate Begum and she vanished into Da'esh. Four years later, as Da'esh collapsed, a British journalist found her, heavily pregnant, in a Syrian refugee camp. Having already lost two children to war and malnutrition, she asked the UK government to help her return home. Its response was categorical. Using powers granted to him by the British Nationality Act 1981, Home Secretary Sajid Javid stripped Begum of her British citizenship, meaning she would no longer be eligible either to receive UK consular assistance or to return to the UK. Similar measures have been taken against around 150 individuals, mostly suspected Islamist terrorists (Javid 2019). Following her infant's death shortly afterwards, Foreign Secretary Jeremy Hunt (2019) said that Begum "knew ... she was going into a country where there was no ... consular assistance, and I'm afraid those decisions ... have consequences." Despite the fact that Javid's action effectively rendered her stateless, Begum's attempt to contest it through the courts failed, and the government faced no real political pushback. She remains in Syria.

Economic and Social Dimension

The UK offers very limited economic and social support for its nationals abroad, and makes no real effort to co-opt them. It does offer some support for business networks, for example in the US and the UAE (Hampshire 2013: 314). But in the absence of a diaspora policy, a ministry with specific responsibility for the diaspora, or a pressing economic need to generate remittances from expatriates to support the domestic economy, these activities remain limited compared to those put on by other states.

Other than immigrants to Britain returning "home," the majority of UK migrants fall into two groups: a large number of professionals who leave the UK for work and a smaller number of sun-seeking retirees. Most UK migrants are relatively wealthy, secure individuals moving from one English-speaking developed country to another (Consterdine 2020: 442). Although the UK receives significant remittances sent home by migrants working abroad – £4.1bn in 2021 (Knomad 2022) – these account for just 0.1 percent of GDP, rendering them irrelevant to government decision-making (Hampshire 2013: 319). Reflecting the fact that many immigrants to the UK come from less wealthy countries, it is perhaps unsurprising that remittances *from* the UK are about twice as large as remittances *to* the UK (Vargas Silva and Klimaviciute 2020). In this sense, the UK looks more like Germany (Brummer and Oppermann, Chapter 10) or the US (Hogan and Krebs, Chapter 13), and very different to countries such as the Philippines (Roldan, Chapter 7) and Indonesia (Murphy and Freedman, Chapter 9) that rely on remittances and actively try to protect the rights of migrant workers abroad.

The UK does not incentivize migrants to return to the UK, in part because it has a surplus of the sort of highly skilled professionals who typically migrate internationally. Although it has experienced sector-specific pressures in recent years, especially in the fields of medicine and healthcare, the UK has continued to rely on its ability to attract immigrants rather than trying to entice emigrants back. This policy makes sense. Most outbound migrants feel positive about their experiences of living in the UK (Sriskandarajah and Drew 2006: viii–ix). This suggests that the factors that pull them abroad are ones the UK cannot offer – like better weather, closeness to family members who have already emigrated, or different employment opportunities.

Security Dimension

The UK has a long track record of using military force to support its nationals abroad. It is among the minority of states that claim that the pre-Second World War customary international right of states to use force to protect their nationals abroad survived the signature of the UN Charter (Zedalis 1990: 221; Ruys 2008: 259–260; Schwarck 2016: 37). Since 1945, the UK has threatened or used force to protect nationals in Iran (1946 and 1951), Egypt (1952 and 1956), Zanzibar (1964), the Falkland Islands (1982), Lebanon (2006), Libya (2011), Afghanistan (2021), and Sudan (2023) (Akehurst 1977: 5–6; Ronzitti 2019: 435–440).

Most UN members wanted the UN Charter to supersede states' historic right to protect their nationals abroad because it was often abused (especially by Britain) to provide pretexts for imperial interventions (Wingfield 2000: 461). In 1850, for example, Foreign Secretary Lord Palmerston ordered a naval blockade of Greece to force the Greek authorities to compensate Don Pacifico, a Gibraltar-born British subject, for damage done to his property during anti-Semitic riots three years earlier. Facing criticism for having co-opted Don Pacifico as a tool of British imperialism, Palmerston insisted that "as the Roman, in days of old, held himself free from indignity, when he could say *Civis Romanus sum*; so also a British subject, in whatever land he may be, shall feel confident that the watchful eye and the strong arm of England, will protect him" (Denza 2018: 464). Britain launched what became the Second Opium War against China in 1856 in response to the Chinese seizure of the *Arrow*, a British-flagged Chinese vessel. It intervened in the Boxer Rebellion in 1900 (ostensibly) to protect British nationals, and in 1927 sent troops to Shanghai to help put down pro-nationalist mobs (Zedalis 1990: 239–240).

A more recent example of the relationship between imperial politics and the desire to protect nationals abroad arose in 1982. Pursuing its long-running claim to sovereignty over the South Atlantic archipelago it calls Las Malvinas, Argentina invaded the Falkland Islands, a self-governing British overseas territory with a predominantly English-speaking population of a little over two thousand. In response, the UK government dispatched a military task force which recaptured the islands at the cost of 907 lives on all sides. Speaking after the initial invasion, Prime Minister Margaret Thatcher made clear that the UK acted primarily to defend its "sovereign territory." She also made clear, however, that the inhabitants of that territory were "British in stock and tradition, and ... in allegiance" and insisted that the UK "cannot allow the democratic rights of the islanders to be denied" (Thatcher 1982: 633–634). Though the war was mainly about territory, in other words, it was also about the British diaspora. The two are difficult to separate for a (post) imperial power.

Subsequent operations have generally complied with the standards set out by UK Foreign Secretary Selwyn Lloyd, ironically at the time of the (distinctly illegitimate) 1956 invasion of Suez. They have responded to "an imminent threat of injury" linked to a "failure or inability" of the host state to protect UK nationals, and have been "confined to the object of protecting the nationals against injury" (Wingfield 2000: 447–448). The three most obvious recent examples are Operation *Deference* in Libya in 2011, Operation Pitting in Afghanistan in 2021 and the unnamed operation in Sudan in 2023.

Operation Deference was a quintessential Non-combatant Evacuation Operation (NEO). UK officials, working in close collaboration with representatives of the other members of the NEO Coordination Group (NCG)[2],

[2] Australia, Canada, France, Germany, Hungary, Ireland, Italy, Malta, the Netherlands, Sweden, and the United States participated in the NEO Coordination Cell formed in 2011.

successfully planned and executed the evacuation of several thousand nationals from Libya during the early stages of its civil war (Sutherland 2012: 15). NCG members, operating out of the British High Commission in Malta, shared information and assets to maximize the number of citizens secured; British forces evacuated 600 UK nationals and 1,170 nationals of other NCG states, while other states evacuated 202 UK nationals (Schwarck 2016: 37). In some cases, UK Special Forces deployed within Libya to locate and transport UK and partner state nationals to extraction points (Grimal and Melling 2011: 165–166). Others were directed to open commercial routes out of the country, or evacuated via less dramatic military means.

Operation Pitting, the withdrawal of UK nationals and UK-affiliated Afghan nationals from Kabul ahead of the city's capture by the Taliban in 2021, was larger but less successful. Both operations were hampered by the relatively limited information UK officials held about the numbers and locations of UK nationals. But the situation in Afghanistan was complicated further by the UK's failure to prepare for the Taliban's rapid takeover (House of Commons Foreign Affairs Committee 2022: 9). Over 15,000 people were eventually evacuated over the course of thirteen days. Unusually, this figure included some 5,000 Afghan nationals eligible for UK support under the Afghanistan Relocations and Assistance Policy (ARAP). ARAP was established by the UK National Security Council in December 2020 to offer protection to Afghan nationals who had worked for the UK government, as well as (in exceptional circumstances) individuals whose activities had supported the UK's goals and would potentially make them targets for retribution (House of Commons Foreign Affairs Committee 2022: 4, 19–20). However, the process was chaotic, and many people who were eligible for evacuation were left behind. At one point, UK officials, acting on instructions apparently issued within the Prime Minister's Office (no one would confirm by whom) in response to social media pressure, used scarce resources helping to evacuate the British founder of Nowzad, a Kabul-based animal rescue charity, and its animals, on a 230-seat privately chartered aircraft. No other human passengers were evacuated on the flight (House of Commons Foreign Affairs Committee 2022: 31–33). Clearly the UK has the capacity to conduct military evacuation operations on a large scale, but clearly, too, the existence of such military capacity does not necessarily translate into effective organizational capacity.

Things went more smoothly in Sudan, with the UK completing what the government described as the "largest and longest" Western evacuation operation following the outbreak of civil conflict in April 2023 (HM Government 2023b). Over the period between April 25 and May 4, 2023, a military task force evacuated 2,450 UK nationals and 1,200 citizens of allied states (House of Commons Library 2023). This operation was aided by co-operation from Sudanese authorities, but hindered by the decision to evacuate UK embassy personnel before other nationals. Minister of State Andrew Mitchell (2023a) told the House of Commons, "we have a duty to all British citizens, of course, but we have a particular duty of care to our own staff and diplomats." Mitchell also confirmed that the majority of British nationals evacuated were dual UK–Sudanese citizens. Under parliamentary pressure the government also evacuated some Sudanese nationals who normally live and work in the UK as NHS clinicians (Mitchell 2023b).

The UK does not always use military measures to protect its nationals when otherwise it might. It has not kept up its nineteenth-century willingness to use force to override judicial proceedings in other sovereign states. It has generally also been reluctant to engage directly in hostage-rescue missions, preferring to work with local partners. When Shamima Begum asked for military assistance to return to the UK from Syria, Defence Secretary Ben Wallace (2019) said she was on her own: "I'm not putting at risk British people's lives to go looking for terrorists or former terrorists in a failed state." The UK government has even been willing not merely to abandon, but actually to harm, UK nationals associated with Islamist terrorism (Sykes 2016: 749–750). The most dramatic example of this was the case of Reyaad Khan and Ruhul Amin. Khan and Amin were British Da'esh operatives. In August 2015, Prime Minister David Cameron ordered an RAF drone strike near Raqqa in Syria that killed both men. It was, as Cameron (2015: 30) admitted, a "new departure" for the UK, which had never previously carried out the targeted killing of one of its own nationals, and which finally abolished the death penalty for treason in 1998. In a heavily redacted report, the parliamentary Intelligence and Security Committee (2017) concluded that the UK government probably reacted proportionately to the security threat posed by Khan, and that Amin's death was justifiable. Nevertheless, it is significant that the UK government was willing and able – without questions being raised about its legitimacy – to kill two of its own nationals without any semblance of legal due process, simply because they were abroad.

The key point, as Begum's case exemplifies, is that the UK government denies that such individuals *are* UK nationals, and therefore accepts no responsibility for protecting them (Sykes 2016: 749–750) and no limitations on its right to kill them (Govier and Boutland 2020: 97–98). At the same time, however, the fact that the UK was only legally able to strip Begum of her citizenship because of her Bangladeshi ancestry suggests that this position relies on an implicit racial hierarchy (Mironova 2021: 3). It implies that dual nationals – or, as in Begum's case, UK nationals with a theoretical right to dual nationality owing to their parents' or grandparents' migrant past – have a less secure form of citizenship than those with no migrant heritage.

Conclusion

The single biggest driver of UK government efforts to engage with national communities abroad is domestic politics. Parliament and public opinion would not normally consider government attempts to co-opt or repress national communities abroad legitimate. The main exceptions to this are extreme circumstances: China's partial repudiation of the Sino-British Joint Declaration, which came at a time of rising hawkishness towards China within the governing Conservative Party, and the involvement of British nationals in Da'esh. Most of the time, Parliament and public opinion support the UK government's laissez-faire approach to supporting national communities abroad. There is no real need to support the British diaspora economically or socially, and most British people accept that tourists and business travelers should have private insurance. In exceptional circumstances, however, such as the conflicts in Libya, Afghanistan, and Sudan, or during the early stages of the Covid-19 pandemic, the press, public, and parliamentarians alike expect the government to leap into action, deploying diplomatic and military assets to get UK nationals home. Even then, who exactly gets prioritized depends on whose supporters lobby government most effectively, as the evacuation of the Nowzad rescue animals from Kabul or of non-UK national NHS staff from Sudan shows.

Since most members of the UK diaspora integrate into their host communities – communities that could often themselves be considered part of that diaspora – UK governments pay little attention to them. The only real exception to this rule is UK nationals resident in EU member states after Brexit. Given how much domestic political debate focuses on immigration over emigration, it is perhaps unsurprising that the interests of UK migrant communities elsewhere in the EU played little part in the negotiations around the UK's withdrawal. Nevertheless, the government did agree to a process that permitted EU nationals who moved to the UK prior to Brexit to remain in the country, thereby ensuring that EU members would grant similar concessions to UK nationals. It has also taken steps to inform UK nationals in the EU about the implications of Brexit for them, and has offered some targeted support to vulnerable individuals who might otherwise struggle (Consterdine 2020: 442) – such as Kathleen Poole, a 74-year-old UK national threatened with deportation from Sweden when her advanced dementia prevented her applying for post-Brexit residency rights (BBC News 2023a).

Generally speaking, UK national communities abroad have limited agency towards the UK. Although they are numerous, they are not sufficiently economically important to require government attention. While they retain voting rights for a period after departure, they do not constitute a distinct voting bloc. Non-resident voters vote in the constituency in which they were last resident before leaving the UK, meaning their influence is distributed across the country rather than concentrated in dedicated expatriate constituencies (as in the French model). While a small number of individual nationals abroad have succeeded in exercising agency towards the UK through their involvement in acts of terrorism, their efforts have tended to reinforce rather than to change government policy, and they have been relatively comprehensively repressed through a combination of consular and security tools.

Most UK nationals abroad are economically secure and socially well integrated into their developed, democratic, English-speaking host states. They are reasonably wealthy on average, but not wealthy or numerous enough to make their remittances economically significant. Nor are they politically significant. Because the UK is a liberal democracy, its governments cannot legitimately co-opt or repress its nationals abroad except in extreme circumstances. Because the UK diaspora is larger than the UK population, and UK nationals continue to travel abroad as tourists and migrants in enormous numbers, UK governments attempt to limit their liability for them. This generally works; travelers cover the cost of routine consular assistance through direct fees and an indirect tax on passport holders. Those who follow travel advice – including the general injunction not to travel without adequate private insurance, but also advice against travel to regions where consular support may not be available – rarely need non-routine assistance. Only in extreme cases – involving terrorism, state hostage-taking, natural disasters or wars – is more robust support required. Here the UK's significant power-projection capabilities, and ability to work effectively in conjunction with diplomatic and military allies ensures it generally can deliver, albeit not necessarily without difficulty. In Afghanistan, the UK struggled thanks to its failure to anticipate the speed of the Taliban takeover and to prepare evacuation plans accordingly. In the conflict with Da'esh, the UK proved willing to reject and even kill its own nationals should their conduct appear "undesirable" in some way – a judgement difficult to distinguish from broader questions about institutionalized racism and the multinational, multicultural nature of national identity in the post-imperial UK.

There is little immediate prospect of a major change in the UK's approach. It has a well-established culture of assuming its nationals can take care of themselves. It has undertaken major overseas operations in extreme situations to rescue its nationals abroad, and it seems unlikely to shift towards the active promotion of social and economic activities among its diaspora in future. Indeed, it seems unlikely that the UK will even begin to use the language of diaspora any time soon. At the same time, there have been some recent hints at possible change. In September 2023, following a ruling from the Parliamentary Ombudsman, the FCDO apologized and paid compensation to a British academic who had been detained in the UAE accused of spying. It accepted, in effect, that it had fallen short in its support obligations and promised to review its internal guidance on similar cases (BBC News 2023b). Moreover, the dislocation caused by the UK's withdrawal from the European Union – the largest destination other than Australia for UK nationals moving abroad in the years leading up to "Brexit" – may become more salient as a political issue over time. Given the mismatch between promises made during the withdrawal process, and the actual impact of third-party status on UK nationals' rights in the EU, it is possible that further action might be required in future.

References

Ahmad, Lord (2020) Covid-19: Repatriation of UK Nationals. Hansard House of Lords Debates: Volume 803. April 30, 2020, London.

Akehurst, Michael (1977) The Use of Force to Protect Nationals Abroad. *International Relations* 5(5), 3–23.

BBC News (2023a) Kathleen Poole: Deportation of Grandmother with Alzheimer's Paused. Available at: www.bbc.co.uk/news/uk-65196484 (last accessed August 23, 2023).

BBC News (2023b) Matthew Hedges: Foreign Office Apology to UAE Academic. Available at: www.bbc.co.uk/news/uk-england-tyne-66711297 (last accessed September 21, 2023).

Bell, Duncan (2007) *The Idea of Greater Britain: Empire and the Future of World Order, 1860–1900*. Princeton, NJ: Princeton University Press.

Bell, Duncan (2020) *Dreamworlds of Race: Empire and the Utopian Destiny of Anglo-America*. Princeton, NJ: Princeton University Press.

Bi, Suriyah (2020) Racialisation of Rescuehood: Contextualising British Muslims Stuck Abroad during Covid-19 Pandemic. Available at: www.researchgate.net/publication/341575190_Racialisation_of_Rescuehood_Contextualising_British_Muslims_stuck_abroad_during_COVID-19_pandemic (last accessed June 21, 2022).

British Hajj Delegation (2011) What Is the British Hajj Delegation? Available at: www.britishhajjdelegation.org.uk/about.php (last accessed June 28, 2022).

Cameron, David (2015) Syria: Refugees and Counter-Terrorism. Hansard House of Commons Debates, Sixth Series: Volume 599. September 7, 2015, London.

Charsley, Katharine (2006) Risk and Ritual: The Protection of British Pakistani Women in Transnational Marriage. *Journal of Ethnic and Migration Studies* 32(7), 1169–1187.

Coles, Anne, and Katie Walsh (2010) From 'Trucial State' to 'Postcolonial' City? The Imaginative Geographies of British Expatriates in Dubai. *Journal of Ethnic and Migration Studies* 36(8), 1317–1333.

Constantine, Stephen (2003) British Emigration to the Empire-Commonwealth Since 1880: From Overseas Settlement to Diaspora? *Journal of Imperial and Commonwealth History* 31(2), 16–35.

Consterdine, Erica (2020) Diaspora Policies, Consular Services and Social Protection for UK Citizens Abroad. In Jean-Michel Lafleur and Daniela Vintila (eds.), *Migration and Social Protection in Europe and Beyond, Volume 3: A Focus on Non-EU Sending States*. Cham: Springer, 433–452.

Cusumano, Eugenio (2015) The Scope of Military Privatisation: Military Role Conceptions and Contractor Support in the United States and the United Kingdom. *International Relations* 29(2), 219–241.

Denza, Eileen (2018) Nationality and Diplomatic Protection. *Netherlands International Law Review* 65, 463–480.

Foreign and Commonwealth Office (2013) FCO Launches New Twitter Service Offering Travel Advice and Help. Available at: www.gov.uk/government/news/fco-launches-new-twitter-service-offering-travel-advice-and-help (last accessed June 28, 2022).

Foreign and Commonwealth Office (2020) 30,000 Stranded Brits Returned to the UK on Government Charter Flights. Available at: www.gov.uk/government/news/30000-stranded-brits-returned-to-the-uk-on-government-charter-flights (last accessed June 28, 2022).

Foreign, Commonwealth and Development Office (2022a) About Us. Available at: https://assets.publishing.service.gov.uk/government/uploads/system/uploads/attachment_data/file/1083349/FCDO_posts_overseas_June_2022.csv/preview (last accessed June 28, 2022).

Foreign, Commonwealth and Development Office (2022b) Living in Country Guides. Available at: www.gov.uk/government/collections/overseas-living-in-guides (last accessed June 28, 2022).

Foreign, Commonwealth and Development Office (2022c) Consular Assistance: How the Foreign, Commonwealth & Development Office Provides Support. Available at: www.gov.uk/guidance/consular-assistance-how-the-foreign-commonwealth-development-office-provides-support (last accessed November 21, 2022).

Geyer, Florian (2007) The External Dimension of EU Citizenship: Arguing for Effective Protection of Citizens Abroad. *CEPS Policy Brief*, July.

Govier, Trudy, and David Boutland (2020) Dilemmas Regarding Returning ISIS Fighters. *Ethics & Global Politics* 13(1), 93–107.

Grimal, Francis, and Graham Melling (2011) British Action in Libya 2011: The Lawful Protection of Nationals Abroad? *Denning Law Journal* 23(1), 165–177.

Hague, William (2012) Foreign Secretary Speaks at Launch of New Crisis Centre. Available at: www.gov.uk/government/speeches/foreign-secretary-speaks-at-launch-of-new-crisis-centre (last accessed June 28, 2022).

Hague, William (2013) The Foreign Secretary Gave an Update on the Situation in Algeria Today. Available at: www.gov.uk/government/news/the-foreign-secretary-gave-an-update-on-the-situation-in-algeria-today (last accessed June 28, 2022).

Hampshire, James (2013) An Emigrant Nation without an Emigrant Policy: The Curious Case of Britain. In Michael Collyer (ed.), *Emigration Nations: Policies and Ideologies of Emigrant Engagement.* Basingstoke: Palgrave MacMillan, 302–326.

HM Government (2012) Forced Marriage to Become a Criminal Offence. Available at: www.gov.uk/government/news/forced-marriage-to-become-a-criminal-offence (last accessed June 28, 2022).

HM Government (2020) Flying Home: The FCO's Consular Response to the Covid-19 Pandemic: Government Response. Available at: https://committees.parliament.uk/publications/3158/documents/40229/default/ (last accessed June 28, 2022).

HM Government (2021) Government Response to the House of Commons Foreign Affairs Committee Fifth Report of Session 2019–21. Available at: https://committees.parliament.uk/publications/4844/documents/48609/default/ (last accessed June 28, 2022).

HM Government (2022a) Get Travel Smart. Available at: https://travelaware.campaign.gov.uk/ (last accessed June 28, 2022).

HM Government (2022b) Types of British Nationality. Available at: www.gov.uk/types-of-british-nationality (last accessed June 28, 2022).

HM Government (2023a) Government Announces a Third Year of Support to Help Hong Kongers Settle into Life in the UK. Available at: www.gov.uk/government/news/government-announces-a-third-year-of-support-to-help-hong-kongers-settle-into-life-in-the-uk (Last accessed August 23, 2023).

HM Government (2023b) UK Government Completes Largest and Longest Western Evacuation from Sudan. Available at: www.gov.uk/government/news/uk-completes-largest-and-longest-western-evacuation-from-sudan (Last accessed August 13, 2023).

HM Passport Office (2020) Freedom of Information Request: Mr Luke Lo. Available at: www.whatdotheyknow.com/request/634155/response/1523562/attach/2/FOICR%2057241%20Luke%20Lo%20final%20response.pdf (last accessed June 28, 2022).

House of Commons Foreign Affairs Committee (2014) Support for British Nationals Abroad: The Consular Service. Available at: https://publications.parliament.uk/pa/cm201415/cmselect/cmfaff/516/516.pdf (last accessed June 28, 2022).

House of Commons Foreign Affairs Committee (2020a) Flying Home: The FCO's Consular Response to the Covid-19 Pandemic. Available at: https://committees.parliament.uk/publications/2159/documents/20049/default/ (last accessed June 28, 2022).

House of Commons Foreign Affairs Committee (2020b) No Prosperity without Justice: The UK's Relationship with Iran. Available at: https://committees.parliament.uk/publications/3987/documents/40221/default/ (last accessed June 28, 2022).

House of Commons Foreign Affairs Committee (2022) Missing in Action: UK Leadership and the Withdrawal from Afghanistan. Available at: https://committees.parliament.uk/publications/22344/documents/165210/default/ (last accessed November 21, 2022).

House of Commons Library (2023) UK Response to Unrest in Sudan: Research Briefing 9778. Available at: https://researchbriefings.files.parliament.uk/documents/CBP-9778/CBP-9778.pdf (last accessed August 13, 2023).

Hunt, Jeremy (2019) Interview with the *Andrew Marr Show. BBC One.* March 10, 2019, London.

Intelligence and Security Committee (2017) UK Lethal Drone Strikes in Syria. Available at: https://isc.independent.gov.uk/wp-content/uploads/2021/01/20170426_UK_Lethal_Drone_Strikes_in_Syria_Report.pdf (last accessed June 28, 2022).

Javid, Sajid (2019) Deprivation of Citizenship Status. Hansard House of Commons Debates, Sixth Series: Volume 654, 20 February 2019.

Knomad (2022) Remittances Data. Available at: www.knomad.org/data/remittances (last accessed June 28, 2022).

Ministry of Defence (2021) *Non-combatant Evacuation Operations.* Joint Doctrine Publication 3–51. London.

Mironova, Vera (2021) *The Challenge of Foreign Fighters: Repatriating and Prosecuting ISIS Detainees.* Washington, DC: Middle East Institute Policy Center.

Mitchell, Andrew (2023a) Sudan. Hansard House of Commons Debates, Sixth Series: Volume 731, April 24, 2023.

Mitchell, Andrew (2023b) Sudan: Repatriation. Available at: https://questions-statements.parliament.uk/written-questions/detail/2023-04-28/183226# (last accessed August 13, 2023).

Office for National Statistics (2021) Number of UK Dual Citizens in London. Available at: www.ons.gov.uk/aboutus/transparencyandgovernance/freedomofinformationfoi/numberofukdualcitizensinlondon (last accessed June 28, 2022).

Office for National Statistics (2022) Overview of the UK Population: 2020. Available at: www.ons.gov.uk/peoplepopulationandcommunity/populationandmigration/populationestimates/articles/overviewoftheukpopulation/2020 (last accessed November 18, 2022).

Okano-Heijmans, Maaike, and Matthew Caesar-Gordon (2016) Protecting the Worker-Citizen Abroad: Duty of Care Beyond the State? *Global Affairs* 2(4), 431–440.

Raab, Dominic (2020a) British Citizens: Repatriation. Hansard House of Commons Debates: Volume 676. May 11, 2020, London.

Raab, Dominic (2020b) Foreign Secretary Advises All British Travellers to Return to the UK Now. Available at: www.gov.uk/government/news/foreign-secretary-advises-all-british-travellers-to-return-to-the-uk-now (last accessed June 28, 2022).

Raab, Dominic (2021) Letter to Tom Tugendhat MP. Available at: https://committees.parliament.uk/publications/4650/documents/46941/default/ (last accessed June 28, 2022).

Richards, Eric (2018) British Emigrants and the Making of the Anglosphere. *History* 103(355), 286–306.

Ronzitti, Natalino (2019) Rescuing Nationals Abroad Revisited. *Journal of Conflict & Security Law* 24(3), 431–448.

Ruys, Tom (2008) The 'Protection of Nationals' Doctrine Revisited. *Journal of Conflict & Security Law* 13(2), 233–271.

Schwarck, Edward (2016) UK–China Cooperation on Non-Combatant Evacuation Operations. *RUSI Journal* 161(5), 36–45.

Sriskandarajah, Dhananjayan, and Catherine Drew (2006) *Brits Abroad: Mapping the Scale and Nature of British Emigration*. London: IPPR.

Sturge, Georgina (2022) Migration Statistics: House of Commons Library Research Briefing No. CBP06077. Available at: https://researchbriefings.files.parliament.uk/documents/SN06077/SN06077.pdf (last accessed June 28, 2022).

Sutherland, Craig (2012) Operation Deference: The Multinational NEO Evacuation Coordination Cell Concept. *RUSI Journal* 157(3), 15–20.

Sykes, Patrick (2016) Denaturalisation and Conceptions of Citizenship in the 'War on Terror'. *Citizenship Studies* 20(6–7), 749–763.

Thatcher, Margaret (1982) Falkland Islands. Hansard House of Commons Debates, Fifth Series: Volume 21. April 3, 1982, London.

Tsinovoi, Alexei, and Rebecca Adler-Nissen (2018) Inversion of the 'Duty of Care': Diplomacy and the Protection of Citizens Abroad, from Pastoral Care to Neoliberal Governmentality. *The Hague Journal of Diplomacy* 13(1), 1–22.

UN Population Division (2020) *International Migrant Stock 2020*. UN Department of Economic and Social Affairs.

Vargas Silva, Carlos, and Luka Klimaviciute (2020) *Briefing: Migrant Remittances to and from the UK*. Oxford: The Migration Observatory at the University of Oxford.

Walker, Nigel, and Tim Robinson (2021) Debate Pack: Consular Support for British Citizens. Available at: https://researchbriefings.files.parliament.uk/documents/CDP-2021-0210/CDP-2021-0210.pdf (last accessed June 28, 2022).

Wallace, Ben (2019) Interview with the Today Programme. *BBC Radio*. February 13, 2019, London.

Warbrick, Colin (1988) Protection of Nationals Abroad. *International & Comparative Law Quarterly* 37(4), 1002–1012.

Wingfield, Thomas (2000) Forcible Protection of Nationals Abroad. *Dickinson Law Review* 104(3), 439–470.

Zedalis, Rex (1990) Protection of Nationals Abroad: Is Consent the Basis of Legal Obligation. *Texas International Law Journal* 25(2), 209–270.

9 Indonesia

Protecting Migrant Workers at Home and Abroad

Ann Marie Murphy and Amy Freedman

Introduction

Indonesia has long been the country of origin for millions of migrant workers. Indonesian men and women have left their homes in search of work to provide a better life for themselves and their families. Most migrant workers are in semi-skilled or unskilled positions in fields such as construction, agriculture, manufacturing, and domestic work, which are mostly low-wage and difficult jobs. Indonesian workers are found in other countries in Asia, such as Malaysia, Singapore, Taiwan, and Hong Kong, and in wealthy countries in the Persian Gulf, such as Saudi Arabia, Kuwait and the United Arab Emirates (UAE) (Aswatini et al. 2022). Migrant workers leave Indonesia both through official, legal channels, as well as through illegal, unofficial channels. Those using the illegal, unofficial channels are often referred to as "irregular" migrants. Throughout the world, migrant workers are often treated poorly and found in dangerous, undesirable jobs. Increasingly, home governments are compelled to try and address abuses to their citizens (IOM 2010). The Indonesian government is very attuned to the treatment of its citizens abroad and has embarked on many measures to try and improve their safety overseas. The government is motivated to better support citizens abroad both because of the economic benefits of remittances and because the treatment of migrant workers abroad has become an important political issue at home. Political leaders who need to win a re-election know that they have to address the concerns and vulnerabilities of migrants and their families. Ultimately, the government has seen some successes in protecting compatriots but it continues to face significant challenges in doing so for more of their workers overseas.

This chapter will detail what the Indonesian government has been able to do to support Indonesians abroad and will assess the obstacles it faces in its efforts to protect its own citizens. Most of the government's efforts are focused on the treatment of migrant workers and as will be discussed later in this chapter, although some of the efforts underway include measures to keep better track of migrants abroad, the motivation for such measures is to improve support and assistance for Indonesian workers overseas, rather than to co-opt or suppress them. While there are some Indonesian students studying abroad, as well as some Indonesian (particularly ethnic Chinese) women who travel overseas for marriage, a number of Indonesians are refugees and asylum seekers (e.g., Achenese fleeing violence from the 1970s to 2004; Chinese Indonesians after the ethnic riots in 1998; and Ahmadiyya, a Muslim religious minority, and Papuans fleeing persecution), and there are also Indonesian business elites working for multinational corporations who require government assistance, the vast majority of Indonesians abroad are migrant workers, thus government attention disproportionately reflects their needs and interests (Missbach and Palmer 2018). Many of the problems Indonesian workers encounter abroad originate from problems in the country's migrant worker-placement process. Our chapter, therefore, examines the efforts made to reform this process and discusses official attempts to protect migrants overseas and negotiate bilateral, multilateral, and international protocols to this end. We find that while there are efforts to try and improve processes and protection within Indonesia for how migrant workers are recruited, trained, and placed in jobs overseas, the changes have been modest and the implementation of better processes have been weak. Internationally, the government has made significant efforts to strengthen the role of the Ministry of Foreign Affairs and to negotiate agreements with countries where Indonesians work. Nevertheless, the government faces an uphill struggle to get policies changed and protection put into place for Indonesian migrant workers in destination countries.

Indonesia's efforts to help its migrating workers are similar to those we see in the case of Mexico (Hernández Joseph and Schiavon, Chapter 3), Pakistan (Khan, Chapter 6), the Philippines (Roldan, Chapter 7), and Egypt (Norman, Chapter 11). In all of these cases, the states want to protect the economic remittances sent back home by their nationals working abroad, and in all of these countries we see efforts to bolster consular services and legal protection for citizens abroad. Mexico, in particular, as Hernández Joseph and Schiavon describe (Chapter 3), has a robust consular network in the United States to address the needs of Mexicans. However, there are some important differences to note. In the case of Mexico and to some extent Pakistan, their migrants are concentrated in the US and the UK, countries with relatively decent systems for the rule of law and protection of human rights. For Filipino, Egyptian, and Pakistani workers in Persian Gulf States and in Southeast Asia, like the Indonesian workers we will describe in this chapter, where the rule of law is weak and there are only low levels of the protection of human rights, it is not surprising that migrant workers are vulnerable.

Overview of the Indonesian Community Abroad

The migration of Indonesians reflects interlocking trends: the liberalization of the global economy between 1980 and 2008, both for goods and labor; the growing wealth disparity between developed and lesser developed countries; and high oil prices after the OPEC embargos of the 1970s led to windfall profits and a huge building spree in the Gulf States, leading to a need for increased labor. In part, this is why we see migrant workers in the Gulf from Pakistan and Egypt as well (Khan and Norman, Chapters 6 and 11, respectively). In the 1980s in Indonesia, then President Suharto promoted economic development through his "New Order" policies. The New Order included following export-oriented policies, coupled with state-led marketization/liberalization policies that encompassed promoting foreign investment. As part of its overall development plans, the Indonesian state promoted labor exportation as a way to deal with high levels of unemployment or underemployment. Unemployment was particularly severe on the densely populated island of Java. The number of Indonesians going abroad for work increased steadily through the 1970s and 1980s, then spiked in response to the economic crisis of 1997/1998 and again with the global boom prior to the 2008 financial crisis, the number of migrants then fell as the global economy contracted from the financial crisis, before growing again after 2015 (World Bank 2020). Until recently, the Indonesian government allowed private agencies a lot of control over recruiting men and women to work in the Gulf States and neighboring countries in Asia. The goal was to shrink Indonesia's unemployment rate, while boosting foreign exchange from remittances as well as increasing economic growth and reducing the country's deficits (Park 2017).

Indonesian workers abroad earn on average four to six times more than in Indonesia and remittances improve the welfare of their families at home (World Bank 2017a). Migrant remittances in the early 1980s were less than 0.01 percent of gross domestic product (GDP), but climbed through the 1980s and 1990s, and has been fairly steady since then with sums averaging around 1 percent of Indonesia's GDP for the last ten years. Remittances got as high as 1.9 percent of GDP in 2006/2007 (just before the financial crisis of 2008) (World Bank 2020). Estimates show that Indonesian workers sent back $11 billion in remittances in 2019 (Pinandita 2020).

Table 9.1 *Total number of official Indonesian migrants, 1990–2020*

Year	Total	Men	Women	Women %
1990	1,622,259	948,258	674,001	41.54706
1995	1,937,233	1,103,287	833,946	43.04831
2000	2,415,077	1,344,276	1,070,801	44.33817
2005	2,781,287	1,544,224	1,237,063	44.47808
2010	3,415,963	1,903,542	1,512,421	44.27510
2015	4,065,095	2,272,231	1,792,864	44.10386
2020	4,601,369	2,560,770	2,040,599	44.34765

Source: UN 2020.

Table 9.2 *Top destination countries for Indonesians abroad*

	Malaysia	Saudi Arabia	Taiwan	Hong Kong	Singapore
% of Indonesian migrant workers	55	13	10	6	5

Source: World Bank, Indonesia's Global Workers, November 2017, 11–12.

By 2020, just before the Covid-19 pandemic, there were over 4.5 million Indonesians officially working overseas (Table 9.1). The figures from the UN only represent migrants who leave Indonesia through official channels. Similarly, a World Bank report in 2017 found that 4.9 million Indonesians were working legally overseas, which constituted 3.8 percent of the Indonesian labor force. The same report estimated that there might be a total of up to 9 million overseas workers if irregular or undocumented workers were counted (World Bank 2017b). Many of the "irregular" migrants are women employed in domestic labor.

The top destination countries for Indonesian migrant workers are Malaysia, Taiwan, Saudi Arabia, Hong Kong, Singapore, and the UAE (Aswanti et al. 2022) (Table 9.2). Malaysia is by far the largest recipient of Indonesian workers, with approximately 2 million legal Indonesian migrants. It has the broadest range of employment opportunities: Indonesians can be found working on Malaysian fishing boats, rubber and palm oil plantations, manufacturing and construction, and domestic service. Given the proximity of the two countries, a common language and religion, the Muslim faith, a long history of people crossing borders between the two for work, and higher standards of living and higher wages in Malaysia, it is not surprising that such large numbers of Indonesians migrate there (Freedman and Murphy 2018). Saudi Arabia is the second most populous destination. The need for workers in the Saudi Kingdom reflects the great levels of wealth and desire for domestic workers (for female migrants), and the huge need for construction workers (for male migrants). We will examine more closely the problems faced by migrants in Malaysia and Saudi Arabia to illustrate larger challenges in improving opportunities and experiences for Indonesian migrants.

Most Indonesians overseas are Muslim and tend to come from East, Central and West Java, East Nusa Tengara (Retno et al. 2021), and Kalimantan (IOM 2010). Many of the destination countries are also Muslim-majority states. There is a feeling among migrants and employers that co-religionists will be a better "fit" for labor needs, yet, this commonality has not prevented nativism, both in the form of anti-immigrant sentiment and political discourse and violence towards migrants in destination countries, nor has it prevented the horrific abuse of migrants on the job (Freedman and Murphy 2018). Similar experiences are shared by Egyptian and Pakistani workers in the Persian Gulf (Khan and Norman, Chapters 6 and 11, respectively).

Indonesian men can be found working in construction, on plantations and other agricultural settings, in the fishing industry, manufacturing, and in the cruise ship industry. Women are employed in factories and as domestic workers (cleaning, caring for children and the elderly). Some women are trafficked into the sex industry, and some men are trafficked and end up as virtual slaves on fishing boats. Migrant workers face significant hardships and dangers on the job. Almost all Indonesian migrant workers are in low or at best semi-skilled positions (IOM 2010). They are extremely vulnerable to exploitation and abuse, and this affects the Indonesian government's diplomatic and policy responses to the need to safeguard their own citizens.

Diplomatic and Consular Dimension

The nature of the problems Indonesian workers face abroad and hence the type and degree of protection they may require from the Indonesian state depends on how they migrate and the type of work they get abroad. Indonesian citizens who migrate illegally to work overseas are more vulnerable than citizens who migrate through formal channels (ETI 2022). Workers who migrate formally and therefore have a right to be in the host country legally have proper documentation such as passports and work permits, and are typically required to have health insurance and accident insurance which can protect them in case of sickness and on-the job accidents (Missback and Palmer 2018). They are often covered by agreements which regulate wages and working conditions and contain provisions regarding housing conditions and stipulations that migrants can hold their own passports, access their cell phones, and are entitled to some degree of privacy when living in their employer's home.

In contrast, workers who migrate illegally lack proper documentation and because they have no right to be in the country, are vulnerable to exploitation by immigration officials, who may demand bribes or other favors from migrants to escape deportation (IOM 2010). Illegal workers are also more vulnerable to exploitation from employers in terms of receiving low wages and going unpaid, working long hours, and enduring poor working conditions as well as physical abuse. Protecting workers in the informal sector, particularly when they migrate illegally, poses the greatest challenge for Indonesian officials. It is worth noting that many of the destination countries (excepting Singapore and Taiwan) have weak rights protection for their own citizens and even fewer codified rights for non-citizens.

Despite differences in how workers migrate and whether they work in the formal or informal sectors, all migrants can face a variety of problems for which they may seek redress from Indonesian officials. In turn, the Indonesian government has grown increasingly concerned about the treatment of migrant workers overseas, more so than ever before. Part of the concern is economic, since remittances are a critical component of Indonesia's economy, but there is also a clear political incentive for elected officials to want to do more to protect Indonesians abroad. Since democratization in the country in the early 2000s, migrant worker advocates, labor groups, and migrants' families more generally have become a more powerful political force. Elected officials therefore face pressure on many fronts to try and respond to migrant needs (Freedman and Murphy 2018). Many employers take their workers' documents, such as passports and visa paperwork, making it impossible for workers to leave or find other employment. This imposes severe restrictions on the migrant workers' movement as many countries, such as Malaysia, require migrants to have their paperwork on them at all times or risk police detention. Some migrants report that employers take their cell phones – domestic workers, in particular, report this frequently occurs. It is common for migrant workers to face wage theft, withholding of wages to pay for recruitment fees, underpayment, or being paid less than they were originally promised. Workers may be forced to work long hours with little or no time off and in dirty and dangerous conditions with minimal safety precautions (ETI 2020). Additionally, some women are tricked into or forced to take oral or injected contraceptives, so that employers do not have to deal with a pregnant worker. Indonesians who migrate through unofficial channels are more likely to be subjected to these risks. Domestic workers face the additional danger of being isolated. Working in an employer's home makes women incredibly vulnerable to a myriad of abuses listed above and they also face the risk of physical and sexual abuse at the hands of employers (Varagur 2017). As the chapter on the Philippines (Roldan, Chapter 7) details, Filipina women face many of the same challenges.

There are heartbreaking cases of the extreme danger suffered by Indonesian migrant workers. In Malaysia, there are several examples of migrant workers who were subject to horrific abuse by their employers. Nirmala Bonat, a nineteen-year-old Indonesian woman who was a domestic worker in Malaysia, was physically assaulted repeatedly by her employer. "She was attacked, using any nearby object, such as a clothes hanger and an iron mug. The most serious physical attacks that Nirmala was subjected to, however, were scalding with boiling water and being burnt by a hot iron on her breasts" (IOM 2010: 48). Nirmala survived and her employer was put on trial in Malaysia and convicted of abuse. Not all workers survive their torment. Abuse of domestic workers is common in Singapore:

> Between 1999 and 2005, at least 147 labour migrants, of whom 122 were Indonesian citizens, died from falling or jumping from their employer's apartments (Human Rights Watch 2005). These incidents included both workplace accidents, such as unsafe methods of cleaning windows, and suicides that were the consequence of inhumane working conditions, which caused depression and anxiety amongst these labour migrants. (IOM 2010: 55)

Indonesian migrants also face significant problems in the Gulf States. Men work in construction and women as domestic workers. Working conditions are especially dangerous with the heat and poor living quarters for construction workers, coupled with coercive and restrictive work contracts, and high recruitment fees to pay back makes it hard for men to leave abusive jobs. Women face even greater dangers:

> Stinah B. J. Ahmad, an Indonesian maid that ended up killing her Saudi employer out of self-defence back in 2007, was placed on death row; she was scheduled to be beheaded unless a bail of 2 million USD was paid to the Saudi state. Ahmad's case is not uncommon. In the same month, the Saudi state beheaded an Indonesian maid for allegations similar to that of Ahmad's case: homicide out of self-defence. As of 2015, 236 Indonesian maids have been sentenced to death row. Such phenomenon indicates the seriousness of the risk and injustice that entail from being employed as a maid in Saudi Arabia (Iaccino 2014 and Park 2017).

Indonesians working in the Gulf and across the Middle East are subject to the *kafala* system, whereby the government awards individuals or companies sponsorship permits to employ foreign workers. The sponsors provide travel and housing and the sponsor assumes all responsibility for the workers. This results in workers being totally beholden to their employers. In addition, there is little oversight of the sponsors by the labor ministries, so workers are not afforded any of the protections that might exist through labor laws. "Furthermore, because workers' employment and residency visas are linked and only sponsors can renew or terminate them, the system endows private citizens – rather than the state – with control over workers' legal statuses, creating a power imbalance that sponsors can exploit" (Robinson 2021).

The government of Indonesia has focused on three distinct ways to improve the well-being of Indonesians who go abroad to work: (1) address the processes within Indonesia by which workers are recruited, trained, and prepared to go overseas; (2) work with governments in destination countries to change policies and oversight there for migrant workers; (3) advocate for regional and international agreements that help countries comply with international standards and best practices for migrant worker protection.

There are several Indonesian government bureaucracies that have overlapping jurisdiction for issues relating to migrant workers. The Ministry of Manpower (MOM) is responsible for overseeing the recruitment and placement processes of migrant workers and is often the organization that negotiates memoranda of understanding (MOUs) with their counterparts in destination countries. In countries where there are high numbers of migrant workers, the government presence is larger. MOM has labor attachés within some Indonesian embassies and consulates abroad in countries with big numbers of migrants. In Malaysia, Indonesia has an embassy in Kuala Lumpur, four consular offices in different parts of the country, a Manpower office, an immigration office, and a legal office, and the staffing levels are higher than in countries with fewer migrants such as the Philippines (Kemlu 2019 official and staff information). In Malaysia and Saudi Arabia, Indonesia operates shelters on its embassy premises to house migrants fleeing abuse. The Ministry of Foreign Affairs (MOFA, or Kemlu) supervises all consular activities like issuing passports before departure and replacing documents overseas. Kemlu is also responsible for providing (or advocating for) legal representation and financial assistance (both to the migrant themselves and to their families) when there are incidents overseas. In 2002, Indonesia established the Directorate for the Protection of Citizens and Legal Entities within the consular section of Kemlu. It is responsible for drawing up and implementing policies to better protect citizens abroad, and has over time both increased its personnel and training for its officials (Kemlu 2019). The

Ministry of Transport has some control over licensing for migrants working in the fishing industry, as well as a certain amount of control over travel arrangements for other migrants (Palmer and Hasbiyalloh 2022). The Tax Bureau helps coordinate remittances.

Indonesia does not have a national ministry dedicated to overseas citizens. However, in 2006, then President Yudhoyono created the National Authority for Placement and Protection of Indonesian Overseas Workers (BNP2TKI) to coordinate all of the relevant government actors involved in the migrant worker process in order to ensure that the placement and protection of workers was done in an integrated manner. BNP2TKI reported directly to the president, not to MOM. However, it lacked any enforcement authority over the recruitment agencies or other actors involved in Indonesia's fragmented migration process (Freedman and Murphy 2018: 172). The fundamental problems that need to be dealt with are weak coordination among agencies, competition for resources, and endemic problems of corruption, making the government's policies hard to implement and enforce. As discussed in greater depth further on, in 2020, BNP2TKI was replaced by the Agency for the Protection of Indonesian Migrant Workers (BP2MI) to better implement the changes in the 2017 Migrant Worker Law.

Better Protection Abroad Begins at Home: Reforming the Domestic Recruitment and Placement Process

Under President Suharto's New Order, Indonesians seeking work abroad were called "migrant worker exports," which is an example of Suharto's focus on economic development (Freedman and Murphy 2018: 165). Until the 2000s, the Indonesian government's primary interest in migrant workers was economic. When workers suffered abuse overseas, diplomatic responses were muted. In 2001, in a backlash against labor importation, Malaysia's Parliament passed legislation reducing work permits from six years to three and started a massive campaign to detain and deport illegal workers. Overnight, many migrant workers found their legal status evaporate. Malaysia also announced new corporal punishment regulations, including flogging for first-time immigration offenders. In January 2002, violent riots by Indonesian workers broke out, similarly, riots broke out among detained Indonesians. Instead of rallying to their citizens' defense, the Indonesian ambassador to Malaysia apologized for the riots (Freedman and Murphy 2018: 168–169).

The year 2002 marked a turning point. As more and more workers went overseas after the 1998 financial crisis, and as increased reports of abuse and denigration of Indonesian migrants became more widely known, there was increasing pressure on the government to do more to protect them. The early 2000s was also a period of significant democratization in Indonesia. Non-governmental organizations (NGOs) and migrant worker advocacy groups pushed for greater reforms to address migrant worker problems. In 2004, Law No. 39 was passed which stipulates that migrant workers can only be sent to countries that have laws to protect them. This was a lofty goal but difficult to enforce (Rahayu 2018).

The law also delegates authority and power to private recruitment agencies to find, train, and place workers. Many Indonesians argue that the problems Indonesians encounter overseas are rooted in a corrupt, high-cost placement system working in collusion with local officials who have an interest in the remittances locals send home. Many placement companies will recruit underage migrants and falsify birth certificates and school records, and sometimes even change migrants' names or otherwise falsify emigration papers (Rahayu 2018). The official process stemming from Law 39/2004 was convoluted, complicated, long, and costly. Since costs were born by the migrants themselves, it led many to borrow money from the agencies or from village lenders at exorbitant rates to cover the costs, often leaving migrants indebted to shady networks until the debts were repaid. Placement firms are supposed to train the migrants, but often fail to do so (IOM 2010). The law was revised in 2006 to try and streamline the recruitment process but it often exploited poorly educated migrants and favored the interests of well-connected placement firms and corrupt officials in the MOM instead. There was a distinct conflict of interest in that the MOM was responsible for overseeing placement companies, but many MOM officials were compensated to overlook violations of placement companies, as is common with other government regulatory attempts, and officials often found lucrative positions working for placement firms after retirement from government (US Department of State 2020).

In 2017, in response to increased activism and public concern, Indonesia enacted a new law for the protection of Indonesian migrant workers (Law No. 18/2017). The new law reinforces policies to provide end-to-end protection for overseas workers as they go through recruitment and training prior to working overseas, as well as the re-entry process on their return to Indonesia. The goal is to give migrant workers the tools to be prepared for their work assignment abroad, be more able to react to abuses abroad should they occur, and to provide services for when they return home. A key goal of migrant worker advocates, including Kemlu, was to reduce the costs of the formal migration placement system so as to incentivize workers to migrate legally and be better protected abroad. Some of the main aspects of the law aim to: provide a social security system for migrants, facilitate more integrated services, establish standards for training, limit the private sector companies' role in placement ("placement" means connecting workers to employers overseas, differentiated from recruitment which is finding and signing up more people to migrate), and create a "One-Stop Service Program" at the district level which provides government services. Since its inception in 2015, the One -Stop Service has been established in thirty-two districts (ASEAN 2017; Global Forum on Migration 2019).

In 2019, in an effort to further strengthen protection for migrant workers and improve government agencies charged with this task, President Jokowi signed a presidential decree to replace the BNP2TKI with a new institution, the BP2MI, the Agency for the Protection of Indonesian Migrant Workers. BP2MI aims to coordinate and oversee the domestic processes of recruiting and training migrant workers, including issuing permits for recruitment agencies (GOI, Cabinet Secretary 2020). The new agency reflects both a change in terminology used for migrant workers (in Indonesian, migrants are now referred to as *Pekerja Migran Indonesia*, Indonesian migrant workers, or MI, whereas previously they were referred to as *Tenaga Kerja Indonesia*, Indonesian workers, or TKI. BP2MI reduces the role of private placement agencies and increases the government's capabilities to stay in touch with migrants while they being recruited and during their time working overseas. The agency also aligned itself with the 2017 migrant worker law which devolved responsibility to local areas (rather than within agencies in Jakarta) (Pinandita 2020). The overarching goals are to reduce recruitment costs for migrants and make it easier for them to use official channels so that fewer will end up migrating through illegal channels. In addition, BP2MI aimed to create more government-to-government coordination to promote these goals.

Despite efforts to improve the conditions under which migrants are recruited, trained, and receive their overseas placements within Indonesia, it is not clear how much the process has improved. Advocates for migrant workers have argued that the One-Stop Service program that was to be implemented in villages to facilitate the process for would-be migrants has not been implemented in many places because local officials and others with vested interests oppose it. Critics argue that the law still favors private businesses and the central government over NGOs, advocacy organization, and local governments, and therefore does not significantly enhance worker protection (Husni et al. 2020).

Protecting Migrant Workers by Banning Migration

In theory, one way to protect citizens is to ban them from working outside the country. The government's response to the worst atrocities against migrants abroad has been to enact bans on sending people to work in the country (countries) where the abuse occurred. Indonesia banned migrants from going to Malaysia in 2009–2011, and again in 2015 (Freedman and Murphy 2018: 177), and in 2022. The Indonesian government banned workers from going to Kuwait in 2009, Jordan in 2010, Saudi Arabia in 2011, and in 2015 it banned migrant workers from going to twenty-one countries in the Middle East, including major destination countries such as Saudi Arabia, the UAE, and Qatar. The ban was triggered by the execution of two Indonesian maids who killed their Saudi employers in self-defense (Varagur 2017). The Indonesian government's concern for the well-being of their citizens, particularly women, is understandable. President Jokowi in 2015 is quoted as saying the following: "The practice of Indonesian women going overseas to work as housemaids must stop immediately. We should have pride and dignity" (Whiteman 2015).

At the same time, many migrant advocates argue that bans have the unintended consequence of rendering Indonesian citizens even more vulnerable (Yi 2017). Indonesia's domestic economy struggles to create enough high(er)-paying jobs to give workers alternatives to migrating. With few opportunities at home, migrant workers still go to the Gulf States but do so without any legal protection, and the recruitment agencies in Indonesia do little to uphold the ban. Many women did not even know that Jakarta had banned women from working as domestics in the Middle East. While the moratorium or ban did not stop migrants from leaving Indonesia to work, it made it harder to address the systemic problems they faced.

Protecting Migrant Workers Abroad: Negotiating Bilateral MOUs with Labor-Receiving Countries

One of the key things the Indonesian government does to protect migrant workers is negotiate formal bilateral MOUs with the governments of receiving countries to improve the oversight of working conditions abroad. Over the last twenty years, Indonesia has signed about a half dozen MOUs with the countries that receive the largest numbers of Indonesian workers, including Hong Kong, Taiwan, Malaysia, and Saudi Arabia (Freedman and Murphy 2018). Indonesia also attempts to create formal, government-to-government placement systems to reduce the role of private placement agencies. In the critical cases of Saudi Arabia and Malaysia, Indonesian efforts to negotiate MOUs, usually through the Ministry of Manpower, have vacillated with bans on migration, which as noted earlier often force Indonesians with few job opportunities at home to migrate illegally, thereby enhancing rather than reducing their vulnerability abroad.

Indonesia and Saudi Arabia signed an MOU on domestic workers in 2014, stipulating that migrant workers would have key protection while working in the kingdom, such as the ability to hold onto their own documents, open bank accounts, have stipulated time off, and other provisions. The MOU did not do enough to prevent the physical and legal abuses of Indonesian workers that lead to the death sentences mentioned earlier in the chapter, and so even with the MOU in place, Indonesia enacted a ban on female worker migration to many Middle East countries in 2015 that remains in place (Antara News 2022).

Indonesia and Malaysia have a contentious history regarding Indonesian migrant workers on plantations, in factories and construction, on fishing boats, and in domestic work. An MOU between the two countries in 2004 aimed to improve conditions for workers on palm oil plantations, in factories, and in construction. However, the MOU did not include domestic workers or fishermen. The MOU ultimately did little to improve working conditions for migrant workers, particularly domestic workers and a ban on the migration of Indonesian female domestic workers was announced in 2009 and was subsequently lifted in 2011 (Freedman and Murphy 2018: 174).

As noted earlier, the most vulnerable Indonesian migrants are female domestic workers. Yet, Malaysian authorities have long been unwilling to enter into MOUs for domestic workers since Malaysian families find it cheaper and often easier to employ household workers through informal networks and, with the advent of the internet, through the Malaysian-based "Maid Online" system. Labor surplus countries like Indonesia with poorly skilled workers have often had little leverage to press governments in destination countries to enact MOUs to cover this sector. This changed recently, in part because Malaysia expelled many migrants across all sectors during the Covid-19 pandemic, leaving both the formal sector and families short of help (Emont 2021; Lee et al. 2022). Indonesia refused to send migrants to the plantation sector unless Malaysia agreed to an MOU on domestic workers, and one was signed on April 1, 2022, after the last one lapsed in 2016. The new MOU stipulates a monthly wage of RM1,500, which must be paid directly to the worker's bank account no later than the seventh day of the month. The agreement stipulates a minimum of ten hours a day off, with seven uninterrupted hours for sleep. Critically, the entire recruitment process is supposed to take place through Indonesia's One Channel portal, which enables the government to track the placement of migrants with employers (Channelnews Asia 2022). Indonesian government officials lauded the MOU as the best one it had ever entered into.

Only months later, in mid July 2022, the Indonesian government froze the migration of workers after claiming that Malaysia was still recruiting Indonesians through its Maid Online system, which was a clear breach of the new MOU. According to Indonesian Ambassador to Malaysia Hermono (who goes by one name), "Malaysia keeps recruiting Indonesians workers through their Maid Online system" (Reuters 2022), making it impossible for Indonesia to track their Malaysian employers, which is critical to protecting them. On July 28, 2022 Indonesia announced that it would lift the freeze following Malaysia's agreement to the One Channel system which will integrate the Indonesian government system overseen by Indonesian representatives in Malaysia and the online system managed by the Malaysian immigration authorities. Given the Malaysian economy's shortfall of 1.5 million workers, particularly in the palm oil plantation sector, Indonesia's freeze was an important source of external pressure, while demands from Malaysian employers was a critical internal source of pressure (Reuters 2022).

MOFA Reforms

Once Indonesians migrate, the responsibility to protect them falls on the MOFA. A key prerequisite to protecting citizens overseas is knowing where they are, and in recent years the Indonesian government has made significant investments to improve the databases it uses to track its citizens living overseas. The government first adopted a tracking system named "Lapor Diri" (Report Yourself) in 2012. This was an electronic database into which migrants could enter their data and movements. There were a number of flaws with this reporting system, the most significant problems being the need to provide extensive personal information, and the hurdle that information had to be entered in person at embassies and consulates abroad, or at the office in Jakarta. Illegal migrants were not included in this system.

In 2018, Kemlu launched a new online portal" Peduli WNI" ("Concern/Protect Indonesian Citizens") to better track Indonesian migrants. Citizens can access it in person at consulates or online from anywhere in the world. The increasing use of technology in government bureaucracies allowed Kemlu to integrate data in other government databases into Peduli WNI, so migrants no longer needed to input personal data since it was transferred from existing databases, thereby reducing the burden on citizens living abroad. Instead, all that migrants need to input is new data on their addresses overseas and update contacts at home. The database can also be used by Indonesians who migrate illegally. Given that migrants are often highly mobile once overseas, it allows citizens on the move to update the government about their whereabouts (GOI, Direktorat Perlindungan 2020). Although such tracking would give the government a greater ability to surveil their citizens abroad, there is no evidence that these tools are being used for purposes other than assisting Indonesian nationals overseas.

In addition to creating new and better databases, the Indonesian government has been reforming its consulates, embassies, and diplomatic practices to protect migrant workers from extortion from officials who had traditionally preyed on migrant workers. Corruption in Indonesian bureaucracies continued overseas, with consular officials demanding bribes to process paperwork such as passport renewals, birth and marriage certificates, and other official documentation. Consular officials often also charged fees for services that should have been done at no cost, such as intervening in disputes between migrants and their employers, helping migrants recover wages and passports that had been illegally confiscated by employers, and other issues (Jones 2000).

Kemlu has cracked down on internal corruption. The ministry did not protect Sudjadnan Parnohadiningrat, a former ambassador to the US who skimmed money from the budget to build a new embassy in Singapore while serving as the Secretary General of Kemlu (Halim 2014). Instead, he was prosecuted and jailed to set an example to others. To reduce not only the incentive but also the opportunity for corruption in embassies and consulates abroad, the ministry adopted a cashless system for most consular activities, with only electronic payments accepted for consular services such as passport renewals. To make migrants more aware of their rights, reduce their vulnerability to bad actors, and encourage them to use official channels rather than illegal ones, Kemlu's website not only lists all of the services available to citizens overseas, but also repeatedly emphasizes that these services are provided free of charge.

While domestic changes should improve the Indonesian migrant workers' understanding of, and preparation for, what they are undertaking when going abroad for work, and provide some financial insurance for their economic protection, these domestic changes alone cannot fully address what happens to the migrant workers once they are overseas. To that end, the government of Indonesia has worked to draft MOUs with receiving countries to better protect the Indonesian migrants' physical safety and rights abroad. And we have found that Indonesia has done more on the ground overseas over the last few years to provide services to their citizens when they are abroad. Several factors have increased pressure on the Indonesian government to do more to help migrant workers through the increased role within Indonesian politics of civil society organizations, and the growing use of cell phones and social media to raise awareness of conditions and problems overseas. The increased political space for civil society has meant that organizations like Migrant Care and the Indonesian Migrant Workers' Union put considerable pressure on elected officials to create better policies and to hold leaders accountable for problems in the system. More widespread use of cell phones for texting and social media means that more people within Indonesia become instantly aware if there is a crisis or problem overseas. This in turn generates a nationalist outpouring of sympathy and pressure on elected officials to take a stand and act to protect Indonesians abroad (BBC News 2013; Bal and Palmer 2020).

Multilateral Efforts

In the early 2000s, Asian counties with large numbers of overseas workers, such as Indonesia, Bangladesh, India, China, Pakistan, and the Philippines, gathered in Sri Lanka to create common protocols (which became known as the "Colombo Process") to protect their workers and encourage the use of formal mechanisms for remittances. In 2005, recipient countries like Bahrain, Italy, Kuwait, Malaysia, Qatar, and others joined the discussions to develop a framework for managing labor mobility. In 2007, at the ASEAN Summit in Cebu, Philippines, leaders signed the Declaration on the Protection and Promotion of the Rights of Migrant Workers. This specified that sending and receiving countries would take measures to protect and promote the rights of migrant workers and signatories pledged to prevent trafficking and smuggling (IOM 2010: 4).

In 2007, the Association of Southeast Asian Nations (ASEAN), agreed to the Declaration on the Protection and Promotion of the Rights of Migrant Workers and set up the ASEAN Committee to Implement the Declaration on the Protection and Promotion of the Rights of Migrant Workers (ACMW) to operationalize it (Freedman and Murphy 2018). The goals are to improve governance, protect migrants' rights, and fight human trafficking in the region (ASEAN 2007). ASEAN officials, through the ASEAN Forum on Migrant Labor (AFML), convene annual meetings to provide information on safe migration to various stakeholders. There is, however, a fundamental disconnect between the respective priorities and interests of sending and receiving countries. Sending states like Indonesia would like to see a legally binding agreement for the protection of their workers overseas, while recipient countries like Malaysia and Singapore resist greater regulations and the codification of workers' rights, thus, the Declaration is only a set of recommendations, not a legally binding document (Freedman and Murphy 2018: 180).

The UN's International Convention on the Protection of the Rights of All Migrant Workers and Members of Their Families is a multilateral treaty which came into force in 2003. The aim of the treaty is to protect the rights of migrant workers and their families and it does so by stipulating that migrant workers should be afforded the same human rights as other groups of people. The Convention has been signed by over fifty countries, including Indonesia. However, the signatories to the treaty are migrant-sending countries. Recipient countries have not signed off on the Convention, making it harder to change norms and actual laws in those countries where migrants work (UN Office of the High Commissioner of Human Rights n.d.).

Economic and Social Dimension

The Indonesian government has been involved in providing a range of social and economic benefits to citizens abroad. In 2012, the foreign ministry under SBY negotiated a large expansion of "community learning centers" to educate children of migrant workers in Malaysia, particularly in Sabah. Malaysia does not formally allow migrants to have families in the country, so almost all children of migrant workers are unrecognized by the Malaysian government and thus have no right to access to education or healthcare services (AP Migration 2012). The agreement reached in 2012 stipulated that Malaysia was to allow the opening of 22 more schools in Sabah. These schools (more appropriately, community learning centers) were an extension of Indonesian schools currently run by Indonesian officials. The schools are paid for by civil society organizations, religious groups, and the government of Indonesia (AP Migration 2012). The need for these schools reflects a reality that the Malaysian government does not acknowledge: that migrants often stay in Malaysia for an extended period of time, sometimes even generations, and that they have families and put down roots. Prior to the pandemic, estimates show there were 290,347 stateless children under the age of eighteen in Malaysia. Some of them were refugees and others were children of migrant workers. None of these children are eligible for state schools and healthcare under Malaysian law. So, to this day, the Indonesian government tries to step in and provide some of the social and economic facilities that Malaysia refuses to provide (Allerton 2014; Azizan 2018).

Repatriation

Protecting compatriots sometimes means bringing them home from overseas. This occurs in cases where Indonesian citizens are studying or working in places that become conflict zones; in cases of kidnappings by terrorist organizations such as Abu Sayyaf; in cases where workers are trafficked; and more recently in the Covid-19 pandemic. During the wars in the Middle East in the 2010s, for example in Afghanistan, Iraq, Libya, and Syria, and the subsequent rise of ISIS, many Indonesian workers and some students were trapped in the conflict. The Covid-19 outbreak in Wuhan, China, was the first time that Indonesia faced the prospect of repatriating its citizens because of a biohazard. Indonesians stranded in Wuhan were students studying abroad, as well as businessmen and businesswomen, and some migrant workers. The Indonesian government, through the foreign ministry both in Jakarta and in the embassy in Beijing, had the task of arranging air transport, coordinating with local authorities, and issuing documents (Gorbiano et al. 2020).

When Covid-19 became widespread in the spring of 2020 and countries began closing their borders, millions of Indonesians were stranded overseas. As low-wage laborers whose jobs cannot be done virtually, Indonesian migrants were hit with multiple calamities all at once: many lost their jobs, were faced with long quarantines without any source of income to buy food and pay their rent. Others were forced to continue working but were not given personal protective equipment (PPE) to guard against the spread of Covid-19. Those who lost their jobs also faced the risk of detention and deportation, and an uncertain future with unpaid loans (Fitriani 2021). Once it became clear that lockdowns were going to last for a while and that the pandemic would not be easily beaten, the Ministry of Foreign Affairs coordinated the repatriation of more than 120,000 Indonesians from 53 countries. The ministry also provided emergency food to migrants in need, and transportation and logistics to migrants who faced joblessness and possible harassment around the world (Fitriani 2021).

The Foreign Ministry facilitated the repatriation of 123,319 Indonesian nationals, of whom the details are as follows: 10,093 were self-repatriated; 408 were members of the Tablighi Jamaat missionary movement and were repatriated from 11 different countries; 306 people were evacuated from Wuhan and the *Diamond Princess* cruise ship; and 24,721 were crew members working aboard ships all over the world. Evacuations were completed using commercial airlines, often the Indonesian national carrier Garuda (Jakarta Post 2020). Aside from the repatriation program, the Ministry of Foreign Affairs distributed free essential food supplies for the duration of the Covid-19 lockdowns. Through its foreign mission offices, it facilitated the distribution of 522,859 free essential food supplies for Indonesian nationals most affected by Covid-19. The distributed supplies included 451,325 packages in Malaysia; 43,227 in the Middle East; 13,374 in the US; 9,384 in Asia and Pacific regions (excluding Malaysia); 5,264 packages in Europe; and 285 packages in Africa. Meanwhile, the free essential food supplies for Indonesian migrant workers in Malaysia came from six Indonesian foreign mission offices in Malaysia (308,960 packages) and the general public (142,365 packages) (Government of Indonesia, House of Representatives 2020).

The Indonesian government, through Kemlu's databases, attempted to trace the number of Indonesian citizens infected by Covid-19. Indonesian citizens in Saudi Arabia proved to have the highest rates, reportedly because many migrants worked as drivers and were thus in enclosed spaces with others. The Indonesian government used public diplomacy to urge employers to provide their citizens with PPE, especially facemasks. Once vaccines became available, the government helped in the vaccination of Indonesian citizens. One of the biggest challenges was convincing undocumented migrants to go to vaccination centers because they feared deportation. As of January 2022, the Indonesian government had successfully vaccinated 88,000 Indonesians abroad (Septiari 2021). These economic efforts were a significant expansion of the role the Indonesian government usually has when addressing the needs of citizens abroad.

Covid-19 also prompted the government to rethink how it communicates with migrants and with other governments on issues regarding migrant workers. The Kemlu initiated "digital diplomacy," making much greater use of Instagram and YouTube to provide information, advice, and assistance to Indonesians abroad. It became deliberate in framing these services as available to all Indonesians overseas, regardless of their immigration status (Fitriani 2021). The government also used a "Safe Travel" app, which sends information to Indonesians abroad about where it is safe to go, and worked with the large telecom providers to be able to send SMS/text messages directly to citizens.

The Ministry of Foreign Affairs furthermore played a significant role in evacuating Indonesians from Ukraine in March of 2022 after the start of the Russian invasion. Eighty Indonesians were repatriated. As with the Covid-19 response, the Indonesian government paid to fly Indonesians home (Coconuts Jakarta 2022). These efforts reflect the government's desire to be seen as being able to protect its citizens abroad and Foreign Ministry officials have received a great deal of domestic and international support for the measures.

Security Dimension

The Indonesian military is rarely used to assist citizens abroad, its involvement is limited to rescuing kidnapped fishermen and citizens caught up in conflict zones. Indonesian fishermen from parts of Kalimantan that boarder Sabah Malaysia often go to work for Malay fishing fleets.

Malaysian fleets travel further and have better storage and processing facilities for fish, so workers earn more there than if they fished in Indonesia. However, fishing boats traveling further into the Celebes Sea risk being taken hostage by Abu Sayyaf militants. The Abu Sayyaf Group (ASG) is partly a terrorist organization that launches attacks on the Philippine government for thwarting its efforts to gain autonomy for Muslim Filipino. It is also partly a crime syndicate, kidnapping tourists and fishermen for ransom (Joubert 2020). Kidnappings have become so frequent now that Indonesia, Malaysia, and the Philippines conduct coordinated maritime patrols to try and deter ASG attacks and protect fishing fleets in the area. Between 2016 and 2020, approximately fifty Indonesians were captured by ASG (Renaldi 2020). The Indonesian government denies paying ransoms for their citizens, but it is likely that it has done so through the use of third parties. ASG may be bringing in as much as $25 million a year in ransoms (Renaldi 2020).

The Indonesian Navy and Coast Guard may again be used to try and deter Abu Sayyaf as needed, but it is a unique situation. Similar tactics have not been used when Indonesian workers suffered horrible abuse by their employers or foreign governments. The reasons for this are primarily that a military response would be out of proportion to the issue at hand and it would do little to alleviate the enduring systems that produce the problems to begin with.

The second use of the Indonesian military occurs when Indonesian citizens are trapped in quickly deteriorating security situations such as Afghanistan and Sudan. The Indonesian Air Force assisted in evacuating 33 people from Afghanistan as the Taliban took control of Kabul. There were 26 Indonesian citizens, including embassy personnel, along with 2 Afghan nationals, and 5 Filipinos rescued in August, 2021. Following the outbreak of conflict in Sudan in 2023, the Indonesian military sent a military aircraft and 39 military officers, including intelligence officials, medical officers, and a 15-member team from the Air Force Quick Reaction Force to help evacuate 291 Indonesian nationals. The elite team helped secure the airport at Port Sudan, where Indonesian officials had urged its citizens to gather (Antara News 2023). The evacuation of citizens was a relatively new use of Indonesia's military and the examples demonstrate the increased importance that the country places on protecting their citizens abroad (Widianto 2021).

Conclusion

The government of Indonesia has spent considerable effort addressing the needs of their citizens overseas, particularly their economic and social needs, and these efforts have expanded over the last few years.

The motivations for this assistance for Indonesian migrant workers are both financial and political. Remittances sent home by migrant workers are an important financial component, both for families with workers overseas and for the government as it provides some relief from a labor surplus at home. Likewise, providing help to migrants both at home during the recruitment process and once they are abroad, is both good policy and an attempt at preventing abuses that can become a political liability for elected officials. Migrant workers, particularly those who migrate unofficially, have very few ways of advocating for their rights within states like Malaysia, Singapore, and the Gulf States. Thus, it is left to the government of Indonesia to advocate on their behalf.

The outlook for the government's ability to better protect citizens abroad is mixed. Indonesian officials have achieved the greatest successes in cases where they have provided humanitarian and economic support and assistance with logistics for citizens needing to be evacuated overseas. The government's ability to provide food and medical aid during the early months of Covid-19 is an example of this, as is their generosity and success in evacuating Indonesians out of Ukraine at the outbreak of the war with Russia. The areas where improvements can be made are arguably much harder problems to solve. Domestically, Indonesia needs to clarify and improve lines of responsibility among different bureaucratic agencies and better regulate recruitment agencies, as well as crack down on unscrupulous recruiters involved in illegal migration channels and human trafficking. These measures are extremely difficult to achieve, in part because of institutional challenges that arose following the decentralization of power and the deeply entrenched problems of corruption. On the bilateral side, Indonesia's focus on creating memorandums of understanding with receiving countries makes a great deal of sense. If the Kemlu and MOM staff in countries with MOUs can help hold those governments (like Malaysia and Saudi Arabia) accountable for maintaining the terms and practices set out in the MOUs, Indonesia's migrant workers would be much better off. Ultimately, the well-being of migrant workers will rest on how well or poorly their working conditions and rights are protected by the governments of the states in which they work.

References

Antara News (2022) Indonesia Saudi Arabia Expedite Drafting of MoU on PMI Placement. June, 2022. Available at: https://en.antaranews.com/news/234325/indonesia-saudi-arabia-expedite-drafting-of-mou-on-pmi-placement (last accessed December 10, 2022).

Antara News (2023) TNI Deploys Kopasgat to Support Evacuation of Indonesians from Sudan. April 25, 2023. Available at: https://en.antaranews.com/news/279666/tni-deploys-kopasgat-to-support-evacuation-of-indonesians-from-sudan (last accessed August 16, 2023).

Al Arabiya News (2021) Three Indonesian Fishermen Rescued One Year after Abu Sayyaf Militant Kidnapping, March 19.

Allerton, Catherine (2014) Statelessness and the Lives of the Children of Migrants in Sabah, East Malaysia. *Journal of International and European Law* 19(1–2): 26–34.

AP Migration (2012) ILO Regional Office for Asia and the Pacific. Malaysia Opens Schools for Migrant Workers' Kids, October 24.

ASEAN (2007) ASEAN Committee to Promote the Rights of Migrant Workers Establishment of the ASEAN Committee on the Implementation of the ASEAN Declaration on the Protection and Promotion of the Rights of Migrant Workers. Available at: https://hrasean.forum-asia.org/wpcontent/uploads/files/documents/Statement%20of%20the%20Establishment%20of%20the%20ACMW%202007.pdf (last accessed December 13, 2022).

ASEAN (2017) On Protection of Indonesian Migrant Workers. Available at: https://asean.org/indonesia-policy-repository-migrant-workers-legislation-practices-asean-member-states/law-of-indonesia-no-18-of-2017-on-protection-of-indonesian-migrant-workers/ (last accessed December 13, 2022).

Aswatini, Anaf, Fitranita Ibnu, Haning Romdati, and Mita Noveria (2022) Indonesian Migrant Workers: The Migration Process and Vulnerability to Covid-19. *Journal of Environment and Public Heath*, June 15.

Azizan, H. (2018) Stateless Children Trapped in a Vicious Cycle. *The Star*, April 1. Available at: www.thestar.com.my/news/nation/2018/04/01/stateless-children-trapped-in-a-vicious-cycle (last accessed November 25, 2022).

Bal, Charanpal, and Wayne Palmer (2020) Indonesia and Circular Labor Migration. *Asian and Pacific Migration Journal* 29(1), 3–11.

BBC News (2013) Indonesia Under Pressure to Protect Its Migrant Workers, January 9.

Channel News Asia (2022) Indonesia-Malaysia Domestic Workers MoU Protection Rights. Available at: www.channelnewsasia.com/asia/indonesia-malaysia-domestic-workers-mou-protection-rights-2615711 (last accessed December 12, 2022).

Chong, Debra (2022) Don't Delegate Anymore, Indonesian Workers Can Return Right Away If You Intervene, Guan Eng Tells Prime Minister. *Malay Mail*, May 1.

Coconuts Jakarta (2022) 80 Indonesians Evacuated from Ukraine Arrive in Jakarta. March 4.

Emont, Jon (2021) In Covid Era Experiment, Malaysia Tries Dramatic Reduction in Migrant Labor. *Wall Street Journal*, November 14.

ETI (2022) Why are Migrant Workers So Vulnerable to Exploitation? *Ethical Trading Initiative*. Available at: www.ethicaltrade.org/events/why-are-migrant-workers-so-vulnerable-to-exploitation (last accessed December 11, 2022).

Fitriani (2021) Indonesia's Foreign Policy and the Covid 19 Pandemic. *Think Global Health*, October 26.

Foley, Laura, and Nicole Piper (2021) *The Challenges Faced by Malaysia's Migrant Workforce during Covid-19 Movement Restrictions*. Fiesole: Migration Policy Centre, Robert Schuman Centre.

Freedman, Amy, and Ann Marie Murphy (2018) *Nontraditional Security Challenges in Southeast Asia*. Boulder, CO: Lynne Rienner.

Global Forum on Migration (2019) Law on Protection of Indonesian Migrant Workers March 12. Available at www.gfmd.org/pfp/ppd/11056 (last accessed November 20, 2022).

GOI (2020) Cabinet Secretary, Republic of Indonesia, President Jokowi Signs Presidential Regulation on BP2MI, January 14. Available at: https://setkab.go.id/en/president-jokowi-signs-presidential-regulation-on-bp2mi/ (last accessed November 10, 2022).

GOI, Direktorat Perlindungan (2020) Information and Forms for Migrant Workers. Available at: https://peduliwni.kemlu.go.id/beranda.html (last accessed December 14, 2022).

Gokkon, Basten (2022) Indonesia Issues Long-Delayed Rules to Protect Migrant Fishing Workers. *Mongabay*, June 14.

Gorbiano, Marchio Irfan et al. (2020) Indonesia to Repatriate Nationals from Epicenter of Coronavirus Outbreak. *Jakarta Post*, January 31.

Government of Indonesia (2020) House of Representatives, Government Ensures Protection of Indonesians Overseas, July 7.

Halim, Haeril (2014) Former Senior Envoy Sent to Prison Again. *Jakarta Post*, July 24. Available at: www.thejakartapost.com/news/2014/07/24/former-senior-envoy-sent-prison-again.html (last accessed August 10, 2022).

Hamidi, Mashitah (2016) Indonesia Female Factory Workers: The Gendered Migration Policy in Malaysia. *PEOPLE: International Journal of Social Sciences* 2(1): 643–664.

Handcock, Adam (2022) Singapore Migrant Workers Labor under Covid Curbs. *Al Jazeera*, January 30.

Human Rights Watch (2005) Maid to Order: Ending Abuses against Migrant Domestic Workers in Singapore. *Human Rights Watch* 17(10).

Husni, Lalu, RR Cahyawati, and Mansur (2020) Legal Protection for Indonesian Migrant Workers Based on Law Number 18 of 2017. *Journal of Legal, Ethical and Regulatory Issues* 23(25).

Iaccino, Ludovica (2014) #SaveSatinah: 'Abused' Indonesian Maid to Be Beheaded in Saudi Arabia Unless Family Pays £1m. *International Business Times UK*, March 24.

IOM (2010) Labour Migrants from Indonesia. *IOM*. Available at: www.iom.int/sites/g/files/tmzbdl486/files/jahia/webdav/shared/shared/mainsite/published_docs/Final-LM-Report-English.pdf (last accessed December 13, 2022).

Jakarta Post (2020) Coronavirus: Indonesian Citizens Aboard Diamond Princess to Be Put in 28 Day Quarantine after Returning Home. February 22.

Jones, Sidney (2000) *Making Money off Migrants: The Indonesian Exodos to Malaysia*. Center for Asia Pacific Social Transformation Studies. Wollongong: University of Wollongong.

Joubert, Lydelle (2020) Abu Sayyaf: The Chameleon in the World of Terror. *Stable Seas*, April 30.

Kaur, Amarjit (2020) Labour Migration Trends and Policy Challenges in Southeast Asia. *Policy and Society* 29(4), 385–397.

Kemlu (2019) Government of Indonesia, Ministry of Foreign Affairs, Director for the Protection of Citizens and Legal Entities Overseas, April 6. Available at: https://kemlu.go.id/portal/en/struktur_organisasi/82/director-for-the-protection-of-citizens-and-legal-entities-overseas (last accessed November 10, 2022).

Koh, Heng Hwee, and Serene Koh (2022) How Can We Encourage Migrant Domestic Workers to Seek Help? *Behavioral Insights*, March 11.

Kok, Xinghui (2021) Could A Singapore Scheme for Domestic Workers Be a Model for Changing Hong Kong's Live in Rule for Helpers? *South China Morning Post*, September 19.

Lee, Liz, Razanna Latiff, and Mei Mei Chu (2022) Malaysian Firms Turndown Orders as Migrant Labor Shortages Hit. *Reuters*, June 13.

Lim, Huey Teng (2022) Indonesia Imposes Temporary Freeze on Sending Migrant Workers to Malaysia. *Reuters*, July 28.

Mahardika, Angga Putra, and Sonny Saptoajie Wicaksono (2020) Human Trafficiking and Migrant Workers: Analysis of Indonesian Migrant Workers Protection Overseas. *Contemporary Development in Legal Studies and Crimes Law Research Quarterly* 6(2), 173–180.

Mahy, Petra (2022) Indonesia's Omnibus Law on Job Creation: Legal Hierarchy and Responses to Judicial Review in the Labour Cluster of Amendments. *Asian Journal of Comparative Law* 17(1), 51–75.

McBeth, John (2019) ISIS Headed Home to Indonesia. *Asia Times*, June 21.

Minter, Adam (2022) Malaysia Migrant Labor Abuse Is a Shot in the Economic Foot. *Bloomberg*, July 10.

Missbach, Antje, and Wayne Palmer (2018) Indonesia: A Country Grappling with Migrant Protection at Home and Abroad. *Migration Policy*, September 19.

Nashirudin, Muh, M. Usman, Layyin Mahfiana, Mudofir (2020) Islam and Gender Issues in Indonesia Government Policy on the Protection of Female Migrant Workers in Malaysia. *PalArch's Journal of Archeology of Egypt* 17(6), 8267–8290.

Ong, Alex (2022) Indonesian Migrant Workers Face Dangers along Sea Routes to Malaysia. *The Observers France24*. January 14. Available at: https://observers.france24.com/en/tv-shows/the-observers/20220114-indonesian-migrant-workers-face-dangers-along-sea-routes-to-malaysia (last accessed January 26, 2023).

Palmer, Wayne and Benni Yusriza Hasbiyalloh (2022) The Government Now Has a Much-Needed Regulation on the Recruitment of Migrant Fishers from Indonesia. What Next? *The Conversation*, June 30.

Park, Daniel C. (2017) The Diaspora of Indonesian Female Domestic Workers in Saudi Arabia: A Case of Abuse and Mistreatment. *Journal of Contemporary Asian Studies* 2(1), ISSN 2369-8217 (online).

Pinandita, Aprisa (2020) Government to Revamp Migrant Labor Management Body. *Jakarta Post*, January 3.

Rahayu, D. (2018) Is the State of Indonesia in Charge to Provide Law Protection to the Indonesian Migrant Workers? *Journal of Physics* 953, 012131.

Renaldi, Adi (2020) Why So Many Indonesians Are Being Kidnapped in the Philippines. *Vice*, April 16.

Reuters (2022) Indonesia, Malaysia Sign Agreement on Protection of Migrant Workers, April 1.

Retno, Agustin et al. (2021) The Impact of the Moratorium of Indonesian Migrant Workers Placement on Society's Attitudes Towards Human Trafficking in East Nusa Tenggara. *Migrant Care*. Available at: www.zerohumantrafficking.org/wp-content/uploads/2021/03/Publications-The-Impact-Of-The-Moratorium-Of-Indonesian-Migrant-Workers-Placement-On-Society-Attitudes-Towards-Human-Trafficking-In-East-Nusa-Tenggara.pdf (last accessed November 10, 2022).

Robinson, Kali (2021) What is the Kafala System? *Council on Foreign Relations*, March 23.

Septiari, Dian (2021) High Saudi Death Toll Overshadows Indonesia's Plans to Allow 'Umrah'. *Jakarta Post*, January 18.

Siregar, Kiki (2021) Indonesian Migrant Workers, Civil Society Welcome New Placement Fee Plan; Employers to Bear Costs from Jan. 15. *Channel News Asia*, January 8.

Song, Yihang (2022) Covid-19 Shedding Light on the Plight and Laws Regulating Migrant Workers. National University of Singapore Faculty of Law. Blog post. Available at: https://law.nus.edu.sg/impact/covid-19-shedding-light-on-the-plight-and-laws-regulating-migrant-worker-dormitories-in-singapore/ (last accessed September 20, 2022).

Strangio, Sebastian (2022) 'Just a Maid': Report Highlights Emotional Abuse of Migrant Domestic Workers in Singapore. *The Diplomat*, June 24.

Sukumaran, Tashny (2022) In Malaysia, Oppressive Policies Marginalized Migrant Workers. *Routed Magazine*, February 21.

Sumeda (2022) Explained | Indonesia's Controversial Jobs Law and Fresh Debate over It. *The Hindu*, June 25.

Tan, Lester (2022) More Employers in Malaysia Will Be Allowed to Hire Foreign Workers. *HumanResources.online*, July 19.

Telling, Oliver (2022) Migrant Workers Suffer in Singapore's Hidden Lockdown. *Financial Times*, June 5.

United Nations (2019) Office of the High Commissioner for Human Rights, International Convention on the Protection of the Rights of All Migrant Workers and Members of their Families.

United Nations Department of Economic and Social Affairs (2020) Population Division, International Migrant Stock 2020.

United States Department of State (2020) 2020 Country Report on Human Rights Practices: Indonesia.

Varagur, Krithika (2017) Indonesia Ban Hasn't Stopped Horrors of Migrant Work in the Gulf. *The New Humanitarian*, October 24.

Whiteman, Hillary (2015) Indonesia Maid Ban Won't Work in Mideast, Migrant Groups Say. *CNN*, May 6.

Widianto, Stanley (2021) Indonesia's Air Force Evacuates Citizens from Afghanistan. *Reuters*, August 20.

World Bank (2017a) *Indonesia Can Improve Opportunities for and Protection of Its Migrants Working Abroad*, November 28.

World Bank (2017b) *Indonesia's Global Workers*, November.

World Bank (2018) Remittances from Overseas Workers. *The Global Economy. Com*.

World Bank (2020) *Covid-19 Crisis through a Migration Lens*. Migration and Development Brief 32. Washington, DC: World Bank Group.

Yi, Ben Lih (2017) Trafficked and Abused: Indonesia's Middle East Ban Backfires. *Reuters*, March 6.

10 Germany

Supportive in Times of Crisis

Klaus Brummer and Kai Oppermann

Introduction

Germany has been a primary destination for migration for decades. Since 2012 alone, over 1 million people have been arriving in Germany each year, leading to a constant annual net migration gain for the country (Statistisches Bundesamt 2022b). However, a different picture emerges when focusing on the migration patterns of German citizens only. Here, the country has seen a net annual migration loss for almost twenty years (Statistisches Bundesamt 2022c). Today, close to 4 million Germans reside abroad (United Nations 2020a). In addition, several million Germans temporarily leave their country each year as tourists.

Overall, Germany's engagement with its national communities abroad is quite limited compared to the activities of other countries covered in this volume, such as India (see Blarel, Chapter 2). Its activities focus on supporting and assisting its national communities abroad, for example through the provision of consular assistance or emergency evacuations in crisis situations. Conversely, co-optation plays a much more limited role, barring, for example, efforts to enable overseas voting or the initiation of return programs for highly skilled citizens. There was no indication of repression, as would be expected for a liberal democracy like Germany. In terms of the targets of state action, emphasis is placed on German citizens (i.e., tourists and first-generation emigrants) rather than the diaspora more broadly. What is more, since the vast majority of Germans either travel to or live in other stable democracies in Western European or North America, the need for support is typically limited. The fact that Germany, contrary to most of the other countries covered in this volume, does not have a ministry dedicated to its citizens living abroad is indicative of the overall limited salience of the issue, as is also the case, for example, in the United Kingdom (see Strong, Chapter 8). However, this is not to suggest that Germany is unwilling or unable to assist or protect its citizens abroad if need be, in particular in times of crisis, indicating another parallel to the British case. Indeed, the following discussion illustrates that, centered around its globe-spanning diplomatic network, Germany does systematically engage in support activities along the three dimensions covered in this volume, namely diplomatic and consular, economic and social, and military. Those activities comprise not only routine measures for example in the consular domain but occasionally also emergency measures in response to civil conflict, natural disasters, or, more recently, a global pandemic.

Overview of the German Community Abroad

Germany has seen several major waves of migration, with people moving both to and from the country (for overviews, see Oltmer 2013; Ette and Erlinghagen 2021). Examples include the emigration of some 5.5 million Germans to the United States in the nineteenth and early twentieth century and of around 300,000 Jewish Germans fleeing from Nazi tyranny to escape to various parts of the world, as well as the arrival of about 14 million German citizens or members of German minorities from Eastern Europe after the Second World War, and of another 14 million originally temporary guest workers from countries like Greece, Spain, and Türkiye, of whom some 3 million remained in the country (Oltmer and Hanewinkel 2021). Since unification, Germany has seen an annual net migration gain for all years except 2008 and 2009 (Statistisches Bundesamt 2022b). In 2021, roughly 1.3 million people moved to the country compared to around 1 million people leaving it. A different picture emerges, however, when focusing only on the migration patterns of German citizens (Statistisches Bundesamt 2022c). While there was also a net migration gain until 2004, more German citizens have left the country than returned to it since then (Figure 10.1).

Resulting from the aforementioned waves of outward migration, there is a significant number of people worldwide claiming German descent. For example, in the US alone, more than 40 million people identify as having German ancestry (Max Kade Institute for German-American Studies n.d.). However, the German diaspora in a stricter sense is much more limited in number and also more concentrated geographically. Above all, German minorities can be found in Central and Eastern Europe and the former Soviet Union as well as in Southern Denmark. For example, some 200,000 ethnic Germans are estimated to be in Hungary, some 150,000 in Poland, and some 15,000 in Denmark (Federal Government Commissioner for Matters Related to Ethnic German Resettlers and National Minorities n.d.).

Today, Germany is the most populous member state of the European Union (EU), with a total population of 83.2 million people. Close to 12

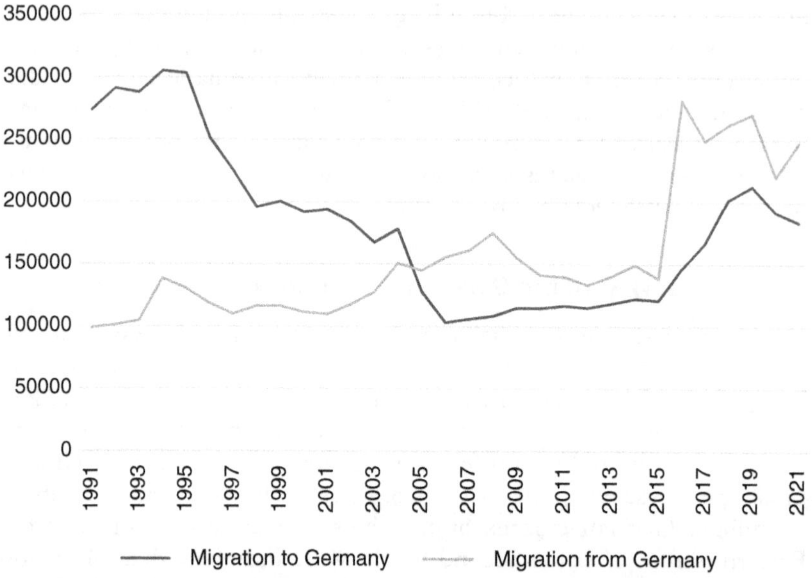

Figure 10.1 Migration of Germans to and from Germany
Source: Own depiction based on Statistisches Bundesamt (2022c).

million people residing in Germany by the end of 2021 were foreigners (Statistisches Bundesamt 2022a). Conversely, around 3.9 million Germans resided abroad in 2020, which represented an increase of roughly 25 percent compared to 1990, when approximately 2.9 million Germans lived outside the country (United Nations 2020a) (Table 10.1). Making up 85 percent of Germans who lived abroad, the vast majority resided in developed regions, most notably Europe (63 percent of the total) and North America (19 percent of the total). Conversely, some 15 percent lived in less developed regions and least developed countries (Table 10.2).

In terms of remittances, Germans living abroad sent some US$19.4 billion back to Germany in 2020, which amounted to 0.5 percent of German GDP. In comparison, there was an outflow of remittances from Germany of US$15.7 billion that same year (World Bank 2022). While paling in comparison to other cases discussed in this volume such as India or Mexico, those numbers are significantly higher than is the case, for example, for the UK in both absolute terms (3.3 billion in case of the UK) and regarding the share of GDP (0.1 percent in the case of the UK) (World Bank 2022).

Last but not least, in addition to those residing abroad permanently, several million Germans leave their country annually as tourists. Indeed,

Table 10.1 *Overview of Germans living abroad*

	1990	1995	2000	2005	2010	2015	2020
World	2,929,448	3,045,354	3,235,247	3,442,933	3,696,638	3,630,278	3,855,268
Among which living in …							
… *developed regions*	2,488,935	2,616,327	2,801,648	3,000,101	3,250,761	3,183,649	3,294,912
… *less developed regions*	440,513	429,027	433,599	442,832	445,877	446,629	560,356

Source: United Nations (2020a).

Table 10.2 *Regional breakdown of Germans living abroad in 2020*

Region	Total by region	Countries with larger groups of German citizens
Africa	49,559	South Africa (16,595); Namibia (9,494); Egypt (7,771); Libya (7,503)
Asia	437,270	Türkiye (376,288); Israel (22,971); Uzbekistan (8,543); Japan (7,477)
Europe	2,446,317	Switzerland (357,112); UK (310,043); Austria (232,836); Italy (211,223); France (203,426); Spain (200,659); Russia (141,947); Netherlands (123,702); Greece (116,644); Poland (100,688)
Latin America and the Caribbean	80,610	Brazil (20,625); Peru (9,733); Argentina (9,332); Chile (7,559); Mexico (7,272)
North America	691,476	US (534,203); Canada (157,059)
Oceania	150,036	Australia (124,818); New Zealand (24,824)

Source: United Nations (2020a).

for many years, Germans were considered “travel world champions” (Welt 2013), and they still rank close to the top of the list today. Even during the Covid-19 pandemic in 2021, some 24 million Germans spent their main holidays abroad (Statista 2022).

The following discussion of Germany’s activities towards its national communities abroad along the dimensions of diplomacy, economy, and security suggests that considerations of support and assistance are the main drivers for its engagement. The focus is on German citizens traveling temporarily or residing permanently abroad as opposed to engaging with the German diaspora more broadly. While Germany has the capabilities to systematically and continuously interact with its citizens abroad, those activities are typically low-key and not politically salient. Unforeseen crisis situations, like civil wars or the global pandemic, provide occasional punctuations to this equilibrium.

Diplomatic and Consular Dimension

Germany has global diplomatic reach. It currently operates a total of 226 missions abroad. Around 3,050 members of the foreign service work at those missions, which is slightly more than the close to 3,000 staff members located at headquarters (Federal Foreign Office 2022d). The missions include: 152 embassies, 53 consulate generals, 7 consulates, 12 permanent missions (e.g., to the United Nations), 1 "representative office" (in Ramallah) and 1 "German institute" (in Taipei City) (Federal Foreign Office 2022f). In addition, there are 327 honorary consuls, who often times are citizens of the host country and, based on their local knowledge and connections, are considered particularly helpful for "provid[ing] valuable assistance to Germans in emergency situations" (Federal Foreign Office 2022f). With those numbers, Germany ranks seventh in the "Global Diplomacy Index" (Lowy Institute 2019).

The location and size of Germany's national communities abroad, with emphasis being placed on those holding German citizenship, are among the main drivers for the density of German diplomatic representations. As outlined in the preceding section, the vast majority of German citizens living abroad reside in Europe (some 2.5 million out of 3.9 million). Another 700,000 or so Germans live in the US and Canada (see Table 10.2). For this reason, but also for political and economic ones, it is little surprising that Germany's diplomatic representation – and ensuing activities to support and assist German citizens abroad – is particularly strong in Europe and North America (Federal Foreign Office 2022f). Since Germany does not have a special ministry dedicated to its citizens living abroad, the diplomatic representations, which are explicitly tasked with "helping German citizens in emergencies, carrying out crisis protection measures, and assisting Germans living abroad with regard to certificates and legal documents" (Federal Foreign Office 2022e), are key for the subsequent discussion.

German citizens abroad are legally entitled to consular assistance under the Consular Act of 1974, last revised in 2021 (Federal Ministry of Justice 2021). However, they do not normally have a right to specific forms of assistance, which largely remain at the discretion of consular officials, within the boundaries of the law (Lenz 2017: 84–89). The

Consular Act defines three broad categories of consular assistance pertaining to individual German citizens in need (§5), support in cases of natural disasters and violent conflicts (§6), and German citizens who have been arrested abroad (§7). These types of consular assistance need to be distinguished from diplomatic protection in a narrower sense, which is concerned with defending German citizens against violations of international law by foreign authorities. While there may be overlaps in practice, for example in civil wars, consular assistance refers to situations that do not originate in violations of international law (Lenz 2017: 11–17).

Germany's missions abroad provide consular assistance to German citizens in their consular district who face individual emergencies, "if the emergency cannot be resolved by any other means" (§5 Consular Act). Under certain conditions, such assistance can be extended to non-German relatives of German citizens. The beneficiaries are expected to incur any financial expenses that arise. For the most part, this category involves rather low-key day-to-day consular work, such as issuing replacements for lost or stolen passports, organizing emergency money transfers, providing contact details of lawyers, doctors, or translators, or informing the relatives of German citizens who have died while abroad (Federal Foreign Office 2022b).

Far more high-profile, consular assistance for German citizens in need also extends to hostage situations (Lenz 2017: 142–150). Given the large number of German tourists abroad and the extensive international activities of German businesses, in both cases including in regions with poor safety records, the risk of German citizens being taken hostage in other countries is considerable. This can be seen in a number of prominent cases in which German citizens have been abducted for financial or political gain around the world (SZ 2010). Consular efforts to free German hostages abroad are coordinated by the crisis management unit (Krisenstab) in the Foreign Office, often involving the Chancellery, the intelligence services as well as consular officials on the ground. Ever since a string of politically motivated kidnappings in the 1970s, the official line in such cases is that the German state is not susceptible to blackmail and does not respond to political or financial demands of hostage-takers. However, it is common knowledge that the German authorities have paid ransom money in the past or facilitated such payments by private citizens or companies. While never officially confirmed, for example, Germany is said to have paid several million Euros in "development aid" to secure the release of sixteen German tourists who were taken hostage in Algeria in 2003. In another case, in 2000, the widespread assumption is that Germany was behind the €20 million which the Libyan Gaddafi

Foundation allegedly paid to arrange for a German family to be freed by their kidnappers in the Philippines (Graw 2007).

The second category of consular assistance applies to actual or imminent disaster situations "which cause harm to the population, or parts thereof" in the respective host country (§6 Consular Act). This covers natural disasters as well as man-made threats to life and liberty, such as in warlike or revolutionary situations. In these circumstances, assistance is to be provided to German citizens and their descendants, as well as non-German citizens who live, or have lived, in a common household with a German citizen. This type of consular assistance usually involves large-scale logistical efforts which are coordinated in the Federal Foreign Office, may enlist support by the German armed forces (Bundeswehr), and rely on the local expertise and networks of Germany's missions abroad. To facilitate such assistance, German citizens, both travelers and permanent residents abroad, have the opportunity to register on a crisis prevention list ("ELEFAND") on the Foreign Office website, enabling the respective German embassies to reach out quickly in cases of emergencies. The Foreign Office website serves as a key information hub for German citizens traveling or living abroad, setting out legal aspects and the domestic political situation of the respective countries as well as detailing health and security risks. The website also provides country-specific travel advice and travel warnings and is used to communicate government requests for German citizens to leave particular countries, for example in cases of natural disasters or civil unrest.

As for natural disasters, the most challenging effort to provide consular assistance followed the massive tsunami that hit Southeast Asia on December 26, 2004, resulting in over 227,000 deaths (Telford et al. 2006: 16), including 534 German citizens, mainly tourists (Spiegel online 2014b). Most immediately, consular assistance came in the form of decentralized and largely ad hoc initiatives of consular officials to help local rescue operations and provide contact points for German citizens. For example, this included setting up mobile consular offices in particularly affected tourist areas, providing financial assistance to cover basic needs, and assisting survivors in finding friends and relatives. Subsequently, attention shifted to providing medical aid, identifying German victims, and organizing the homeward journey of German citizens and their relatives. German consular officials were instrumental in drawing up lists of German citizens in the region and in coordinating the modalities of return flights with local authorities and private tour operators (FAZ 2004a: 7). The evacuation of German citizens was supported by special flights in military aircraft, including a Bundeswehr air ambulance, for example from Thailand and Sri Lanka. The scale of the operation is evidenced by the fact that around 3,000 German citizens had to be flown out by commercial and military flights from Sri Lanka alone (FAZ 2004c: 1). EU members cooperated in their rescue efforts, with seats on flights organized by other EU states being made available to German citizens and vice versa (FAZ 2004b: 9).

Evacuations of German citizens abroad have also taken place from conflict zones, which in turn point to a gray area between diplomatic and military activities. A major example is the rescue staged after the escalation of the civil war in South Sudan in July 2016, which led Germany to fly out around 100 of its citizens, for the most part aid workers and diplomats, as well as other European nationals. The flights were organized by the Federal Foreign Office and conducted in Bundeswehr transport aircraft (Deutsche Welle 2016). More recently, the Federal Foreign Office has conducted, on the request and with the agreement of the affected families, at least six secret operations between 2020 and 2022 to bring back to Germany more than 100 German citizens, mainly children and their mothers, from camps in northeast Syria. The children were originally brought to Syria by parents who sympathized with the so-called Islamic State and suffered, like their mothers, disastrous humanitarian conditions in the camps. All affected individuals were carried to safety in Germany, while some of the mothers were held accountable in German courts for their decisions to go to Syria (Federal Foreign Office 2022a). The evacuations were made possible by close collaboration with local actors and were conducted in cooperation with international partners, including the US (ZDF 2022). In other cases, in which evacuations were seen as either not feasible or not desirable, the German government has used the website of the Federal Foreign Office and other media channels to request German citizens to leave conflict zones, offering advice through the crisis hotline of the Foreign Office. Recent examples from 2022 include the war in Ukraine and the violent repression of protests in Iran.

The "biggest evacuation effort in German history" (Spiegel online 2020) took place during the Covid-19 pandemic. Between March 17 and April 24, 2020, the federal government instituted an "air bridge" (FAZ 2020b), bringing back to Germany around 240,000 German citizens from all over the world. To the extent possible, this relied on regular flights and private tour operators, but also involved around 260 special flights from 65 countries on aircraft chartered by the government, including a Bundeswehr aircraft flight from Wuhan early on in the pandemic (FAZ 2020a). The chartered flights carried around 66,000 passengers, including more than 6,000 citizens from other EU countries and more than 3,000 non-EU citizens (Spiegel online 2020). The operation was led and coordinated by around fifty staff in the Foreign Office's crisis management unit, which was significantly ramped up for this purpose and involved around 1,000 diplomatic staff in total, both in the ministry in Berlin and in Germany's missions abroad (SZ 2020a, b). The operation was supported by a specially created website on which German citizens who needed return flights to Germany could register (FAZ 2020d), after the regular crisis prevention list on the Foreign Office website crashed due to overload (SZ 2020b). Germany's efforts were also embedded in EU-level coordination, including an EU crisis response center in Brussels, to enable an efficient sharing of flights to Europe between EU members (FAZ 2020c). The Foreign Office received a special budget of around €100 million from the federal government to pay for the chartered flights, but passengers on these flights, in line with §6 of the Consular Act, were later requested to cover parts of the costs (Spiegel online 2020). While there were, perhaps inevitably, some complaints about a lack of information and coordination on the ground (SZ 2020a), the unprecedented scale of the evacuations still represents a significant logistic achievement that speaks to the resources and capabilities of the German consular services.

The third and final category of consular assistance detailed in the Consular Act concerns German citizens who have been arrested abroad (§7 Consular Act) and who have an international legal right to seek support from Germany's diplomatic representation in the respective country or region. Following a request from the affected individual, foreign authorities have an obligation to inform the relevant German embassy or consulate, which then establishes contact with the person under arrest. Consular officials can offer different kinds of practical assistance, for example advising on suitable lawyers, informing relatives, or helping with day-to-day needs in prison. They also observe if the accused gets a fair trial and if the conditions of confinement meet international minimal standards, speaking out on behalf of the arrested German citizen if necessary (Federal Foreign Office 2022c). A prominent example is the – ultimately unsuccessful – efforts of German diplomats to prevent the execution in the US of two German citizens, Walter and Karl LaGrand, on the grounds that they were not informed of their rights to consular assistance under the Vienna Convention when they were arrested for bank robbery and murder in 1984 (ICJ 2001). A more recent case concerns German diplomatic support for Deniz Yücel, a journalist with dual German and Turkish citizenship, when he was arrested for allegedly disseminating terrorist propaganda in Istanbul in 2017 and held without charge for more than a year in Turkish prisons. The German consulate general in Istanbul closely monitored Yücel's treatment by the Turkish authorities, with the consul general paying regular visits to him in prison, and diplomatic negotiations, at times at the highest political level, ultimately led to his release and departure to Germany in February 2018 (Spiegel online 2018).

Another notable area of consular assistance provided by Germany's diplomatic representations that does not directly originate from the Consular Act relates to the right – under certain conditions – of German citizens living abroad to vote in German federal elections (Pautsch and Müller-Török 2016). In addition to supporting German citizens abroad by extending a fundamental democratic right that comes with German citizenship, this can also partly be seen as co-optation, by way of sustaining a sense of national identity and loyalty to the German state among German citizens living abroad. In order to exercise their voting rights, however, prospective voters need to file a written application to be put on the local voter registration roll in the municipality where they were last resident in Germany. As a matter of fact, only a fraction of the estimated 2.5 million Germans living abroad who are eligible to vote in German elections actually make the effort to go through this process – for example, in the case of the 2017 federal elections, as few as around 113,000 of them registered to vote (Business Insider 2021). While German embassies and consulates, unlike the diplomatic missions of many other countries, do not double as polling stations on election day, they offer some logistical support in the election process. Specifically, they can provide German citizens with application forms to request voter registration and they can send the postal votes to polling stations in Germany if the local postal service is deemed unreliable (Klekowski von Koppenfels 2020: 216). By way of international comparison, however, the application and voting process of German citizens living abroad is often being criticized as unwieldy and impractical (SZ 2021).

In providing consular assistance to its citizens, Germany collaborates closely with other EU member states. Under the European treaties, it is party to an EU-wide reciprocal arrangement, according to which EU citizens are eligible for consular support from diplomatic missions of any EU member in cases of emergency if their own country has no diplomatic representation in a particular country (Federal Foreign Office 2019). On the subject of the special relationship with Israel (Oppermann and Hansel 2019), Germany extends consular assistance to Israeli citizens in countries where Israel has no diplomatic offices, most notably some Muslim-majority countries, such as Indonesia or Malaysia (Spiegel online 2014a). On a case-to-case basis, the Federal Foreign Office also works with non-governmental actors in delivering consular assistance, as could be seen, for example, when the German Red Cross helped in implementing quarantine requirements for German citizens who were flown out of Wuhan at the beginning of the Covid-19 pandemic (FAZ 2020a). Germany does not, however, outsource any significant diplomatic activities on a permanent basis to private actors, either in Germany or abroad.

Beyond the information disseminated through the Foreign Office website and traditional media channels, Germany's missions abroad have also widely taken to social media to engage with audiences in their host countries and in Germany. As of 2016, 136 German embassies, permanent representations, and consulates were active on social media, with Facebook and Twitter (now: X) being the most popular sites (Politik and Kommunikation 2016). However, no systematic data exist about how German missions abroad use social media, making it impossible to disentangle to what extent their social media activities specifically support their consular work or serve other purposes, for example as tools of public diplomacy. At the same time, case study evidence on the Twitter feed of Germany's ambassador to Pakistan points to a highly diverse use of the platform, including to communicate information about the work of the embassy and visas that would be relevant for German citizens in Pakistan (Khan et al. 2021).

Economic and Social Dimension

On the economic and social dimension, co-optation plays a bigger part in complementing considerations of support as the main driving force of Germany's activities than is the case on the diplomatic, consular, and security dimensions. Economic and social activities are also often less narrowly targeted to German citizens, but tend to reach beyond German passport holders. Overall, however, Germany undertakes only quite limited economic and social activities that focus on German communities abroad, as by and large Germany does not see much need for specific economic or social support for Germans outside its borders (Klekowski von Koppenfels 2020: 224).

The main exceptions are social and cultural programs for the German diasporas in Central and Eastern Europe and the former Soviet Union as well as Southern Denmark. The Federal Office of Administration (BVA) operates a website that points German emigrants to information centers across Germany which are not run by the Germany state, however, but rather by private service providers or religious and church-associated groups, such as the Catholic Raphaelswerk and the Protestant Diakonie. The most comprehensive online source of information for German citizens about the social, economic, and cultural aspects of living and working abroad is provided by Deutsche im Ausland e.V., a charitable, non-religious association aiming to provide, according to its statute, "selfless support for Germans abroad" (DIA 2022).

Germany's support for its diasporas in Central and Eastern Europe and in the former Soviet Union – counting around 1 million people altogether – is part of its policy of reconciliation since the Second World War (Feldman 2012). Building on bilateral agreements between Germany and the respective countries, government assistance aims at strengthening a sense of community and identity amongst German minorities, including, for example, through programs to promote the German language or through funding and organizing cultural and educational events. As a recent case in point, the German government decided to allocate €5 million in the 2023 federal budget for extracurricular German-language teaching for the German minority in Poland (Federal Government Commissioner for Ethnic German Resettlers and National Minorities 2022). Similarly, albeit on a smaller scale, the German government supports social and cultural projects for the around 15–20,000 members of the German diaspora in Denmark, based on a 1955 agreement between the two countries. Germany's policy towards these diasporas is coordinated by the office of the Federal Government Commissioner for Ethnic German Resettlers and National Minorities in the Federal Ministry of the Interior, Building and Community (BMI 2022). While the German diasporas that benefit from this support are mostly not German citizens, they claim a German ethnic affiliation and cultural background.

More indirectly, Germans living abroad can take advantage of Germany's worldwide network of cultural and educational institutions. This is true, first and foremost, for Germany's 158 Goethe institutes in 98 countries, employing around 4,000 staff and offering more than 1,000 contact points through collaboration with international partners (Goethe Institute 2022). While the main purpose of the Goethe institutes is to engage with their host societies and to cultivate Germany's image abroad, its cultural and social events are also opportunities for German diasporas to foster bonds of community and to nurture their ties to the German language, culture, and customs. These activities thus aim at strengthening a German identity among members of German diasporas and can be seen through the lens of efforts at co-optation. Germany also maintains 140 German schools abroad, which are partly funded by the Federal Foreign Office and which constitute a key dimension of Germany's foreign cultural and educational policy (Federal Foreign Office 2020: 74–76). These schools are open both to non-German and German nationals, with about one third of the 82,000 students enrolled at German schools worldwide being German citizens (Klekowski von Koppenfels 2020: 218).

Moreover, Germany provides support for German students and academics who study, research, or teach abroad. This support comes from the German Academic Exchange Service (DAAD), which has a yearly budget (in 2021) of around €635 million and is financed mainly by the Federal Foreign Office, the Federal Ministry of Education and Research, and the Federal Ministry for Economic Cooperation and Development, but also receives funding from the European Union and other international organizations (DAAD 2022a). The DAAD supports more than 100,000 German (and international) students and academics traveling abroad from German universities each year, making it the biggest funding body for international academic exchange worldwide (DAAD 2022c). It operates a diverse range of schemes, covering both short- and long-term stays abroad, and addresses students and academics at different career stages. German students going abroad can also receive financial support through the Federal Training Assistance Act (BAföG) and draw on a federal program for student loans. In addition, German students are eligible to apply for funding under the EU's Erasmus program, which supports, on average, around 32,000 German students per year (Statistisches Bundesamt 2021: 13).

The DAAD also makes some effort to facilitate the return of German academics to Germany from abroad (for similar efforts in other countries, see, for example, Ghiseli on China, Chapter 5). While these efforts are very narrowly targeted, they represent a case of co-optation to avoid or reverse "brain drain." For one thing, the DAAD gives its long-term lecturers abroad the opportunity to apply for "return fellowships" after they have taught at a foreign partner institution for at least three years (DAAD 2022b). For another, the DAAD has a small program that provides funding for postdoctoral researchers to continue their research at a German university after a research project at an international host institution (DAAD 2019). Beyond students and academics, Germany does not have public programs to incentivize German citizens living abroad to return to Germany. It does, however, provide practical advice for German citizens planning to do so, for example through the website of the Federal Office of Administration (BVA 2022) and the Federal Employment Agency's "virtual welcome center" (BfA 2022). This advice covers legal requirements and information about how to re-enter into the German social system as well as support for job seekers.

Finally, German citizens abroad are covered by certain German social policies. Their access to benefits from these policies is highly constrained and very limited, however, since payments are, in the main, tied to

German residency. For example, German citizens abroad are not eligible for social benefits (*Sozialhilfe*), with the possible exception, in individual cases, of emergencies and when a return to Germany is unfeasible (§24 SGB 12). The most notable divergence from the principle of residence-based rights in the German social system concerns pensions. Under the German pensions system, German (and non-German) citizens who have earned an entitlement to German pensions are eligible to receive their pensions while living abroad, either temporarily or permanently. This is possible without detriment within EU and EFTA countries as well as in about twenty further countries with which Germany has bilateral social security agreements, including, for example the US, Türkiye, and Japan. However, restrictions may apply for pension payments to other countries (Deutsche Rentenversicherung 2022). In 2021, approximately 250,000 German pensioners have indeed used the opportunity to draw German pensions from abroad, mainly from Austria, Switzerland, and the US (Fokus 2022).

Security Dimension

As is the case for the diplomatic and consular dimension, Germany's activities in the security domain are driven first and foremost by considerations of support-and-assist and are aimed primarily at its citizens traveling or residing permanently abroad. Germany's predominant national role conception is that of "civilian power" (Maull 1990; Brummer and Kießling 2019). While this role does not foreclose the use of military force as a tool of statecraft, the deployment of the country's military is considered as an instrument of last resort. This, together with the fact that the vast majority of German citizens living or traveling abroad are located in countries which are politically stable, are the key reasons why there have been only few occasions in which the Bundeswehr has been sent abroad to protect or outright rescue Germans. Still, the Bundeswehr had conducted a total of fourteen "evacuation operations" by 2022 (Deutscher Bundestag 2022c: 100), plus a more recent operation in Sudan in April 2023, most of which have not seen much political debate or scholarly attention. Four of those operations, in Albania, Libya, Afghanistan, and Sudan, respectively, qualify as military evacuation operations, whereas the other operations should be seen as diplomatic evacuations or national air lifts (on Germany's diplomatic security policy, see Brummer and Krotz 2019), like the above mentioned ones following the 2004 Tsunami in the Indian Ocean and during the Covid-19 pandemic. The military evacuation operations are not only interesting in themselves but also with respect to their broader political ramifications.

On March 14, 1997, the Bundeswehr conducted a military evacuation operation codenamed Libelle (dragonfly) in Albania, which had experienced major economic and political unrest since the beginning of that year. For their operation, the German armed forces used half a dozen helicopters which were already present in the region as part of the country's contribution to the NATO-led Stabilization Force (SFOR) in Bosnia and Hercegovina. The Bundeswehr used the helicopters to fly out around 100 people, of whom around 20 were Germans, from 22 different countries from Tirana, Albania, to Podgorica, Montenegro (Deutscher Bundestag 2000: 8). From there, two transport Bundeswehr planes which had been dispatched earlier that day from a military base in Germany brought the evacuees to Köln/Bonn Airport.

The operation in Albania, in which some 320 members of the Bundeswehr participated (Deutscher Bundestag 2016: 3), was noteworthy in several respects. For starters, it was the first time that the Bundeswehr conducted such a rescue operation, which according to commentators "opened a new chapter" in the history of the German armed forces (FAZ 1997a). Another first was that the Bundeswehr was engaged in a firefight during an operation abroad which erupted when the evacuees tried to get onto the helicopters. Moreover, by flying out not only its citizens but also, and even primarily so, people from other countries, Germany was in a position to reciprocate similar efforts undertaken by other countries when German citizens were brought out of harm's way, for example by Belgium in Rwanda in 1994 (FAZ 1997a). In this sense, Foreign Minister Klaus Kinkel stated that: "In the past we have been helped, this time we have helped" (SZ 1997b).

Finally, the operation at the time highlighted the still ambiguous legal situation surrounding the foreign deployment of Germany's armed forces beyond the territory of NATO members ("out of area"). That such activities are principally in accordance with the German constitution (*Grundgesetz*) had been established in 1994 by the Federal Constitutional Court (Bundesverfassungsgericht). In their ruling, the judges assigned a strong role to the German Parliament (Bundestag), granting the parliamentarians ex ante veto power for foreign deployments. However, in the Albanian case, the Conservative–Liberal government led by Chancellor Helmut Kohl did not ask the Bundestag for permission prior to the rescue operation. True, the Constitutional Court had foreseen such emergency measures, and the government had informed the chairpersons of the Bundestag's parliamentary groups in advance, who in turn gave their consent to the operation (FAZ 1997a). However, the "quasi-involvement of the parliament" (SZ 1997a) called the legality of the operation in question, as did the fact that Germany had acted unilaterally rather than, as was also stipulated by the Constitutional Court, within a system of mutual collective security such as NATO (Fastenrath 1997). Still, six days after the operation, the Bundestag approved ex post the operation with a large majority. Ensuing calls for a law specifically to regulate emergency military measures outside of NATO territory (FAZ 1997b) have not been heeded to date. Having said that, in response to the experience in Albania, the Bundeswehr set up a special forces unit (Kommando Spezialkräfte) in early April 1997, among whose core tasks is to rescue Germans held hostage abroad (SZ 1997c).

The second military evacuation operation by the German armed forces was conducted in the context of the Libyan Civil War in 2011. Contrary to the operation in Albania, where the decision was essentially taken overnight, there was more time for preparation. On February 22, the Federal Foreign Office issued a travel warning for Libya and called on all of the estimated 500 Germans who were still in the country to leave immediately (FAZ 2011). In the following days, the majority of Germans was flown out using either commercial airlines or Bundeswehr aircraft. The latter also brought to safety citizens from other countries, just like other countries, such as Türkiye, helped evacuate German citizens (FAZ.net 2011). Then, on February 26, Operation Pegasus was launched. Assisted by British forces and local militias, two Bundeswehr aircraft flew out an additional 130 or so people, including 22 Germans from the eastern Libyan Desert where a German company ran an oil production facility. Overall, a total of 262 people, of whom 125 were Germans, were brought to safety during this operation (Deutscher Bundestag 2011: 1).

Like in the Albanian case, the Bundestag was not asked for approval prior to the operation, though the government again informed in advance the chairpersons of the parliamentary groups. However, contrary to the Albanian case, the Bundestag was not asked for ex post approval either. Rather, the Conservative–Liberal government under Chancellor Angela Merkel argued that the operation was merely an evacuation mission for humanitarian ends which did not involve the use of weapons, thus also not requiring parliamentary approval (Deutscher Bundestag 2011: 3). This argument failed to convince the political opposition, however. Indeed, the Greens lodged a complaint before the Federal Constitutional Court arguing that the Bundestag's rights were violated by the government. In its ruling, which came only in 2015, the court somewhat surprisingly rejected the complaint. The key argument was that since the operation had already ended prior to the earliest possible referral to Parliament, the Bundestag had never been in a position to influence the operation. In such cases, the government must merely quickly and thoroughly inform Parliament rather than ask for an ex post approval of its decisions (FCC 2015).

The Bundeswehr conducted another military evacuation operation in Afghanistan in the summer of 2021 where, to the surprise of Germany and its allies (Deutscher Bundestag 2022b: 30), the Taliban had regained power just a few weeks after the withdrawal of the international security forces in late June–early July. Due to the increasingly volatile security situation, the crisis management unit (Krisenstab) of the German government decided on August 15, which was also the day when the German embassy was evacuated (Deutscher Bundestag 2022b: 18), to deploy a military operation (MilEvakOp) to evacuate not only German citizens but also members of the international community and the Afghan civil society. The government confirmed that decision three days later, and the Bundestag approved the operation ex post (like it did in the Albanian case) on August 25. Overall, between August 16 and 27 some 500 German soldiers were involved in conducting 37 evacuation flights by which around 5,350 people – the large majority of whom were Afghans (Deutscher Bundestag 2022b: 23–24) – from 45 countries were flown out of Kabul Airport in close coordination with American forces (Deutscher Bundestag 2022b: 16, 2022c: 16).

The evaluation of the evacuation operation was inconclusive. While the German armed forces did successfully rescue several thousand people from Afghanistan, it became clear that the Bundeswehr would not have been able to conduct the operation without help from third parties, and the US in particular. What is more, the rescue operation was perceived as merely the culmination of various problematic political developments that had paved the way for the eventual withdrawal of Western security forces from Afghanistan. Against this background, the Bundestag set up a committee of inquiry (Untersuchungsausschuss) in July 2022, which is tasked with scrutinizing the withdrawal and evacuation process as well as German Afghanistan policy since early 2020 more broadly (Deutscher Bundestag 2022c).

The most recent military evacuation operation of the German Bundeswehr took place in Sudan in April 2023. The operation involved up to 1,000 Bundeswehr personnel and four military aircraft which flew out around 780 people from Khartoum, including around 200 German citizens as well as citizens of more than 40 other states. The evacuation was considered necessary because of a dramatic worsening of the security situation in Sudan in the context of a violent power struggle between rival elites and was implemented during a 72-hour ceasefire (Federal Government 2023). The political decision for the operation was taken by the federal government's crisis management unit on April 22, with the first Bundeswehr forces deployed one day later. Following the precedents of the military evacuations from Albania and Afghanistan, the decision was confirmed in cabinet on April 25 and mandated ex post by a unanimous vote (with seven abstentions) in the German Bundestag on April 26, while the chairpersons of all parliamentary groups were already informed at the beginning of operations on April 23 (Deutscher Bundestag 2023). The government invoked §5 of the 2005 Parliamentary Participation Act (*Parlamentsbeteiligungsgesetz*) as legal basis for the operation, which stipulates that deployments of the armed forces, by way of exception, do not require the ex ante approval of the German Bundestag "in cases of imminent danger" or in the case of rescue operations when advance public debate in the Bundestag would threaten the lives of the people to be rescued. In contrast to the military evacuation operation in Afghanistan, the Sudan operation was widely seen as successful, with Defense Minister Boris Pistorius congratulating the Bundeswehr for a "really great success within a short time" in an "extraordinarily complex" operation (Tagesschau 2023).

Finally, the arguably most famous rescue operation ever undertaken by German security forces was carried out by the country's police forces rather than its military. Operation Feuerzauber (Fire Magic) ended the hijacking of a German civilian aircraft on October 13, 1977 by members of the Popular Front for the Liberation of Palestine (e.g., Geiger 2009). The Lufthansa aircraft was taken over by the terrorists on its way from Palma de Mallorca, Spain, to Frankfurt am Main, Germany. On board the aircraft were five German crew members as well as 86 passengers, mostly from Germany (Wiegrefe 2008). After several stops, the plane eventually landed in Mogadishu, Somalia, on October 17. There, the GSG 9, a special unit of the Bundespolizei (German Federal Police) that was set up in response to the terrorist attacks on the Summer Olympic Games in Munich in 1972, managed to end the hostage-taking and bring to safety all the passengers and all but one of the crew members.

Conclusion

This chapter has presented Germany as a resourceful supporter and protector of its national communities abroad that springs to action mainly in times of crisis. On the one hand, Germany's capabilities, commensurate with a highly developed country, put it in a strong position to interact with its communities abroad across various substantive dimensions, ranging from diplomacy and consular activities to economic and social as well as security-related ones. On the other hand, the location of Germany's communities abroad, most of whom live or travel in developed countries, reduce the salience of such undertakings, as does the limited political and economic role that German citizens abroad play in and for domestic politics. Generally speaking, then, Germany's engagement with its communities abroad has a much lower profile than is the case for other countries covered in this volume, including India, the Philippines, and Türkiye. Punctuations in this equilibrium tend to come primarily in the form of sudden eruptions of civilian unrest or military conflict (e.g., Albania, Libya, Afghanistan, Ukraine, Sudan), natural disasters (e.g., the 2004 Tsunami in the Indian Ocean), hostage situations, or, recently, a global health crisis (Covid-19 pandemic). Activities to respond to such crises have been typically undertaken in close cooperation with Germany's European or North American partners, not only out of choice, in terms of solidarity and burden-sharing, but also out of necessity due to limited capabilities.

Among its national community abroad, Germany focuses its activities on German citizens who reside permanently or travel temporarily abroad, as opposed to engaging systematically and in a sustained fashion also with the broader German diaspora whose members are no longer tied to the country by formal citizenship. As regards the motivations for Germany's actions, emphasis is placed on supporting and assisting its citizens abroad. This covers not only routine consular activities but also diplomatic or military measures in man-made or natural emergency situations. In turn, co-optation plays some role, for example by setting up return programs for highly skilled academics or by organizing social and cultural events to nurture a sense of national identity in German diasporas. However, those efforts pale compared to the undertakings by other countries covered in this volume to tap into the political (e.g., Türkiye) or economic (e.g., India, Mexico) potentials of their communities abroad. Lastly, as would be expected by the literature on transnational authoritarianism, repression is not a relevant motive that shapes Germany's relations with its communities abroad.

In terms of the agency of Germany's communities abroad, we found no indications that they themselves exerted significant influence on policymakers in Germany. Rather, similar to the British case (see Strong, Chapter 8), the pressure to act seemed to emerge mainly from media and public attention to international crises, sporadically raising the domestic political profile of Germans living or traveling abroad. While we do not discern clear linear trends in how Germany engages with Germans living or traveling abroad, with the unsurprising exception of an increasing role for technology, this chapter suggests that crisis situations demanding rapid and decisive action, for example due to natural disasters, political instability, or civil conflict in host countries, seem to come in ever closer succession. If this is indeed a systematic and lasting development, it would enhance the political salience of how Germany engages with its communities abroad, potentially motivating demands for more sustained policies to support (and co-opt) these communities. With climate change leading to an increase in extreme weather events, for instance, the chances are that rescue-and-evacuation operations in response to, say, severe floods will become more frequent. Similarly, the medium- and long-term ramifications of the Covid-19 pandemic and the Russian invasion of Ukraine could trigger political unrest and civil conflict, particularly in areas of fragile statehood, which too might increase the need to bring German citizens out of harm's way. However, given the location of the German communities abroad, this might concern first and foremost a limited number of tourists, as has been the case in the past.

With the exception of extreme crisis situations, even if they increase in number, Germany's engagement with its national communities abroad is therefore likely to remain of limited salience for most of the time in the years to come. In terms of the provision of more routine support measures, the implementation of novel technical solutions (ranging from communication to digital services) is as likely as are additional efforts in burden-sharing, most notably with other EU member states, possibly through an increased use of the European External Action Service.

References

BfA (2022) Ihre Rückkehr nach Deutschland. Available at: www.arbeitsagentur.de/vor-ort/zav/content/1533737785059 (last accessed November 30, 2022).

BMI (Federal Ministry of the Interior, Building and Community) (2022) Beauftragte für Aussiedlerfragen und nationale Minderheiten. Available at: www.bmi.bund.de/DE/ministerium/beauftragte/beauftragte-aussiedlerfragen/beauftragte-aussiedlerfragen-node.html (last accessed November 29, 2022).

Brummer, Klaus, and Friedrich Kießling (eds.) (2019) *Zivilmacht Bundesrepublik? Bundesdeutsche außenpolitische Rollen vor und nach 1989 aus politik- und geschichtswissenschaftlichen Perspektiven*. Baden-Baden: Nomos.

Brummer, Klaus, and Ulrich Krotz (2019) German Diplomatic Security Policy: A Federal Police Response. In Eugenio Cusumano and Chris Kinsey (eds.), *Diplomatic Security: A Comparative Analysis*. Stanford, CA: Stanford University Press, 90–108.

Business Insider (2021) Wahlen sollen für etwa 2,5 Millionen Deutsche im Ausland leichter möglich werden. Available at: www.businessinsider.de/politik/deutschland/wahlen-sollen-fuer-millionen-deutsche-im-ausland-leichter-werden-a/ (last accessed August 29, 2023).

BVA (Bundesverwaltungsamt) (2022) Informationen für Auswanderer und Rückkehrer nach Deutschland. Available at www.bva.bund.de/DE/Das-BVA/Aufgaben/A/Auswanderer_Auslandstaetige/_documents/Laenderauswahl/

Laender_Deutschland_Inhalt.html;jsessionid=18E43A3914C43BECE08429D10FF74B16.intranet671 (last accessed November 30, 2022).

DAAD (German Academic Exchange Service) (2019) Einmal Ausland und zurück. Available at: www2.daad.de/presse/pressemitteilungen/de/31325-einmal-ausland-und-zurueck (last accessed November 30, 2022).

DAAD (German Academic Exchange Service) (2022a) Budget und Geldgeber des DAAD. Available at www.daad.de/de/der-daad/was-wir-tun/zahlen-und-fakten/budget-und-geldgeber-des-daad (last accessed November 30, 2022).

DAAD (German Academic Exchange Service) (2022b) Kurz- und Langzeitdozenturen. Available at: www.daad.de/de/im-ausland-studieren-forschen-lehren/lehren-im-ausland/dozenturen/kurz-und-langzeitdozenturen (last accessed November 30, 2022).

DAAD (German Academic Exchange Service) (2022c) So unterstützt Sie der DAAD – Überblick. Available at: www.daad.de/de/im-ausland-studieren-forschen-lehren/stipendien-finanzierung/ueberblick (last accessed November 30, 2022).

Deutsche Rentenversicherung (2022) Umzug als Rentner ins Ausland. Available at: www.deutsche-rentenversicherung.de/DRV/DE/Rente/Ausland/Rente-im-Ausland/rente-im-ausland-umzug-detailseite.html?nn=c29ef28f-8ca5-42fa-934c-44004c078da6 (last accessed November 29, 2022).

Deutsche Welle (2016) Evacuations from Juba, July 13. Available at: www.dw.com/en/eu-citizens-evacuated-from-south-sudan/a-19397576#:~:text=Germany%20and%20Italy%20have%20begun%20evacuations%20from%20South,were%20also%20being%20airlifted%20to%20Uganda%20and%20Djibouti (last accessed November 23, 2022).

Deutscher Bundestag (2000) Unterrichtung durch die Bundesregierung: Bericht der Bundesregierung über die deutsche Humanitäre Hilfe im Ausland 1994 bis 1997. Document 14/3981. Berlin.

Deutscher Bundestag (2011) Evakuierungseinsatz “Pegasus” der Bundeswehr in Libyen. July 11, 2011. Document 17/6564. Berlin.

Deutscher Bundestag (2016) Gesamt- und Folgekosten aller Auslandseinsätze seit Gründung der Bundeswehr. March 9, 2016. Document 18/7820. Berlin.

Deutscher Bundestag (2022a) Antrag der Fraktionen SPD, CDU/CSU, BÜNDNIS 90/DIE GRÜNEN und FDP: Einsetzung des 1. Untersuchungsausschusses der 20. Wahlperiode. June 21, 2022. Document 20/2352. Berlin.

Deutscher Bundestag (2022b) Aufarbeitung der Einschätzungen, Entscheidungen und Maßnahmen vor und nach der Machtübernahme der Taliban in Afghanistan. September 20, 2021. Document 19/32505. Berlin.

Deutscher Bundestag (2022c) Unterrichtung durch die Wehrbeauftragte. Jahresbericht 2021 (63. Bericht). March 15, 2022. Document 20/900. Berlin.

Deutscher Bundestag (2023) Antrag der Bundesregierung: Einsatz bewaffneter deutscher Streitkräfte zur militärischen Evakuierung aus Sudan. April 26, 2023. Document 20/6528. Berlin.

DIA (Deutsche im Ausland e.V.) (2022) Satzung. Available at: www.deutsche-im-ausland.org/fileadmin/inhalte/pdf/Downloads/Satzung_DIAeV_01.pdf (last accessed November 28, 2022).

Ette, Andreas, and Marcel Erlinghagen (2021) Structures of German Emigration and Reimigration: Historical Developments and Demographic Patterns. In Marcel Erlinghagen, Andreas Ett, Norert F. Schneider, and Nils Witte (eds.), *The Global Lives of German Migrants: Consequences of International Migration across the Life Course.* Cham: Springer, 43–64.

Fastenrath, Ulrich (1997) Neues Kapitel der Bundeswehrgeschichte ohne rechtliche Grundlage? *Frankfurter Allgemeine Zeitung,* March 19, p. 8.

FAZ (Frankfurter Allgemeine Zeitung) (1997a) In Tirana mußte die Regierung handeln. *Der Segen des Bundestages kommt später, March* 17, p. 2.

FAZ (Frankfurter Allgemeine Zeitung) (1997b) SPD fordert Gesetz für Notensätze im Ausland, March 20, p. 1.

FAZ (Frankfurter Allgemeine Zeitung) (2004a) Auf der Straße des Todes, December 29, p. 7.

FAZ (Frankfurter Allgemeine Zeitung) (2004b) Am Mittwoch war der Boden noch voll Blut, December 31, p. 9.

FAZ (Frankfurter Allgemeine Zeitung) (2004c) Hilfsbereitschaft in aller Welt, December 31, p. 1.

FAZ (Frankfurter Allgemeine Zeitung) (2011) Reisewarnung für Libyen, February 22, p. 5.

FAZ (Frankfurter Allgemeine Zeitung) (2020a) Auf das Ungewisse vorbereiten, February 1, p. 6.

FAZ (Frankfurter Allgemeine Zeitung) (2020b) Operation Luftbrücke, March 19, p. 2.

FAZ (Frankfurter Allgemeine Zeitung) (2020c) Rückholaktion für gestrandete Europäer, March 24, p. 2.

FAZ (Frankfurter Allgemeine Zeitung) (2020d) Zehntausende warten auf Rückkehr nach Deutschland, March 28, p. 4.

FAZ.net (2011) EU schließt Militäreinsatz nicht aus, February 24. Available at: www.faz.net/aktuell/politik/ausland/naher-osten/eskalation-in-libyen-eu-schliesst-militaereinsatz-nicht-aus-1591782.html (last accessed November 9, 2022).

FCC (Federal Constitutional Court) (2015) Leitsätze zum Urteil des Zweiten Senats vom 23. September 2015–2 BvE 6/11. Available at: www.bundesverfassungsgericht.de/SharedDocs/Entscheidungen/DE/2015/09/es20150923_2bve000611.html (last accessed November 9, 2022).

Federal Foreign Office (2019) Konsularhilfe-Kooperation der Europäischen Union, December 12. Available at: www.auswaertiges-amt.de/de/service/konsularinfo/konsularhilfe-eu (last accessed November 25, 2022).

Federal Foreign Office (2020) 24. Bericht der Bundesregierung zur Auswärtigen Kultur- und Bildungspolitik für das Jahr 2020, Berlin.

Federal Foreign Office (2022a) Außenministerin Baerbock zur Rückholaktion aus Nordostsyrien, October 5. Available at: www.auswaertiges-amt.de/de/newsroom/baerbock-rueckholung-nordostsyrien/2556468 (last accessed November 23, 2022).

Federal Foreign Office (2022b) Hilfe für Deutsche in Notfällen: Konsularische Hilfefälle. Available at: www.auswaertiges-amt.de/de/service/konsularinfo/hilfe-notfaelle (last accessed November 22, 2022).

Federal Foreign Office (2022c) Konsularische Betreuung in ausländischer Haft, October 19. Available at: www.auswaertiges-amt.de/de/service/konsularinfo/konsularische-betreuung-haftfaelle (last accessed November 24, 2022).

Federal Foreign Office (2022d) Mitarbeiterinnen und Mitarbeiter. Available at: www.auswaertiges-amt.de/de/aamt/auswdienst/mitarbeiter/214948 (last accessed October 28, 2022).

Federal Foreign Office (2022e) Tasks of the German Missions Abroad. Available at: www.auswaertiges-amt.de/en/about-us/auslandsvertretungen/-/229722 (last accessed October 28, 2022).

Federal Foreign Office (2022f) Verzeichnis der Vertretungen der Bundesrepublik Deutschland im Ausland sowie der Honorarkonsulinnen und Honorarkonsuln. Available at: www.auswaertiges-amt.de/blob/199314/3dc8cd0ba6b40d1bb164a6ae36962604/dtauslandsvertretungenliste-data.pdf (last accessed October 28, 2022).

Federal Government (2023) Rund 780 Menschen aus dem Sudan evakuiert, April 28. Available at: www.bundesregierung.de/breg-de/aktuelles/bundeswehr-sudan-2185846#:~:text=Die%20Soldatinnen%20und%20Soldaten%20des%20Bundeswehr%20evakuierten%20rund,B%C3%BCrger%20weiterer%2040%20Staaten%20aus%20dem%20Sudan%20evakuiert. (last accessed August 29, 2023).

Federal Government Commissioner for Ethnic German Resettlers and National Minorities (n.d.) Deutsche Minderheiten in Europa. Available at: www.aussiedlerbeauftragte.de/Webs/AUSB/DE/themen/minderheiten-ausland/europa/europa-node.html (last accessed August 30, 2023).

Federal Government Commissioner for Ethnic German Resettlers and National Minorities (2022) 5.000.000 € zusätzliche Mittel zur außerschulischen Sprachförderung im Bundeshaushalt 2023, November 17. Available at: www.aussiedlerbeauftragte.de/SharedDocs/pressemitteilungen/Webs/AUSB/DE/2022/bundesmittel-sprachfoerderung.html (last accessed November 29, 2022).

Federal Ministry of Justice (2021) Gesetz über die Konsularbeamten, ihre Aufgaben und Befugnisse (Konsulargesetz). Available at: www.gesetze-im-internet.de/konsg/BJNR023170974.html (last accessed May 22, 2024).

Feldman, Lily Gardner (2012) *Germany's Policy of Reconciliation: From Enmity to Amity*. Lanham, MD: Rowman & Littlefield.

Fokus (2022) Rente im Ausland genießen? Auf diese Fallstricke müssen Sie achten, August 25. Available at: www.focus.de/finanzen/altersvorsorge/rente/das-gilt-wenn-sie-woanders-leben-wollen-auswandernde-gastarbeiter-immer-mehr-renten-werden-ins-ausland-gezahlt_id_136708737.html (last accessed November 29, 2022).

Geiger, Tim (2009) Die "Landshut" in Mogadischu. Das außenpolitische Krisenmanagement der Bundesregierung angesichts der terroristischen Herausforderung 1977. *Vierteljahreshefte für Zeitgeschichte* 57(3), 413–456.

Goethe Institute (2022) Annual Report 2021/2022, Munich. Available at: www.goethe.de/resources/files/pdf270/jahrbuch-2021_20222021.pdf (last accessed November 29, 2022).

Graw, Ansgar (2007) Wer bezahlt für verschleppte Deutsche? *Die Welt*, July 31. Available at: www.welt.de/103891334 (last accessed November 22, 2022).

ICJ [International Court of Justice] (2001) LaGrand (*Germany* v. *United States of America*), Judgements, I.C.J. Reports 2001, 466–517.

Khan, M. Laeeq, Muhammad Ittefaq, Yadira Ixchel Martínez Pantoja, Muhammad Mustafa Raziq, and Aqdas Malik (2021) Public Engagement Model to Analyze Digital Diplomacy on Twitter: A Social Media Analytics Framework. *International Journal of Communication* 15, 1741–1769.

Klekowski von Koppenfels, Amanda (2020) Diaspora Policies, Consular Services and Social Protection for German Citizen Abroad. In Jean-Michel Lafleur and Daniela Vintila (eds.), *Migration and Social Protection in Europe and Beyond (Volume 2): Comparing Consular Services and Diaspora Policies*. Cham: Springer, 207–226.

Lenz, Susanne (2017) *Der konsularische Schutz. Notfälle Deutscher im Ausland.* Universität Potsdam.

Lowy Institute (2019) Global Diplomacy Index. 2019 Country Ranking. Available at: https://globaldiplomacyindex.lowyinstitute.org/country_rank.html (last accessed October 28, 2022).

Maull, Hanns W. (1990) Germany and Japan: The New Civilian Powers. *Foreign Affairs* 69(5), 91–106.

Max Kade Institute for German-American Studies (n.d.) How German is American? Settling in America. Available at: https://mki.wisc.edu/exhibits/virtual-exhibits-2/how-german-is-american-3/how-german-is-american-settling-in-america/ (last accessed August 30, 2023).

Oltmer, Jochen (2013) *Migration im 19. und 20. Jahrhundert*, 2nd ed. München: Oldenbourg.

Oltmer, Jochen, and Vera Hanewinkel (2021) Geschichte der Migration nach und aus Deutschland. Available at: www.bpb.de/themen/migration-integration/laenderprofile/deutschland/341068/geschichte-der-migration-nach-und-aus-deutschland/ (last accessed November 14, 2022).

Oppermann, Kai, and Mischa Hansel (2019) The Ontological Security of Special Relationships: The Case of Germany's Relations with Israel. *European Journal of International Security* 4(1), 79–100.

Pautsch, Arne, and Robert Müller-Török (2016) Das Wahlrecht der Auslandsdeutschen nach §12 Abs. 2 BWG auf dem neuerlichen Prüfstand? Eine Analyse aus juristischer und verwaltungswissenschaftlicher Sicht. *Zeitschrift für Parlamentsfragen* 47(4), 851–866.

Politik & Kommunikation (2016) Warum das Auswärtige Amt auf digitale Kanäle setzt, October 26. Available at: www.politik-kommunikation.de/politik/warum-das-auswaertige-amt-auf-digitale-kanaele-setzt (last accessed November 24, 2022).

Spiegel Online (2014a) Deutschland vertritt künftig israelische Bürger weltweit, February 21. Available at: www.spiegel.de/politik/deutschland/abkommen-deutschland-vertritt-kuenftig-israelische-buerger-weltweit-a-954951.html (last accessed November 25, 2022).

Spiegel Online (2014b) Rückkehr an den Ort des Unglücks, December 26. Available at: www.spiegel.de/panorama/tsunami-2004-deutsche-gedenken-der-opfer-in-thailand-a-1010333.html (last accessed November 23, 2022).

Spiegel Online (2018) The Long Road to Freedom for German Journalist Yücel. Available at: www.spiegel.de/international/world/german-journalist-yuecel-s-long-road-to-freedom-a-1195149.html (last accessed November 30, 2022).

Spiegel Online (2020) Nicht umsonst geflogen, June 13. Available at: www.spiegel.de/reise/coronakrise-auswaertiges-amt-treibt-rueckholkosten-ein-a-ca95b388-5105-41ad-86b4-5989235b4c4d (last accessed November 24, 2022).

Statista (2022) Anzahl der Urlaubsreisenden in Deutschland in den Jahren von 2005 bis 2021 (in Millionen). Available at: https://de.statista.com/statistik/daten/studie/151940/umfrage/anzahl-der-urlaubsreisenden-in-deutschland-seit-2005/ (last accessed November 16, 2022).

Statistisches Bundesamt (2021) Deutsche Studierende im Ausland. Ergebnisse des Berichtsjahres 2019. Available at: www.destatis.de/DE/Themen/Gesellschaft-Umwelt/Bildung-Forschung-Kultur/Hochschulen/Publikationen/Downloads-Hochschulen/studierende-ausland-5217101217004.pdf?__blob=publicationFile (last accessed November 30, 2022).

Statistisches Bundesamt (2022a) Ausländische Bevölkerung nach Familienstand und ausgewählten Staatsangehörigkeiten am 31.12.2021. Available at: www.destatis.de/DE/Themen/Gesellschaft-Umwelt/Bevoelkerung/Migration-Integration/Tabellen/auslaendische-bevoelkerung-familienstand.html (last accessed November 14, 2022).

Statistisches Bundesamt (2022b) Migration between Germany and Foreign Countries. Available at: www.destatis.de/EN/Themes/Society-Environment/Population/Migration/Tables/migration-total.html;jsessionid=3017B5B4619A85D3B3481DA3EC3C2862.live722 (last accessed November 14, 2022).

Statistisches Bundesamt (2022c) Migration of German Citizens between Germany and Foreign Countries. Available at: www.destatis.de/EN/Themes/Society-Environment/Population/Migration/Tables/migration-german.html;jsessionid=3017B5B4619A85D3B3481DA3EC3C2862.live722 (last accessed November 14, 2022).

SZ (Süddeutsche Zeitung) (1997a) Bundeswehr-Einsätze erleichtern, March 19, p. 5.

SZ (Süddeutsche Zeitung) (1997b) Schnelle Hilfe am Parlament vorbei, March 15, p. 1.

SZ (Süddeutsche Zeitung) (1997c) Spezialeinheit für alle Fälle gerüstet, April 2, p. 5.

SZ (Süddeutsche Zeitung) (2010) Deutsche Geiseln im Ausland, May 11, Available at: www.sz.de/1.635904 (last accessed November 22, 2022).

SZ (Süddeutsche Zeitung) (2020a) Abreise ungewiss, March 31, p. 2.

SZ (Süddeutsche Zeitung) (2020b) Wie in der Arche Noah, March 28/29, p. 10.

SZ (Süddeutsche Zeitung) (2021) Ungehört in der Ferne, September 27, p. 7.

Tagesschau (2023) Ein Rennen gegen die Zeit, April 24. Available at: www.tagesschau.de/inland/bundeswehr-sudan-103.html (last accessed August 29, 2023).

Telford, John, John Cosgrave, and Rachel Houghton (2006) *Joint Evaluation of the International Response to the Indian Ocean Tsunami: Synthesis Report.* London: Tsunami Evaluation Coalition.

United Nations Department of Economic and Social Affairs, Population Division (2020) International Migrant Stock 2020 Available at: www.un.org/development/desa/pd/content/international-migrant-stock (last accessed October 26, 2022).

Welt (2013) Chinesen lösen Deutsche als Reiseweltmeister ab. Available at: www.welt.de/reise/article112792396/Chinesen-loesen-Deutsche-als-Reiseweltmeister-ab.html (last accessed December 1, 2022).

Wiegrefe, Klaus (2008) "Wo sind die Schweine?". Protokoll der "Landshut"-Entführung. Available at: www.spiegel.de/geschichte/protokoll-der-landshut-entfuehrung-a-947933.html (last accessed November 9, 2022).

World Bank (2022) Indicators. Available at: https://data.worldbank.org/indicator (last accessed November 14, 2022).

ZDF (2022) Aus Lager in Syrien: Deutschland holt IS-Frauen und Kinder zurück, October 6. Available at: www.zdf.de/nachrichten/politik/deutschland-holt-is-anhaengerinnen-kinder-aus-syrien-100.html (last accessed November 23, 2022).

11 Egypt

Cultivating Loyalty Abroad, Repressing When Necessary

Kelsey P. Norman

Introduction

Egypt is the most populous state in the Arab world, with just over 100 million citizens residing in the country. Unsurprisingly, Egyptian nationals have long looked abroad for educational and work opportunities, to reunite with family, and in, some instances, to escape repression at home. Since the establishment of the modern state in the mid twentieth century, the Egyptian government has intertwined the management of its emigrant population with a number of goals, including building the country's soft diplomatic power, developing and funneling remittances back to Egypt, and cultivating and maintaining loyalty among its expatriates. While the majority of Egyptians abroad reside in other Arab countries – considered to be "temporary migrants" – the government has developed a bifurcated approach to its diaspora, devoting much of its attention to citizens and their offspring residing in Western states, considered by Egypt to be "permanent" migrants (Tsourapas 2019; Abdel Fattah, Rietig, and Fakhry 2021).

This chapter examines the evolution of the Egyptian state's polices toward its citizens abroad – both within the Arab world and beyond – and seeks to understand how the Egyptian government has attempted to protect, assist, and cultivate loyalty among its diaspora, as well as how it has sought to exert further control over this population. While initially the modern Egyptian state discouraged emigration in the early decades after its founding, engagement with its diaspora has, since the 1970s, come to constitute a critical component of the country's diplomatic and external economic policy. The current Egyptian government has several ministries responsible in part for the management of its expatriates – among them, the Ministry of Foreign Affairs, Ministry of Manpower, and Ministry of State for Emigration and Egyptian Expatriate Affairs – although these various entities have overlapping roles and do not always work in concert. And while the Egyptian state has historically been unwilling to intervene militarily in the affairs of its expatriates, this chapter describes a number of initiatives the Egyptian government has taken to engage with, protect, and in some cases, suppress, its citizens abroad.

Overview of the Egyptian Community Abroad

After the 1952 coup – celebrated in Egypt as a revolution – and during the presidency of Gamal Abdel Nasser, Egyptian emigration was generally discouraged. Tsourapas (2019) argues that the ruling Free Officers regime was concerned with both high- and low-skilled labor shortages, leading the state to develop a rigid system of exit visas that forbade the migration of most professions. The exception to this was Egyptian teachers – and a smaller subset of other skilled workers – who were seconded across the Arab world, in addition to some who were sent to sub-Saharan Africa and Latin America. The secondment policies explicitly encouraged public sector employees to take leaves of absence, sometimes paying their salaries both at home and abroad, with the guarantee that their position would remain available upon return (Sell 1988). This served the dual purpose of depopulating Egypt's overstaffed public sector while simultaneously spreading Nasserite, pan-Arab ideology to newly independent states that needed to educate and build their work forces (Sell 1998).

It was not until after Egypt's 1967 military defeat by Israel, the worsening of the domestic economic situation, and increasing agitation among student protestors that the Egyptian regime began to explore more lenient emigration policies as a "safety valve," signing several labor agreements with other Arab states (Tsourapas 2019). This was accelerated under President Anwar Sadat, who came to power following Nasser's death in 1970. Sadat sped up passport processing, provided amnesty to young Egyptians who had emigrated abroad under Nasser's tenure to avoid conscription, and intentionally stopped collecting data on emigration in order to minimize state control of the process (Tsourapas 2019). These changes were in line with Sadat's broader economic liberalization policies and aimed to capitalize on migration – and specifically remittances – as a critical economic resource for the Egyptian state. While the Egyptian Central Agency for Public Mobilization and Statistics (CAPMAS) estimated the number of Egyptian emigrants to be about 70,000 in 1970, this number jumped to 1.4 million by 1976 (Zohry 2005).

Sadat particularly focused on selling the image of hard-working, non-political Egyptian emigrants to the newly oil-rich states of the Persian Gulf, which were eager to replace Palestinian workers who were perceived as too politically contentious (Tsourapas 2019). The 1971 Egyptian Constitution also stated that all Egyptians were granted the right to emigrate and to return home any time they wished (Abdel Fattah, Rietig, and Fakhry 2021). While Egyptian workers were expelled *en masse* from other Arab states after Egypt signed the Camp David Accords in 1977, which normalized its relations with Israel and which was perceived as a betrayal by most Arab states, Egypt managed to use the reliance of other Arab states on Egyptian labor to regain political favor by the early 1980s (Tsourapas 2019). The first and only emigration law in Egypt – Law No. 111 – was passed in 1983, aiming to further promote Egyptian migration abroad (Abdel Fattah, Rietig, and Fakhry 2021).

However, an overreliance on emigration to Arab states ultimately left Egypt vulnerable when opportunities for labor emigration diminished (Tsourapas 2019). This process began in 1979 when oil prices fell, but was amplified as the Gulf Cooperation Council (GCC) countries began to favor labor migration from Asia rather than other Arab states throughout the 1980s. The Gulf Crisis of 1990, when Iraq invaded Kuwait, revealed Egypt's unpreparedness to absorb its repatriated citizens, with more than half a million Egyptian migrants forced to return to Egypt within two months of the invasion (Tsourapas 2019). Later, during the 1990s, the Gulf countries became increasingly interested in employing their own citizens in public sector jobs, leading to fewer opportunities for Egyptian migrants to find work abroad. Coupled with rising inflation and unemployment at home, Tsourapas (2019) argues that the diminishing of Egypt's emigration "safety valve" primed the country for broad-scale discontent that eventually fueled the uprising of 2011.

As of 2020, the United Nations calculates the number of Egyptians residing abroad as 3.6 million (United Nations Population Division 2020). Egyptian government figures place the number much higher, claiming at the time of writing that between 10 and 14 million Egyptians live abroad (Sada Elbalad News 2022). This is partly an issue of accounting. The Egyptian government considers its expatriates to include not only individuals who hold Egyptian citizenship, but also second- and third-generation emigrants who may not be citizens. That the Egyptian government utilizes the largest estimates available may also reflect that it views its diaspora as a resource for remittances, as subsequent sections will explain. At the end of 2016, CAPMAS estimated that there were 9.5 million Egyptian expatriates, with 6.2 million Egyptians residing in other Arab countries, 1.6 million in the Americas, 1.2 million in Europe, 285,000 in Australia, and 46,000 in Africa (predominantly South Africa) (Table 11.1).

Tsourapas (2015b) characterizes Egypt's emigration policy as "multi-tier." Those who emigrate to the United States and Western Europe are believed by the Egyptian state to do so permanently, and are thus

Table 11.1 *Top destination countries for Egyptians abroad*

Country	Number of Egyptians nationals
Saudi Arabia	3,500,000
Jordan	1,250,000
United States	1,131,000
UAE	982,375
Canada	700,000
Kuwait	700,000
Italy	400,000
France	366,000
Australia	285,000
Qatar	250,000

Source: CAPMAS (2017).

considered "permanent" migrants. In reality, however, emigration options to Western states are limited for Egyptian nationals. For example, Europe began phasing out its guest-worker system in the 1980s, making it more difficult for the regular migration of third-country nationals, including Egyptians (Castles 2006). In 2017, approximately 1.2 million Egyptians resided in Europe, with nearly 50 percent – or 560,000 settling in Italy (IOM 2019). The population of Egyptian emigrants and their second- and third-generation offspring residing in North America is also relatively small: approximately 980,00 in the US and about 600,000 in Canada as of 2017 (CAPMAS 2017).

Instead, most Egyptian emigrants reside in other Arab states. The Egyptian government believes that its citizens migrating to Arab countries intend to eventually return to Egypt – even if this is not always the case in practice. As such, migrants to other Arab countries have been characterized as "temporary workers" (Tsourapas 2015b). According to Egyptian government statistics in 2017, Saudi Arabia hosted 2.9 million Egyptian workers, Jordan 1.6 million, the United Arab Emirates (UAE) 765,000, Kuwait 500,000, and Qatar 230,000. A 2020 Gallup poll found that 78 percent of Egyptians residing in the countries of the GCC and 79 percent of those residing outside of MENA wished to remain where they were and would not move onto another country given the opportunity (Esipova, Ray, and Pugliese 2020). The percentage is slightly lower – 58 percent – for Egyptians living in MENA countries outside the GCC, such as Jordan. Tens of thousands of Egyptians also continue to work in Libya despite ongoing political violence and civil war (Tsourapas 2015a).

While the Egyptian diaspora is fairly diverse in terms of its ethnic and religious background, some concentrated patterns exist. For example, Coptic Christians fleeing persecution traditionally escaped to the US, establishing numerous Coptic-focused organizations (Migration Policy Institute 2015). This pattern intensified following the Egyptian uprising of 2011, when violence against Coptic Christians once again escalated. In contrast, large numbers of Muslim Brothers, or Ikhwan, and other Islamists began leaving in mid 2013 after the military coup and primarily fled to Qatar and Türkiye since these countries had strained relations with the Egyptian military regime at the time (Mandour 2022). Secular intellectuals and activists also fled Egypt from 2014 onward after repression intensified against them, primarily seeking refuge and work or educational opportunities in Europe and North America. While these groups – liberal activists, Coptic Christians, or Muslim Brotherhood members – also faced persecution in previous decades, Dunne and Hamzawy argue that the post-2011 period is unique in that so many groups have faced political or social persecution at the same time (Dunne and Hamzawy 2019), leading to the formation of new centers of activism – whether religious or secular in tone – among Egypt's diaspora.

Remittances from Egyptians abroad are an important component of Egypt's GDP, estimated at 8.1 percent in 2020 or $29.6 billion (World Bank 2020). Between 1975 and 1995, remittances generally made up approximately 7–14 percent of the country's GDP, reaching a high of 14.6 percent in 1992 and a low of 2.9 percent in 2000 (World Bank 2020). Remittances steadily increased throughout the 2000s, followed by another dip in 2009 to 3.8 percent, likely as a result of the global economic crisis of 2008 (World Bank 2020). Remittances remained consistently high in the years following the Egyptian uprising, and nearly doubled between 2016 and 2017, which may reflect Egyptians abroad attempting to help family members back home weather the economic uncertainties associated with the Egyptian uprising and its aftermath (Migration Policy Institute 2015). The principal sources of remittances to Egypt have been other Arab states – including Saudi Arabia, Jordan, Kuwait, Libya, and the UAE – with the US-based diaspora population constituting Egypt's sixth-largest source of international remittances in 2012 (Migration Policy Institute 2015).

Diplomatic and Consular Dimension

Egypt's representation abroad totals 119 embassies and 32 consulates in different nations. Egypt has consulates in 21 countries, including some that host multiple consulates such as Iraq, the US, Brazil, and Australia.

Finally, Egypt has two special missions to the European Union and the United Nations as well as an interest section in Iran and a representative office in the Occupied Palestinian Territories (Embassy Worldwide 2022).

The Ministry of Manpower traditionally held purview over the issue of Egyptian emigration, with a special committee created in 1977 for handling migration affairs. However, in 1981, the government placed responsibility for migration under the Ministry of State for Emigration and Egyptian Expatriate Affairs,[1] which continued to operate as a separate ministry until 1990. The primary reason for its creation in 1981 – the first year of the presidency of Hosni Mubarak – was an interest in monitoring the activities of Muslim Brotherhood members residing in Egypt's diaspora and countering dissident narratives concerning Egyptian governance at home.

However, the responsibilities of the Ministry of State for Emigration and Egyptian Expatriate Affairs were collapsed back under the Ministry of Manpower in 1990, which was renamed the Ministry of Manpower and Emigration in 1996 under Executive Order No. 165. In 1997, Resolution No. 2000 created a Higher Committee for Migration (HCM) that incorporated all government entities concerned with the issue of emigration, headed by the Minister of Manpower and Emigration. This included establishing professional training centers for potential migrants, providing Egyptians abroad with media and cultural materials to maintain ties with Egypt, support for Arabic-language learning among the diaspora, and supporting efforts for religious education (Zohry 2005). However, the committee has not met regularly and its proposals have failed to be implemented (Abdel Fattah, Rietig, and Fakhry 2021).

Between 1996 and 2015, the Ministry of Manpower and Emigration, in collaboration with the Ministry of Foreign Affairs, remained the primary body responsible for Egyptians abroad,[2] even though its mandate was somewhat narrow, focusing specifically on assisting Egyptian workers abroad. In comparison to Egypt's many consular offices across the world run by the Ministry of Foreign Affairs, the Ministry of Manpower has a presence in only nine countries, which include those of the GCC, Italy, and Jordan.[3] The Ministry of Manpower has a domestic strategy within Egypt to train and equip Egyptian workers so that they can find employment opportunities abroad, and it also works closely with

[1] The Ministry of State for Emigration and Egyptian Expatriate Affairs will be referred to as the Ministry of Emigration for the purposes of brevity.

[2] In reality, other government entities also claim involvement over the issue of emigration, including the Ministries of Education, Health, and Finance, and the Central Bank of Egypt. See Abdel Fattah, Rietig and Fakhry (2021).

[3] Author interview, deidentified, Cairo, July 2023.

Egyptian consulates – managed by the Ministry of Foreign Affairs – to provide assistance and advice regarding contractual issues to Egyptian laborers. Finally, it handles any disputes or problems that workers might face while outside Egypt.

Despite its technical purview over the issue of Egyptian emigration, the Ministry of Manpower plays second fiddle to the Ministry of Foreign Affairs, which remains the focal point between the various ministries involved with Egyptian emigration as well as the international organizations covering the issue – particularly the International Organization for Migration (IOM) – and foreign governments. The Ministry of Foreign Affairs manages all of the country's consulates, issues documents, and assists the Egyptian diaspora abroad – not just workers – providing consular services should issues arise. The Ministry of Foreign Affairs is also more engaged at a policy level, reporting on the negotiation of international conventions and treaties and representing Egypt at international forums and discussions related to emigration. As one official explained, "MFA is more important, just look at the size of the consulates compared to nine Manpower offices."[4]

In September 2015, President Abdel Fattah el-Sisi reinstated the Ministry of State for Emigration and Egyptian Expatriate Affairs as the ministry responsible for managing and coordinating outreach to Egyptians abroad. Because it is a ministry of state, the Ministry of Emigration does not have as strong a purview or mandate as full ministries like the Ministry of Manpower or the Ministry of Foreign Affairs. Under the auspices of the Council of Ministers, the Ministry of Emigration cooperates with other ministries, agencies, and government bodies, including the Ministry of Foreign Affairs, which remains responsible for diplomatic and consular activities, and the Ministry of Manpower, which remains responsible for establishing and maintaining bilateral worker contracts with receiving countries as well as managing any contractual or labor problems that arise.

Technically it is the responsibility of the Ministry of Foreign Affairs to communicate with and manage any diplomatic issues among expatriates, but the Ministry of Emigration is also sometimes involved. Nabila Makhram, who was Minister of Emigration during 2015–2022, attempted to differentiate the work of her ministry, stating, "Now, the foreign service, they have their embassies and their consultants. And the consultants are involved with the expatriates. But the work was bureaucratic. They needed more, they needed someone to talk to, someone

[4] Author interview, deidentified, Cairo, July 2023.

to reach out when [they] have an idea and want to serve the country."[5] As with its earlier creation in 1981, it is likely that el-Sisi reinstated the Ministry of Emigration for the purpose of countering opposition abroad, especially as Muslim Brotherhood members once again fled the country *en masse* after the military coup of 2013. Former Minister Makhram specifically described the work of her ministry as one focused on improving Egypt's image, and "to clear [expatriates'] minds about wrong ideas."[6]

While the Egyptian diaspora has historically been divided along political, ideological, and religious lines, opposition to the presidency of Hosni Mubarak in late 2010 and support for the 2011 uprising united disparate groups, including members of the Muslim Brotherhood, Coptic activists, liberals, and Nasserists (Ashour 2010). The el-Sisi regime, which has ruled with an even more repressive hand than former President Mubarak, is determined to prevent a diasporic opposition from mobilizing (Hamzawy 2017). Furthermore, in 2011, following the uprising and after persistent activism from Egypt's diaspora, the Egyptian cabinet's legislative committee approved modifications to the political participation law allowing Egyptian citizens living abroad to cast a vote in presidential elections and public referendums (Müller-Funk 2016). The 2014 Constitution also reemphasized rights for Egyptians abroad, including the right to vote and to be represented in the House of Representatives (Abdel Fattah, Rietig, and Fakhry 2021). As such, maintaining political support among the diaspora electorate became increasingly important.

The Ministry of Emigration uses in-person visits coupled with social media initiatives to garner goodwill and interest in fostering stronger connections with Egypt, and to build the country's "soft power." One official described the Ministry of Emigration's role as, "engaging the diaspora to maximize their contribution to Egypt, whether through remittances or through economic and cultural contributions," and "enhancing relations between diaspora members and development back in Egypt."[7] According to former Minister Makhram, trips abroad to visit Egyptian consulates and embassies allowed her to meet with community members as well as representatives from banks and other influential leaders in order to raise financial support for el-Sisi's many infrastructural initiatives.[8] The minister also organized summer camps in collaboration with the Egyptian

[5] Author interview, Minister of State for Emigration and Expatriate Affairs, Cairo, March 2022.

[6] Author interview, Minister of State for Emigration and Expatriate Affairs, Cairo, March 2022.

[7] Author interview, deidentified, Cairo, July 2023.

[8] Author interview, Minister of State for Emigration and Expatriate Affairs, Cairo, March 2022.

Ministry of Defense that brought diaspora youth to spend time with the Egyptian Army for the purposes of building allegiance. In the aftermath of Russia's invasion of Ukraine in 2022, the Ministry of Emigration served as the lead ministry for coordinating the return of approximately 3,000 Egyptian nationals – primarily students – who had been residing in the country, working with the Ministry of Foreign Affairs to ensure their ability to cross into neighboring countries like Poland, and then subsequently collaborating with the Ministry of Education to find the students new spots at Egyptian universities.[9]

Finally, the former minister explained that she considered the diaspora to not only include citizens, but also second and third generation Egyptians who may not possess Egyptian nationality, potentially encompassing a population of 40 million.[10] The ministry therefore sees its mission as building and spreading a national identity among its "lost citizens." For example, the ministry organized a trip to Alexandria in collaboration with her counterparts in Greece and Syria to bring Greek and Syrian citizens – whose ancestors used to live in Egypt but who left during the xenophobic years of the early Nasser era – to reconnect with Egypt by visiting hospitals, churches, and touristic venues. The ministry also arranges Arabic-language classes abroad for second- and third-generation Egyptians abroad. It has become more adept at using social media – Twitter, Facebook, Instagram and WhatsApp, among others – to amplify its outreach and respond to the needs of diaspora members, with former Minister Makhram describing instances of engaging via WhatsApp with Egyptians experiencing difficulties at consulates or dealing with other administrative problems.[11] Yet at the same time, the Egyptian government has become more adept at monitoring and – in some cases – curtailing the voices of oppositional diaspora members, as will be detailed in the following section.

Despite these outreach efforts, Egypt has been reluctant to defend its citizens abroad when doing so requires a confrontation with an economically important receiving country. For example, Egypt has sided with Gulf host countries in cases where its citizens were physically accosted or even killed. An Egyptian physician was brutally assaulted by a Kuwaiti patient in her examination room in 2020, leaving her with bruises and the partial loss of her tongue (*Al-Monitor* 2020). That same year, an

[9] Author interview, Minister of State for Emigration and Expatriate Affairs, Cairo, March 2022

[10] Author interview, Minister of State for Emigration and Expatriate Affairs, Cairo, March 2022.

[11] Author interview, Minister of State for Emigration and Expatriate Affairs, Cairo, March 2022.

Egyptian supermarket cashier was assaulted by a Kuwaiti customer and a video recording angered Egyptians across social media (*Al-Monitor* 2020). An anonymous source from the Egyptian Ministry of Foreign Affairs explained that, "These incidents will not disturb the longstanding fraternal and historical relations between the two countries" (quoted in *Al-Monitor* 2020). In Saudi Arabia, two Egyptian workers were killed in 2020 by a Saudi employer after a dispute over construction work on his residence, and that same year an Egyptian teacher was shot and killed by two of his Saudi students (Aftandilian 2021). However, a representative from the Egyptian Ministry of Foreign Affairs downplayed the deaths, stating, "These are mere separate incidents that people carry out, and do not rise to the level of a systematic phenomenon against Egyptian workers in Saudi Arabia" (quoted in *Al-Monitor* 2021). Egypt has been reluctant to criticize countries such as Kuwait and Saudi Arabia both because of their hosting of Egyptian workers, but also due to other economic links, such as the importation of Egyptian goods and Gulf-driven investment in Egypt (Aftandilian 2021).

Economic and Social Dimension

Remittances represent up to 10 percent of Egypt's GDP, in addition to an estimated 20 percent that comes in through informal remittance channels (Fattah et al. 2021). Remittances therefore constitute one of Egypt's largest sources of foreign currency, comparable to earnings from the Suez Canal transit fees and tourism (Fattah et al. 2021). However, the reliance on remittances from Gulf countries – where more than half of all remittances to Egypt come from – has meant that Egyptian workers abroad are highly subject to the volatility of oil pricing. According to the chairman of the Division of Recruitment Companies at the Cairo Chamber of Commerce, the Gulf's demand for Egyptian workers decreased by 80 percent between 2017 and 2019 as a result of the war in Yemen, a drop in oil prices, and an increasing preference for employing nationals (Rabie 2019). Furthermore, 200 of the approximately 1,200 recruitment agencies officially registered with the Egyptian Ministry of Manpower closed their doors between 2015 and 2019 (Rabie 2019).

Traditionally, Egyptians have also looked across the Mediterranean to Europe for employment, though since the 1980s, migrating via regular routes has proven difficult. As a result, irregular migration toward Europe increased, including the migration of Egyptians, either directly from Egypt's North Coast or via Libya. However, Egypt faces a dilemma in its cooperation with Europe on the issue of irregular migration. While the Egyptian government would like to see further opportunities for regular migration of its low-wage workers – and benefits via informal remittances even for those who migrate irregularly – Europe's agenda is almost entirely focused on preventing migration from Egypt.

Egypt became more concerned with the issue of irregular migration in late 2014, when larger numbers of both foreign and Egyptian nationals departed Egypt's North Coast for Italy. Following the proliferation of EU migration deals across the Mediterranean in the wake of the 2015 "crisis," the international incentives were in place for Egypt to approach Europe about a deal of its own. However, it was not until a domestic tragedy in September 2016 that Egypt decided to respond. On September 21, 2016, a fishing boat carrying as many as 450 individuals left the North Coast of Egypt – most of them Egyptian nationals – embarking on an unauthorized trip for Italy. After traveling only 12 miles, the overcrowded ship sank off the coast of the city of Rasheed (in English, Rosetta), killing more than 200 people (Al Hurra 2016). While government officials and government-controlled media outlets were quick to blame smugglers and victims, independent media accused the Egyptian coastguard of failing to respond to calls that the boat was sinking (Magid 2016). The highly publicized tragedy was deeply embarrassing for the government (Ali 2016), especially as so many of those killed were Egyptian nationals (Youm7 2017).

Following the tragedy, the government quickly passed new domestic legislation, which eventually paved the way for a deal between Egypt and the EU. In March 2017, the European Commission announced an agreement to launch a formal EU–Egypt dialogue on migration, and in July 2017 Egypt and the EU adopted a series of "partnership principles," among which was a commitment to "managing migratory flows for mutual benefit," including supporting "Egypt's efforts to prevent and combat irregular migration, trafficking and smuggling of human beings, including identifying and assisting victims of trafficking" (General Secretariat of the Association Council 2017). Under the EU Emergency Trust Fund for Africa (EUTF), Egypt received €60 million spread across seven projects, the largest of which was used to support infrastructure development, livelihood training, and small loans for Egyptians living in poorer governorates who were "at-risk" of migration. While the Trust Fund was allegedly also meant to support regular pathways to migration for Egyptian nationals hoping to find work in Europe, most funding went toward incentivizing Egyptians to remain in Egypt through the procurement of livelihood support – viewing development aid as a substitute for migration – or toward support for Egyptian security forces in order to physically prevent irregular migrants from departing Egypt.[12] Despite cooperation between the EU and Egypt, Egyptians continue to seek opportunities in Europe, primarily Italy, where Egyptians accounted for one in every five disembarkations in 2022 (European Union Agency for Asylum 2022). This is partly due to the draw of an existing Egyptian diaspora that has managed to find work in informal sectors such as the restaurant industry, as previously mentioned. The Egyptian Ministry of Emigration has collaborated with the Italian government, aided by the International Organization for Migration, to launch a series of actions to engage the Egyptian expatriate community in Italy in order to raise awareness of the risks of irregular migration and to facilitate remittances to assist poorer governorates in Egypt where potential migrants are likely to originate (IOM 2019).

The Egyptian state has begun to look beyond the countries of the GCC and Europe in order to diversify the destination options for its emigrant workers. Relying so heavily on other oil-producing Arab states has led to extreme volatility when oil prices drop, and the Egyptian state has been unable to quickly reabsorb its returned workers. With Europe unwilling to recruit low-wage workers from Egypt on any meaningful level, Egypt has started to investigate the possibility of sending more Egyptian workers to sub-Saharan African states. When President el-Sisi was Chairman of the African Union (AU) in 2019 2020, the Division of Recruitment Companies at the Cairo Chamber of Commerce put forward several proposals to negotiate labor agreements with AU countries, mainly Nigeria, South Africa, Niger, and Ghana (Rabie 2019).

Simultaneously, Egyptian "brain drain" – or the emigration of high-wage nationals – has been an acknowledged problem since the 1970s (Ayubi 1983). Historically, the Egyptian state offered housing and employment perks to some Egyptians willing to return from North America and Europe (Tsourapas 2022). The Egyptian Academy of Scientific Research and Technology also financed a program to invite Egyptian scientists employed abroad to return to Egypt for brief periods in order to transfer expertise to domestic Egyptian scientists, in partnership with the United Nations Development Programme (Tsourapas 2022). Yet these programs did not yield the expected results, partly because a return to Egypt meant lower living standards for returnees, and partly because some Egyptians residing in the West – whom these policies targeted – had emigrated for political, rather than purely economic, reasons (Tsourapas 2022).

[12] Author Interview, deidentified, Cairo, October 2022.

Concern over brain drain has only become more pronounced in the last decade due to Egypt's increasingly worse post-revolution economic situation. The introduction of austerity measures in 2016 after Egypt accepted a new loan from the International Monetary Fund (IMF) pushed the state to reduce spending on sectors like health and education, and between 2019 and 2022, nearly half of Egypt's doctors fled the country (Dalloul 2022; Egyptian Medical Syndicate 2022). According to former Minister of Emigration Makhram, Egypt is actively working to entice its educated diaspora to come home and to help reverse the country's brain drain phenomenon:

> We do not push them to return, but [instead] incentivize. When they visit Egypt and they see how the country has become, a lot of people are thinking of returning. A lot. Before, with immigrants, we used to look at them as traitors who left the country, saying, 'you cannot talk about your country, you do not belong here.' Now, this has changed.[13]

Another official from a different ministry claimed, "We don't entice people to come back."[14] Yet if Egyptians do return, various ministries can assist with finding employment in Egypt. For example, when the Covid-19 pandemic led to mass layoffs of Egyptians and other nationals working in the GCC, the Ministry of Foreign Affairs helped individuals to return to Egypt from abroad. The Ministry of Emigration and the Ministry of Planning then assisted returnees with finding new jobs and opportunities in Egypt.

Despite the official rhetoric of a welcoming reception for those wanting to return to Egypt, the state has also engaged in an increasingly intensive campaign of transnational repression toward its dissident citizens abroad since 2013. To suppress activism within its diaspora, the Egyptian state has used several forms of transnational repression, which Adamson (2020) sorts into three categories: punishment, compellence, and deterrence. Adamson gives several examples of punishment-by-proxy in Egypt, including the arrest of the brother of blogger Wael Ghonim after his refusal to work with the Egyptian embassy or silence himself, and recounts twenty-nine documented cases of Egyptian journalists and political and human rights activists living abroad who had family members in Egypt targeted by the regime between 2016 and 2019. Comparatively, deterrence involves holding families of emigrant laborers hostage so that they do not defect, and compellence can involve threatening to arrest family members if information is not given. And while Egypt has long

[13] Author interview, Minister of State for Emigration and Expatriate Affairs, Cairo, March 2022.

[14] Author interview, deidentified, Cairo, July 2023.

used its embassies and consulates to coordinate information-gathering and monitor the political activities of its diaspora (Müller-Funk 2016), the state's actions have become more brazen since 2013, with two separate individuals arrested in the US and Germany on accusations of spying for the Egyptian state (Al-Anani 2022). The Egyptian government has also made extraditing Brotherhood members residing abroad a high priority (Egypt MFA Blog 2021). The Egyptian public prosecution office has used bilateral instruments to cooperate with Saudi Arabia, Kuwait, and the UAE to return Muslim Brotherhood members since 2014 (Aman 2014), and while relations with Türkiye and Qatar were antagonistic throughout much of the 2010s, the warming of ties since 2021 with both countries could lead to further extraditions in the future (Mandour 2022).

Security Dimension

Tsourapas (2019) argues that the Egyptian state has been notoriously unwilling to directly intervene to protect citizens' rights in host states. Despite Egyptian workers facing violations in countries such as Libya and Iraq, the Egyptian government has mostly been reluctant to frame issues such as torture or the deportation of its citizens as human rights abuses, instead characterizing such treatment as either isolated instances or political affronts that could be solved by other Arab states absorbing Egypt's workers. Various administrations – whether under the leadership of Sadat, Mubarak, or el-Sisi – generally refrained from disrupting relations with powerful receiving countries that Egypt relied upon to host its foreign worker populations.

Examples of the Egyptian state refraining from military or diplomatic intervention on behalf of its citizens abound. During the 1980s in Iraq, Egyptian workers were recruited to fill the vacant posts of conscripted Iraqi soldiers fighting against Iran. When the Iran–Iraq War ended in 1988, returning Iraqi soldiers treated Egyptians with contempt and even brutality. According to Tsourapas (2019: 196), "Violent attacks by the returning Iraqi soldiers were not uncommon: 1,052 bodies were flown in from Baghdad in the first ten months of 1989, many with bullet holes and other marks of violence, while reports of police brutality and mass attacks against Egyptians were quite common". Later, more than half a million Egyptians were returned from Iraq and Kuwait during the 1990–1991 Iraqi invasion of Kuwait and subsequent Gulf War. While Egypt dispatched troops along with Western allies to drive Iraqi soldiers out of Kuwait, it struggled to absorb and protect its returned workers at home. However, in 2012 – two decades later – the Egyptian state finally managed to secure $408 million in "yellow remittances," or payments to offset the lost property and wages of Egyptians returned between 1990–1991 (Reuters 2012). Egypt's reluctance to retaliate against Iraq for the poor treatment of its workers can be understood through the country's dependence on a consistent outflow of workers, not only to Iraq, but across the Arab world. As Tsourapas (2015b: 2210) argues, "Egyptian emigrant labour continued to be attractive partly due to the absence of the state's involvement in its affairs, refusing to intervene even at instances of human rights violations."

Libya is the one exception in which the Egyptian state has intervened militarily on behalf of its citizens abroad, which can be explained by worsening political relations between Egyptian leaders and Colonel Muammar Gaddafi – and later, Islamic factions after Gaddafi's fall – rather than a direct result of the abuse of Egyptian workers. Historically, the government was unwilling to take action in retaliation for the ill treatment of Egyptian nationals working in Libya. When President Sadat abandoned plans in 1973 for a Federal Arab Republic encompassing Egypt, Libya, and Syria, Gaddafi deported hundreds of thousands of Egyptian workers, many of whom were tortured or assaulted in other ways during their departure (Tsourapas 2019). Rather than confront Libya directly, Sadat called on other Arab nations – particularly Saudi Arabia – to absorb the deported Egyptian workers. In 1976, Libya expelled a further 5,500 migrants, many of whom were tortured before being bused to the border with Egypt. While the Egyptian Ministry of the Interior organized transport for the stranded workers, the state did not take action against Libya, with Sadat stating that he did not, "take the situation so seriously. We are ready to absorb our workers; they can find work here, or in other Arab countries" (quoted in Tsourapas 2019: 192).

Egyptian–Libyan relations further deteriorated in 1977, resulting in a four-day war, with border skirmishes and Egyptian air attacks on Libyan soil, and again in 1985 when hundreds of thousands of Egyptians were deported *en masse*. Tsourapas (2019) views the expulsion of Egyptian workers as part of a broader confrontation between the Egyptian regime – headed by former President Mubarak at the time – and Colonel Gaddafi, which also involved an Egyptian troop mobilization along the Libyan border and the Libyan hijacking of an Egyptian airplane in 1985. In 1989, after Libya normalized its relations with Arab states, including Egypt, Libya agreed to pay $6 million in reparations to expelled Egyptian workers (Tsourapas 2019).

By far the most direct military action taken by the Egyptian government was in 2015 after twenty-one Coptic Christian Egyptian construction workers were kidnapped in the Libyan city of Sirte and beheaded by Islamic State militants. President el-Sisi proclaimed that Egypt reserved the right for retaliation, and on February 16 the Egyptian Air Force conducted airstrikes on Islamic State training facilitates and weapons stockpiles (BBC News 2015). While the airstrikes demonstrated el-Sisi's commitment to fighting terrorism – helping to further drum up political and financial support from the West and the Gulf – the airstrikes did little to safeguard Egyptian workers still residing in Libya in the midst of a civil war (Tsourapas 2015a).

Conclusion

Since the establishment of the modern Egyptian state in 1952, the government has used a bifurcated approach to its emigration policy – differentiating between "permanent" emigrants and their offspring residing in Western states and "temporary" emigrants to other Arab states who are presumed to eventually return to Egypt, even if this is not always the case in practice. For the Egyptian state, emigration policies have been used to address a number of domestic and foreign policy goals. Beginning with targeted secondment policies that aimed to spread pan-Arabist ideology and broadening to mass labor-exportation agreements directed primarily toward other Arab nations – especially the oil-rich countries of the Persian Gulf – Egypt has sought to address demographic concerns of overpopulation, an overburdened and underfinanced public sector, and to reap the benefit of remittances as a major contribution to the country's GDP. To maintain a robust emigration system to meet these goals, Egypt developed a series of outreach programs to induce investment and cultivate loyalty among the diaspora, also offering policies aimed at encouraging return migration in some instances.

Nonetheless, Egypt continues to face systemic barriers to the effective governance of, and engagement with, its diaspora. First, the overlapping responsibilities of various ministries prevent coherent management of the issue of emigration. While the Ministry of State for Emigration and Egyptian Expatriate Affairs has held responsibility for diaspora outreach since 2015, the Ministry of Manpower also retains significant purview over the issue as concerns Egyptian laborers abroad, in addition to the Ministry of Foreign Affairs and other tertiary government entities. Rather than coordinated responsibility-sharing, these ministries act without coherence in aim or practice, as their mandates overlap. For example, the Ministry of Manpower and the Ministry of State for Emigration and Egyptian Expatriate Affairs have at times existed as the same entity and at other points, including presently, existed separately, with the Ministry of State of Emigration and Egyptian Expatriate Affairs serving a clear political role. The Ministry of Foreign Affairs and Ministry of Manpower also have overlapping roles, as Egyptian workers – covered by the Ministry of Manpower – are a subcategory of Egyptian citizens more broadly, purview over whom is handled by the Ministry of Foreign Affairs.

There are examples of the three ministries working in concert; they are all members of the National Coordinating Committee for Combating and Preventing Illegal Migration and Trafficking in Persons (NCCPIM&TIP), which falls under the Prime Minister's Office, and for which there are regular meetings. Yet a more streamlined and transparent structure would help both the government and its citizens abroad. Abdel Fattah, Rietig, and Fakhry (2021) note that, "a recent proposal of a long-awaited national migration strategy by the IOM and the Egyptian government for the period 2022–2025 is meant to improve the coordination and governance of Egypt's migration policy," but it is unclear how exactly the strategy will alter the current ministerial structure or the government's overall approach.

Second, Egypt will have to address domestic economic issues in order to prevent further brain drain and incentivize the return of Egyptians abroad. The country faces a debt crisis that preceded the 2011 uprising, but which has worsened drastically over the last decade (Momani 2018). It has been slow to implement the fiscal reforms required by its 2016 IMF loan, and as a major importer of wheat, it has been negatively impacted by the 2022 Russian invasion of Ukraine and subsequent war. In November 2022, the Egyptian pound hit a new low when the government implemented a flexible exchange rate to secure another loan from the IMF (Gbadamosi 2022). Unless the government can address the challenges to its political economy – including tackling poverty, inequality, and corruption – highly skilled migrants, especially those working in the public sector, will likely continue to look for opportunities elsewhere, and skilled emigrants – as well as second- and third-generation Egyptians – will be reluctant to return.

Finally, Egypt will continue to have difficulty fully engaging with its citizens abroad unless the state ends its practices of transnational repression. By utilizing tactics of direct repression, compellence and punishment of its citizens abroad or their families still in Egypt – as well as by arbitrarily arresting citizens returning to Egypt upon arrival – the Egyptian state has instilled fear and uncertainty in its citizens abroad, leading its nationals to question their own safety and whether they too might be detained if they attempt a return to Egypt. To cultivate a trusting relationship with its diaspora that will lead to stronger associations with the home state, further investment from abroad, and the development of a sense of belonging among members of the second and third generation, the Egyptian state must learn to engage with and govern its diaspora without resorting to repression.

References

Abdel Fattah, Dina, Victoria Rietig, and Alia Fakhry (2021) Egypt, the EU, and Migration: An Uncomfortable Yet Unavoidable Partnership. German Council on Foreign Relations. Available at: https://dgap.org/en/research/publications/egypt-eu-and-migration.

Adamson, Fiona B. (2020) At Home and Abroad: Coercion-by-Proxy as a Tool of Transnational Repression. *Freedom House Special Report*. Available at: https://freedomhouse.org/report/special-report/2020/home-and-abroad-coercion-proxy-tool-transnational-repression.

Aftandilian, Gregory (2021) Egyptian-Saudi Relations: Strategic Ties with Some Political Strains. Arab Center Washington, DC. Available at: https://arabcenterdc.org/resource/egyptian-saudi-relations-strategic-ties-with-some-political-strains/.

Al Hurra (2016) "2016, الحرة ".حادث رشيد. النيابة المصرية تأمر بحبس مالك المركب. Available at: www.alhurra.com/a/egypt-boat-illegal-immigrants/324790.html.

Al-Anani, Khalil (2022) Sisi's Transnational Repression: Silencing Political Dissidents in Exile. Arab Center Washington, DC. Available at: https://arabcenterdc.org/resource/sisis-transnational-repression-silencing-political-dissidents-in-exile/.

Al-Monitor (2020) Egyptian Government Fires Official Who Insulted Kuwait to Avoid Diplomatic Crisis. *Al-Monitor*. Available at: www.al-monitor.com/originals/2020/11/egypt-kuwait-assaults-criticism-dismissal-action.html.

Al-Monitor (2021) Egyptians Living in Saudi Arabia Face Attacks. *Al-Monitor*. www.al-monitor.com/originals/2021/01/egypt-saudi-arabia-release-fishermen-killed-attacks.html.

Ali, Noura (2016) Egyptian Officials and Pro-regime Media Blame Victims of Rashid Tragedy for Their Fate. *Middle East Observer*. Available at: www.middleeastobserver.org/2016/09/26/egyptian-officials-and-pro-regime-media-blame-victims-of-rashid-tragedy-for-their-fate/.

Aman, Ayah (2014) Egypt Seeks Extradition of Brotherhood Members. *Al-Monitor*. Available at: www.al-monitor.com/originals/2014/03/egypt-muslim-brotherhood-qatar-saudi-kuwait-uae-summit.html.

Arab Republic of Egypt Central Agency for Public Mobilization and Statistics (CAPMAS) (2017) Egyptians Abroad. Fact sheet. *CAPMAS*. www.capmas.gov.eg/Admin/Pages%20Files/2017109144221Egy.pdf.

Ashour, Omar (2010) ElBaradei and the Mobilization of the Egyptian Diaspora. Carnegie Endowment for International Peace. Available at: https://carnegieendowment.org/sada/41631.

Ayubi, Nazih (1983) The Egyptian 'Brain Drain': A Multidimensional Problem. *International Journal of Middle East Studies* 15: 431–450.

BBC News (2015) Egypt Bombs IS in Libya after Beheadings Video. *BBC News*. Available at: www.bbc.com/news/world-middle-east-31483631.

Castles, Stephen (2006) Guestworkers in Europe: A Resurrection? *International Migration Review* 40 (4): 741–766.

Dalloul, Motasem (2022) When Will Egypt's Brain Drain End? *Middle East Monitor*. Available at: www.middleeastmonitor.com/20220620-when-will-egypts-brain-drain-end/.

Dunne, Michelle, and Amr Hamzawy (2019) *Egypt's Political Exiles: Going Anywhere But Home. Carnegie Endowment for International Peace.* Washington, DC: Carnegie Endowment for International Peace. Available at: https://carnegieendowment.org/research/2019/03/egypts-political-exiles-going-anywhere-but-home?lang=en.

Egypt MFA Blog (2021) The Egyptian State's Efforts and Comprehensive Approach to Countering Terrorism and Extremist Ideology Conducive to Terrorism. Available at: https://mfaegypt.org/2021/08/02/national-report-on-countering-terrorism-2021/.

Egyptian Medical Syndicate (2022) لجان نقابيةنقابة الأطباء تدق ناقوس الخطر. Available at: www.ems.org.eg/ar/news/Committees/2430?fbclid=IwAR3rCqTgo7gwX8t9-ZwWDTvzxDZsn8tCA1wwHdfpIMDUWUXnR60rG48nuqM.

Embassy Worldwide (2022) List of Diplomatic Missions in Egypt & Egyptian Diplomatic Missions Abroad. *Embassy Worldwide*. Available at: www.embassy-worldwide.com/country/egypt/.

Esipova, Neli, Julie Ray, and Anita Pugliese (2020) Inside Egypt's Diaspora: Who Wants to Come Home Again? *Gallup*. Available at: https://news.gallup.com/opinion/gallup/284159/inside-egypt-diaspora-wants-home-again.aspx.

European Union Agency for Asylum (2022) Egypt as a Country of Origin. Available at: https://euaa.europa.eu/sites/default/files/publications/2022-08/2022_07_MDR_Egypt_Origin_EN.pdf.

Gbadamosi, Nosmot (2022) What Caused Egypt's Economic Tailspin? *Foreign Policy*. Available online: https://foreignpolicy.com/2022/11/02/egypt-economy-sisi-imf-cop-27-united-nations-climate/.

General Secretariat of the Association Council (2017) EU-Egypt Partnership Priorities 2017–2020. Available at: www.consilium.europa.eu/media/23942/eu-egypt.pdf.

Hamzawy, Amr (2017) Legislating Authoritarianism: Egypt's New Era of Repression. Available at: https://carnegieendowment.org/2017/03/16/legislating-authoritarianism-egypt-s-new-era-of-repression-pub-68285.

IOM (2019) Italy, IOM Sign Agreement to Implement Development Project in Egypt. Available at: www.iom.int/news/italy-iom-sign-agreement-implement-development-project-egypt.

Magid, Pesha (2016) Report from Rashid: Where Was the State When Hundreds Drowned? *Mada Masr*. Available at: https://madamasr.com/en/2016/10/13/feature/politics/report-from-rashid-where-was-the-state-when-hundreds-drowned/.

Mandour, Mohamed (2022) A Homeland Lives Within Us, but We Cannot Live in It: Egyptian Organizing and Activism from Exile. *The Tahrir Institute for Middle East Policy*. Available at: https://timep.org/commentary/analysis/a-homeland-lives-within-us-but-we-cannot-live-in-it-egyptian-organizing-and-activism-from-exile/.

Migration Policy Institute (2015) The Egyptian Diaspora in the United States. *Migration Policy Institute*. Available at: www.migrationpolicy.org/sites/default/files/publications/RAD-EgyptII.pdf.

Momani, Bessma (2018) Egypt's IMF Program: Assessing the Political Economy Challenges. *Brookings*. Available at: www.brookings.edu/research/egypts-imf-program-assessing-the-political-economy-challenges/.

Müller-Funk, Lea (2016) Diaspora Mobilizations in the Egyptian (Post) Revolutionary Process: Comparing Transnational Political Participation in Paris and Vienna. *Journal of Immigrant & Refugee Studies* 14 (3): 353–70, doi.org/10.1080/15562948.2016.1180471.

Rabie, Hossam (2019) Egypt Finds Its Nationals New Job Markets Abroad. *Al-Monitor*. Available at: www.al-monitor.com/originals/2019/03/job-nationalization-gulf-countries-affect-work-egyptians.html.

Reuters (2012) Iraq to Pay $408 Million Gulf War Debt to Egyptians. *Retuers*. Available at: www.reuters.com/article/ozatp-iraq-egypt-remittances-20120317-idAFJOE82G06020120317.

Sada Elbalad News, dir. (2022) وزيرة الهجرة: عدد المصريين بالخارج يتراوح بين ١٠ إلى ١٤ مليون مصري. Sada Elbalad News.

Sell, Ralph R. (1988) Egyptian International Labor Migration and Social Processes: Toward Regional Integration. *International Migration Review* 22 (3): 87–108.

Tsourapas, Gerasimos (2015a) The Politics of Egyptian Migration to Libya. *Middle East Research and Information Project*. Available at: https://merip.org/2015/03/the-politics-of-egyptian-migration-to-libya/.

Tsourapas, Gerasimos (2015b) Why Do States Develop Multi-tier Emigrant Policies? Evidence from Egypt. *Journal of Ethnic and Migration Studies* 41 (13): 2192–214, doi.org/10.1080/1369183X.2015.1049940.

Tsourapas, Gerasimos (2019) *The Politics of Migration in Modern Egypt: Strategies for Regime Survival in Autocracies*, doi.org/10.1017/9781108630313.

Tsourapas, Gerasimos (2022) Migration and Development in Egypt – A Holistic View. *Revue Internationale de Politique de Développement* 14 (January), doi.org/10.4000/poldev.4803.

United Nations Population Division (2020) *International Migration Stock*. Available at: www.un.org/development/desa/pd/content/international-migrant-stock.

World Bank (2020) *Personal Remittances, Received*. Washington, DC: World Bank.

Youm7 (2017) "تأجيل محاكمة المتهمين بمركب الموت الغارق على سواحل رشيد إلى 9 يناير." اليوم السابع, 2017. Available at: bit.ly/3wS4phR.

Zohry, Ayman (2005) *Interrelationships between Internal and International Migration in Egypt: A Pilot Study*. Development Research Centre on Migration, Globalisation and Poverty. Sussex, UK; Sussex Centre for Migration Research.

12 Türkiye
Home State Reimagined

Yasemin Akbaba

Introduction

The defeat of the Ottoman Empire in the First World War and the subsequent occupation by the Allied Powers of the Ottoman territory initiated the Turkish War of Independence. The Republic of Türkiye was founded in 1923 as a result of this war. Emigration of Turkish citizens took place in the early years of the republic and expanded with the labor movement to Western Europe in the 1960s and 1970s (Aksel 2019).[1] Today, the Turkish national communities abroad are spread globally across seventy-two countries (Akçapar 2018: 157). As the nature of emigration evolved, home agencies' roles, policies, services, and motivations have shifted (Aydin and Østergaard-Nielsen 2020; Bruce 2019; Akcapar and Aksel 2017; Kilic and Biffl 2021). Both the 1980 coup d'état (Aksel 2019: 68) and the 2001 economic crisis (Ünver 2013: 181) altered Türkiye's outlook on communities abroad. While the former politicized the relationship, the latter led to events that eventually advanced Türkiye's cultural engagement abroad. Beyond these turning points, many domestic and international factors created incentives to support, selectively support, co-opt, and at times limit national communities abroad.

Türkiye's support for nationals abroad has increased significantly over the decades with noticeable improvement in consular services, as well as access to information. In addition, there has been an increase in cultural engagement of nationals abroad. However, in some cases, this support has been selective. For example, the state-based cultural initiatives tend to highlight conservative values. This selective support mechanism can also be categorized as co-optation since emphasis on conservative values could easily translate into promotion of such political opinions among national communities abroad. Given the overseas voting rights of citizens and the public diplomacy potential of the diaspora, this could also tilt the balance towards conservative parties at home. Arguably, the labor

[1] Turkey officially changed its name to Türkiye in 2022.

migration era provides the best co-optation example for Türkiye. At this time Türkiye's interaction with nationals aboard was predominantly shaped by economic benefits. Sending young men to Europe for employment meant lower unemployment rates at home, and the remittances translated into economic growth (Kilic and Biffl 2021). This was a transactional relationship centered around mutual economic benefits. The focus on financial benefits changed after the 1980 coup d'état. Members of politically marginalized communities left Türkiye and created diaspora organizations (Yabanci 2021). As national communities abroad started to become more political and at times critical of Turkish politics, Türkiye started to pay more attention to the political discourse of its nationals abroad. Türkiye's attention to specific communities abroad has been associated with the security concerns at home. Yet the target of such scrutiny changed over time. Right after the 1980 coup, it was supporters of communist ideology. During 1990s, the rise of religious movements, especially in Europe, was a concern for the secular establishment of the time. After the failed coup attempt in 2016, it was Gülen movement, which is named after the Islamic cleric Fethullah Gülen.

In this chapter, after an overview of the current numbers, locations, and composition of the Turkish communities abroad, I will describe transformations in the diplomatic, economic/cultural, and security dimensions to engage national communities with a focus on how the Turkish state's role in this regard has changed over time. Collectively, the discussions will reveal various forms of support and selective support as well as examples of co-optation and repression. They will also show how Türkiye reimagined its relationship with its citizens abroad, which in turn eventually allowed national communities abroad to reimagine their home state.

Overview of the Turkish Community Abroad

Developments over Time

Aksel (2019) identifies six partially overlapping "emigration waves" from Türkiye, the first of which originated in the pre-republic era. Those are: (1) "the emigration of non-Muslim communities" which started in the late nineteenth century and continued throughout the twentieth century (Içduygu et al. 2008); (2) "labor and family migration to Europe and Australia"; (3) "brain drain migration towards Northern America"; (4) "political migration to Europe" following the 1980 coup; (5) "temporary labor migration to the Middle East and North Africa" and "former Soviet countries"; and (6) "divergent patterns … including high-skilled and student migration to Europe, USA, Canada and Australia" (Aksel 2019: 51).

As a result of the first wave, there has been a significant decline of the non-Muslim population, particularly from 1950 to 1980 (Icduygu and Aksel 2013: 173). The second wave started in the 1960s to address low-skilled labor needs in Western Europe. Türkiye concluded guest-worker agreements with Germany, Belgium, Austria, and the Netherlands (Aydin 2014: 9). Similar arrangements were made with Switzerland and Denmark in 1970s and with Norway in 1981 (Aksel 2019: 60). At this point, to accommodate the needs of guest workers in Western Europe, Türkiye focused on the "transfer of funds, the organization of practical issues for workers (visas, official documents, etc.), and potentially facilitate their return to the national labour force after a period of time abroad" (Bruce 2019: 76).[2] Economic recession during the 1970s in a number of European host countries eventually stopped the flow of guest workers, but movement of Turkish citizens to European countries nonetheless continued through family reunification (Aydin and Østergaard-Nielsen 2020).

Since the 1960s and continuing to this day, as part of the third and fourth waves, there has been movement of more skilled workers seeking employment outside of Türkiye, which raised concerns of a "brain drain" (Kilic and Biffl 2021; Aksel 2019). With a decline of interest in guest labor in Europe, workers started to seek other regional possibilities such as the Middle East and North Africa (MENA) as well as Australia (Kilic and Biffl 2021; Icduygu and Aksel 2013: 174). The temporary outflow of labor from Türkiye to MENA continued in the 1980s and early 1990s (Aksel 2019: 51). With the end of the Cold War, this fifth wave also expanded to the former Soviet states in the 1990s (Aksel 2019: 51). As part of the sixth wave, from the 1990s onward, European and North American countries continued to attract high-skilled labor (Aksel 2019: 51). In addition, many young people pursued postgraduate degrees internationally with the intention to remain abroad (Tansel and Güngör 2003).

Through these waves, gender, age, ethnic origin, political leanings, and skill sets of Turkish citizens abroad diversified. Guest workers of the 1960s were predominantly low-skilled men leaving their homes to provide for their families who remained in Türkiye. Through family reunification, women and children emigrated in 1970s (Yabanci 2021). Asylum seekers of the 1980s and 1990s diversified the political and ethnic profile of Turkish communities abroad (Sahin-Mencutek and Baser

[2] Since unemployment was a serious concern (Icduygu and Aksel 2013: 173), this was an opportunity to export labor surplus and promote economic growth through remittances (Kilic and Biffl 2021).

2017: 2; Sahin-Mencutek and Erdogan 2016: 177). During the last decades, more young people have been seeking higher and postgraduate education abroad, which expanded the skill sets, demographics, and political leanings of Turkish diaspora.

Numbers, Location, and Composition

Türkiye is considered among the top ten "emigration countries in the world" (Sahin-Mencutek and Baser 2017: 2). According to the United Nations (UN) International Migrant Stock (2020) data, there were 3,411,408 migrants originating from Türkiye in 2020. Europe, specifically Western Europe, was the most popular region. Germany was the top destination,[3] followed by France and the Netherlands. While the United States had smaller numbers in comparison to Western Europe, as well as Northern Europe and Asia for that matter (Table 12.1), the Turkish diaspora there achieves higher degrees in education in comparison to Turks in Europe (Kaya 2005: 428). This could be due to the educational goals of immigrants. Many come to the US to purse undergraduate or graduate degrees. In fact, in 2014, Türkiye sent "more students" to the US "than any other European country" (Karaçay 2018). While Turkish national communities abroad are dispersed to all parts of the US (Kaya 2005: 428), "the largest concentration of Turkish Americans" is in the New York City metropolitan area (Kaya 2005: 426).

Table 12.1 *Top destination countries for migrants originating from Türkiye*

Destination region/state	Number of migrants in 2020
Europe	3,052,762
Western Europe	2,721,502
Germany	1,837,282
France	340,271
Netherlands	199,280
Austria	159,999
Northern Europe	203,288
Asia	166,275
North America	141,712
United States	112,943

Source: United Nations International Migrant Stock (2020).

[3] The Minorities at Risk (MAR) project estimates 20–25% percent of Türkiye's diaspora in Germany to be Kurdish.

It is important to note that while the ranking of destinations is similar in varying sources, the UN numbers reported above do not fully overlap with the other estimates. For example, according to Türkiye's Ministry of Foreign Affairs, there are approximately 6.5 million Turkish people living abroad. Roughly 5.5 million of them reside in Western European countries (Republic of Türkiye, Ministry of Foreign Affairs: Turkish Citizens Living Abroad n.d.). Others suggested that "more than 3 million people of Turkish origin" reside in Germany (Aksel 2019: 8) and "1,383,040 of them have Turkish citizenship and are eligible voters" (Sahin-Mencutek and Erdogan 2016: 178). France, with an estimated 450,000 Turkish citizens, and the Netherlands, with an estimated 372,000, follow Germany as the Western European states with the largest Turkish diasporas (Sahin-Mencutek and Erdogan 2016: 178). Outside of Western Europe, the US with approximately 250,000 Turkish citizens (Sahin-Mencutek and Erdogan 2016: 178) estimated to have the largest Turkish diaspora (Akçapar 2018: 157).

With the exception of the first wave, immigrants from Türkiye have been largely Muslim with a Sunni majority and an Alevi minority. There is a wide network of cultural organizations based on the Sunni sect of Islam. There are also Alevi organizations in many countries, such as Germany, France, the Netherlands, and the US (Massicard 2012: 185).

Diplomatic and Consular Dimension

The Turkish state was expecting the labor movement of the 1960s to be temporary and referred to emigrants as "Turkish Nationals Working Abroad" (Sahin-Mencutek and Baser 2017: 6). Accordingly, there was very little investment in the development of a diaspora policy at this point. Instead, the institutional structure was "fragmented," with the Ministry of Foreign Affairs and the Presidency of Religious Affairs (Diyanet İşleri Başkanlığı, hereinafter Diyanet) as the main state agencies in charge of serving citizens abroad (Sahin-Mencutek and Baser 2017: 6).[4]

The Ministry of Foreign Affairs had a central role as Turkish consular officials were in charge of processing passports and related documents of workers abroad (Sahin-Mencutek and Baser 2017: 6). Since the 1960s, the diplomatic and consular activities of the Turkish state have expanded. According to the Ministry of Foreign Affairs website, there are 247 Turkish representations worldwide. This includes 143

[4] The Diyanet is a government agency that engages with various aspects of religion (Öktem 2012: 40), including domestic and international outreach. It will be discussed further on as part of cultural activities.

embassies, 91 consulate generals, 12 permanent missions and 1 trade office (Ministry of Foreign Affairs, Turkish Representations n.d.). There has been an increase in foreign representation from 163 in 2002 to 236 in 2017 (Aksel 2019: 114) and to 247 as of 2022 (Ministry of Foreign Affairs, Turkish Representations n.d.). Currently, Germany with 14 representations (1 embassy and 13 consulate generals), France with 10 representations (1 embassy, 6 consulate generals, and 3 permanent missions), and the US with 8 representations (1 embassy, 6 consulate generals, and 1 permanent mission) are countries with the highest number of representations, which is consistent with the distribution of Turkish national communities.

Embassies and consulate generals provide many services to Turkish citizens living abroad, such as the management of compulsory military service for eligible men, issuing passports and ID cards, processing marriage, birth, and citizenship documents, and providing certificates of criminal records. Military service is obligatory for all male citizens from twenty-one years of age. However, the requirement of military service for male citizens residing abroad has been relaxed over time, with opportunities to postpone and paid shorter service options: "As of 2016, emigrants can be exempted from service by paying €1,000 without any obligation to complete the prior 21 days of obligatory service in Turkey" (Aksel 2019: 128). Consulates and embassies guide citizens who need to postpone or be exempted from their military service. Since 2009, part of the consular services can be done through an online platform called e-Konsolosluk (e-consulate) (Aksel 2019: 123).[5] Starting in 2001, citizens have access to free legal assistance for various concerns, with a focus on experiences of discrimination through embassies and consulates. There is also guidance and legal support provided on custody related matters (Ministry of Foreign Affairs: Turkish Citizens Living Abroad n.d.). In addition, there has been an improvement in the overall treatment of emigrants since the 1960s (Sahin-Mencutek and Baser 2017: 6–10). All of these services function as support for national communities abroad.

Under the Ministry of Foreign Affairs, the Directorate General for Consular Affairs is responsible for consular relations and the attendance at and coordination of the associated meetings (Mevzuat 2013). Under the directorate, there are three agencies: the Deputy Directorate General for Immigration, Refuge and Visa; the Deputy Directorate General for Citizens Living Abroad and Estates; and the Deputy Directorate General for Consular Affairs (Ministry of Foreign Affairs Organization Chart n.d.).

[5] Turkish citizens can make appointments, contact call centers, and download relevant forms for various services through e-Konsolosluk.

The topic of "Turkish Citizens Living Abroad" is mapped under the main foreign policy issues on the Turkish Ministry of Foreign Affairs website, along with other high-profile issues such as Cyprus, Türkiye's security, and terrorism (Ministry of Foreign Affairs website). The entry on "Turkish Citizens Living Abroad" highlights the importance of the integration of the Turkish community to host states for the Turkish government: "It is desired that members of Turkish community actively participate in the social, economic, cultural and political life of host countries while maintaining their ties to their motherland, mother tongue and culture, and live as prosperous, successful individuals respecting local laws and customs" (Turkish Citizens Abroad, Ministry of Foreign Affairs n.d.).

Several steps have been taken to support the political integration of the Turkish communities into their host states. One aspect of integration is through gaining citizenship of host states as this would advance political participation opportunities of Turkish citizens abroad. The 1981 Amendment to the Turkish Nationality Act opened the way to seek dual citizenship, which was not previously allowed (Tiryakioglu 2006: 1). This was a turning point for Türkiye's diaspora politics as it allowed Turkish citizens living abroad to seek citizenship without giving up their Turkish passports (Ünver 2013: 184). Aydin (2014: 8) notes that the dual citizenship law was a "break with the past" diaspora policies that focused on predominantly economic aspects of immigration. With dual citizenship, there was an opening for "achieving profound legal status" abroad and retaining connections with Türkiye (Ünver 2013: 184). This was one of the significant changes that eventually helped national communities to reimagine the home state. The momentum continued in the 1990s with the creation of the Advisory Committee for Turkish Citizens Living Abroad and of the High Committee for Turkish Citizens Living Abroad in 1998 "to research and monitor the problems faced by Turkish citizens abroad and communicate them to the Turkish parliament" (Akçapar 2018: 162). Similarly, in the 2000s, there were attempts to support the political integration of citizens overseas. A 2003 parliamentary inquiry commission report recommended the "acquisition of citizenship from host states" and the protection "against xenophobia, discrimination, and violence" (Bahcecik 2020: 186). Aksel summarizes the impact of this report on the larger diaspora relations as follows:

> The parliamentary report formulated an anticipated emigration regime, which would determine emigrants' relationship with both Turkey and the countries where they resided. As active citizens in two nations, the citizens of Turkey were expected to become intervening actors or "bridges of good relations" between overseas societies/states and the Turkish state/society. The report codified the nature of the relationship between the emigrant society differently with the

Turkish state and host states. It emphasized citizens' access to social, political and cultural rights in host countries and the international arena. Although the groups living overseas were described as active in their new communities, the Turkish state adopted an approach based on proactive involvement to determine forms of allegiance and responsibilities that would be paired with various circles of solidarity (Aksel 2019: 111).

The Presidency of Turks Abroad and Related Communities (Yurtdışı Türkler ve Akraba Topluluklar Başkanlığı, hereinafter YTB) was created in 2010 following the recommendations of the 2003 parliamentary report "to function as a reference point for emigrant related affairs" (Sahin-Mencutek and Erdogan 2016: 180). The creation of YTB was crucial as it was a state agency dedicated to relations with the Turkish nationals abroad. The YTB also expanded the importance of diaspora politics in the institutional framework of the Turkish state. Ünver (2013: 186) suggests that the YTB "tries to be active in many fields that were mostly untouched by the state in the past." The YTB as a government department has "the objective to maintain and strengthen the relationship of the Turkish state with Turkish citizens living abroad, those of Turkish origin living outside of Turkish territories and with the foreign students in Turkey" (Icduygu and Aksel 2013: 183). It is charged with "awareness raising, rights protection, and advocacy" (Bahcecik 2020: 186) and promotes "active citizenship" and political participation in host states through knowing their rights (Bahcecik 2020: 187–188). The creation of YTB highlights the increasing importance of emigrants for Tukey. Sahin-Mencutek and Erdogan (2016: 180) suggest that "[s]uch a new national-level institution reflects the institutional crystallization of Turkey's growing interest in engagement with citizens abroad as well as how the government policy turned into state policy." While some of the YTB's work qualifies as diplomatic activities, most of the duties concern economic and social activities, which will be explored in the next section.

For citizens abroad, political participation opportunities have advanced over the years as well. Turkish citizens living abroad have the right to vote at specified custom points since 1987 (Aksel 2019: 125). Although a constitutional amendment of 1995 gave external voting right to citizens abroad, without "additional electoral legislation provisions" to regulate "applicable measures for implementation," it was not implemented (Sahin-Mencutek and Erdogan 2016: 178). The voting location options were expanded to diplomatic offices in 2012 (Akcapar and Aksel 2017: 148). External voting was finally implemented in the 2014 Turkish presidential election. According to Sahin-Mencutek and Erdogan (2016: 178), the extension of out-of-country voting rights to citizens abroad was partly a response to demands of diaspora populations dating back to the 1970s.

In 2018, there were roughly 3.5 million registered voters abroad (Yabanci 2021). On the YTB website, participation in elections in Türkiye is featured in detail (YTB, Türkiye'deki Seçimlere Katılım n.d.).

At times, protecting Turkish citizens abroad calls for uncommon diplomatic approaches. Indeed, Türkiye has engaged in some high-profile activities to protect its citizens. While most of these activities were rescue operations in conflict zones, some were responses to environmental disasters and the Covid-19 pandemic. The National Intelligence Organization (Millî İstihbarat Teşkilatı, hereinafter MIT) was involved in many of these operations. One could speculate that for countries like Türkiye, which are located close to zones of instability and have citizens spread across different regions of the world, the following examples of sensitive activities could be signaling challenges of protecting and serving citizens abroad in an ever more complex world.

From the US invasion of Iraq in 2003 and subsequent withdrawal in 2011 to regime changes following the Arab uprisings that began in 2010, recent decades have witness a change in the security environment of the MENA. Some of these changes, such as the outbreak of civil wars, made it harder to protect the Turkish diaspora in the region. For example, forty-six Turkish citizens taken captive by the Islamic State were rescued in September 2014. The special operation was conducted by MIT. Hostages included Turkish diplomats, staff, and their family members (WSJ 2014; Insider 2014). Similarly, in November 2021, seven Turkish citizens who were held hostage in Libya were rescued with the participation of Türkiye's Tripoli embassy and the MIT. Türkiye's Foreign Ministry acknowledged the help of the Libyan and Qatari governments (TRT World 2021).

The war in Ukraine has also initiated multiple rescue operations. Since the start of the Russian invasion of Ukraine in early 2022, Türkiye has been helping its citizens who were residing in various Ukrainian cities to return home. It is estimated that at least 12,306 Turkish citizens were evacuated from the country (*Daily Sabah* 2022).

There have also been various non-conflict-related rescue operations. For example, in November 2021, the National Defense Ministry sent a plane with Disaster and Emergency Management Authority (AFAD) personnel to Bosnia to help in a rescue operation of a Turkish citizen following a severe flood (Hurriyet Daily News 2021). In April 2020, Turkish Airlines, the national flag carrier, rolled out its plan to bring home to Türkiye roughly 25,000 Turkish citizens who were trapped in fifty-nine counties due to Covid-19-related closures (Travel and Tour World 2020; Simple Flying 2020). A handful of emigrants were also transferred from Germany to Türkiye to receive healthcare. For example, a 59-year-old Turkish emigrant was brought to Türkiye by the Ministry of Health in July 2022 (AA 2022). Similarly, in November 2022, a young woman was transferred after her family got in touch with the diplomatic offices in Cologne (TRT Haber 2022). A teacher working in Germany was also brought to Türkiye through the assistance of the Ministry of Education to seek healthcare (Ministry of Education 2022).

Economic and Social Dimension

The bilateral treaties that Türkiye signed with various Western European states in the 1960s and the 1970s to govern labor movements stemmed from the economic needs of both sides. Indeed, Türkiye had unskilled labor surplus and Western countries needed workers. In addition to lowering unemployment rates, Türkiye's economy benefited tremendously from the remittances at this time, which shows co-optation. However, with family reunification, changes in labor demand, and shifting economic circumstances, the flow of remittances to Türkiye has diminished over time. The ratio of remittance inflows to GDP peaked in 1974 at 4 percent. In turn, in 2020, remittance inflows to GDP were a mere 0.11 percent (World Bank, Remittance Inflows to GDP for Türkiye n.d.).

Although not as critical as before, remittances are still important for Türkiye's economy. Pew, using World Bank data, estimates that in 2017, the amount of $1,045 billion was sent as remittances to Türkiye from abroad. Germany, with $503 million, was the top source, followed by France, the Netherlands, Austria, and US (Pew Research Center, Remittance flows worldwide in 2017). This overlaps with the population distribution of the Turkish diaspora. As previously shown, Western Europe has the highest number of Turkish citizens outside of Türkiye, and Germany, France, and the Netherlands have the highest number of Turkish immigrants (Aydin and Østergaard-Nielsen 2020).

In many ways, the needs of the Turkish communities in Western Europe shaped economic and social services. Under the Ministry of Labor and Social Security, the Directorate General for International Affairs is charged with protecting and promoting the rights of Turkish workers on matters such as social security and services (Ministry of Labor and Social Security n.d.). It has a broad set of responsibilities, including, but by no means limited to, coordinating social security agreements with other nation states, working with international organizations with a focus on labor or social security, and working towards solving cultural, economic, and family concerns of workers abroad (Ministry of Labor and Social Security n.d.). There are forty-seven attachés (*ataşelik*) and advisory offices (*müşavirlik*) of the Directorate General for International Affairs operating in more than twenty countries.

Although the economic and social activities of the state intersect with population and remittance dynamics, they are not the only factors with such an impact. Starting in the early 2000s, there has been an expansion of economic and social services provided by Türkiye along with a changed diaspora policy (Kilic and Biffl 2021). Akcapar and Aksel note a shift in the perspective and co-optation strategies of Türkiye in regard to citizens living abroad, with a focus on how Türkiye discovered the latter's economic power and public diplomacy potential:

> Departing from the former perspectives of classifying Turkish skilled migrants as a total loss for the homeland and labour migrants as machines for remittances, Turkey finally realized the potential of its diaspora with strong connections to homeland. This is certainly related with the increasing economic power of the diaspora and the intensifying transnationalism with return migrants, circular migrants, and upcoming generations who are more versed and politically mobilized. It is also related with the rising global trend in which migrant populations are increasingly being re-labelled as diasporas and in which there is growing interest on behalf of nation-states to engage with their diasporas (Akcapar and Aksel 2017: 138).

Aydin (2014: 13) suggests that in the 2010s, Türkiye pursued "an active diaspora policy" that was connected to "economic, political and cultural interests" of the country. This policy is consistent with co-optation as well as support motives. The aforementioned creation of YTB as a state agency in 2010 is the most visible evidence of change in the diaspora policy of Türkiye. YTB is charged with "the task to coordinate the activities for Turks living abroad, related (sister) communities and Türkiye Scholarship Program, and develop the services and activities carried out in these fields" (YTB, About Us, Institutions n.d.). Three objectives of Türkiye's diaspora policy include: (1) "Maintaining ties of Turkish citizens living abroad with the homeland"; (2) "Preserving the native language, culture and identity of Turkish citizens living abroad"; and (3) "Strengthening social status of Turkish citizens living abroad" (YTB, General Information n.d.).

To realize these objectives, YTB supports language and cultural education through initiatives such as "Anatolia the Weekend School Program" and "Turkish Language Training Program" (YTB, Turkish and Education n.d.). In addition, there are "mobility programs" that aim to culturally engage the youth (YTB, Cultural Mobility n.d.). The YTB also has an application called *cep rehberi* (pocket guide) (YTB, Pocket Guide n.d.). This guide provides updated guidelines on various topics relevant to the diaspora (Aksel 2019: 124). For citizens abroad, there are several general categories of guidance on YTB site-citizenship. Those are: participation in elections in Türkiye; Turkish-language education; cultural mobility programs; and FAQs that include information on various diplomatic, bureaucratic, and legal needs of citizens abroad (YTB, FAQ n.d.). The YTB aims to connect the Turkish state with the diaspora through cultural and social support as well as providing information and resources.

With the changeover to a presidential system in 2018, YTB's supervision transitioned from the prime minister's office to the Ministry of Culture and Tourism (Aydin and Østergaard-Nielsen 2020: 406). Under the supervision of the Minister of Culture and Tourism, the YTB's institutional structure includes many agencies that have specific goals and responsibilities (YTB Organization Chart n.d.). Annual activity reports include detailed content on goals, activities, budget, performance, and strengths/weaknesses of the YTB from 2010 to 2021 (YTB Annual Activity Reports n.d.). The 2021 report indicates that YTB had a budget of 401,962,800 TL[6] for the year 2021. Among the YTB agencies, the Department of Citizens Abroad (*Yurtdışı Vatandaşlar Daire Başkanlığı*) specifically focuses on citizens living abroad and their social, economic, and cultural development (YTB Organization Chart n.d.). Legal Advisory (*Hukuk Müşavirliği*) provides information on the law in host states as well as on international law (YTB Organization Chart n.d.). The Department of Cultural and Social Affairs (*Kültürel ve Sosyal İlişkiler Daire Başkanlığı*) is charged with supporting and coordinating cultural and social activities and engagement of Turkish diaspora (YTB Organization Chart n.d.). Although the YTB is a symbol of change in Turkish diaspora politics, the process is made up of various small shifts in cultural and social services provided to citizens abroad. Religious services and language education have been key components of such social activities of the Turkish state for its citizens abroad.

Religious Services

Among Muslim majority states, Türkiye stands out in its approach to religion as "one of the rare states that does not refer to Islam in its constitution and yet has not seen a decline in the role of Islam in society and politics" (Cesari 2014: 45). Turkish laicism excludes religion from public life while keeping religion under the control of the state (Cesari 2014: 45). The Diyanet, as a state agency, is responsible for the management of the religious affairs of Türkiye.

Since the early labor migration years, the Turkish state has provided and facilitated religious services for the Turkish diaspora. The Diyanet

[6] This roughly equals $45,215,163 based on the average conversion rate for 2021 (i.e., 1 USD=8.8922 TL as reported by Exchange Rates UK). This is an important note since in 2022 the Turkish lira lost value against the US dollar.

has been central in coordinating such efforts. While the Diyanet is predominantly in charge of domestic management, due to both the rising number of emigrants and a greater interest in public diplomacy over the years, its international role has expanded. The increasing number of religious staff working abroad is an example of this.[7] Since the 1970s, the Turkish government has been sending religious officers overseas (Bruce 2020: 1169; Icduygu and Aksel 2013: 174; Aksel 2014: 202). Bruce (2019: 82) notes that until the early 1980s, the "sending of religious personnel abroad was primarily undertaken on a case-by-case basis and was the result of requests by individual mosque associations." However, the presence of religious officials expanded noticeably in the 1980s and 1990s (Aksel 2019: 65; Bruce 2019: 87). There were 20 religious officials in 1980; 320 in 1985; 628 in 1989; 797 in 1990; and 948 in 1995 (Aksel 2019: 65; Bruce 2019: 87). The Diyanet's Department of Foreign Affairs was also founded in the midst of this trend in 1984 (Bruce 2019: 91).[8] Indeed, the role of religion in Türkiye advanced in 1980s. When the military took over to stop the tensions between leftists and ultranationalists in 1980, it adopted the Turkish–Islamic synthesis approach, which merges nationalist and religious sentiments. This was inconsistent with Kemalist ideology, which promotes secular governance, and eventually Turkish–Islamic synthesis paved the way for the rise of political Islam in Türkiye (Eligür 2010). It also modified the role of Diyanet. Maritato explains this change as follows:

> Article 136 of Turkey's 1982 Constitution affirms that the Diyanet is responsible not only for religious services but also the protection of national sovereignty and integrity. It is precisely the Diyanet's Janus-faced nature that situates religious officers' activities between Islam and the state. The Turkish-Islamic synthesis in the official doctrine of the Turkish state during the Cold War included a new reference to Islam as a relevant element with which to define the national identity (Maritato 2021: 122).

In fact, Türkiye's relationship with its nationals became complicated at the time and included support, selective support, cooptation, and repression. The 1982 constitution was the first one to outline the state's responsibilities towards citizens outside of Türkiye (Aksel 2019: 53; Ünver 2013: 184), which qualify for support. The Turkish–Islamic synthesis and the 1980 coup were in many ways shaped by the larger politics

[7] The Ministry of Foreign Affairs lists two responsibilities of religious officers working abroad: "to provide religious services to the Turkish community" and "help them perform their religious duties" (Ministry of Foreign Affairs: Turkish Citizens Living Abroad n.d.).

[8] The Director of Turks Abroad, under Diyanet's General Directorate for Foreign Affairs (*Dış İlişkiler Genel Müdürlüğü)*, regulates religious personnel to be sent abroad (Bruce 2019: 170).

of the Cold War and how religion was considered a counter-strategy for communist ideology. This ushered in tendencies to selectively support conservative components. It also meant tendencies to repress (or at least control) political opinions of citizens abroad that were perceived to be dangerous. Ironically, roughly a decade later, Islamist movements were perceived to be a threat. Since the failed attempted coup d'état in 2016, people associated with the Gülen movement have been considered a security threat. The Turkish government blames Fethullah Gülen, an exiled Turkish cleric, for plotting the 2016 coup against the government. After the failed coup attempt, Swedish Radio reported that Türkiye asked national communities living abroad to report supporters of Fethullah Gülen (Reuters 2016). The Parliamentary Assembly of the Council of Europe (2023) in Resolution 2509 noted the following: "Türkiye has also used some of the tools of transnational repression, particularly following the coup attempt of July 2016 and its consistent policy of pursuing, among others, anyone allegedly related to the 'Gülen movement', which is referred to as the 'Fethullahist Terrorist Organisation (FETÖ)' by the Turkish authorities."

In 1984, the Turkish–Islamic Union for Religious Affairs (DITIB, Diyanet İşleri Türk İslam Birliği) was founded (Sahin-Mencutek and Baser 2017: 6). DITIB self-describes as a civil society organization (DITIB About n.d.). Aydin and Østergaard-Nielsen (2020: 407) note that DITIB started as a "religious association" and evolved to be "the umbrella organization of the mosque associations in Germany," and was followed by similar organizations in Belgium, the Netherlands, and France (Aydin and Østergaard-Nielsen 2020: 407). There is a long list of services provided by DITIB, including religious education, cultural activities, generating funeral funds for burial in Türkiye, and helping in the organization of the Diyanet's hajj and umrah trips. They also have services tailored to youth and women. Ünver (2013: 185) suggests that DITIB is "the largest Turkish diaspora organization" with affiliation with "more than 1000 mosque associations." According to Aydin (2014: 17), DITIB "is subject to the management and control of the Turkish state Presidium for Religious Affairs (DİB) and thus represents a view of Islam that is compatible with the official policy of a secular state." Similar connections are noted elsewhere: "The Diyanet sends Turkish imams to DITIB mosques; the imams' salaries are then paid by the respective Turkish consulate general for the duration of their stay. In other words, the Diyanet determines the theological guidelines behind what is preached in the mosques" (Heinrich 2018).

Diyanet's bureaucratic footprint has been expanding since the 1980s (van Bruinessen 2018; Çitak 2017) with implications for Türkiye's foreign policy. Çitak (2010: 620) considers the Diyanet as a foreign policy instrument for the Turkish government. This is not surprising, given the role of religion in Türkiye's foreign policy (Özturk 2021: 1). The Justice and Development Party (*Adalet ve Kalkınma Partisi*, hereinafter AKP) governments have aimed to expand Türkiye's influence. Religion was centralized in advancement of Türkiye's soft power as the leader of the Muslim world (Akbaba and Özdamar 2019: 99).

Öztürk and Sözeri (2018: 630) note a steady increase in the Diyanet's budget between 2002 and 2017. With a budget allocation of €1.5 billion for 2018 (van Bruinessen 2018: 3), it has the financial means to operate effectively. In the same vein, the Diyanet's international administrative capacity (Öktem 2012: 41–42) and its presence in diaspora populations increased (Çitak 2017: 388). Bruce (2019: 1) argues that, "[i]n 2015, Turkey had over 1,800 imams serving in foreign countries. The vast majority of these state-employed religious officials are appointed to mosques in Western Europe to provide religious services to local Turkish communities." Until 2000, only male religious officers were sent abroad. Starting from the early 2000s, the Diyanet has also been sending female religious officers abroad to organize "sermons, Qur'an readings and preaching sessions in Diyanet mosques" and "provide religious knowledge and moral support to women and families" (Maritato 2018: 1). Akcapar and Aksel (2017: 146) give a snapshot of the geographical expansion. In 2017, there were Diyanet counsellor offices in 15 countries "and attachés from religious affairs hold 21 offices in nine countries around the world, with the majority being positioned in Germany" (Akcapar and Aksel 2017: 146).

The Diyanet's activities abroad aimed "to provide religious services and moral guidance, to maintain loyal relations with the diaspora, and to reach families and young people" (Maritato 2021: 122). These goals led to a plethora of initiatives. For example, in 2006, the Diyanet initiated an "international program of theology to train students from abroad with Turkish roots as imams working in diaspora communities" (Maritato 2018: 4). The International Theology Programme (Uluslararası İlahiyat Programı) was created by the Turkish government in 2006 with the idea of training religious officials who are citizens of their host countries. Bruce (2020: 1167) writes the following about this initiative:

> From a small initiative with uncertain prospects for success, the programme has grown enormously and now counts upwards of 600 to 700 students from 15 different countries, including most of Western Europe, North America, and Australia. Moreover, since 2010, hundreds of students have graduated and have now begun to take up positions as teachers and religious leaders back home.

Such expansion of religious services and cultural activities also indicate selective support targeting only conservative segments of nationals abroad.

Language and Culture-Related Services

The state also prioritized supporting language and the cultural education of Turkish citizens living abroad. Like religion, language is considered part of the larger cultural identity and as a key connection between Türkiye and future generations of the Turkish communities abroad:

[T]he Turkish Government closely follows the conditions of the Turkish community to learn their mother tongue. The Turkish citizens who are bilingual and have the opportunity to preserve their own identity would be more equipped individuals in today's globalized world and would contribute to the furtherment of bilateral relations between Turkey and the host countries. To this end, Turkey appoints, in cooperation with host countries, teachers for Turkish language and culture (Republic of Turkey, Ministry of Foreign Affairs: Turkish Citizens Living Abroad n.d.).

Starting in the mid-1970s, Turkish language and culture teachers were sent abroad (Aksel 2019: 65). In the 1980s, Türkiye focused on "exportation of culture and ideology in order to strengthen emigrants' sense of belonging towards Turkey" through "religion and education" (Akcapar and Aksel 2017: 145). While in 1985 "there were 1,015 teachers sent from Turkey," in 2014 the number of overseas teachers and instructors employed by the Ministry of Education was 1,700, "primarily settled in Germany (495 teachers) and France (190 teachers)" (Aksel 2019: 65, 121).

In addition, there are cultural initiatives with a broad scope. For example, the Yunus Emre Foundation (YEV), created in 2007 through Law No. 5653, has cultural purposes such as "presenting Turkish cultural heritage, promoting cultural exchange, making information about Turkey available and providing educational services on Turkish language and culture and on the country's arts" (Aydin 2014: 16). YEV's Board of Trustees is led by the Minister of Culture and Tourism (Management of Yunus Emre Foundation n.d.). The Yunus Emre Institute (YEI), which was established as a foundation (Yunus Emre Institute n.d.), is affiliated to YEV. It provides language education and organizes cultural activities (Yunus Emre Institute, Corporate n.d.) and is funded from the state budget (*Daily Sabah* 2017). The External Cultural Policy (ECP) Monitor reports a budget of the YEI of €25.8 million for 2019, with the institute having a presence in forty-eight countries (ifa ECP Monitor Fact Sheet Turkey 2021).

Security Dimension

While most rescue operations are done through civilian agencies, the Turkish Armed Forces (*Türk Silahlı Kuvvetleri*, TSK) have engaged in activities to protect citizens abroad as well. Many such efforts were designed to evacuate citizens trapped in conflict zones and fit closely to the support category. Prior to the political upheaval of 2011 in Libya that eventually led to Muammar Gaddafi's overthrow, many Turkish contractors were working in the country (Caglayan 2020). There were around 25,000 Turkish citizens employed in various construction projects at that time (Butler 2011a). In February 2011, during the early stages of the instability in Libya, Türkiye rescued around 17, 157 Turkish citizens. Part of this operation was carried out using Turkish Air Force military aircraft (T24 2011). Türkiye's navy also contributed to the rescue operation with ships and frigates (Butler 2011b). Similarly, after the Taliban's takeover of Afghanistan in 2021, Turkish military aircraft evacuated 1,129 Turkish citizens (*Daily Sabah* 2021).

In February 2021, the Turkish military initiated a rescue operation in Northern Iraq to save thirteen hostages who were kidnapped by the Kurdish militant organization PKK (Kurdistan Workers' Party) in 2015 and 2016 (US Department of State Country Reports on Human Rights Practices 2021). The PKK executed the hostages and the Turkish military discovered bodies of victims during the rescue operation in Iraq. (*The Guardian* 2021).

Conclusion

Türkiye's relationship with its national communities has changed tremendously over the decades. Widening support is most visible in the diplomatic dimension. Both the quality and the scope of diplomatic outreach expanded tremendously. While the general motivation is to (selectively) support nationals abroad, there are many examples of co-optation that are associated with economic and/or political interests. In the early years of labor migration, Türkiye's economy benefited from remittances. Later on, Türkiye started seeing the public policy potential of national communities abroad. Overseas voting gave citizens the opportunity to participate politically. In some cases, the outcome was in favor of politically established figures. For example, in the May 2023 presidential runoff election, Erdogan secured 59.4 percent of international votes and Kilicdaroglu received 40.6 percent (Al Jazeera 2023). There have also been tendencies to limit or repress groups that are perceived to be a security threat.

While it is helpful to distinguish examples of support, co-optation, and repression to analyze the relationship between the state and its national communities abroad, it is equally important to understand how they are interconnected. For example, in the 1980s, Türkiye's relationship with its citizens included support, selective support, co-optation, and repression. The Turkish–Islamic synthesis and the 1980 coup, as previously described, were in many ways shaped by larger Cold War politics and how religion was considered a counter-strategy for communist ideology. This brought tendencies to repress (or at least control) critical political opinions. Aksel (2019: 6) marks the 1980s as the "transition in Turkish state policies towards the management of emigrants." Icduygu and Aksel (2013: 175) connect this to changes in the nature of emigration: "the management of social and cultural affairs became increasingly important in maintaining ties with the now-permanent emigrants abroad." All of these also influenced a growing interest in providing social and specifically religious services to Turkish citizens abroad, which brought in selective support to more conservative segments. At the same time, this was a period of increased support in general. The 1982 constitution was the first one to outline the state's responsibilities towards citizens outside of Türkiye (Aksel 2019: 53; Ünver 2013: 184). Article 62, which was introduced with the new constitution (Sahin-Mencutek and Baser 2017), states the following about Turkish citizens working abroad: "The State shall take the necessary measures to ensure family unity, the education of the children, the cultural needs, and the social security of Turkish citizens working abroad, and to safeguard their ties with the home country and to help them on their return home." In this article, the Turkish state assumed key responsibilities for non-resident Turkish citizens. These responsibilities bring in the social and cultural policy dimensions, which were not present in the early years of guest-worker migration.

Like many aspects of recent Turkish politics, it is difficult to understand Türkiye's relations with communities living abroad without understanding the AKP, which came into power after the 2002 general elections. The AKP focused on projecting influence and acting as a regional leader. Connecting with citizens abroad was part of a larger foreign policy goal that sought to geographically expand Türkiye's soft power (Baser and Ozturk 2020: 16–19; Aksel 2019: 129). The AKP governments prioritized diaspora politics and public diplomacy (Baser and Ozturk 2020: 13; Akcapar and Aksel 2017). With interests in advancing the position and influence of Türkiye in Europe and the MENA region, the AKP viewed citizens abroad as cultural bridges and showed interest in connecting with various external networks (Baser and Ozturk 2020: 14). Türkiye's rising interest in its diaspora and co-optation strategies also overlapped with its economic growth in the 2000s. Türkiye's economy started to recover after the 2001 economic crisis. This upward trend continued for almost two decades. Economic growth allowed various initiatives such as the foundation of YTB in 2010. However, as of 2023, Türkiye's economy is in crisis, with high inflation and a declining value of the Turkish lira. In addition, the February 2023 earthquake devastated parts of the country, causing death and displacement. Such changes will pull the attention towards citizens at home. However, considering the size of national communities abroad as well as the opportunities that diaspora politics present, Turkish emigrants are likely to remain crucial for Türkiye in the long term. Public diplomacy and economic opportunities that come with engaging citizens abroad are simply too important to ignore.

References

AA (2022) Almanya'da 'bitkisal hayata girdigi' öne sürülen gurbetçi ambulans uçakla Türkiye'ye getirildi. Available at: www.aa.com.tr/tr/gundem/almanyada-bitkisel-hayata-girdigi-one-surulen-gurbetci-ambulans-ucakla-turkiyeye-getirildi/2603645 (last accessed December 14, 2022).

Akbaba, Yasemin, and Özgur Özdamar (2019) *Role Theory in the Middle East and North Africa*. New York and London: Routledge.

Akçapar, Şebnem Köşer (2018) Diaspora Engagement in the United States: The Case of India and Turkey. In Smita Tewari Jassal and Halil Turan (eds.), *New Perspectives on India and Turkey: Connections and Debates*. London and New York: Routledge, 155–167.

Akcapar, Sebnem Koser, and Damla Bayraktar Aksel (2017) Public Diplomacy through Diaspora Engagement: The Case of Turkey. *Perceptions* 22(4), 135–160.

Aksel, Damla B. (2014) Kins, Distant Workers, Diasporas: Constructing Turkey's Transnational Members Abroad. *Turkish Studies* 15(2), 195–219.

Aksel, Damla B. (2019) *Home States and Homeland Politics: Interactions between the Turkish State and Its Emigrants in France and the United States*. London and New York: Routledge.

Al Jazeera (2023) How Did Turks Living Abroad Vote in Turkey's Run-Off Election? Available at: www.aljazeera.com/news/2023/5/29/how-did-turks-living-abroad-vote-in-turkeys-run-off-election#:~:text=Erdogan%20received%2059.4%20percent%20of,managed%20to%20garner%2040.6%20percent.&text=Turkey's%20President%20Recep%20Tayyip%20Erdogan,%2Dcontested%20run%2Doff%20election (last accessed September 19, 2023).

Aydin, Yasar (2014) *The New Turkish Diaspora Policy: Its Aims, Their Limits and the Challenges for Associations of People of Turkish Origin and Decision-Makers in Germany*. Berlin: Stiftung Wissenschaft und Politik.

Aydin, Seda, and Eva Østergaard-Nielsen (2020) Diaspora Policies, Consular Services and Social Protection for Turkish Citizens Abroad. In J. M Lafleur and D. Vintila (eds.), *Migration and Social Protection in Europe and Beyond (Volume 3)*. IMISCOE Research Series. Cham: Springer, 401–418.

Bahçecik, Şerif Onur (2020) Constructing Liberal Subjects? Turkey's New Diaspora Strategy. In Hazal Pabuççular and Deniz Kuru (eds.), *A Transnational Account of Turkish Foreign Policy*. Cham: Palgrave MacMillan, 175–194.

Baser, Bahar, and Ahmet Erdi Ozturk (2020) Positive and Negative Diaspora Governance in Context: From Public Diplomacy to Transnational Authoritarianism. *Middle East Critique* 29(3), 319–334.

Bruce, Benjamin (2019) *Governing Islam Abroad*. The Sciences Po Series in International Relations and Political Economy. Switzerland: Palgrave MacMillan.

Bruce, Benjamin (2020) Imams for the Diaspora: The Turkish State's International Theology Programme. *Journal of Ethnic and Migration Studies* 46(6), 1166–1183.

Butler, Daren (2011a) Erdogan Warns Libya on Violence as Turks Await Rescue. *Reuters*. Available at: www.reuters.com/article/uk-libya-protests-turkey-idUKTRE71L34U20110222 (last accessed October 4, 2022).

Butler, Daren (2011b) Turks Wait at Benghazi Port for Ships Out of Libya. Available at: www.reuters.com/article/libya-protests-turkey-idAFLDE71L0RG2011 0222 (last accessed October 4, 2022).

Caglayan, Ceyda (2020) Turkey Aims to Sign Deal with Libya over Gaddafi-Era Compensation. *Reuters*. Available at: www.reuters.com/article/us-libya-security-turkey/turkey-aims-to-sign-deal-with-libya-over-gaddafi-era-compensation-idUSKBN1Z913A (last accessed November 30, 2022).

Constitution of Republic of Turkey. Available at: www5.tbmm.gov.tr/yayinlar/2021/TC_Anayasasi_ve_TBMM_Ic_Tuzugu_Ingilizce.pdf (last accessed September 7, 2022).

Cesari, Jocelyne (2014) *The Awakening of Muslim Democracy: Religion, Modernity and the State*. Cambridge: Cambridge University Press.

Çitak, Zana (2010) Between 'Turkish Islam' and 'French Islam': The Role of the Diyanet in the *Conseil Français du Culte Musulman*. *Journal of Ethnic and Migration Studies* 36(4), 619–634.

Çitak, Zana (2017) National Conceptions, Transnational Solidarities: Turkey, Islam and Europe. *Global Networks* 18(3), 377–398.

Daily Sabah (2017) Yunus Emre Institute Head Ateş: As an Element of Soft Power, Our Aim Is to Introduce Turkey, Its Culture to the World. Available at: www.dailysabah.com/diplomacy/2017/07/24/yunus-emre-institute-head-ates-as-an-element-of-soft-power-our-aim-is-to-introduce-turkey-its-culture-to-the-world (last accessed November 30, 2022).

Daily Sabah (2021) Turkey Begins Withdrawing Military Forces from Afghanistan. Available at: www.dailysabah.com/politics/turkey-begins-withdrawing-military-forces-from-afghanistan/news (last accessed September 30, 2022).

Daily Sabah (2022) Turkey Evacuates over 12,300 Citizens from Ukraine. Available at: www.dailysabah.com/politics/diplomacy/turkey-evacuates-over-12300-citizens-from-ukraine (last accessed September 30, 2022).

DITIB About (n.d.) Kuruluş ve Teşkilat Yapısı. Available at: www.ditib.de/default1.php?id=5&sid=8&lang=en (last accessed October 13, 2022).

e-Konsolosluk (n.d.) Republic of Türkiye. Available at: www.konsolosluk.gov.tr/ (last accessed October 5, 2022)

Eligür, Banu (2010) *The Mobilization of Political Islam in Turkey*. Cambridge: Cambridge University Press.

Exchange Rates UK (n.d.) US Dollar to Turkish Lira Spot Exchange Rates for 2021. Available at: www.exchangerates.org.uk/USD-TRY-spot-exchange-rates-history-2021.html (last accessed December 16, 2022).

Giglou, Roya Imani, Leen d'Haenens and Baldwin Van Gorp (2019) Determinants of Degree of Integration of Turkish Diaspora in Belgium, the Netherlands and Germany. *International Communication Gazette* 81(3), 259–282.

Heinrich, Daniel (2018) What You Need to Know about DITIB. *DW*. Available at: www.dw.com/en/erdogan-in-germany-what-you-need-to-know-about-ditib-mosque-association/a-45676937 (last accessed October 13, 2022).

Home and away: Turks in Europe (2017, September 2). *The Economist*. Available at: http://ezpro.cc.gettysburg.edu:2048/login?url=https://www.proquest.com/magazines/home-away-turks-europe/docview/1934443792/se-2 (last accessed October 18, 2022).

Hurriyet Daily News (2021) Turkey Sends Team to Rescue National Missing in Bosnia. Available at: www.hurriyetdailynews.com/turkey-sends-team-to-rescue-national-missing-in-bosnia-169336 (last accessed September 30, 2022).

Içduygu, Ahmet, and Damla B. Aksel (2013) Turkish Migration Policies: A Critical Historical Retrospective. *Perceptions* 18(3), 167–190.

Içduygu, Ahmet, Şule Toktas, and B. Ali Soner (2008) The Politics of Population in a Nation-building Process: Emigration of Non-Muslims From Turkey. *Ethnic and Racial Studies* 31(2), 358–389.

ifa ECP Monitor Fact Sheet Turkey (2021) Available at: https://opus.bsz-bw.de/ifa/frontdoor/deliver/index/docId/13/file/ECP_Monitor_Turkey_At_a_Glance.pdf (last accessed June 4, 2024).

Insider (2014) 46 Turkish Hostages Kidnapped by ISIS Militants Freed. Available at: www.businessinsider.com/46-turkish-hostages-kidnapped-by-isis-militants-freed-2014-9 (last accessed September 30, 2022).

Karaçay, Bahri (2018) Turkey Sends More Students to the United States Than Any Other European Country. *Tassa*. Available at: www.tassausa.org/Newsroom/2014/item/2087/Turkey-Sends-More-Students-to-the-United-States-Than-Any-Other-European-Country#:~:text=Turkey%20currently%20ranks%2011th%20worldwide,currently%20in%20the%20United%20States (last accessed October 21, 2022).

Kaya, Ilhan (2005) Identity and Space: The Case of Turkish Americans, *Geographical Review* 95(3), 425–440.

Kilic, Hakan and Godrun Biffl (2021) Turkish Migration Policy from the 1960s Until Today: What National Development Plans Tell Us. *Journal of International Migration and Integration*. Available at: https://doi.org/10.1007/s12134-021-00912-3 (accessed September 9, 2022).

Management of Yunus Emre Foundation (n.d.) Management of Yunus Emre Foundation. Available at: www.yee.org.tr/en/corporate/management-yunus-emre-foundation (last accessed November 30, 2022).

Maritato, Chiara. (2018) Addressing the Blurred Edges of Turkey's Diaspora and Religious Policy: Diyanet Women Preachers Sent to Europe. *European Journal of Turkish Studies* 27, doi.org/10.4000/ejts.6020.

Maritato, Chiara. (2021) Islam, the Homeland, and the Family: Diyanet's Narrative and Practices Aimed at Shaping a Loyal Muslim Turkish Diaspora. *Diaspora: A Journal of Transnational Studies* 21(2), 121–138.

Massicard, Elise (2012) *The Alevis in Turkey and Europe: Identity and Managing Territorial Diversity*, Taylor & Francis Group. ProQuest Ebook Central, https://ebookcentral.proquest.com/lib/gettysburg/detail.action?docID=1047069.

Mevzuat (2013) Available at: www.mfa.gov.tr/data/BAKANLIK/mevzuat-2013.pdf (last accessed October 4, 2022).

Ministry of Education (2022) Almanya'da Yogun Bakimda Tedavi Gören Ögretmen, Bakan Özer'in Girisimleriyle Ambulans Uçakla Türkiye'ye Getirildi. Available at: www.meb.gov.tr/almanyada-yogun-bakimda-tedavi-goren-ogretmen-bakan-ozerin-girisimleriyle-ambulans-ucakla-turkiyeye-getirildi/haber/28303/tr (last accessed December 13, 2022).

Ministry of Foreign Affairs, Turkish Representations (n.d.) Available at: www.mfa.gov.tr/yurtdisi-teskilati.tr.mfa (last accessed September 29, 2022).

Ministry of Foreign Affairs Organization Chart (n.d.) Available at: www.mfa.gov.tr/data/merkez-teskilatimiz-en.pdf (last accessed October 4, 2022).

Ministry of Labor and Social Security (n.d.) Gorevlerimiz. Available at: www.csgb.gov.tr/digm/contents/genel-mudurluk/gorevlerimiz/ (last accessed October 12, 2022).

Minorities at Risk Project (2009) *Minorities at Risk Dataset*. College Park, MD: Center for International Development and Conflict Management. Available at: www.mar.umd.edu/ (last accessed October 18, 2022).

Oldac, Yusuf Ikbal, and Nigel Fancourt (2021) "New Wave Turks" Turkish Graduates of German Universities and the Turkish Diaspora in Germany. *British Journal of Educational Studies* 69(5), 621–640.

Öktem, Kerem (2012) Global Diyanet and Multiple Networks: Turkey's New Presence in the Balkans. *Journal of Muslims in Europe* 1(1), 27–58.

Özturk, Ahmet Erdi (2021) Islam and Foreign Policy: Turkey's Ambivalent Religious Soft Power in the Authoritarian Turn. *Religions* 12(38).

Öztürk, Ahmet Erdi, and Semiha Sözeri (2018) Diyanet as a Turkish Foreign Policy Tool: Evidence from the Netherlands and Bulgaria. *Politics and Religion* 11(3), 624–648.

Parliamentary Assembly of the Council of Europe (2023) Transnational Repression as a Growing Threat to the Rule of Law and Human Rights. Resolution 2509, June 23, 2023.

Pew Research Center, Remittance flows worldwide in 2017. Available at: www.pewresearch.org/global/interactives/remittance-flows-by-country/ (last accessed October 3, 2022).

Republic of Turkey, Ministry of Foreign Affairs: Turkish Citizens Living Abroad (n.d.). Available at: www.mfa.gov.tr/the-expatriate-turkish-citizens.en.mfa#:~:text=The%20total%20population%20of%20Turkish,live%20in%20Western%20European%20countries (last accessed August 30, 2022).

Reuters (2016) Turkey Asking Turks Abroad to Report Gulen Supporters Whereabouts – Swedish Radio. Available at: www.reuters.com/article/turkey-security-sweden-idINKCN1021RY (last accessed September 18, 2023).

Sahin-Mencutek, Zeynep, and Bahar Baser (2017) Mobilizing Diasporas: Insights from Turkey's Attempts to Reach Turkish Citizens Abroad. *Journal of Balkan and Near Eastern Studies* 20(1), 86–105.

Sahin-Mencutek, Zeynep, and M. Murat Erdogan (2016) The Implementation of Voting from Abroad: Evidence from the 2014 Turkish Presidential Election. *International Migration* 54(3), 173–186.

Simple Flying (2020) Turkish Airlines Will Operate Almost 200 Rescue Flights This Week. Available at: https://simpleflying.com/turkish-airlines-rescue-flights/ (last accessed September 30, 2022).

T24 (2011) Davutoğlu: 17.734 kişinin Libya'dan tahliye edildi. Available at: https://t24.com.tr/haber/davutoglu-17734-kisinin-libyadan-tahliye-edildi,130005 (last accessed October 4, 2022).

Tansel, Aysit and Nil Demet Güngör (2003) "Brain Drain" from Turkey: Survey Evidence of Student Non-return. *Career Development International* 8(2), 52–69.

Tiryakioglu, Bilgin (2006) Multiple Citizenship and Its Consequences in Turkish Law. *Ankara Law Review* 3(1), 1–16.

The Guardian (2021) Erdoğan Vows to Expand Fight against PKK after Deaths of 13 Hostages. Available at: www.theguardian.com/world/2021/feb/16/erdogan-vows-to-expand-fight-against-pkk-after-deaths-of-13-hostages (last accessed October 20, 2022).

Travel and Tour World (2020) Turkish Airlines to Operate Hundreds of Rescue Flights This Week. Available at: www.travelandtourworld.com/news/article/turkish-airlines-operate-hundreds-rescue-flights-week/ (last accessed September 30, 2022).

TRT Haber (2022) Almanya'da hastanede yatan genç kız, ambulans uçakla Türkiye'ye getirildi. Available at: www.trthaber.com/haber/gundem/almanyada-hastanede-yatan-genc-kiz-ambulans-ucakla-turkiyeye-getirildi-723218.html (last accessed December 13, 2022).

TRT World (2021) Turkey Rescues Nationals Held Hostage in Eastern Libya for Two Years. Available at: www.trtworld.com/turkey/turkey-rescues-nationals-held-hostage-in-eastern-libya-for-two-years-51871 (last accessed September 30, 2022).

Turkish Citizens Abroad (n.d.) Ministry of Foreign Affairs. Available at: www.mfa.gov.tr/the-expatriate-turkish-citizens.en.mfa#:~:text=The%20total%20population%20of%20Turkish,live%20in%20Western%20European%20countries (last accessed October 5, 2022).

United Nations Department of Economic and Social Affairs, Population Division (2020) *International Migrant Stock (2020)*. Available at: www.un.org/development/desa/pd/content/international-migrant-stock (last accessed October 17, 2022).

United Nations International Migrant Stock (2020) Available at: www.un.org/development/desa/pd/content/international-migrant-stock (last accessed December 14, 2022).

US Department of State Country Reports on Human Rights Practices (2021) Available at: www.state.gov/reports/2021-country-reports-on-human-rights-practices/turkey/ (last accessed September 30, 2022).

Ünver, O. Can (2013) Changing Diaspora Politics of Turkey and Public Diplomacy. *Turkish Policy Quarterly* 12(1), 181–189.

Uysal, Nur, and Jared Schroeder (2019) Turkey's Twitter Public Diplomacy: Towards a "New" Cult of Personality. *Public Relations Review* 45(5), doi.org/10.1016/j.pubrev.2019.101837.

Uysal, Nur, Jared Schroeder and Maureen Taylor (2012) Social Media and Soft Power: Positioning Turkey's Image on Twitter. *Middle East Journal of Culture and Communication* 5(3), 338–359.

van Bruinessen, Martin (2018) The Governance of Islam in Two Secular Polities: Turkey's Diyanet and Indonesia's Ministry of Religious Affairs. *European Journal of Turkish Studies*, 27, online since January 10, 2019, doi.org/10.4000/ejts.5964.

World Bank (n.d.) Remittance Inflows to GDP for Turkey, retrieved from FRED, Federal Reserve Bank of St. Louis. Available at: https://fred.stlouisfed.org/series/DDOI11TRA156NWDB (last accessed October 3, 2022).

WSJ (2014) Turkey Secures Release of Hostages Held by Islamic State. Available at: www.wsj.com/articles/turkey-secures-release-of-hostages-held-by-islamic-state-1411209683 (last accessed September 30, 2022).

Yabanci, Bilge (2021) Home State Oriented Diaspora Organizations and the Making of Partisan Citizens Abroad: Motivations, Discursive Frames, and Actions towards Co-opting the Turkish Diaspora in Europe. *Diaspora: A Journal of Transnational Studies*. Advance Access Version, doi.org/10.3138/diaspora.21.2.2021.05.20.2.

YTB, About Us, Institutions (n.d.) Available at: www.ytb.gov.tr/en/corporate/institution (last accessed September 7, 2022).

YTB, Cultural Mobility (n.d.) Available at: www.ytb.gov.tr/en/abroad-citizens/cultural-mobility (last accessed September 8, 2022).

YTB, FAQ (n.d.) Available at: www.ytb.gov.tr/soru-cevap/sosyal-hizmetler (last accessed October 12, 2022).

YTB, General Information (n.d.) Available at: www.ytb.gov.tr/en/abroad-citizens/general-information-2 (last accessed September 7, 2022).

YTB, Pocket Guide (n.d.) Available at: www.ytb.gov.tr/guncel/ytb-cep-rehberi (last accessed September 28, 2022).

YTB, Turkish and Education (n.d.) Available at: www.ytb.gov.tr/en/abroad-citizens/turkish-and-education (last accessed September 8, 2022).

YTB, Türkiye'deki Seçimlere Katılım (n.d.) Available at: www.ytb.gov.tr/yurtdisi-vatandaslar/turkiyedeki-secimlere-katilim (last accessed October 13, 2022).

YTB Annual Activity Reports (n.d.) Available at: www.ytb.gov.tr/kurumsal/faaliyet-raporlari (last accessed October 12, 2022).

YTB Organization Chart (n.d.) Available at: www.ytb.gov.tr/teskilat-semasi (last accessed October 12, 2022).

Yunus Emre Institute (n.d.) Home Page. Available at: https://yeelondon.org.uk/ (last accessed November 30, 2022).

Yunus Emre Institute, Corporate (n.d.) Available at: www.yee.org.tr/tr/kurumsal/yunus-emre-enstitusu (last accessed November 30, 2022).

13 The United States
A (Mostly) Hands-Off Superpower

Drew A. Hogan and Ronald R. Krebs

Introduction

The United States differs from other countries included in this volume. It is a relatively large country, with respect to both geography and population. It is one of the world's largest exporters of population in absolute terms, though not relative to its total population, nor relative to the number of immigrants it absorbs. Since the Second World War, the United States has exercised unmatched power and influence around the globe. While other nations have adopted exceptionalist narratives, America's exceptionalism has been unusually thoroughgoing and persistent, and its national narrative has been unusually focused on a central idea known as the American creed – the notion that all Americans, regardless of national origin, race, religion, or any other categorical identity, succeed by dint of their talents and industry alone (Shklar 1991). As a result, only America's exceptionalist narrative is tied up with immigration: while Americans' actual relationship to immigrants has been ambivalent at best, both pro- and anti-immigrant forces share the belief that America's inherent superiority has made it a magnet for people around the world desperately searching for freedom and opportunity (Bon Tempo 2011).

The US's approach toward its citizens abroad reflects its unique configuration of power, interests, and ideas. In this regard, it has, more often than not, been a "hands-off" superpower. With millions of Americans residing outside the United States, the US government takes little responsibility for their physical safety. It does not force them to leave dangerous territories, it rarely helps facilitate their evacuation, and it does not collaborate with host nations in protecting its citizens. Until recently, the US government only occasionally and reluctantly got involved when Americans were taken hostage, and even more recently, its role has been quite limited, if somewhat more proactive. The US plays little role in promoting the social and cultural activities that would maintain expatriate Americans' attachment to their home country. US policy toward Americans abroad has certainly not been "hands-off," however, when it has come to the pursuit of their economic interests. The US government has offered some direct support, from the use of financial coercion, backed by US diplomacy, to advance US commercial interests at the start of the twentieth century – so-called Dollar Diplomacy – to the promotion of US exports today via diverse government agencies.

However, and significantly, the United States has *indirectly* used its military and economic power to further its citizens' interests and ambitions – by constructing the conditions in which (White) Americans could thrive. It cleared the continent of Native Americans, it worked to open the door to commerce in Latin America and Asia, and it built a postwar multilateral order that steadily ground down obstacles to trade and investment (Ostler 2019; Boot 2014; Cohen 2013). Yet, like liberal empires of old, the US government typically denied that its policies were designed to benefit primarily its citizens. Informed and impelled by a universal vision, it claimed to be advancing the natural interests of all people, everywhere (Packenham 1973; Mazower 2012).

The distinctive US approach to supporting its citizens abroad – limited direct support, significant indirect support – likely derives from a mix of pragmatism, historical identity, and ideology. Pragmatically, the immense number of US citizens located abroad at any given time has made expansive government support prohibitively expensive and logistically challenging. Historically, the US has been, and has seen itself as, a land of immigrants rather than emigrants. Its policy-makers and intellectuals have devoted their energies to integrating millions of newcomers into the nation's economy and culture. Ideologically, America's laissez-faire traditions likely underpinned its mostly "hands-off" approach to its citizens abroad, while its liberal commitments led it to construct a global order in which capitalism in general, and US businesses in particular, could thrive.

In contrast, we find that the US government has undertaken virtually no efforts to co-opt citizens abroad. This may be because doing so would raise intense challenges of logistics and coordination and invite questions about legality, but it also may be because the postwar hegemonic United States has had little need: it has had, at its disposal, a vast military, diplomatic, and surveillance infrastructure and alliance system to conduct matters of state. Finally, the US government has at times engaged in repression of its citizens abroad, in a distinctly American style – primarily by surveilling them and controlling their travel. The most intrusive and illegal Cold War measures were rolled back, but the mission and impulses of US security agencies have led them regularly to embrace repression, especially during periods of intense insecurity – notably after 9/11 (Theoharis 2011).

The remainder of this essay substantiates these claims. It follows the same template as other chapters. It first briefly reviews the past and present of US citizens living abroad. It then examines what the US government has done to support and promote its expatriate citizens – through, in turn, diplomacy and consular work, social and economic activities, and security and surveillance affairs. The conclusion reflects back on the larger analytical lessons and offers some predictions about the future.

Overview of the American Community Abroad

The number of Americans living abroad is not known – and indeed is contested. The US Census Bureau stopped counting citizens living abroad after the 1970 census, largely because of concerns of data reliability and because, at the time, no federal programs required data on Americans overseas. Furthermore, the Department of Defense and the Office of Personnel Management maintained their own records of military-service people and government employees residing abroad (Mills 1993), so different government agencies have generated their own estimates, which can diverge wildly (American Citizens Abroad 2017). Per Table 13.1, in 2020, the Federal Voting Assistance Program (FVAP) estimated that approximately 4.8 million US citizens live abroad. That same year, the US Department of State offered a figure of approximately 9 million Americans (US FVAP 2020; US Department of State 2020).[1]

Table 13.1 *US citizens residing abroad*

Country	Number
Canada	516,309
United Kingdom	327,245
Israel	183,499
France	181,393
Australia	126,703
Japan	92,879
Switzerland	87,705
Mexico	80,887
Germany	75,142
Hong Kong	64,809

Source: FVAP (2020).

[1] The FVAP relies on foreign government estimates and US administrative records and data, such as the number of social security beneficiaries and number of foreign-earned income returns. The Department of State does not explain its methodology.

The United Nations estimated that there were under 3 million US citizens located abroad (World Population Review 2022). One reason for this wide discrepancy is that American citizens, whether living in the US or abroad, and unlike citizens of most other nations, are not required to register a place of residence (Costanzo and Klekowski von Koppenfels 2013). Regardless of the estimate, however, the number of Americans residing abroad is fairly small relative to the total US population, which in 2020 was nearly 330 million.

Immigration to the United States has dwarfed emigration from the country throughout its history. The very reasons that made the United States a magnet for immigrants also made emigration relatively unappealing. This disparity grew as US power and wealth increased after the Second World War. In 1970, 1.7 million Americans were thought to reside abroad. By 1990, that number had fallen to just 925,000 (Mills 1993). However, the rise of neoliberalism and the end of the Cold War removed some impediments to emigration (Solimano 2010), and the "rise of the rest" meant that opportunities have abounded elsewhere. The result has been an apparently significant increase over the last thirty years in the number of Americans located abroad. Still, the United States in 2020 had over 50 million foreign-born residents – more than the next four countries combined (World Population Review 2022).

The reasons for emigration from the US are diverse. A 2008 survey found that marriage/partnership was the chief motivation, accounting for 28.8 percent of Americans living abroad. Professional opportunities were another top reason Americans had left the country, as was dissatisfaction with the political and social atmosphere in the United States (Klekowski von Koppenfels 2014). Given these reasons, along with the United States' geographic location and the national origins of its naturalized citizens, it is not surprising that US citizens residing abroad have long tended to cluster in Europe and the Western Hemisphere (Dulles 1966). In 1970, Americans chiefly resided in Canada, Mexico, the United Kingdom, and Germany (US Census Bureau 1973). In 2015, the Department of State estimated there were 3.7 million US citizens in the Western Hemisphere, and another 2.02 million in Europe and Eurasia, compared to 1.13 million in East Asia and the Pacific and even fewer in other regions (U.S GAO 2018). Nor is it surprising that US citizens abroad tend to be highly educated compared to the US population. In 2020, FVAP estimated that 45 percent of Americans living abroad had a bachelor's degree, and 35 percent had a graduate degree. In contrast, in 2021, 37.9 percent and 14.3 percent of Americans over age twenty-five held undergraduate and graduate degrees (FVAP 2020).

Finally, with regard to remittances, US citizens sent far more remittances to foreign countries than they received. In 2017, approximately $148 billion in remittances flowed out of the United States, compared to just $6.62 billion that came in. The largest source of remittance inflows came from workers in Mexico – $1.77 billion (Pew Research Center 2019). In 2008, just 1 percent of total US households reported receiving a remittance from outside the country in the previous twelve months. This number rose to just 4 percent among foreign-born households (Grieco et al. 2010).

While emigration is not part of the American historical or present narrative, it remains the case that there are millions of Americans located all over the world – between 3 and 9 million. This is a notably smaller than the nearly 18 million Indians abroad, but the upper estimate would rank the United States fifth in the world (World Population Review 2022). What does the United States do to ensure their safety, protect their rights, and otherwise meet their many needs?

Diplomatic and Consular Dimension

The United States maintains a far-reaching system of embassies – in nearly every country. The size of US embassy staff is less a function of the number of US citizens living in the country than of US interests in that nation. For example, in 2012, the US embassy in Iraq had approximately 16,000 employees (Arango 2012), while the US embassy in Canada currently employs roughly 250 people (U.S. Embassy & Consulates in Canada n.d.). In 2022, although the UK had the second largest number of US citizens living abroad, the embassy staff totaled only 1,000 (US Embassy London: About n.d.) – far less than the embassy in Iraq at its peak, with far fewer US citizens.

The size of US embassies and US expatriate populations are not correlated for two reasons. First, as a global power, the United States has significant and varied interests all over the globe, and US embassies are, first and foremost, a tool for advancing those interests. Embassy staff perform significant diplomatic, security, economic, and intelligence functions that dwarf the US interest in serving the needs of its expatriate citizens. Second, as explained further on, the United States provides relatively few services to its citizens located abroad and thus does not require corresponding embassy staff. Intertwined material and ideological forces may account for the relative paucity of services provided. Traditional American antipathy toward the state provision of benefits, which has produced a less generous welfare state at home, may be at work abroad as well in limiting the scope of state-provided services (Bailyn 1968;

Huntington 1981; Friedberg 2000). At the same time, because so many Americans reside abroad, dispersed widely around the globe, providing equal access to such services would be very costly. However, the United States also has large numbers of military personnel permanently stationed abroad. Because the US government has different legal and ethical responsibilities to them, the discussion addresses separately US protections for active-duty military.

With respect to diplomatic functions, the United States provides its citizens abroad with travel information and assistance and basic consular services. The U.S. State Department has travel advisory and alert programs, and, in emergency situations, it reaches out to US travelers and expatriates enrolled in its Smart Traveler Enrollment Program. US consulates and embassies also help US citizens traveling and residing abroad with limited problems, by issuing new passports, providing logistical assistance in the event of medical or legal emergencies, and reporting missing persons or deaths abroad (U.S. Government n.d.). However, US consulates and embassies do not help citizens with more routine challenges such as recovering stolen property, assisting in paying for lodging, or mailing items back to the United States (Elliott 2022). Although the U.S. State Department is the main agency tasked with assisting overseas citizens, other agencies – such as the aforementioned Federal Voting Assistance Program – also provide citizens abroad with limited support. Regarding diplomatic functions, the United States is most similar to the UK (see Strong, Chapter 8) and Germany (see Brummer and Oppermann, Chapter 10) in providing relatively limited direct diplomatic support to its citizens abroad.

US citizens residing abroad retain the right to vote, but very few exercise that right – whether because voting at the local embassy or consulate is difficult or because expatriate Americans have low motivation. For example, in the high-turnout 2016 presidential election, 71.9 percent of eligible domestic voters cast a ballot, but only 6.9 percent of eligible US citizens overseas did. Turnout among overseas voters increased slightly in 2020 to 7.8 percent (FVAP 2020). Accounting for this 65-point difference in turnout, FVAP estimates that in 2016, 30.5 percent of eligible overseas voters did not vote because of obstacles to voting, and 34.4 percent did not cast a ballot because of "lack of interest or motivation" (FVAP 2018). One reason for the turnout gap is that voting in the United States is managed largely by the states, not the federal government. While federal law requires that each state provide a ballot in electronic form to overseas voters at least forty-five days before an election, states are ironically not required to accept electronically submitted ballots, and in fact, nineteen states do not (National Conference of State Legislatures 2020).

However, the peculiarities of the US federal system cannot be blamed for all the logistical challenges of overseas voting. Germans are also legally permitted to vote while residing abroad, but exercise that right to only a limited degree (Brummer and Oppermann, Chapter 10).

In addition to these more regular activities, the US government assists citizens abroad when two exceptional challenges to personal security arise. First, some 270 times between 1988 and 2007 the State Department has ordered an evacuation of its staff when a host state's security situation declines precipitously or a disease or natural disaster strikes the region (U.S. GAO 2007). When this happens, the US government urges, but cannot compel, US citizens to leave the country. It relies on a variety of tools – notably, social media – to warn US citizens of impending crises and to encourage them to leave. In these cases, the State Department generally does not directly provide US citizens who are not government employees with transportation. The US government has sometimes asked, or even compelled, US-based airlines to offer more commercial flights in support of the evacuation (Cullen and Josephs 2021), but the US military only rarely uses its own resources to transport citizens out of a country. The airlift of approximately 124,000 people, including an estimated 6,000 US citizens, from Afghanistan in August 2021 was the exception, not the rule. Other prominent evacuations took place from Libya in 2014, from Lebanon in 2006, from Haiti in 2004 (Fuentes 2021), and from Sudan in 2023 (Bowman et al. 2023). These operations were generally quite small, usually numbering in the hundreds of Americans, and most Americans in danger abroad have received just limited help from the US government. The Ukraine–Russia War is a more typical case: the Biden administration instructed US citizens in Ukraine to leave the country immediately, and, although the State Department provided logistical help and information, it did not coordinate a large-scale evacuation, and US citizens had to make their own arrangements (Chappell 2022).

Moreover, the US government does not take significant measures to protect US citizens worldwide. It has responsibility for the physical security of US government employees abroad, and in recent decades it has hired private security companies to ensure their security (Singer 2007). But this does not extend to private citizens, and the United States does not work closely with host states to protect them. Protecting US citizens worldwide would presumably present a great logistical challenge, and it might prove counterproductive: per the logic of "moral hazard," the guarantee of such protections might encourage US citizens to engage in riskier behaviors. In contrast, China has partnered closely with host states to protect its citizens (see Ghiselli, Chapter 5). But the fact that

China has focused on countries that employ thousands of Chinese workers on projects funded under its Belt-and-Road initiative raises questions about whether China is protecting its citizens – or its investments.

However, in response to the Covid-19 pandemic, the State Department facilitated a massive ad hoc repatriation program, ultimately repatriating 100,000 citizens over four months. The government arranged commercial flights, private charters, and flights on government aircraft. Many citizens paid the commercial or charter airline directly, although nearly 26,000 citizens signed promissory notes agreeing to repay the government for the cost of the flights. Unlike the normal State Department repatriation program, this one served citizens from all socioeconomic backgrounds and prospects. By June 5, 2020, the State Department had overseen 1,135 flights from 139 countries (US GAO 2021). Other Western countries, including Germany and the UK, that have normally been reluctant to help citizens abroad return home also provided extraordinary, direct assistance during the Covid crisis (see Strong, Chapter 8 and Brummer and Oppermann, Chapter 10).

US policy has been most notably tested when Americans are taken hostage. Because the United States cannot prevent its citizens from traveling or living anywhere across the world, including hostile and dangerous territories, US citizens have long been vulnerable to kidnapping. Hostage taking, in exchange for ransom, led to the first US war outside North America – against the Barbary Pirates in 1801–1805 and again in 1815–1816. It became a high-profile problem for the United States beginning in the 1970s, with a wave of airplane hijackings. US citizens have been taken captive abroad by either (1) non-state violent actors, for either political or pecuniary reasons, or (2) autocratic adversaries seeking political leverage. First, violent non-state actors have kidnapped dozens of Americans every decade over the last fifty years, seeking either policy concessions or ransom money. The geographical focus has shifted, from Latin America in the 1970s to Lebanon in the 1980s back to Latin America in the 1990s to the Middle East and North Africa in the twentieth-first century (Gilbert 2020; Jenkins 2018).

Second, America's nation-state adversaries have also periodically arrested US citizens under charges that have a veneer of legitimacy and subjected them to wrongful or arbitrary imprisonment. The case of US college student Otto Warmbier, who was arrested by North Korea in January 2016 on the pretext of stealing a propaganda poster from his hotel, suffered an unspecified injury and fell into a coma while in North Korean custody and then died very shortly after his release in June 2017, is particularly tragic. The basketball star Brittney Griner was arrested in February 2022 in Russia on minor drug charges amidst the outbreak of the Ukraine War and was released from custody ten months later in a negotiated swap for a convicted Russian arms dealer. *Wall Street Journal* reporter Evan Gershkovich was arrested by Russian authorities in March 2023 on espionage charges and, at the time of writing, remains in custody. These detainees then become bargaining chips, released after the US government offers the desired concessions (Gilbert 2019). The data for "hostage diplomacy" victims are less reliable, because it is not always clear when criminal charges are politically motivated. However, the best estimates suggest that this form of hostage-taking has become more prevalent – rising from no US hostages held by foreign governments in 2000 to 15 in 2010, to almost 40 in 2015, and peaking at nearly 60 in 2018 (Woodsome, Rezaian, and Whitehouse 2021). "Hostage diplomacy" can be effective at creating leverage for two reasons. First, it generates embarrassing and politically damaging media attention focused on the stories of particular victims (Gilbert 2020). Second, it constitutes a bilateral monopoly of one buyer and one seller, and "the target cannot take its recovery business elsewhere to protest the perpetrator's price" (Gilbert and Gaëlle Rivard 2021). Whether the hostage returns home or languishes in prison – or even faces execution or death from neglect – depends on whether the hostage's home state is willing to pay the demanded price.

Hostage-taking presents the US government with a dilemma. Paying the demanded ransom or making the desired policy concessions might only encourage more hostage-taking. For this reason, the US government's official long-standing policy has been not to negotiate with hostage-takers – "no concessions" – and US law technically forbids private individuals from paying ransoms to designated foreign terrorist organizations.[2] However, hostage families have often been vocally critical of the US government for neglecting their loved ones, and their personal plight generates pressure on the government to take action (Bergengruen 2022). In recent years, the civil society organizational network devoted to hostage advocacy and recovery has become better established and developed, notably with the setting-up of the James W. Foley Legacy Foundation in 2014, boosting families' advocacy efforts.

Subject to these contending considerations and stresses, the US government's policy in practice has been less absolute than its official "no

[2] See United States, 18 U.S. Code § 2339B – Providing Material Support or Resources to Designated Foreign Terrorist Organizations, n.d. U.S. law does not forbid the payment of ransoms to foreign governments, or non-state actors not designated terrorist groups, that hold Americans hostage, but there is no record of the U.S. government ever having done so.

concessions" rhetoric. Unlike Germany, which has on occasion paid ransoms to free captured citizens, the US government does not pay ransoms to secure hostages' release (Brummer and Oppermann, Chapter 10). However, the US also does not prevent families and friends from paying, and it has never strictly applied the law and prosecuted an individual for doing so (Gilbert 2019). There is some evidence that US government agents have on occasion facilitated ransom payments to foreign terrorist organizations (Barrett and Entous 2015). Backed by two presidential executive orders – Presidential Policy Directive 30 (PPD-30) and Executive Order 13698 – representatives of the US government have often worked with families of detained Americans and pursued negotiations to seek the release of hostages. Under pressure from the Foley Foundation and hostage families (Moriarty 2021), these practices were codified into law by the 2020 Levinson Act, named after Robert Levinson, a former FBI agent who disappeared in Iran in 2007 during an unauthorized mission for the CIA and was presumed by the US government to have died in Iranian custody in 2020 (CBS News 2020). According to his daughter, Sarah Moriarty, the Magnitsky Act, which empowered the US government to sanction individuals deemed responsible for human rights offenses, inspired similar powers in the Levinson Act (Hostage Aid Worldwide and James Foley Foundation 2021). The latter law granted the president authority to sanction individuals who are involved or "complicit in the unlawful or wrongful detention of a US national abroad" (United States 2020). Additionally, the act calls upon the US government to seek the release of US nationals held hostage and requires the president to appoint a Special Presidential Envoy for Hostage Affairs and establish an interagency Hostage Recovery Fusion Cell, which is staffed by officials from the Defense, Treasury, Justice, and State Departments, intelligence agencies, and other agencies deemed necessary (United States, *22 U.S. Code § 1741b – Hostage Recovery Fusion Cell* 2020).

In July 2022, President Biden signed Executive Order 14078 – "Bolstering Efforts to Bring Hostages and Wrongfully Detained Unites States Nationals Home" – in response to growing pressure from the families of US citizens held abroad (Pamuk and Alper 2022). When the secretary of state determines that a citizen has been "wrongfully detained," the order directs US government agencies to increase communication and coordination with the families of Americans held abroad, authorizes government agencies to impose financial sanctions on individuals directly or indirectly involved in Americans' wrongful detention, and declares the issue a national emergency (Hansler 2022). A determination of "wrongful detention" is warranted, according to the order's expansive list of criteria, if, among other factors, the citizen is thought to be innocent; the charges are likely politically motivated; the country does not have an independent judiciary; the individual is being detained to create leverage against the US government; the individual is being held in inhumane conditions; and the detention appears to be because the individual "sought to obtain, exercise, defend or promote freedom of the press, freedom of religion, or the right to peacefully assemble" (United States 2020). To try to secure the release of those wrongfully detained, the US government will pursue diplomatic solutions, boost public and international pressure, and conduct high level meetings to raise attention (United States Department of State n.d.c).[3] Some detainee advocates have criticized the executive order for adding little additional capacity beyond existing executive orders and legislation and for granting US officials excessive discretion in how they pursue detainees' release (Pamuk and Alper 2022). It is true that the US government's approach to specific cases of wrongful detention has been tailored to the circumstances, but the 2022 executive order reflects the fact that high-profile wrongful detentions of US citizens have been increasingly prominent in geopolitics. The UK has charted a similar course with respect to hostage-taking: becoming involved reluctantly, but recently developing a more formal system for coordinating response (Strong, Chapter 8).

The increase in "hostage diplomacy" may also be responsible for this recent shift in US government policy and practice. A "hostage" is any American blocked from leaving a foreign country. It is simpler, both legally and politically, for the US government, led by the State Department, to negotiate with governments, rather than non-state actors, over the return of "wrongfully detained" US citizens. Furthermore, other options, like hostage rescue operations, are much less likely to be successful when a citizen is held by a foreign government (Gilbert and Gaëlle Rivard 2021). When it comes to hostages, the FBI and other intelligence organizations lead the effort to secure their release (Jakes and Kannapell 2023). The case of Brittney Griner is instructive about the circumstances under which the US government intervenes in such cases. Griner is a WNBA star, who had entered Russia to play in the Russian Premier League. She was arrested at the beginning of the Russia–Ukraine War in February

[3] Assistance to citizens that have been legally detained – i.e. the Secretary of State has determined that they have not been "wrongfully detained" – is more limited. It generally includes only coordinating communication with the detainee's family, monitoring their conditions, providing the family with an overview of the country's legal system, and referring them to local attorneys (Arrest or Detention of a U.S. Citizen Abroad 2023).

2022, after Russian customs officials found minuscule amounts of hashish oil in vape cartridges in her luggage. Swift, direct US government involvement in Griner's case was the result of a unique confluence of circumstances: Griner's unusually high profile as a famous professional athlete and the geopolitical context of Russia's open violation of Ukraine's sovereignty. The US government would surely not have involved itself in Griner's case, let alone freed a notorious Russian arms smuggler in exchange for her release, if not for the impressive power of Griner's family, friends, and professional networks to generate public awareness of and sympathy for her cause. Even that might not have been enough if not for the context of the Ukraine War.

US efforts to seek the release of its citizens taken hostage by Palestinian militants on October 7, 2023 are similarly revealing of the idiosyncratic and uncertain nature of US hostage diplomacy. After ten US citizens were taken prisoner in the Hamas-led attacks on Israel, President Biden took a personal interest in their release. The US government pressured Israel's government to agree to a pause in military operations to facilitate hostage swapping (Baker 2023), flew drones over Gaza to help locate captured US citizens (Stewart and Ali 2023), and sent U.S. Special Operation Forces to Israel to help locate the hostages (Schmitt 2023). The US government has devoted unusual resources to seeking these hostages' release because the October 7 attacks were unprecedented in their scale and brutality, the larger hostage crisis was international in scope (with an estimated 240 hostages holding citizenship from 25 different countries), and the hostages' families were very effective in garnering attention in major US and international media outlets and political forums, including the United Nations. The case though also reveals the limits of US power: at the time of writing, over two months after the attacks, just 1 US citizen has been released.

Finally, the US government takes a particularly assertive role in protecting its active-duty military citizens abroad. The United States is globally unique in its large number of military personnel permanently stationed abroad. Those numbers have fluctuated over the last thirty years, from around 400,000 at the end of the Cold War and the height of the Iraq War in 2003 to approximately 170,000 in 2021 (Siebens, Lucas, and Wang 2021). Yet, as of 2021, the US still had roughly 750 military installations across roughly 80 countries and territories (Vine 2021). It maintains Status of Force Agreements (SOFAs) with many countries that host US military personnel, which detail the "rights and responsibilities of military forces stationed on foreign soil" and provide legal protection for US servicepeople (Gher 2002). The number of SOFAs grew alongside the US military's global footprint after 9/11, and these newer SOFAs increasingly granted the United States "exclusive jurisdiction," stipulating that US military personnel must be tried in US military courts rather than host-nation courts (Herrin 2020; Efrat 2022a, 2022b). In 2003, the United States stipulated that all future SOFAS should aim to provide US troops nearly full diplomatic immunity (Efrat 2022b). Even when the host country maintained criminal jurisdiction, however, US influence remained substantial. According to Department of Defense data, between 1954 and 1970, in over half the cases in which US military personnel were charged with crimes committed on foreign soil, the host government waived its jurisdiction. Although, over this span, thousands of US servicemembers were charged with serious violent crimes – robbery, rape, aggravated assault, and murder – just 121 were sent to jail for more than five years (Efrat 2022a). Nevertheless, the US government has so prioritized legal protections for its soldiers that the failure to negotiate an acceptable SOFA has had significant consequences for US foreign policy – notably leading the Obama administration in 2011 to withdraw from Iraq even residual US forces that advised and trained the Iraqi army.

Like US civilians, US military personnel are sometimes taken hostage abroad, and the US military has then taken the lead role in hostage recovery. Its specific policies have varied depending on the circumstances and the geopolitical situation. For example, in 1999, three US peacekeepers were captured while conducting patrols at the Serbian–Macedonian border and held hostage for over a month by Serbia. The US civil rights leader Jesse Jackson, without official support from the White House, led a delegation to Belgrade that successfully negotiated their release. In exchange, Jackson reportedly carried a letter from President Slobodan Milosevic to President Clinton, outlining Milosevic's proposals for a settlement of the Kosovo Crisis (Page 1999; Rodgers et al. 1999). In contrast, in May 2007, several US soldiers on patrol south of Baghdad were kidnapped in Iraq by a Sunni insurgent group. Fearing their execution, the US military unsuccessfully conducted large-scale searches for the captured soldiers, and they were eventually killed (Morgan 2008). In contrast, Bowe Bergdahl, at the time a Private First Class in the U.S. Army,[4] deserted his post in Afghanistan in 2009 and was subsequently captured by Taliban forces. The US government's decision to secure Bergdahl's release in exchange for five high-ranking Taliban held in

[4] Bergdahl was subsequently promoted, in absentia, to Specialist and then Sergeant, but he was later then demoted to Private as part of his dishonorable discharge from the Army.

Guantanamo Bay proved very controversial – especially after Bergdahl was court-martialed and pled guilty to misbehavior before the enemy and desertion.

Economic and Social Dimension

The scholarly consensus is that the US government's outreach to and engagement with American expatriates is paltry. Klekowski von Koppenfels finds that "there is no consistent or institutionalized engagement by the United States with its own overseas population as a distinct diaspora" (2019). Dashefsky speculates that this may be because "emigration doesn't fit the narrative of the United States. Our ideological bias is that we are a country of immigrants. Why would anybody want to leave the United States?" (Best 2020). Whatever the reason, the US government has neither created nor funded a robust system to provide Americans living abroad with social and cultural activities that remind them of home and sustain their attachments to the United States. This stands in marked contrast to Germany and Türkiye, which fund significant cultural programs to cultivate community amongst their expatriates and encourage ties to their homeland (Brummer and Oppermann, Chapter 10 and Akbaba, Chapter 12).

The US government does run significant programs that bring American culture to foreign audiences. These programs benefit the Americans who participate in them and expatriates may enjoy them as well, but the primary audiences are foreign nationals. The leading cultural exchange program funded by the US government is the Fulbright Program. For US citizens who are recent college graduates and graduate students, as well as young professionals and artists, the Fulbright U.S. Student Program offers the opportunity to study, conduct research, and teach English abroad. A second track sends established professionals, artists, and scholars abroad to teach, conduct research, and work in their area of expertise. There are also more specific programs, such as the Fulbright Arctic Initiative. The program also famously provides non-US citizens with opportunities in the United States, but those are not our concern here. In total, the Fulbright program awards roughly 8,000 fellowships each year across all programs and initiatives, with on average roughly 3,000 going to US citizens. Overall, the program has awarded about 400,000 fellowships over the course of its history (United States Department of State n.d.a). Although the Fulbright program is an established and prestigious means of forging connections between Americans and foreign nationals, it is not aimed at providing assistance to US citizens already living abroad.

US embassies offer cultural programs that include film, music, sports, and educational activities. Some embassies have built "American Spaces" to educate local residents about US culture, politics, economics, and education. The US embassy in India has established these sites in New Delhi, Chennai, Hyderabad, and Ahmedabad, and they also offer workshops on various topics including helping participants study for English-language exams (U.S. Embassy & Consulates in India n.d.). Such programs are typically modest: in 2021, the State Department spent just $15 million worldwide on the American Spaces program – out of its overall annual budget of $53 billion (United States Department of State 2020). Embassy cultural programs are also not designed for US citizens living abroad. Their primary purpose is bolstering America's "soft power": facilitating knowledge of, sympathy for, and the appeal of American culture and society. US citizens traveling and living abroad may avail themselves of these programs, but they are not the intended audience.

By contrast, support for US businesses that operate abroad is far more robust. There are generally three areas in which the US government advances the fortunes of American businesses: negotiating international trade and investment agreements and insisting on their enforcement; bolstering protection for Americans' property, including intellectual property, through multilateral organizations, the prospect of economic sanctions and other forms of punishment, and strong laws prohibiting counterfeit products from being sold or distributed in the United States; and promoting exports. The first two categories mostly entail policy development and enforcement. Only the last category involves providing services abroad to the representatives of US corporations.

The Congressional Research Service estimates that twenty government agencies assist US businesses in export promotion. These agencies use four distinct strategies to promote exports: direct export assistance services, such as trade missions and business matchmaking services; feasibility studies of proposed projects abroad; export financing and insurance; and government-to-government advocacy (Ilias, Hanrahan, and Villarreal 2013). For example, in 2010, US export promotion agencies conducted 35 trade missions abroad with over 400 companies participating. Additionally, in FY2011, the Export–Import Bank authorized $32.7 billion in loans, guarantees, and export credit insurance. Furthermore, in 2010, commercial advocacy led to the sale of American aircraft to Saudi Arabia and Türkiye for a total US export content of $5.1 billion (Ilias et al. 2011).

One especially notable agency is the United States Commercial Service (USCS) located within the International Trade Administration (ITA). It promotes the "export of goods and services from the United States, particularly by small- and medium-sized businesses." The agency also helps US businesses find international trading partners abroad and represents US companies internationally. USCS has 106 locations throughout the United States but also maintains significant presence abroad, with officers in approximately 150 cities across 80 countries (United States Trade Representative n.d.). Within the US, these offices are generally U.S. Export Assistance Centers (USEACs) that help businesses expand or develop their exports. They provide "counseling, planning, and financing services," and also help identify target markets, financing opportunities, and market strategies. The staff located abroad help US businesses connect with local counterparts by facilitating trade shows and by bringing foreign businesses and governments to the United States (Ilias, Hanrahan, and Villarreal 2013). In 2022, the USCS budget was roughly $340 million. The agency claimed it helped over 42,000 clients "achieve nearly $92 billion in US exports and inward investment." Among them was a company in Oregon that USCS claimed it helped negotiate a $3.5 billion contract with Romania to export and deploy clean energy technology throughout the country to replace coal-fired powerplants (United States International Trade Administration 2022). The Export–Import Bank also plays an important role in federal export promotion by providing direct loans and export credit guarantees and insurance. In FY2012, it approved nearly 4,000 credit and insurance support transactions totaling $35.8 billion, with much of this activity supporting the export of capital-intensive goods. Although an important part of US export promotion, in FY2012, the bank supported less than 5 percent of US exports (Ilias, Hanrahan, and Villarreal 2013).

Export promotion, however, is no longer the responsibility of the federal government alone. State governments also help businesses promote their exports abroad. In 2018, the US government awarded $18 million in grants designed to promote small-business exports to 47 states through the State Trade Expansion Program (STEP) (U.S. Small Business Administration 2020). Sometimes states will set aside their own funds for export promotion, although these funds are often quite limited. For example, in 2022, the state of Michigan announced $1.4 million in funds to promote export assistance for small and medium-sized businesses by providing grants for trade missions, international sales trips, website translation, trade show attendance, and international certifications, among other activities (Michigan Economic Development Corporation 2022).

Finally, the US government does not maintain any programs to encourage or incentivize citizens living abroad to return home. It does have several temporary assistance programs. The first, run by the U.S.

Department of Health & Human Services, dates back to 1935, for citizens living abroad who return to the United States "because of destitution, illness, war, threat of war, or a similar crisis, and are without available resources" (U.S. Department of Health & Human Services n.d.). Through this program, US citizens and their dependents can be provided with housing assistance, counseling, money payments, medical care, and transportation. Assistance is provided as a loan that must be repaid, although the program will consider forgiveness if the citizen is unable to repay. However, this program assists only a tiny number of US citizens in any given year – far less than 1,000 per year, over the last decade (U.S. Department of Health & Human Services n.d.; Congressional Research Service 2020). Its budget is capped at just $1 million annually, but Congress has increased its budget during emergencies. In 2010, because of a major earthquake in Haiti, the program repatriated 28,500 citizens. Congress increased the caps in 1990–1991 due to the first Iraq War and then again in 2003 because of the second Iraq War. Some state governments maintain their own repatriation programs, with similar emergency terms (e.g., Texas Health and Human Services, Texas Repatriation Program n.d.). The State Department also repatriates citizens through a similar loan process that is designed for citizens and their families who face extreme poverty if they remain abroad (U.S. Embassy in Albania n.d.) Between 2015 and the beginning of 2019, it had repatriated only 6,000 people. In contrast, China maintains major programs, notably the Thousand Talents Plan, to encourage citizens – especially highly educated citizens – to return home (Ghiselli, Chapter 5).

Security Dimension

The US military infrequently engages in operations to provide protection to US civilians traveling and residing abroad. It has rarely been involved in evacuations of citizens during crises, and it has even more rarely attempted to rescue Americans located in precarious security situations or being held hostage. Given the preponderance of US military power since the end of the Second World War, this might seem surprising. But the reasons seem clear. First, there are simply too many Americans living and traveling abroad to offer them meaningful protection. Second, if Americans traveling and residing abroad thought US intervention on their behalf was guaranteed, they would have little incentive to refrain from risky behavior. Third, rather than deterring attacks on US civilians, the prospect of US military intervention could ironically invite their targeting – as local political actors eager to burnish their credentials might be even more likely to target Americans.

However, the connections between US military power and its citizens' interests run deeper. For much of the nineteenth century, with the important exception of the Barbary Wars (1801–1805 and 1815–1816), US military force was rarely deployed outside North America. The US military was nevertheless quite busy protecting US citizens and advancing their economic interests – by hounding, expelling, and slaughtering Native Americans and conquering the continent. The nation's westward expansion at Native Americans' expense created numerous opportunities, especially for White Americans, to profit from the bountiful land that they would settle, farm, log, and mine. The U.S. Army's missions included preventing and avenging attacks on White settlers and more generally clearing the land for its "productive" use (Ostler 2019; Immerwahr 2019). Once the nation's Manifest Destiny – its providential mission to spread its supposedly superior institutions across the continent – was fulfilled, however, and as US military power grew, it began to set its sights abroad (Stephanson 1996).

At the turn of the twentieth century, the US began conducting frequent military interventions to protect American citizens, as well as their property and business interests abroad, especially in Latin America and Asia. A critical turning point came in 1898, when President William McKinley reluctantly dispatched the warship *Maine* to Cuba to protect US citizens and property after a revolt and subsequent harsh crackdown by the Spanish government (LaFeber 2013). A few years later, President Theodore Roosevelt announced that the United States had an obligation to intervene in Latin America to ensure foreign governments paid their debts and maintained solvency – the so-called "Roosevelt Corollary" (Boot 2014). US policy-makers' goals included establishing regional stability and increasing US geopolitical influence, but this policy was also surely designed to protect the business and financial interests of US citizens. The United States often employed financial coercion in enforcing the Roosevelt Corollary, but military force lurked in the background, bolstering the efficacy of these economic instruments. And, with some frequency between 1890 and the 1930s, it burst into the foreground, as U.S. Marines intervened some 180 times in Cuba, Panama, Nicaragua, Haiti, the Dominican Republic, the Philippines, and China (Boot 2014). Financial coercion, backed by military power, underpinned Dollar Diplomacy, which drew little distinction between the private interests of major American corporations and the interests of the nation (Veeser 2002).

US military interventions that directly served the interests of corporate America largely came to an end with the Great Depression, but military power remained an important tool in constructing a global economic system in which US corporations would thrive and in which US capital would circle the globe. After the Second World War, the US military's presence around the world dramatically increased in the name of combatting global communism, but one is hard-pressed to attribute specific military interventions to concrete business interests (Odell 1974).[5] In fact, US-led efforts at regime change generally resulted in less, rather than more, bilateral trade (Zachary, Deloughery, and Downes 2017). However, the US consistently sought to create and sustain a global system that protects financial capital, open access to markets, and private property (LaFeber 2013). The views of US-based business elites frequently coincided with policy-makers in the US government (Jacobs and Page 2005). In the 1950s, many thought that "what is good for General Motors is good for America," and US decision-makers also firmly believed that, by removing the barriers to the free exchange of goods and services and building a liberal international political economy, they were serving the common good. US military forces that kept communism at bay were making possible an international economic order that benefited all and that, by promoting growth and development everywhere, further bolstered peace among the United States and its allies (Packenham 1973; Mazower 2012).

One notable exception to the otherwise limited use of the US military to protect civilians abroad was the failed rescue attempt of American hostages held in Iran after the revolution in 1979. Operation Eagle Claw was a highly risky operation involving eight RH-53 D Sea Stallion helicopters, six C-130 Transport planes, and ninety-seven US troops. The rescue operation was executed on April 24, 1980 but was aborted within several hours when a Sea Stallion helicopter crashed into a transport plane in the midst of a sandstorm in the Iranian desert, killing eight soldiers. It served, if anything, as a negative precedent. First, very few of the hostages were private citizens. Nearly all were government civilian employees or military servicepeople. Second, it was an abject failure and cautionary tale that hurt America's international prestige and called into question its military capabilities (Glad 2009).

[5] A possible exception is 1970s Chile. The CIA and the US-based ITT Corporation drew up a plan to overthrow the Allende regime covertly through financial coercion, in part because ITT was concerned about their investments in the country (Rosen 1974). However, such a close collaboration between the US government and individual US business interests was more the exception than the rule after the Second World War and was certainly less common than in the Dollar Diplomacy era. US foreign policy during the Cold War did prefer right-wing governments for various reasons, including their receptivity to US and international business and economic activities (Rosen 1974). But this was a more general structural imperative to "make the world safe for capital." It was not a result of the US government doing the bidding of particular business interests.

While the specific ways in which the US used military force to protect its citizens and promote their interests evolved alongside America's rise to power, we should not lose sight of a constant thread. The US has, in its foreign policy, not drawn clear distinctions between the interests of its private citizens and those of the nation and globe. That line is necessarily somewhat blurry in any liberal polity, which is committed to responsive government. But that line has been especially blurry in an America long persuaded of its exceptionalism. US policy-makers often believed that those who prevented private citizens from pursuing their economic well-being by impeding the free flow of capital, goods, and services were both preventing America from achieving its destiny and undermining the global public good. By using military force to clear North America of Native Americans, to open the door to commerce in Latin America and Asia, and to support an interlocking system of liberal international economic institutions, the US government saw itself as advancing the interests of its citizens, the United States, and the world.

Overt repression of its citizens abroad has not been a central feature of US policy. But the US government has nevertheless employed coercive authority over its citizens abroad in two main ways: via travel controls and surveillance. Starting with travel controls, the US government has used passport denial and no-fly lists to control Americans' ability to travel. It has thereby, either temporarily or indefinitely, prevented US citizens from moving freely around the globe, leaving the US, and even from returning home. First employed in the early twentieth century as a tool to control the movement of "radicals," passport denial reached its apex in the 1950s, along with the "Red Scare." Exact numbers are difficult to obtain, as different government agencies released conflicting information, and agencies were less than transparent. For example, the U.S. State Department's Division of Passport Control reported that it denied over 8,000 passports in 1956 alone, but it attributed just 275 passport denials between 1952 and 1956 to applicants' communist affiliation. This was surely an understatement, as the division provided no explanation for the vast majority of the denials (Lebovic 2020). Moreover, many on the Left were very likely dissuaded from even applying for a passport in the first place. Court battles in the early 1960s greatly diminished the discretion of the Division of Passport Control to deny passports (Rogers 1985). Today, US citizens cannot be refused passports because of opaque national security concerns, but only if they have outstanding tax debt, face a federal or state criminal court order or a federal warrant for arrest, or if their parole or probation prevents international travel. This potentially affects millions of Americans: in 2018, at least 362,000 Americans were in danger of being denied passports if they did not settle their tax debts (Saunders 2018; United States Department of State n.d.b).

However, US government travel controls still exist in the form of travel watchlists, including no-fly lists. In the over two decades since 9/11, thousands of US citizens have been affected by these lists, which have blocked them from entering or exiting the country and have sometimes stranded them abroad for months. Lawsuits challenging no-fly lists have had limited success. In response to a court decision in 2014, the US government developed procedures ensuring US citizens would be told if they were on a no-fly list and would be provided an opportunity to challenge the decision, but the use of no-fly lists continues (Kahn 2013; Savage 2021). Travel controls are legitimated on the grounds of security, but they are also a means of punishing those the government deems undesirable and compelling others to toe the line.

Surveillance is a less overt, but very powerful means of coercion. The vast US intelligence community constitutes a surveillance system that is "continuous, general, routine, systematic, impersonal, and ubiquitous" (Lyons 2003). US intelligence agencies' abuses at home and abroad are both well documented, but also necessarily impossible to quantify (Theoharis 2011; Reeves 2017). During the Cold War, they conducted domestic surveillance on perceived enemies of the state – communists, homosexuals, and other "radicals" and "subversives," including civil rights activists. Employees of the US government, including those who lived and worked abroad, were frequent targets of surveillance and abuse in the 1950s and 1960s. Many were subjected to forced interrogations that often resulted in dismissal if they were suspected of being (or even just fraternizing with) communists, homosexuals, or other "subversives." Between 1947 and 1956, roughly 5 million federal employees faced these "loyalty screenings," ultimately leading to 2,700 dismissals and 12,000 resignations (Storrs 2015). Investigators would sometimes offer to "forgive" suspected offenses if the employee cooperated with the authorities by naming other "subversives" (Johnson 2006). The 9/11 attacks, along with technological changes that allowed the intelligence community to vacuum up immense swaths of communications data, supercharged the reach and intensity of US surveillance (Reeves 2017). US citizens abroad were not unique targets of US surveillance activities, but nor were they subject to significant protections in practice when they came within its crosshairs.

US citizens have meaningful but imperfect protections from indiscriminate surveillance. Broadly speaking, US citizens and permanent residents cannot be legally, intentionally, and directly surveiled, whether at home or abroad, unless intelligence agencies can show probable cause that the citizen is an "agent" of a foreign power or "knowingly" violated criminal laws (Shults 2011). However, after 9/11, US intelligence agencies were given wide latitude to conduct warrantless surveillance on non-citizens outside the US, which created a "backdoor" to surveilling citizens and permanent residents if they interacted with a foreign surveillance target. Intelligence agencies often searched this data to collect information on Americans, even though they were not the intended target of the initial surveillance. In 2021, the FBI ran 3.4 million searches for data on US citizens, although this number fell to 204,000 in 2022 after data use reforms (Doshi 2023).

Conclusion

The United States has historically provided limited direct services to its citizens who live abroad. It has not generally sought to guarantee their physical safety, it has provided very limited consular and diplomatic assistance, and it has offered few appealing cultural activities to sustain their ties home. A mix of factors – especially logistical challenges, the country's exceptionalist identity, and its limited welfare state at home – are likely contributing factors. Only in rare instances, notably hostage-taking, does the US government reluctantly become directly involved, driven by media pressure. In contrast, the US government's direct and indirect support of American businesses operating abroad has been much more expansive. This is partly due to the congruence of beliefs and preferences between US business leaders and government officials, and perhaps also to the activities of organized business lobbies. Since the Second World War, the US has effectively advanced the interests of its citizens *indirectly* – by using its military, economic, and diplomatic power to shape the larger international order and to foster a web of institutions, organizations, laws, and regulations with which Americans were constitutionally familiar, in which Americans could thrive, and in which American capital could freely invest and reap profits. We found little evidence that the US has co-opted its citizens into serving the interests of the state – perhaps because the postwar US built powerful military, diplomatic, and intelligence organizations with a global reach to advance its interests abroad.

Since its rise to global power amidst the world wars, the US has at times targeted its citizens for coercion. But its repressive hand has, in comparative terms, been fairly light, limited to travel controls and surveillance. US courts, responding to lawsuits initiated by US citizens harmed by US government action, have sometimes reined in US security agencies' worst excesses. But those agencies, despite their immense power, have also recognized limits to their authority, especially where US citizens are concerned. The relative transparency of the US government, its systems of accountability and the rule of law, its ideological commitment to liberal values, all operate less reliably outside the nation's borders and in the arenas of security and intelligence, but they nevertheless do seem to have had a moderating effect on these agencies' natural inclination to repression.

We do not foresee significant changes in most of these arenas in the short-to-medium run. It seems likely that the US will continue to attract more immigrants than it fosters emigrants. Notwithstanding its relative decline, for the foreseeable future, the United States will remain a preeminent global power with global interests. It is possible that, as international terrorism becomes less of a priority for the US government, activities to control travel via no-fly zones and watch lists may be relaxed. If the United States does retrench, shrinking its military footprint, its capacity to protect US citizens will decrease accordingly.

However, there may be two notable exceptions. First, in an increasingly competitive global economic environment, in which US political influence is declining, US citizens located overseas may start to insist that the US government take a more active hand in tilting the economic tables in their direction. They may increasingly come to doubt that indirect, systemic influence can alone ensure their prosperity. The pressures on the US government for more direct intervention, to boost the prospects of its citizens abroad, are likely to build over time. Second, if the geopolitical environment becomes increasingly competitive, revolving around US–China rivalry, US government agencies may intervene more energetically – not only to support its citizens, as the nation's economic foot-soldiers, but perhaps to repress them as well.

References

American Citizens Abroad (2017) *How Are We Counted?* Available at: www.americansabroad.org/how-are-we-counted/ (last accessed July 1, 2022).

Arango, Tim (2012) U.S. Is Planning to Cut Its Staff at Iraq Embassy by as Much as Half. *New York Times*, February 7. Available at: www.nytimes.com/2012/02/08/world/middleeast/united-states-planning-to-slash-iraq-embassy-staff-by-half.html?pagewanted=2&_r=1&hp (last accessed June 6, 2022).

Bailyn, Bernard (1967) *The Ideological Origins of the American Revolution*. Cambridge, MA: Harvard University Press.

Baker, Peter (2023) Biden Hopes to Alter the Trajectory of the War as Hostages Are Released. *New York Times*, November 27. Available at: www.nytimes.com/2023/11/27/us/politics/biden-israel-hamas-hostages.html (last accessed December 6, 2023).

Barrett, Devlin, and Adam Entous (2015) FBI Helped Facilitate Ransom for U.S. Hostage Killed in Drone Strike. *Wall Street Journal*, April 29. Available at: www.wsj.com/articles/fbi-helped-facilitate-ransom-for-u-s-hostage-killed-in-drone-strike-1430328084 (last accessed June 7, 2022).

Bergengruen, Vera (2022) Families of American Hostages Demand Biden Do More. *Time*, May 5. Available at: https://time.com/6173655/american-hostages-joe-biden/ (last accessed June 1, 2022).

Best, Kenneth (2020) Americans Abroad: Escaping or Enhancing Life? *UConn Today*, August 7. Available at: https://today.uconn.edu/2020/08/americans-abroad-escaping-enhancing-life/ (last accessed April 8, 2022).

Bon Tempo, Carl (2011) American Exceptionalism and Immigration Debates in the Modern United States. In S. Söderlind and J. T. Carson (eds.), *American Exceptionalisms: From Winthrop to Winfrey*. Albany, NY: State University of New York Press, 147–166.

Boot, Max (2014) *The Savage Wars of Peace: Small Wars and the Rise of American Power* (Revised edition). New York: Basic Books.

Bowman, Emma, Tom Bowman, and Joe Hernandez (2023) The U.S. Evacuates Some 1,000 Americans from Sudan. *NPR*, April 30. Available at: www.npr.org/2023/04/29/1172916366/sudan-us-e©vacuation (last accessed July 3, 2023).

CBS News (2020) *For First Time, U.S. Formally Blames Iran for Presumed Death of Former FBI Agent Robert Levinson*, December 14. Available at: www.cbsnews.com/news/robert-levinson-death-iran-trump-administration-blame/ (last accessed December 6, 2022).

Chappell, Bill (2022) Biden Tells U.S. Citizens to Leave Ukraine, Saying Military Wouldn't Rescue Them. *NPR*, February 11. Available at: www.npr.org/2022/02/11/1080060546/biden-us-citizens-leave-ukraine (last accessed April 29, 2022).

Cohen, Warren (2013) *The New Cambridge History of American Foreign Relations: Challenges to American Primacy, 1945 to the Present*, Vol. 4. Cambridge: Cambridge University Press.

Congressional Research Service (2020) *U.S. Repatriation Program for Citizens Returned from Abroad*. Available at: https://crsreports.congress.gov/product/details?prodcode=IF11484&__cf_chl_tk=tvaroOvuDF3W46ZkxvURikD6SaMK.4sqGKB8jS5PkvA-1665589302-0-gaNycGzNCOU (last accessed November 2, 2022).

Costanzo, Joe, and Amanda Klekowski Von Koppenfels (2013) Counting the Uncountable: Overseas Americans. *Migrationpolicy.org*, May 17. Available at: www.migrationpolicy.org/article/counting-uncountable-overseas-americans (last accessed May 23, 2022).

Cullen, Terri, and Leslie Josephs (2021) Pentagon Orders U.S. Airlines to Help Fly Afghanistan Evacuees. *CNBC*, August 22. Available at: www.cnbc.com/2021/08/22/biden-administration-activates-civil-reserve-air-fleet.html (last accessed November 1, 2022).

Doshi, Juhi (2023) What Is Section 702? Congress Is Debating the Controversial Surveillance Power. *NBC News*, 31 July. Available at: www.nbcnews.com/politics/congress/section-702-foreign-intelligence-surveillance-act-congress-what-know-rcna96259 (last accessed August 4, 2023).

Dulles, Foster Rhea (1966) A Historical View of Americans Abroad. *Annals of the American Academy of Political and Social Science* 368, 11–20.

Efrat, Asif (2022a) Facing US Extraterritorial Pressure: American Troops in Foreign Courts during the Cold War. *Journal of Politics* 84(1), 242–257.

Efrat, Asif (2022b) How to Handle Offending Troops Overseas: The U.S. Military's Legal Strategy during the Cold War. *Armed Forces & Society*, OnlineFirst, doi.org/10.1177/0095327X211061423.

Elliott, Christopher (2022) When Should Travelers Call a U.S. Embassy or Consulate? *Washington Post*, February 16. Available at: www.washingtonpost.com/travel/2022/02/16/travelers-united-states-embassy/ (last accessed October 17, 2022).

Friedberg, Aaron L. (2000) *In the Shadow of the Garrison State: America's Anti-statism and Its Cold War Grand Strategy*. Princeton, NJ: Princeton University Press.

Fuentes, Gidget (2021) Afghanistan Exit Latest in Long History of U.S. Noncombatant Evacuation Missions. *USNI News*, 17 August. Available at: https://news.usni.org/2021/08/17/afghanistan-exit-latest-in-long-history-of-u-s-noncombatant-evacuation-missions (last accessed November 29, 2022).

Gher, Jaime (2002) Status of Forces Agreements: Tools to Further Effective Foreign Policy and Lessons to Be Learned from the United States–Japan Agreement Comment. *University of San Francisco Law Review* 37(1), 227–256.

Gilbert, Danielle (2019) 'No Concessions'? A Closer Look at U.S. Hostage Recovery Policy. *War on the Rocks*, 27 February. Available at: https://warontherocks.com/2019/02/no-concessions-a-closer-look-at-u-s-hostage-recovery-policy/ (last accessed June 7, 2022).

Gilbert, Danielle (2020) The Oxygen of Publicity: Explaining U.S. Media Coverage of International Kidnapping. *Studies in Conflict & Terrorism*, OnlineFirst, doi.org/10.1080/1057610X.2020.1792723.

Gilbert, Danielle, and Piché Gaëlle Rivard (2021) Caught between Giants: Hostage Diplomacy and Negotiation Strategy for Middle Powers. *Texas National Security Review* 5(1), 11–32.

Glad, Betty (2009) *An Outsider in the White House: Jimmy Carter, His Advisors, and the Making of American Foreign Policy*. Ithaca, NY: Cornell University Press.

Grieco, Elizabeth, Patricia De La Cruz, Rachel Cortes, and Luke Larsen (2010) Who in the United States Sends and Receives Remittances? An Initial Analysis of the Monetary Transfer Data from the Aug. 2008 CPS Migration Supplement. *United States Census Bureau*. Available at: www.census.gov/library/working-papers/2010/demo/POP-twps0087.html (last accessed June 6, 2022).

Hansler, Jennifer (2022) White House Unveils New Executive Order on US Hostages and Wrongful Detainees. *CNN*, July 19, 2022. Available at: www.cnn.com/2022/07/19/politics/executive-order-hostages-wrongful-detainees-biden/index.html (last accessed December 8, 2023).

Herrin, Aubree (2020) *Understanding Status of Forces Agreements: What Shapes Jurisdictional Control?* PhD diss., University of Iowa, Iowa City.

Hostage Aid Worldwide and James Foley Foundation (2021) Hostage Aid Worldwide Launch Event. Available at: www.youtube.com/watch?v=KRinHoK92fM (last accessed December 6, 2022).

Huntington, Samuel P. (1981) *American Politics: The Promise of Disharmony.* Cambridge, MA: Belknap Press of Harvard University Press.

Ilias, Shayerah, Charles Hanrahan, and Angeles Villarreal (2013) U.S. Government Agencies Involved in Export Promotion: Overview and Issues for Congress. *Congressional Research Service.* Available at: https://sgp.fas.org/crs/misc/R41495.pdf (last accessed October 11, 2022).

Ilias, Shayerah, Wayne Morrison, Ian Fergusson, and Angeles Villarreal (2011) Boosting U.S. Exports: Selected Issues for Congress. *Congressional Research Service.* Available at: https://crsreports.congress.gov/product/pdf/R/R41929/8. (last accessed September 10, 2022).

Immerwahr, Daniel (2019) *How to Hide an Empire: A History of the Greater United States.* New York: Farrar, Straus and Giroux.

Jacobs, Lawrence, and Benjamin Page (2005) Who Influences U.S. Foreign Policy? *American Political Science Review* 99(1), 107–23.

Jakes, Lara, and Andrea Kannapell (2023) What Does 'Wrongfully Detained' Mean? *New York Times*, April 10, 2023. Available at: www.nytimes.com/2023/04/10/world/europe/wrongfully-detained-us-citizens.html (last accessed December 5, 2023).

Jenkins, Brian (2018) *Does the U.S. No-Concessions Policy Deter Kidnappings of Americans?* Washington, DC: The RAND Corporation.

Johnson, David K (2006) *The Lavender Scare: The Cold War Persecution of Gays and Lesbians in the Federal Government.* Chicago, IL: University of Chicago Press.

Kahn, Jeffrey (2013) *Mrs. Shipley's Ghost: The Right to Travel and Terrorist Watchlists.* Ann Arbor, MI: University of Michigan Press.

Klekowski von Koppenfels, Amanda (2014) *Migrants or Expatriates? Americans in Europe.* New York: Palgrave Macmillan.

Klekowski von Koppenfels, Amanda (2019) The Disinterested State: Negative Diasporic Policy as an Expression of State Inclusion and National Exclusion. *Journal of Ethnic and Migration Studies* 45(4), 595–612.

LaFeber, William (2013) *The American Search for Opportunity, 1865–1913.* In *The New Cambridge History of American Foreign Relations*, Vol. 2. Cambridge: Cambridge University Press.

Lebovic, Sam (2020) No Right to Leave the Nation: The Politics of Passport Denial and the Rise of the National Security State. *Studies in American Political Development* 34(1), 170–193.

Lyon, David (2003) *Surveillance after September 11.* Malden, MA: Polity.

Mazower, Mark (2012) *Governing the World: The History of an Idea, 1815 to the Present.* New York: Penguin.

Michigan Economic Development Corporation (2022) *Gov. Gretchen Whitmer Announces $1.4 Million in Export Assistance Funds Available for Michigan's Small Businesses.* Available at: www.michiganbusiness.org/press-releases/2022/09/whitmer-announces-$1.4-million-in-export-assistance-funds-available-for-michigans-small-businesses/ (last accessed October 10, 2022).

Mills, Karen M. (1993) Americans Overseas in U.S. Censuses. U.S. Dept. of Commerce, Economics and Statistics Administration, Bureau of the Census, *Technical Paper* 62. Available at: http://purl.fdlp.gov/GPO/gpo35912 (last accessed November 29, 2022).

Morgan, David (2008) Bodies of Missing U.S. Soldiers Identified in Iraq. *Reuters*, July 11. Available at: www.reuters.com/article/us-iraq-usa-soldiers-idUSN1134322320080711 (last accessed July 8, 2022).

Moriarty, Sarah (2021) How Bob Levinson's Legacy Will Help Bring Hostages Home. *James W. Foley Legacy Foundation*, March 10. Available at: https://jamesfoleyfoundation.org/bloghostage-family-perspectives/2021/3/9/how-bob-levinsons-legacy-will-help-bring-hostages-home (last accessed June 23, 2022).

National Conference of State Legislatures (2020) *Electronic Ballot Return*. Available at: www.ncsl.org/research/elections-and-campaigns/internet-voting.aspx (last accessed October 13, 2022).

Odell, John (1974) Correlates of U.S. Military Assistance and Military Intervention. In Steven Rosen and James Kurth (eds.), *Testing Theories of Economic Imperialism*. Lexington, MA: Lexington Books, 143–162.

Ostler, Jeffrey (2019) *Surviving Genocide: Native Nations and the United States from the American Revolution to Bleeding Kansas*. New Haven, CT: Yale University Press.

Packenham, Robert (1973) *Liberal America and the Third World: Political Development Ideas in Foreign Aid and Social Science*. Princeton, NJ: Princeton University Press.

Page, Clarence (1999) Jackson's Serbo-American Ally. *Chicago Tribune*, May 9. Available at: www.chicagotribune.com/news/ct-xpm-1999-05-09-9905090267-story.html (last accessed November 4, 2022).

Pamuk, Humeyra, and Alexandra Alper (2022) As Pressure Mounts, Biden Acts to Deter Wrongful Detentions of Americans Abroad. *Reuters*, July 20. Available at: www.reuters.com/world/us/biden-sign-executive-order-deter-detention-hostage-taking-americans-abroad-2022-07-19/ (last accessed December 8, 2023).

Pew Research Center (2019) *Remittance Flows Worldwide in 2017*. Available at: www.pewresearch.org/global/interactives/remittance-flows-by-country/ (last accessed April 8, 2022).

Reeves, Joshua (2017) *Citizen Spies: The Long Rise of America's Surveillance Society*. New York: New York University Press.

Rodgers, Walter, Jonathan Karl, Alessio Vinci, and David Ensor (1999) Three Captured U.S. Soldiers Released by Yugoslavia; U.S. F-16 Plane Crashes, Pilot Safe. *CNN*, May 2. Available at: http://edition.cnn.com/WORLD/europe/9905/02/captured.soldiers.01/ (last accessed July 7, 2022).

Rogers, Alan (1985) Passports and Politics: The Courts and the Cold War. *The Historian* 47(4), 497–511.

Rosen, Steven (1974) The Open Door Imperative and U.S. Foreign Policy. In Steven Rosen and James Kurth (eds.), *Testing Theories of Economic Imperialism*. Lexington, MA: Lexington Books, 3–14.

Savage, Charlie (2021) Testing an Opaque Security Power, Michigan Man Challenges 'No-Fly List.' *New York Times*, April 6. Available at: www.nytimes.com/2021/04/06/us/politics/no-fly-list-lawsuit.html (last accessed June 30, 2023).

Saunders, Laura (2018) Thousands of Americans Will Be Denied a Passport because of Unpaid Taxes. *Wall Street Journal*, July 6. Available at: www.wsj.com/articles/thousands-of-americans-will-be-denied-a-passport-because-of-unpaid-taxes-1530869401 (last accessed August 2, 2023).

Schmitt, Eric (2023) American Commandos Are in Israel Helping to Locate Hostages, Pentagon Says. *New York Times,* October 31. Available at: www.nytimes.com/2023/10/31/us/politics/us-israel-hostages.html (last accessed December 11, 2023).

Shklar, Judith (1991) *American Citizenship: The Quest for Inclusion.* Cambridge, MA: Harvard University Press.

Shults, Anthony M. (2011) The Surveil or Kill Dilemma: Separation of Powers and the FISA Amendments Act's Warrant Requirement for Surveillance of U.S. Citizens Abroad Note. *New York University Law Review* 86(5): 1590–1629.

Siebens, James, Ryan Lucas, and Jocelyn Wang (2021) US Global Force Posture and US Military Operations Short of War. *Stimson Center,* July 14. Available at: www.stimson.org/2021/us-global-force-posture-and-us-military-operations-short-of-war/ (last accessed June 7, 2022).

Sieff, Kevin (2018) U.S. Is Denying Passports to Americans along the Border, Throwing Their Citizenship into Question. *Washington Post,* September 13. Available at: www.washingtonpost.com/world/the_americas/us-is-denying-passports-to-americans-along-the-border-throwing-their-citizenship-into-question/2018/08/29/1d630e84-a0da-11e8-a3dd-2a1991f075d5_story.html (last accessed August 2, 2023).

Singer, Peter W. (2007) The Dark Truth about Blackwater. *Brookings Institution,* October 2. Available at: www.brookings.edu/articles/the-dark-truth-about-blackwater/ (last accessed May 1, 2022).

Solimano, Andrés (2010) *International Migration in the Age of Crisis and Globalization.* Cambridge: Cambridge University Press.

Stephanson, Anders (1996) *Manifest Destiny: American Expansion and the Empire of Right.* New York: Hill & Wang.

Stewart, Phil, and Idrees Ali (2023) U.S. Flying Drones over Gaza in Search of Hostages. *Reuters,* November 2. Available at: www.reuters.com/world/middle-east/us-flying-drones-over-gaza-search-hostages-2023-11-03/ (last accessed December 6, 2023).

Storrs, Landon R. Y. (2015) "McCarthyism and the Second Red Scare." In *Oxford Research Encyclopedia of American History.* Oxford: Oxford University Press. doi.org/10.1093/acrefore/9780199329175.013.6.

Texas Health and Human Services (n.d.) *Texas Repatriation Program.* Available at: www.hhs.texas.gov/services/financial/cash/repatriation-program (last accessed July 13, 2022).

Theoharis, Athan G. (2011) *Abuse of Power: How Cold War Surveillance and Secrecy Policy Shaped the Response to 9/11.* Philadelphia, PA: Temple University Press.

United States (n.d.) 18 U.S. Code § 2339B – Providing Material Support or Resources to Designated Foreign Terrorist Organizations, 2339B 18.

United States (2020) 22 U.S. Code § 1741b – Hostage Recovery Fusion Cell. December 27. Washington, DC.

United States (2020) S.712 – 116th Congress (2019–2020): Robert Levinson Hostage Recovery and Hostage-Taking Accountability Act. June 18, 2020. Washington, DC.

United States Census Bureau (1973) *1970 Census – Population, Subject Reports: Americans Living Abroad.* Available at: www.census.gov/library/publications/1973/dec/pc-2-10a.html (last accessed June 24, 2022).

United States Department of State (n.d.a) Fulbright Program – Frequently Asked Questions. Available at: https://eca.state.gov/fulbright/frequently-asked-questions (last accessed November 9, 2022).

United States Department of State (n.d.b) Passport Information for Law Enforcement. Available at: https://travel.state.gov/content/travel/en/passports/legal-matters/law-enforcement.html (last accessed June 27, 2023).

United States Department of State (n.d.c) U.S. Government Response to Wrongful Detention. Available at: www.state.gov/u-s-government-response-to-wrongful-detention/ (last accessed December 5, 2023).

United States Department of State (2020) FY 2021 International Affairs Budget. Available at: www.state.gov/fy-2021-international-affairs-budget/ (last accessed October 5, 2022).

United States Federal Voting Assistance Program (2018) FVAP Overseas Voters Interactive Data. Available at: www.fvap.gov/info/interactive-data-center/overseas (last accessed June 10, 2022).

United States Government Accountability Office (2021) COVID-19 State Carried Out Historic Repatriation Effort but Should Strengthen Its Preparedness for Future Crises. Available at: www.gao.gov/assets/gao-22-104354.pdf (last accessed July 9, 2022).

United States International Trade Administration (2022) FY 2023 Congressional Budget Submission. Available at: www.commerce.gov/sites/default/files/2022-03/FY2023-ITA-Congressional-Budget-Submission.pdf (last accessed October 11, 2022).

United States Trade Representative (n.d.) Export Assistance: United States Commercial Service. Available at: http://ustr.gov/trade-topics/trade-toolbox/export-assistance (last accessed August 10, 2022).

U.S. Department of Health & Human Services. (n.d.) Office of Human Services Emergency Preparedness and Response. Available at: www.acf.hhs.gov/ohsepr/repatriation (last accessed August 9, 2022).

U.S. Department of State – Bureau of Consular Affairs (2023) Arrest or Detention of a U.S. Citizen Abroad. Available at: https://travel.state.gov/content/travel/en/international-travel/emergencies/arrest-detention.html?_gl=1*1eb6loq*_gcl_au*MTg2NDc5MzMxMi4xNzAyMDUxOTYw (last accessed December 8, 2023).

U.S. Embassy & Consulates in Canada (n.d.) History of the U.S. Mission in Canada. Available at: https://ca.usembassy.gov/our-relationship/policy-history/io/ (last accessed November, 14, 2022).

U.S. Embassy & Consulates in India (n.d.) Education & Culture. Available at: https://in.usembassy.gov/education-culture/ (last accessed August 9, 2022).

U.S. Embassy in Albania (n.d.) Repatriation to the United States of Destitute U.S. Citizens. Available at: https://al.usembassy.gov/u-s-citizen-services/emergency-financial-assistance/repatriation-united-states-destitute-u-s-citizens/ (last accessed November 10, 2022).

US Embassy London (n.d) US Embassy London: About. LinkedIn. Available at: www.linkedin.com/company/us-embassy-london/about/ (last accessed September 7, 2022).

U.S. Federal Voting Assistance Program (2020) State of the Overseas Voter. Available at: www.fvap.gov/info/reports-surveys/overseas-citizen-population-analysis (last accessed October 1, 2022).

U.S. Government (n.d.) International Travel Issues for Americans. Available at: www.usa.gov/americans-abroad (last accessed June 15, 2022).

U.S. Government Accountability Office (U.S. GAO) (2007) State Department: Evacuation Planning and Preparations for Overseas Posts Can Be Improved (GAO-08–23). Available at: www.gao.gov/products/gao-08-23 (last accessed August 3, 2022).

U.S. Government Accountability Office (U.S. GAO) (2018) Workplace Retirement Accounts: Better Guidance and Information Could Help Plan Participants at Home and Abroad Manage Their Retirement Savings. Available at: www.gao.gov/products/gao-18-19 (last accessed June, 15 2022).

U.S. Small Business Administration (2020) State Trade Expansion Program (STEP). Available at: www.sba.gov/funding-programs/grants/state-trade-expansion-program-step (last accessed November 1, 2022).

Veeser, Cyrus (2002) *A World Safe for Capitalism: Dollar Diplomacy and America's Rise to Global Power.* New York: Columbia University Press.

Vine, David (2021) Lists of U.S. Military Bases Abroad, 1776–2021. *American University Library.* Available at: https://doi.org/10.17606/7EM4-HB13 (last accessed November 4, 2022).

Woodsome, Kate, Jason Rezaian, and Ray Whitehouse (2021) Opinion: More Countries Are Taking Americans Hostage. The U.S. Is Losing Its Ability to Stop It. *Washington Post,* 15 November. Available at: www.washingtonpost.com/opinions/interactive/2021/hostage-taking-americans-foreign-governments/ (last accessed June 6, 2022).

World Population Review (2022) Immigration by Country. Available at: https://worldpopulationreview.com/country-rankings/immigration-by-country (last accessed October 15, 2022).

Zachary, Paul, Kathleen Deloughery, and Alexander B. Downes (2017) No Business Like FIRC Business: Foreign-Imposed Regime Change and Bilateral Trade. *British Journal of Political Science* 47(4), 749–82.

14 Comparative Insights into States' Support, Co-optation, and Repression of Their National Communities Abroad

Šumit Ganguly and Klaus Brummer

Introduction

This volume explores states' interactions with what we refer to as "national communities abroad." The latter term casts a deliberately wide net in that it encompasses groups ranging from tourists to first-generation migrants to members of the diaspora with only loose connections to their ancestors' homeland. The country chapters show that such a broad understanding regarding the possible addressees of state action is expedient since there is indeed great variation in terms of which groups or segments of the national community abroad states primarily target.

The volume suggests that states' interaction with their national communities abroad, or specific segments therein, manifests in very different ways. We refer to them as "support," "co-optation," and "repression." In turn, to explain state action and variation therein towards their national communities abroad, the volume proposes four sets of explanatory factors pertaining to the characteristics of the national communities abroad, legal and institutional aspects, state capacity, and regime type.

Building on this framework, the volume surveyed the interaction of a total of twelve states from both the Global North and the Global South with their national communities abroad. The volume presents states' practices along three substantive dimensions pertaining to core areas of statecraft, namely political and consular, economic and social, and security, with efforts to support, co-opt, or repress national communities abroad cutting across those three dimensions.

The array of countries examined in this book provide us with a range of cross-cutting themes and propositions. Indeed, a careful sifting of the chapters suggest important similarities and differences not only in terms of how these states have handled common problems and challenges in their efforts to interact with their national communities abroad but also in the underlying rationale(s) for engaging (or not) in said activities in the first place. Building on the discussion offered in the introductory chapter (Brummer and Ganguly, Chapter 1), this concluding chapter first discusses general insights concerning the motivations of states' interactions with their national communities abroad and the reasons that explain those interactions. Next, it zooms in on specific themes and trends in some greater detail. The final section offers suggestions for future research.

General Insights Concerning States' Interaction with Their National Communities Abroad

This volume breaks down states' interactions with their national communities abroad into three categories. The first is "support," in the sense of assisting their communities abroad; the second is "co-optation," in the sense of obtaining benefits from their communities abroad; and the third is "repression," in terms of actively acting against their communities abroad. Rather than being confined to a single domain of action (i.e., political/consular; economic/social; security), measures to support, co-opt, or repress national communities abroad can be found in each dimension as the chapters contained in this volume illustrate.

Living up to their "duty of care" (e.g., Melissen and Okano-Heijmans 2018), states strive to *support* and assist members of their national communities abroad, most notably those who hold the country's citizenship (i.e., tourists, expats, or first-generation migrants). Activities to that end contain routine measures such as replacing lost passports in the political/consular realm, the signing of memoranda of understanding with third countries to shore up the rights of the members of the national community living there, and emergency evacuations, for example after natural disasters in the security realm.

Yet states' interaction with their national communities abroad also manifests in more instrumental and self-interested ways. One of them is *co-optation* through which states seek to benefit from their communities abroad, typically economically or politically. In the political/consular realm, enabling overseas voting is one example of how states undertake targeted measures to benefit politically from its communities living abroad. More obvious still are efforts to profit economically, for example by fostering the flow of remittances or enticing highly skilled members of the community to return home.

Last but by no means least, states engage with members of their national community through acts of *repression*. The country chapters contained in this volume reinforce the recent literature on "transnational authoritarianism" (e.g., Tsourapas 2021) by providing multiple examples where states actively act against members of their national community abroad, which can be single individuals or larger, for example ethnically or religiously defined groups. Typical practices in this regard contain the withholding of consular assistance or social services. They also include systematic acts of surveillance, forceful returns of people accused of crimes, or in the most extreme cases, targeted killings.

Overall, the country chapters contained in this volume drive home the point that states' interaction with their national communities abroad is manifested in very different ways. The ensuing question is how states' actions, and variation therein, can be explained in terms of both what states do (support, co-opt, or repress) and whether they engage in such activities in the first place. The literature suggests different sets of possible drivers for state action. Those are: characteristics of the national communities abroad, legal and institutional aspects, state capacity, and regime type.

Regarding the specific characteristics of the national community abroad, location has indeed proven to be crucial in accounting for states' actions, or inaction for that matter. As a rule of thumb, the bigger the share of the national community abroad staying in developed countries is, the less need there is to come to their support. For example, the fact that most British (Strong, Chapter 8) and German (Brummer and Oppermann, Chapter 10) nationals live in or travel to other Western/developed countries is one of the key reasons why those countries have done relatively little to support their citizens, barring extraordinary circumstances such as the Covid-19 pandemic, despite having the wherewithal to do so. Similarly, in the Mexican case, the fact that virtually all of its diaspora is located in a single country (which renders Mexico a clear outlier in this volume), namely the United States, has had a major impact in terms of what the country can, or often times cannot, do in support of their citizens residing across the border (Hernández Joseph and Schiavon, Chapter 3).

The location of national communities has also been important for states' effort to co-opt. For example, India has shown particular interest in those members of national community abroad who reside in OECD countries who tend to be relatively well-off and can thus make important contributions to the economy of their home state (Blarel, Chapter 2). Another example is Russia, whose actions are primarily targeted towards its "stranded citizens" living in post-Soviet countries (Larson, Chapter 4). Lastly, location has also affected states' acts of repression against their communities abroad. Monitoring and surveillance activities tend to focus on locations where larger clusters of the national community that do not sympathize, or actively act against, their home states' regime exist. However, as for example the case of China (Ghiselli, Chapter 5) shows, such measures can also be employed in a less discriminatory fashion against larger segments of the national community abroad.

Another key characteristic of national communities abroad that drives states into in-/action is their economic relevance for the home state. As outlined in the Introduction, in cases like Egypt, the Philippines, and Pakistan, remittances amount to almost 10 percent of the respective country's GDP (Brummer and Ganguly, Chapter 1). Those countries have little choice but to engage with their national communities abroad, which relates not only to acts of co-optation but also of support. Co-optation is driven by states' desire to maintain the flow of remittances but also investments from their national community abroad back home. However, in many instances, the "worker-citizens" (Okano-Heijmans and Caesar-Gordon 2016) abroad are low skilled and face precarious work conditions and an insecure legal status in their host states. Therefore, states try to support them, among other things, through the conclusion of bilateral labor agreements, of which, for example, the Philippines has signed more than seventy (Roldan, Chapter 7).

In terms of legal and institutional matters as drivers for state action, a more mixed picture emerges. We turn first to the legal provisions with regards to supporting and by implication possibly co-opting national communities abroad. The lack of such provisions does not mean that states are inactive nor does the existence of such provisions automatically compel states into action. A straightforward case is the United Kingdom, where a lack of legal provisions to protect citizens abroad corresponds with the country's limited engagement with its national community abroad even in times of distress. The lack of legal provisions means that the issue is one of "moral or political pressure" (Strong, Chapter 8) rather than of legal obligations. Another straightforward case from the opposite end of the spectrum is Indonesia, where legal provisions aimed at supporting migrant workers abroad have been met with sustained state action to that effect (Murphy and Freedman, Chapter 9).

Having said that, the volume also contains cases where legal or even constitutional provisions to assist nationals abroad are not mirrored in corresponding state action. Indeed, the cases of China and Türkiye show that constitutional provisions to protect nationals abroad do not inevitably translate into extensive, sustained, and multifaceted support activities (Ghiselli and Akbaba, Chapters 5 and 12, respectively). A similar finding has been noted for Germany, where legal provisions to support nationals abroad do exist (Brummer and Oppermann, Chapter 10).

Turning to bureaucratic institutions, the existence, or lack thereof, of specific ministries dedicated to the engagement of national communities abroad is also not necessarily an indicator of the breadth and depth of states' activities either. For sure, the existence of such ministries highlights the political importance that a country, or maybe more accurately the "government of the day," ascribes to the topic. Accordingly, countries that have dedicated ministries such as Pakistan (Khan, Chapter 6), Egypt (Norman, Chapter 11), and the Philippines (Roldan, Chapter 7) are indeed among the more active ones in terms of supporting their citizens abroad, not least for the aforementioned reasons of co-optation for economic gains. However, this is not to say that countries that do not have a specialized ministry, and where often times the foreign ministry is the main institution in charge of dealing with citizens abroad, are necessarily less active in terms of engaging their national communities abroad, as, for example, the Russian case illustrates (Larson, Chapter 4).

In terms of state capacity, the expected connection to state action towards national communities abroad has come to the fore. The within-case comparison of Russia, where increasing military interventions to "support compatriots" abroad have gone hand in hand with the augmentation of state capacity (Larson, Chapter 4), serves as illustration. A similar argument is made for India, which until the late 1980s had "very consciously adopted a policy of distancing itself from Indians abroad, due limited material capacities to support a large and diverse overseas community," and which afterwards started to "re-engage" with its national communities abroad when its "own material capacities grew" (Blarel, Chapter 2).

Yet the country chapters similarly highlight that there is no linear relationship between state capacity and state action. True, in principle, the developed countries covered in this volume are by definition much better equipped to interact across the board with their national communities abroad. They have larger diplomatic networks, a broader set of economic tools, and greater military power, which in principle render them highly capable to support, co-opt, or repress their national communities abroad. However, capabilities do not automatically translate into greater activities compared to less developed countries, as the chapters on the UK (Strong, Chapter 8), Germany (Brummer and Oppermann, Chapter 10), and the United States (Hogan and Krebs, Chapter 13) show. If anything, the reverse relationship is true in that less developed countries tend to focus more on their national communities abroad than the more developed ones, not least for the aforementioned economic reasons but possibly also for reasons of regime security.

Finally, the empirical discussions reinforce the ambiguous expectations outlined in the introductory chapter concerning the interaction between regime type and support activities. Clearly, there are significant differences among the democracies covered in this volume concerning their respective efforts to interact with their citizens abroad. In other words, in terms of support, being a democracy does not necessarily lead to a pronounced "duty of care," a proposition which holds true for both stable democracies (Polity score of 6 or higher) and defective ones. The same variation applies to co-optation. While some democracies are heavily engaged in such efforts, for both political and often times even more so economic reasons, others barely act at all. By implication it is not (shared) regime type but differences in other factors such as the location and social status of the national community abroad and the level of state capacity that explains variation in the behavior of democracies. As Strong (Chapter 8) pointedly notes for the UK, which represents a democracy that barely engages its national communities abroad, "They [British national community abroad] generally do not need the UK's help. Nor does the UK generally need them." Hogan and Krebs (Chapter 13) make a similar argument for the US.

In turn, the non-democratic regimes covered in this volume tend to be relatively more active especially compared to the stable democracies. However, here instrumental economic motives associated with co-optation seem to trump more altruistic considerations of supporting and assisting nationals abroad as an end in itself. Having said that, what has by and large been in accordance with our expectations is that non-democratic regimes such as China and Egypt have been particularly involved in acts of repression against specific segments of their national community abroad (Ghiselli and Norman, Chapters 5 and 11, respectively). At the same time, repressive measures against nationals abroad have also not been alien to democracies, as the discussion below on "democratic repression" suggests.

Taken together, the country chapters contained in this volume do provide support for all of the explanatory factors found in the literature on why and how states interact with their national communities abroad. However, they do so to varying degrees, with the characteristics of national communities abroad and state capacity having greater explanatory purchase than legal/institutional factors or regime type. Still, none of the factors can do the explanatory lifting alone. In so doing, the discussions lend support to multicausal explanations for state action, which have also been suggested for state–diaspora relations more broadly (Délano and Gamlen 2014; Ragazzi 2014).

In addition, the chapters speak to two additional themes that the extant literature flags, in the form of the agency of national communities abroad toward their home state on the one hand and the importance of time on the other. Regarding the former, the chapters show that national communities abroad are by no means merely passive recipients of state action. Indeed, while the focus of this volume has rested on states' actions towards their national communities abroad, this relationship must not be seen as running exclusively in one direction. On the contrary, the country chapters contain numerous examples showing that states' actions have been adjusted, expanded, and at times initiated in response to their national communities abroad. To give but two examples: Being cognizant of their country's interest to re-engage with their national communities abroad, particularly those Indians residing in OECD countries (i.e., those in which the government has shown particular interest) have voiced demands to their home state concerning "dual citizenship and schemes to facilitate investments in India" (Blarel, Chapter 2). And in the Mexican case, national communities in the US have been asking for state involvement to shore up or expand their already ongoing activities (Hernández Joseph and Schiavon, Chapter 3).

Further, the discussions also point to the importance of developments over time, thus bringing to the fore a distinctly temporal dimension of the argument. Indeed, examples of changes over time in states' activities towards their national communities abound. In addition to changes in the global institutional set-up (e.g., Gamlen 2019), another key factor highlighted in the chapters for explaining changes in state action over time pertains to changes in state capacity over time, as already mentioned above with respect to India and Russia. Further, the chapters have shown that changes in size of national communities abroad over time have necessitated alterations in state action, typically in the form of the customization and general expansion of such activities, or should usher in such changes in the near future as, for example, Khan (Chapter 6) suggests for the case of Pakistan. Another example is Türkiye, where changes in the ideology of the ruling elite translated into adjustments as to which parts of the national community abroad warranted particular attention from as security standpoint (Akbaba, Chapter 12). In turn, the US has altered over time its repressive measures against its citizens pertaining to travel control in response to changes in the country's security environment (Hogan and Krebs, Chapter 13).

After having outlined general insights with respect to possible drivers for states' interactions with their national communities abroad, the following section explores additional themes and developments as highlighted in the country chapters in greater detail.

Specific Themes and Developments

Contested Definition of National Communities Abroad

The discussion reveals that the very definition of what constitutes – and thus who does or does not belong to – a state's national community abroad is "inherently fluid and voluntaristic" (Larson, Chapter 4). By implication, any definition is also highly contested and politicized. Arguably least contentious is the definition and ensuing number of tourists, which are collected, for example, by the UN World Tourism Organization (UNWTO). In terms of members of a state's national community residing permanently abroad, at times for several generations, the picture is very different. The chapters contained in this volume use data from the UN Department of Economic and Social Affairs' Population Division as their point of departure. However, virtually all the chapters have shown that governments at times use vastly different – and in all cases (much) higher – numbers when accounting for the number of their nationals residing abroad.

One reason for this is technical. Whereas UN data defines people as member of a country when they were born in a particular country, individual countries such as the UK count anyone holding citizenship, which in the British case includes, for example, non-UK-born children of British citizens as well (Strong, Chapter 8). The other reason is political. National communities abroad are increasingly perceived as an opportunity to use and exploit, most notably in terms of economic contributions (remittances) but also with regards to political ones (lobbying the host-country government, etc.). As Akbaba (Chapter 12) reports for Türkiye, the state actively encourages its nationals abroad to take on host-state citizenship in addition to the Turkish one in order to increase the country's influence in the respective states. Even more far-reaching, Larson (Chapter 4) has shown for the Russian case that the country actively distributes passports ("passportization") to "stranded citizens" in former Soviet states, based on which interventions, including military ones, in neighboring countries are justified. Also, the size of national communities abroad, and with it the way in which they are defined in the first place, are important. Generous accounting or the outright "creation" of such groups open up avenues for politicization, and with it (artificially) create, for example, the need to support and provide protection for those groups.

At the same time, inflating one's national communities abroad can come at a cost as it ushers in increasing demands on state actions and services toward that group, which in turn may be challenging to fulfil. In this sense, Blarel points in the case of India "to a possible gap between public rhetoric and actual policy and material tools available to adequately support all its nationals abroad." Thus, too generous definitions of national communities abroad come with opportunity costs and can potentially backfire in the domestic political arena. Not least based on such considerations, British governments have gone in the opposite direction by "attempt[ing] to limit liability" for their national community abroad (Strong, Chapter 8).

Targeting Specific Segments of the National Community Abroad

The country chapters contained in this volume show great diversity in terms of which groups or segments of the national community abroad states primarily target. Variation is driven by several, and partially overlapping, factors. Geography is one of them in that it is typically much easier for states to engage with those groups of their national communities abroad who live closer to their home state. In this sense, Egypt even distinguishes its national community abroad based on geographical grounds, in the form of "temporary migrants" who reside in other Arab states and "permanent migrants" who live in Western states (Norman, Chapter 11).

However, proximity alone does not determine on which part of their national community abroad states focus and which part they neglect. In addition, and at times closely linked to geography, political reasons make states concentrate on different parts of their national communities abroad. This is illustrated by the case of Russia and its emphasis on those members of its national community who live in the post-Soviet space as part of its effort to shore up its influence in the "near abroad" (Larson, Chapter 4).

Another source of variation is legal in that many states' actions are limited to passport holders irrespective of whether they are in another country temporarily (e.g., tourists), for extended periods (e.g., expats), or permanently. Ideology can also lead to selective measures on the part of governments towards their national communities abroad by singling out and assisting those group that support the ruling regime in the home state (Akbaba, Chapter 12).

Lastly, variation can be grounded in economic reasons. While some states place greater emphasis on the more well-off members of their national communities abroad whom they try to co-opt, as Blarel (Chapter 2) has suggested for the Indian case and Strong (Chapter 8) for Britain's recent efforts towards citizens of Hong Kong, other states such as Pakistan (Khan, Chapter 6), the Philippines (Roldan,

Chapter 7), Indonesia (Murphy and Freedman, Chapter 9), and Egypt (Norman, Chapter 11) focus on low-skilled laborers whom they try both to co-opt and support, the latter, for example, by trying to ameliorate their status in their host countries. Taken together, no clear cross-country pattern emerges in terms of which groups of the national community abroad states place particular emphasis on.

Material and Non-material Drivers of State (In-)Action

The country chapters provide multiple examples that underpin the importance of material factors as key drivers for state action towards their national communities abroad. In this context, economic motives and state capacity loomed particularly large. Countries are all the more active and engaged depending on the domestic importance and the economic clout of their national communities abroad. Similarly, and quite obviously, the greater the level of a states' capacity, the more they can, at least in principle, do vis-à-vis their communities abroad, be it in terms of support, co-optation, or repression.

Quite interestingly, economic motives seem to override questions of state capacity in the sense that states with relatively less state capacity seem all the more keen to engage their communities abroad for economic gains, as, for example, the cases of India (Blarel, Chapter 2), the Philippines (Roldan, Chapter 7), and Indonesia (Murphy and Freedman, Chapter 9) illustrate. Conversely, high state capacity does not automatically translate into sustained and extended state action, as the cases of the United Kingdom (Strong, Chapter 8), Germany (Brummer and Oppermann, Chapter 10), and the US (Hogan and Krebs, Chapter 13) show – thus countries that (barring in emergencies) do not exhibit significant interest in their national communities abroad compared to many other states covered in this volume.

Hence, there can be a disconnect between states' ability to act on the one hand and their willingness to act on the other. Economic factors are clearly relevant in explaining this "ability–action gap." For the UK, Germany, and the US, their national communities abroad are simply not so important in economic terms, especially based on remittances as a share of the GDP. However, in addition to those material factors, nonmaterial factors play an important role as well.

For example, as Hogan and Krebs (Chapter 13) show for the US and Strong (Chapter 8) for the UK, both states have a peculiarly laissez-faire attitude toward supporting their nationals abroad. In considerable part, this unwillingness to render assistance to nationals abroad faced with hardship especially in the case of the US stems from what Hogan and

Krebs refer to as the "exceptionalist identity" of the US – namely that citizens should have the capacity to fend for themselves along with a commitment to a limited welfare state at home. Similarly, Strong argues that the limited role that the UK has envisaged for itself can be traced to historical developments in the nineteenth century. First, the British state was mostly unwilling to provide welfare at home as well as abroad. Second, most British emigrants at the time were in British colonies. Consequently, the responsibility for their welfare fell to colonial authorities in far-flung corners of the British Empire. Of course, in both cases (i.e., US and UK) the location of the respective communities abroad, the vast majority of which resides in developed countries, diminishes the need to come to their support in the first place, as is the case also, for example, for Germany (Brummer and Oppermann, Chapter 10).

At the same time, the country chapters suggest that nonmaterial factors pertaining, for example, to identity, ideological dispositions, and political cultures can cut both ways, in the sense of not only dampening states' willingness to engage with their national communities abroad but, quite the opposite, foster activities in this regard. Hernández Joseph and Schiavon (Chapter 3) make such an argument for the Mexican case whose policy towards the US is "connected to the definition of a national identity that includes the diaspora as a consequence of the loss of half the national territory to the US and currently in the huge presence of people of Mexican origin in that country." Thus, next to economic motives which are clearly present as well, Mexican governments have no choice but to pay considerable attention to their national community abroad (living in the US) for reasons of state identity. Roldan (Chapter 7) makes a similar argument for the Philippines by linking state identity and state action in that the country as a democracy "where governance principles of accountability and participation in nation-building, development, and the electoral process" are key "extend[ed] [those principles] to its nationals abroad." Akbaba (Chapter 12) points to another aspect of identity building by suggesting that changes in how the Turkish government has approached and interacted with its national communities abroad has allowed the latter to adjust their perception of the country and thus "to reimagine their home state."

Militaristic at Home, Non-militaristic Abroad?

The country chapters illustrate that a traditionally strong domestic role of the military, which is commonly associated with autocracies, does not necessarily translate into a similarly active involvement of the military in a state's interactions with its national communities abroad. Indeed, several countries covered in this volume in which the military plays a strong role domestically have for the most part refrained from using the armed forces in its interactions with its national communities abroad. This concerns not only possible acts of repression but also measures in support of nationals abroad in distress.

Cases in point include Türkiye, Egypt, and Pakistan. For example, Akbaba (Chapter 12) reports for the Turkish case that most of the rescue operations have been conducted by civilian agencies. In turn, Norman (Chapter 11) shows for Egypt that the country's military has also been rarely involved, though not for a lack of opportunity (e.g., the wars in Iraq and Libya) but rather primarily because the government did not want to jeopardize relations with powerful receiving countries which it relied upon economically. Finally, Khan (Chapter 6) reports a similar outcome for the case of Pakistan, though she argues that this is first and foremost not for a lack of need to engage in such behavior but rather because key host states for the Pakistani diaspora, such as Saudi Arabia, the United Arab Emirates, UK, and the US, are relatively stable (which, however, by no means implies that workers' rights are necessarily guaranteed). At the same time, the military seems keenly interested in forging good relations with the diaspora, not least for economic reasons, and engages in image and outreach campaigns to that end. Those findings are surprising not only in light of the general role of the military in politics but also, more specifically, since it forecloses a possible source of legitimacy for autocracies by standing up for its nationals abroad. That the latter motive can be on autocrats' minds is illustrated by Ghiselli (Chapter 5), who discusses how China has engaged in military actions in support of its nationals in distress abroad.

At the same time, the country chapters suggest that some democracies are at least as, if not more, prone than autocracies to use the military in its (supportive) activities towards their national communities abroad. Strong (Chapter 8) lists a number of occasions when the UK has used its armed forces to protect and rescue its citizens abroad. Indeed, the country's National Security Strategy specifically enjoins it to use armed force to guarantee the security of its citizens abroad. Moreover, despite the highly limited domestic role of the military and a general reluctance to use it overseas, even Germany has repeatedly dispatched the Bundeswehr abroad to take its nationals out of harm's way from conflict zones, most recently in Afghanistan and Sudan.

Having said that, other democracies engage in little or no military activities to protect their nationals abroad. A case in point is Mexico (Hernández Joseph and Schiavon, Chapter 3), though with almost all nationals abroad residing in the US that is arguably little that the country's military would be able (or be asked) to do anyway. In turn, the US has been fairly reticent in using its military capabilities to provide protection to US civilians traveling and residing aboard. Hogan and Krebs (Chapter 13) cite two compelling reasons for the reluctance of the US government to come to the aid of civilians abroad. First, there are simply too many American expatriates dispersed across the world. Second, the government is concerned about the moral hazards of such military intervention. If American civilians could count on their government resorting to force to guarantee their security, they may be tempted to engage in more risky behavior. That being said, the US has taken a far more proactive stance when it comes to "hostage diplomacy" – namely securing the release of American citizen who, in the eyes of the US, have been wrongfully detained abroad.

Irrespective of regime type, the use of the military is typically associated with measures of support of national communities abroad pertaining, for example, to evacuations from conflict zones. Hence, those measures aim at moving nationals out of certain geographic areas to safer neighboring countries or directly back to the home state. Russia's use of the military is the exception here. As Larson (Chapter 4) notes, "unlike many of the countries discussed in this volume, where armed force is typically used to facilitate evacuations, Russian interventions aim not at moving compatriots, but keeping them where they are." Thus, in the Russian case, the military is not used to moving nationals but to makes sure that they (can) stay put, mostly in post-Soviet states. By implication, the underlying goal of state action is not to support but rather to co-opt what is being referred to as "stranded citizens" for domestic political as well as geopolitical purposes.

More than Remittances: Enhancing Power and Status through Co-optation

As expected, several country chapters demonstrate that economic motives are crucial to explain states' efforts to co-opt their national communities abroad. As shown in the introduction (Brummer and Ganguly, Chapter 1), certain states depend heavily on remittances, which make up close to ten percent of national GDP in countries such as Egypt (Norman, Chapter 11), Pakistan (Khan, Chapter 6), and the Philippines (Roldan, Chapter 7). No wonder then that states seek and foster such inflow of revenue.

In addition to "classical" economic motives, the co-optation of national communities abroad by their home states can also be driven by political considerations. The latter are not confined to the domestic arena in the home state but can have much broader implications that extend well beyond national boundaries. In terms of domestic politics, the obvious motivation of states to co-opt members of their national communities abroad is the garnering of electoral support. This, in turn, has been rendered possible, for example, through the introduction of overseas voting. As the most recent presidential election in Türkiye in 2023 has illustrated (Brummer and Ganguly, Chapter 1), overseas ballots can indeed have important effects on national elections. Hence, political leaders in home states seek to cultivate their ties with their national communities abroad to shore up their political survival domestically.

What is more, states' interactions with their national communities abroad can have effects that transcend national boundaries. Indeed, states use their engagement with, and instrumentalization of, their communities abroad to foster regional or global goals. India serves as a case in point which has increasingly sought "to leverage the Indian communities' growing economic and political clout in their host countries" (Blarel, Chapter 2). Another example is Russia, which draws on its actual or alleged communities abroad not only to advance political goals and territorial claims in its geographic neighborhood but also to "recover its status as a global power," as Larson has argued (Chapter 4).

Democratic Repression

Repressing national communities abroad is commonly associated with autocracies. The country chapters in this volume corroborate this assessment in that the majority of examples of states acting against certain groups or individuals of their national communities abroad comes from authoritarian states, including China (Ghiselli, Chapter 5) or Egypt (Norman, Chapter 11). Conversely, democratic states by and large tend not to act against members of their national communities abroad since, as Hernández Joseph and Schiavon (Chapter 3) have argued with respect to Mexico, they have "nothing to gain from it."

Having said that, the country chapters lend some nuance to this assessment by suggesting that it is by no means categorically beyond democracies to undertake repressive measures against members of their national communities abroad. For example, the UK government decided in 2015 to kill two of its nationals who were operatives of Da'esh via a drone strike (Strong, Chapter 8). Similarly, if proven true, the alleged recent involvement of the Indian state through its intelligence services in the murder of a Canadian–Indian activist in Canada is another obvious example of democracies' transgressions in this context (Blarel, Chapter 2).

In addition, at lower levels of intensity, monitoring and surveillance measures by the intelligence services of democracies against members of the national community abroad deemed, for example, a threat to the home states' territorial integrity must also be considered an act of repression against members of their national communities abroad. Such measures have been reported, for example, for India (Blarel, Chapter 2) and the US (Hogan and Krebs, Chapter 13). The same goes for travel control through no-fly lists, for example, by the US (Chapter 13) or the withholding of consular services. As an example for the latter, the British government has stripped some 150 nationals, most of whom have been suspected Islamist terrorists, of their British citizenship. This, in turn, means that those people are no longer eligible to receive consular assistance and also forecloses their return to the UK (Strong, Chapter 8). Thus, there is a democratic complement to transnational authoritarianism.

Avenues for Future Research

States' efforts to interact with their national communities abroad are here to stay. Increases in human migration in terms of travel, work, and residence resulting from technological developments, better economic opportunities, political instability, and invariably the adverse effects of climate change contribute to these population movements. Similarly, advances in communications technology and social media are likely to further increase pressure on governments to interact with their national communities abroad across the spectrum. The latter ranges from providing support in distress not least for reasons of domestic legitimacy all the way to acts of repression out of fear that they instigate unrest in their home country.

It is worth noting that while most consular services, except the "discretionary" ones to which Alan Gamlen (2019: 248) refers, are codified in international conventions, most of the other activities that states undertake towards their national communities abroad in the realms of politics, the economy, or security are not grounded in any extant body of international legal norms that would require states to interact, let alone specifically support their national communities abroad. Instead, legal obligations that a state has toward its nationals abroad primarily stem from domestic law or from bilateral treaties that they may have entered into with various countries. Consequently, a veritable patchwork quilt of legal stipulations and ensuing responsibilities governs this issue area.

Finally, the discussions presented in this volume offer several avenues for future research. While the volume has placed states front and center, additional research should explore from a regional perspective the efforts, actual or potential, of regional and subregional organizations to collectively engage in interactions with the national communities of their member states (e.g., Bicchi and Schade 2022). Besides, from a state-centered perspective, deeper explorations of how domestic factors and developments influence states' activities towards their national communities abroad seems in order. Indeed, the chapters contained in this volume have shown that countries have experienced notable changes over time in the breadth and depth of their efforts in terms of both what they do (support, co-opt, repress) and towards who they target (i.e., which segment or segments of the national community abroad they engage). The ensuing question would be whether those changes can be systematically connected to domestic political factors (e.g., ideology of the governing party) or to domestic economic developments (e.g., periods of high growth or recession).

Such explorations would also help shed light on several related issues located at the nexus of domestic and international politics. One concerns the conditions and effects – domestically or internationally – of the politicization of states' interaction with their communities abroad, for example during election campaigns or as precursor of interstate conflict. Another issue relates to the interplay between material and non-material drivers of state action, for example concerning the extent to which domestic economic ideology translates into states' willingness, or lack thereof, to support their national communities abroad or with regards to the effect that states' interactions with their national communities abroad has on the construction of a state's identity. Finally, regarding acts of "democratic repression," it seems worthwhile exploring further the contexts and conditions under which democracies act against their own fundamental principles, and whether those contexts and conditions are different from what drives autocracies to act against their nationals abroad.

References

Bicchi, Federica, and Daniel Schade (2022) Whither European Diplomacy? Long-Term Trends and the Impact of the Lisbon Treaty. *Cooperation and Conflict* 57(1), 3–24.

Délano, Alexandro, and Alan Gamlen (2014) Comparing and Theorizing State–Diaspora Relations. *Political Geography* 41, 43–53.

Gamlen, Alan (2019) *Human Geopolitics. States, Emigrants, and the Rise of Diaspora Institutions*. Oxford: Oxford University Press.

Melissen, Jan, and Maaike Okano-Heijmans (2018) Introduction: Diplomacy and the Duty of Care. *The Hague Journal of Diplomacy* 13(2), 137–145.

Okano-Heijmans, Maaike, and Matthew Caesar-Gordon (2016) Protecting the Worker-Citizen Abroad: Duty of Care beyond the State? *Global Affairs* 2(4), 431–440.

Ragazzi, Francesco (2014) A Comparative Analysis of Diaspora Policies. *Political Geography* 41, 74–89.

Tsourapas, Gerasimos (2021) Global Autocracies: Strategies of Transnational Repression, Legitimation, and Co-optation in World Politics. *International Studies Review* 23(3), 616–644.

Index